EUROPE

ASIA

D0891759

FRICA

AUSTRALIA

California Clippers ————————
Tea Clippers · · · · · · · · · · · ·
Australian &
New Caledonian Clippers ● ● ● ● ● ● ● ● ● ● ● ●
Nitrate Clippers — — — — — —

CLIPPERS

The Ships that Shaped the World

CLIPPERS

The Ships that Shaped the World

DANIEL J NOLAN

MALBAY PUBLISHING

2011

First published in Ireland in 2011 by
Malbay Publishing
Bray, County Wicklow

The moral right of Daniel Nolan to be
identified as the author of this work has been
asserted in accordance with the Copyright,
Designs and Patents Act, 1988.

A CIP catalogue record for this book is available
from the British Library

ISBN 978-1-908726-00-1

Set in Albertina by Libanus Press Ltd, Marlborough
Printed and bound in Great Britain by Hampton Printing (Bristol) Ltd

Contents

The sea drives truth into a man like salt

HILAIRE BELLOC

PROLOGUE

The 'Golden Age of Sail' extended from the time of the great Portuguese explorers of the fifteenth century to the closing days of the clipper ship era in the twentieth century. Merchant sailing ships reached a peak of perfection with the clipper ships, the greatest wind-propelled vehicles of all time; their sea-worthiness and exceptional beauty were matched by the great speeds they reached, reducing the distance in time between far-flung corners of the globe. These magnificent creations, designed and built for the fast transport of cargo, passengers, and mail, established their reputation for speed during the early days of steam. Clippers were the ultimate refinement of the merchant sailing ship; their revolutionary hull and rig enabled sail to compete favorably with steamships on the long-distance ocean routes well into the twentieth century.

Vasco da Gama was the first known European to reach the Orient by sea after he rounded the Cape of Good Hope in 1497. His discovery of the sea route to the Far East was made possible by the earlier voyages of other Portuguese explorers: Diogo Cão explored and mapped much of the coast of Africa during his two voyages in 1482–1484, and Bartholomew Dias sailed along the coast of Africa and rounded the Cape of Good Hope, before he returned to Portugal in December 1488 with knowledge of an open sea, east of Africa, that could provide a route to the Orient. In 1519 another Portuguese explorer, Ferdinand Magellan, set sail from the Spanish port of Seville in search of a southern route to the South Seas, as the southern part of the Pacific Ocean was then known.

Vasco da Gama

The epic voyages and discoveries of Cão, Dias, da Gama, Magellan, and Christopher Columbus were made possible by the earlier endeavors of a man who had never gone to sea: Prince Henry of Portugal, better known as Prince Henry the Navigator. In 1418 Henry, at the age of 24, was made Governor of the most southerly of Portugal's provinces, the Algarve.

Henry established his court at Sagres, near the headland of Cape St Vincent, at the south-west tip of the Iberian Peninsula; he built his famous observatory and navigation academy there. Henry was determined to provide his captains, pilots, and navigators with the most accurate charts and the finest instruments. He recruited astronomers, mathematicians, and cartographers from around the Mediterranean, mostly Islamic, Italian, Jewish, and Spanish scholars. Seafarers flocked there to learn the most advanced navigation techniques and offer their services.

At the time Henry founded his academy, Europe's knowledge of the world extended no further than the Canary Islands and the coast of Africa as far south as Cape Bojador. Apart from reports of the voyage of the Irish monk St Brendan, the rest of the world was completely unknown.

Henry's enterprise yielded results: in 1444 Gil Eamnes doubled Cape Bojador; in 1445 Dinis Dias and Nuno Tristão reached the Senegal River which was the boundary between the Sahara desert and fertile West Africa; the Azores were re-discovered and colonized by the Portuguese the same year; and shortly afterwards Alvise de Cadamosta discovered the Cape Verde Islands, and charted a stretch of the African coast further south.

Diogo Cão set out in August 1482, on the first of two voyages that took nearly two years. He explored the coast of Africa from Cape Santa Catarina, just south of the equator, to Cape Cross in South West Africa, discovering the mouth of the Congo River in the process. Bartholomeu Dias continued Cão's exploration work, rounding the Cape of Good Hope, the southern tip of Africa, in 1488. Dias provided information that was vital to Vasco da Gama in the planning of his memorable voyage of 1497.

The Portuguese were also the leaders in shipbuilding. Their caravels were the first European vessels to be able to sail close to the wind on the homeward voyage north along the coast of Africa, a feat made possible by the raked masts, lateen sails, and bowsprit; this enabled them to set a large foresail and sail closer to the wind.

From the caravel, the Portuguese developed the larger carrack, a full-rigged ship with three masts. Carracks were large and round-built, fitted out for carrying a large amount of stores; their depth was extraordinary for the time. They were a major advance in ship design and remained unchanged for three centuries, apart from being enlarged and improved.

Caravel at Cueta, North Africa

Vasco da Gama set sail from Lisbon on 8 July 1497 to find a way of sailing to India that could be developed into a lucrative trade route; at the time the overland route between Europe and India was controlled by the Venetians. His fleet of four ships consisted of the 170-ton carrack *São Gabriel* under the command of da Gama himself, a similar vessel *São Rafael* under the command of his brother Paolo da Gama, a 50-ton caravel *Berrio*, and a small store ship. *São Gabriel's* pilot was Pero de Alemquer, who had been with Bartholomeu Dias when they discovered the Cape of Good Hope.

Four months later the fleet anchored in St Helena Bay on the west coast of Africa, and da Gama went ashore there to take astronomical observations with the recently invented mariner's astrolabe. Over the following 150 years, the angle measuring astrolabe would be developed and refined through a number of stages to become the sextant. Da Gama made his observations on the land near St Helena Bay; he mistrusted measurements taken aboard because of the unsteadiness of a ship.

On 22 November, sailing before the wind, de Alemquer guided the fleet past the Cape of Good Hope. The fleet put in at a number of places on the east coast of

The carrack *White Bear*   (Vischer)

Africa before anchoring off the island of Mozambique on 10 March 1498. A month later at Malinda, in what is now known as Kenya, da Gama contracted the services of a pilot who guided the fleet to southern India, landing at Calicut on 20 May. Sixteen months later da Gama arrived back in Portugal to a rapturous reception, and bearing a letter from the Zamorin of Calicut to the King of Portugal:

> "Vasco da Gama, a nobleman of your household, has visited my kingdom, which has given me great pleasure. In my kingdom there is abundance of cinnamon, cloves, ginger, pepper, and precious stones in great quantities. What I seek from thy country is gold, silver, coral, and scarlet."

Clippers, full-rigged ships, represented the single greatest advance in the design of merchant sailing ships since the Portuguese carrack. During the 1840's the first ocean-going clippers were built in the United States. They continued to be built until the early part of the twentieth century but by then steel had replaced wood and iron in the construction of the hulls and spars.

Seafaring nations conducted trade over the seas for thousands of years. But during the clipper ship era, an unprecedented expansion of trade between distant lands took place, making the world seem a smaller place, and setting the scene for what is now known as the 'Global Economy.'

The advances in navigation that had taken place since Henry the Navigator's time, and the peace that followed the Napoleonic Wars in Europe and the Anglo-American War of 1812, allowed the British and United States navies to chart coastlines, and study the winds and ocean currents. Charts and sailing directions gave ships' captains the information required to make safe and swift passages.

Steam tugboats were built in the 1830s and could tow large sailing ships into and out of harbors, and between home ports when winds were light or absent. Otherwise, square-rigged clipper ships, powered solely by the wind, voyaged in isolation on the great oceans, without any means of communication with the outside world. Their navigators, using a mariner's compass, astronomical measuring devices, timepieces, plotting instruments, charts, and sailing directions could read the complex ocean signposts, find their position, and plot their way across the vast empty space of the high seas. Guided by signs in the sky, sea, and air they sailed confidently to distant ports and anchorages.

CLIPPER SHIP ERA

Preceding page: *Royal Family* (ILN)

CHAPTER 1

Rakish Vessels

The centuries-long history of the sailing ship design, not only in
America but also in the rest of the world, reached its culmination
in the clippers. Such ships were never to be seen again.

A B C Whipple, *Tall Ships and Great Captains*

The United States set the scene for the clipper ship era. Their transatlantic sailing
packet liners were a new class of ship, built to carry passengers, freight, and mail
at regular intervals between North America and Europe; the mail contracts alone
were quite lucrative.

Following the Anglo-American War of 1812, there was considerable growth in
commercial traffic across the Western Ocean, as the North Atlantic had been
known since Elizabethan times. In 1815, the famous Black Ball Line of New York
started regular packet sailings across the Western Ocean – the 'Atlantic Ferry.'
The sailings, scheduled for the first day of the month, regardless of weather,
or lack of freight or passengers, provided the only means of communication
between New York and Liverpool at that time. The pioneering Black Ball Line was
founded by Isaac Wright, Francis and Jeremiah Thompson, Benjamin Marshall,
and others; the company's distinguishing mark was the image of a large black
ball sewn or printed on the foresail; the ships were black with green super-
structures.

Earlier commercial sailing ships had registered between 100 and 500 tons.
The first four Black Ball packets were the 500-ton ships *Amity, Courier, Pacific,* and
James Munroe, ships that were fitted out with well appointed cabin arrangements
for passengers. Six months later a further four ships were added to the fleet,
and soon afterwards there were four more. Black Ball Line packets were strongly
built, with the floor of the upper deck continuous from stem to stern, a construction described as a 'flush deck.'

Some of the first captains appointed to command Black Ball packets were former privateer commanders of the War of 1812. Captains sailed their packet ships hard across the Western Ocean, at times reaching speeds of 14 knots. In the early years, the packets took on average 23 days to complete the eastbound voyage, and 40 days westbound. *Canada,* one of the Black Ball's earliest ships, reached Liverpool 15 days and 18 hours out from New York. In the 1850s another Black Ball packet, the 969-ton *Fidelia,* reduced the eastbound transatlantic record to 13 days 7 hours.

But it was the tall-rigged 110-foot-long 359-ton *Emerald,* commanded by Captain Philip Fox and belonging to the Boston & Liverpool Packet Co, that established a westbound record when she crossed from Liverpool in 17 days. Fox had picked up an east wind that followed him west. Arriving in Boston at 3pm on 8 March 1824, Fox produced the Liverpool newspapers of 20 February to the surprised owners. They thought that he had got into trouble when they saw *Emerald* anchored at the mouth of the harbor off Fort Independence. Fox made fast passages; he had a reputation for carrying so much sail that his ship's lee rail was almost constantly under water. The westbound record was set when the 1,679-ton clipper ship *Andrew Jackson* sailed from Liverpool to New York in 15 days during November 1860.

For nearly half a century Black Ball packets continued to dominate the Atlantic Ferry, until sail could no longer compete with steam for transporting passengers and mail. Wind-driven packets were the only regular means of communication between Europe and the United States.

The Black Ball Line was not the first Western Ocean packet service. In 1807 Thomas P Cope started the Philadelphia Line, with the 290-ton *Lancaster* and the 379-ton *Tuscarora* providing regular sailings between there and Liverpool. Larger ships followed. Many of the Philadelphia Line vessels carried cotton to Liverpool from New Orleans and Mobile, in ships that differed little from later Western Ocean packets. Most of Cope's packets were built locally by John Lynn and his family.

An increasing emphasis was being placed on speed. American sailing packets built between 1825 and 1846 were a new class of vessel, based on the French frigate model, an improved and sharper version of the East Indiaman. They reached the height of perfection in the early 1840s. By then fast American packets were criss-crossing the Western Ocean, and sailing into and out of European ports, particularly Liverpool, London, and Le Havre. The Atlantic Ferry was

Packet Ship *Victoria*

almost entirely in the hands of the Americans. Among the best known Western Ocean packets were *Independence, Montezuma, Cornelius Grinnell, Daniel Webster,* and *New World.*

The 734-ton *Independence* was launched from the New York yard of Smith & Dimon in 1833 for the Swallow Tail Line of Grinnell, Minturn & Co, and placed under the command of Captain Ezra Nye, a sailor with a reputation for carrying a large spread of canvas. The 1,045-ton *Montezuma* was built in 1835 at the Brown & Bell yard for the Black Ball Line; *Montezuma* was also fast, and a strong rival to *Independence.* Both vessels were renowned for fast runs eastwards, each making passages of 14 days on a number of occasions. A number of other fast packets regularly crossed from New York to Liverpool in 16–17 days.

A fine representative of the packet class, and at 1,168 tons the largest merchant sailing vessel of the time, was *Queen of the West,* designed by David Brown and launched in 1843 from the New York yard of Brown & Bell at the foot of Stanton Street, East River. A large sailing ship classed as a packet, but more of a cargo carrier, was the 1,750-ton *City of Mobile.* Built by Perrine & Stack at Greenpoint, New York, in 1854 for Harbeck & Co of the same city, she was one of the first of the packets that was illustrated carrying double topsails. *City of Mobile* had three decks, and carried large cargos of grain in the hold and the lower between ('tween) decks, with steerage passenger accommodation in the upper 'tween decks. The last packet built for the Black Ball Line was the 1,600-ton *Charles C Marshall,* launched from Webb's New York yard in 1869.

*

> ... in the North Atlantic, which is haunted by the terrors of the sea, – fogs, icebergs, dead ships bent on mischief, and long sinister gales that fasten upon one like a vampire till all the strength and spirit and even hope are gone, and one feels like the empty shell of a man.
>
> Joseph Conrad *Lord Jim*

Robustly built to cope with the rigors of the cold and stormy Western Ocean winters, the packets were strong and seaworthy. Once clear of land, they were sailed hard in order to maintain speed by continuing to carry a press of sail in heavy weather. The hard driving they received, particularly into the teeth of the prevailing westerlies on the return run to the United States, limited their useful life as passenger carriers to little more than five years.

On the upper deck of the packets, between the fore and main masts, there was a small galley and the securely lashed ship's longboat. The longboat was housed-over, and carried the livestock: pens for sheep and pigs in the bottom; ducks and geese on a deck set between the gunwales; and above them hens and chickens. A companionway aft led to comfortable well-appointed cabins with light, provided by skylights, candles, and whale-oil lamps. Steerage passengers' sleeping accommodation was 'tween decks amidships, and the crew was quartered in the forecastle.

Passengers travelling steerage were nearly all emigrants. They purchased their food before boarding and had to cook it in the small galley. Their accommodation below deck was cramped; during bad weather, with the hatches closed, it was extremely miserable and frightening as the ship battled west against the elements. From 1815 to 1854 over four million emigrants left Britain for North America; in the six years between 1846 and 1854 nearly two-and-a-half million Europeans emigrated to the USA.

New York was the busiest of the packet ports. During the era of the packet and clipper, sailing ships could be seen moored alongside individual piers that extended into the East River from South Street. Bowsprits extended across the

South Street, New York

road, almost touching the upper floor windows of the offices and houses that lined the street, while a forest of masts and yards extended skywards from the decks. Shipping companies had their own individual berths situated across the road from their offices. Halfway along, in pride of place, was pier 23 of the Black Ball Line of Liverpool packets. Piers 19 and 20 belonged to Grinnell & Minturn's Swallow Tail Line; their Liverpool and London packets, and Californian clippers, sailed from there

Packet captains sailed from their berth if the wind was favorable: sail was set, and the yards laid aback; as the wind caught the sails the lines were eased off, allowing the vessel to move slowly astern to the cheers of the spectators on shore and the passengers on deck. When clear of the pier, with room to maneuver, the lines were slipped and taken aboard, the captain put the helm over, the yards were swung round, and the sails trimmed; then, with the wind filling the sails, the majestic craft would slowly get under way on a heading for the open sea. Packets also berthed under sail if conditions were favorable: the incoming ship would glide up to her berth, and as her lines were taken ashore she would bump gently alongside and stop. Tugboats, expensive and underpowered in those days, were used as a last resort.

Most ships ending their voyage at Liverpool did so in full view of the waterfront, an opportunity for the American captains to show off their skills. After picking up a pilot on the Welsh coast, and ignoring the offer of a tug if the wind was favorable, they would continue under a press of canvas in the shipping channel of the estuary and for three miles into the River Mersey, before furling sail, dropping anchor, and coming to a complete stop in style.

> . . . to the Captain and crew of a sailing-ship the operation of coming to anchor was a crowning feat, requiring the utmost nicety of judgement, plus hard work, under the critical eyes of experts on other ships and on shore.
>
> William H S Jones, *The Cape Horn Breed*

Packet captains were highly regarded. Their families moved in the same social circles as the shipowners; and when ashore they were on equal terms with the shipowners and merchants. Tremendous profits were made by the most successful packets. In one round trip of 48 days the medium clipper *Dreadnought,* launched from the yard of Currier & Townsend in Newburyport, Massachusetts, in 1853, earned $40,000. Captains nearly always had an interest in the ships they commanded, and relied on a share of the revenue generated: 5 per cent of all freight charges, 25 per cent of cabin passenger fares, and 5 per cent of the steerage fares, as well as all the revenue generated from carrying mail: two cents for each letter carried from the United States, and tuppence for each one from the United Kingdom. The annual income of a captain could amount to as much as $5,000. Captains that did not have shares in their ships were paid about $360 per month.

On board ship, the packet captain's power was absolute: he drove the crew of 'packet rats' as hard as the ships, sending them aloft with great frequency in the inhospitable North Atlantic weather, to shorten or set sail. The sailors were reasonably well fed, and were allowed plenty of coffee day or night in heavy weather; grog was unknown on American merchant ships, as no alcohol was permitted.

British shipbuilders paid scant attention to the fast American sailing packets; they were not envisaged as a threat because of the Navigation Laws, and because of Britain's lead in steam propulsion. They did, however, catch the eye of some observers. In 1848, Lord William Lennox described fast American liners he had seen at Liverpool and London. In Liverpool he had gone aboard the Swallow Tail

Line's packet *Henry Clay* of New York, commanded by Captain Ezra Nye. Lennox afterwards described her as exceedingly beautiful, with accommodations superior to that of any other sailing vessels he had ever seen. *Henry Clay,* measuring 1,250 tons and built by Brown & Bell in 1845, was one of the first packets with three decks; she had caused a sensation in New York when she first lay alongside Pier 19, opposite the South Street office of Grinnell, Minturn & Co.

Charles Dickens drew attention to the sailing packets by singing their praises following his return home on *Washington* in 1842, after an uncomfortable outward voyage on board a 'smoke box,' the Cunard Steam Ship Company's paddle steamer *Britannia:*

> There was grandeur in the motion of the splendid ship, as overshadowed by her mass of sails, she rode at a furious pace upon the waves, which filled one with an indescribable sense of pride and exultation. As she plunged into a foaming valley, how I loved to see the green waves, bordered deep with white, come rushing on astern, to buoy her upward at their pleasure, and curl about her as she stopped again, but always own her for their lengthy mistress still!
>
> Charles Dickens, *American Notes for General Circulation*

It was the brilliant Boston-based ship designer and builder Donald McKay who, more than anyone else, established America as the leading builder of first-class commercial sailing ships. McKay was apprenticed with John Willis Griffiths and William H Webb at the New York shipyard of William's father, Isaac Webb. McKay was to remain a friend and disciple of Griffiths, the naval architect responsible for the emergence of the American clipper ship. William H Webb took over the family shipbuilding business in New York on the death of his father, Isaac Webb, in 1840 and many fine ships were built by him in the shipyard at the foot of 5th Street to 7th Street, East River.

Released early from his apprenticeship, probably to get married, McKay gained

Donald McKay

employment in the shipyard of Brown & Bell, a yard jointly owned by David Brown and Jacob Bell. Bell was impressed by the young Donald McKay, and recommended him for employment in the Brooklyn Navy Yard. There he was selected from nearly a thousand men as foreman for an important job. But there was great resentment in the yard against anyone who was not born under the 'Stars and Stripes.' McKay, born in Canada to Scottish parents, was bullied out of the yard by the workers. It was not long before ships built by this 'foreigner' would be flying the Stars and Stripes in all corners of the globe, bringing enormous prestige to the United States's maritime achievements. More than 100 years later, the dramatist Arthur Miller worked in the Brooklyn Navy Yard as a ship-fitter third class, from November 1942 for over a year as part of the war effort; Miller laboured from four in the afternoon until four in the morning, working thirteen nights out of fourteen, sometimes in temperatures below freezing.

Donald McKay, a descendant of the 14th-century Scottish Highland chieftain of the same name, was born in Shelburne, Nova Scotia, in 1810. He received a basic education before leaving school to learn the skills of shipbuilding in the New York shipyards. While at Isaac Webb's shipyard, McKay started courting Albenia Martha Boole, the talented and well educated eldest daughter of another New York shipbuilder, John Boole. McKay and Boole married in 1829. The Boole household was steeped in the traditions of shipbuilding: two of Albenia's brothers were in the business, and Albenia was skilled at drafting ships' plans and had considerable knowledge of naval architecture. It was from her that McKay acquired the grounding in mathematics and draftsmanship that enabled him to become a master shipbuilder.

He was a visionary well in advance of his time, who would need recognition by the right shipowners if he was to succeed in the competitive world of shipbuilding. After his expulsion from the Brooklyn Navy Yard, he was sent to Maine to supervise the building of a number of ships for Jacob Bell. At the age of 30, McKay was taken on as a partner by John Currier Jr of Newburyport, Massachusetts, and *Delia Walker* was the first ship from the yard showing signs of the McKay genius. Dennis Condry, the owner, was impressed with McKay's technical skill, and with his ability to maintain good working relationships with his men and to motivate them. *Courier*, the first ship designed by McKay, was launched the following year. The 380-ton ship went into service on the Rio coffee run, and proved to be fast enough to outsail vessels of all sizes that fell in with her. *Courier* was also a great commercial success. The demise of McKay's partnership with Currier was followed by the McKay & Pickett partnership at Newburyport in 1843. Two big New York packets, of just less than 1,000 tons, were completed by McKay & Pickett.

At roughly the same time Enoch Train, a prominent Boston shipowner and merchant with ships in the Baltic and South American trades, was planning to start a packet service between Boston and Liverpool. Train was one of the leading merchants and shipowners in the United States, and in 1844 he travelled to Europe to establish agencies for his new shipping line. On board one of the early Cunard steamships bound for Liverpool, Train fell into conversation with fellow-passenger Dennis Condry. In a discussion on shipbuilding, Condry's effusiveness about Donald McKay's accomplishments at Newburyport convinced Train that McKay was the person to build the ships he required. Train did not wish to have them built in New York, and was of the opinion that there was no shipbuilder in Boston with the necessary experience to construct packets to the degree of perfection he required.

Immediately after his return, Train went to meet McKay in Newburyport. In the words of Arthur H Clark, master mariner, author, and boyhood friend of Donald McKay: 'It was the swift contact of flint and steel, for within an hour a contract had been signed for the building of *Joshua Bates*, the pioneer ship of Train's famous Liverpool Line.' Train frequently visited the yard as *Joshua Bates* took shape, during which time his admiration for McKay's shipbuilding skills soared. As soon as *Joshua Bates* was afloat on the Merrimack River, Train persuaded Donald McKay to move to Boston and open a shipyard there.

> He designed every vessel built in his yard, and personally attended to every detail of her construction.
>
> S E Morrison, *The Maritime History of Massachusetts*

Shortly afterwards, at the age of 34, McKay opened his shipyard at Border Street, East Boston, from where many of the finest commercial sailing ships the world has ever known were launched. Five robust packets, designed to carry a large press of canvas in all weathers, were built there for Train between 1846 and 1851. Train's packets carried a large T on their fore topsail. The packet *Daniel Webster*, launched in 1851, was one of the finest built by McKay, and one of the really great Western Ocean packets of the 1850s. Although not built as a fast ship, *Daniel Webster* passed Cape Clear 13 days 10 hours out from Boston on her maiden voyage.

McKay built impressive packets for other clients, including *New World* and *Cornelius Grinnell* for the Swallow Tail Line. *New World* measured at 1,400 tons and was considered to be the largest and finest American merchant ship when she was launched from McKay's Boston yard in 1847. McKay's strong and fast sailing packets dominated the transatlantic route between 1845 and 1853. They were greatly admired in ports such as New York, Liverpool, and London. The specifications of *Cornelius Grinnell* were described in detail in the *Illustrated London News* in August 1850, accompanied by a lithographic print of her lying at anchor in the Thames.

A classic sailing packet had three masts: fore, main, and mizzen, each carrying square sails, an arrangement defined as 'ship' rigged; the designation 'full-rigged' was applied to any ship with square sails on three or more masts. Square sails referred to any four-cornered sail bent to a yard that was suspended by the middle. McKay's packets were three-masted, full-rigged, and with a 4:1 length-width ratio. They were not fast in light winds; but Western Ocean packets did not sail in the latitudes of light winds! The transatlantic packet ships that McKay

Cornelius Grinnell (ILN)

built were known for their power and strength. During 1853, the worst winter in the North Atlantic for many years, McKay's packets crossed safely.

The wind-propelled Atlantic Ferry reduced most crossing times under sail. Voyages that had previously taken from one to three months took 14–20 days. The fast passages of the packets were achieved by their designers and by how they were driven by their commanders who kept their charges moving as fast as possible, day and night in all weathers, from the moment of cast off in New York until they were alongside the Pier Head at Liverpool. The packet's sails provided a degree of stabilization in the rough North Atlantic.

Samuel Cunard introduced four side-paddle steamers onto the transatlantic route in 1847. Initially there was strong prejudice against steam, but steamships would eventually displace sail, and in time, dominate the transatlantic packet business.

* * *

Developed from the transatlantic sailing packet ships, and built of timber in the shipyards of the American East Coast, early clipper ships quickly established a reputation for speed over long distances. New season's tea from China arrived in New York in record time. Their reputation was further enhanced during the early days of the California Gold Rush. Soon the United States was acknowledged as the world leader in commercial shipping, and British shipowners began chartering and buying American built clippers for the China tea trade. Many of McKay's ships were subsequently bought by Liverpool shipowners for use on the developing Australia run.

The first sailing vessel built on clipper lines was *Scottish Maid*, a 150-ton schooner built in 1839 by Alexander Hall & Sons of Aberdeen, to compete with the paddle steamers then plying between there and London. The Hall brothers had tested various hull models in a water tank and found that those with a sharp bow and raked stem offered the least resistance. *Scottish Maid* was very fast and gave half a century of service before she was wrecked on the coast. As a result of her success, three further clipper schooners, *Fairy, Rapid,* and *Monarch,* of the same design and tonnage, were built at the Hall yard and launched in 1842.

John Willis Griffiths created a sensation in American shipbuilding circles when he attacked the prevailing theory that it did not matter how roughly the wide bows of a vessel advanced through the water, as long as she left smooth water in her wake. 'A codfish head and a mackerel tail' was the way many in

John Willis Griffiths

the industry described the ideal shape of a ship. Ship designers at the time were following Isaac Newton's 'solid of least resistance' theory. Griffiths, who was employed as a naval architect and draughtsman at Smith & Dimon's shipyard in New York, revolutionized the science of merchant shipbuilding by creating the first clipper ship model.

Griffiths had read up on ship design, and concluded that the accepted theories were wrong. He assiduously studied the theories and experiments of the British astronomer and physicist Mark Beaufoy. Beaufoy, the first Englishman to climb Europe's highest mountain, Mont Blanc, was taught astronomy by William Bayly, the astronomer on Captain Cook's third voyage. At age fifteen, Beaufoy conducted his first experiments on the resistance of solids moving through water in one of the vats of his father's vinegar brewery near London. His interest was aroused when he heard an eminent mathematician state that a cone pulled through the water with the blunt end first offered less resistance than

Col Mark Beaufoy FRS

if the sharp end was in front, a hypothesis he found difficult to believe. He soon established that a cone-shaped object, drawn with equal force, moved more slowly with the blunt end forward. Beaufoy was a founding member of the Society for the Improvement of Naval Architecture (1791), which was formed to deal with Britain's inferiority to France in the art of shipbuilding. During the latter half of the 18th century France led the world in the modeling and construction of ships, and the Royal Navy's finest vessels were frigates that that had been

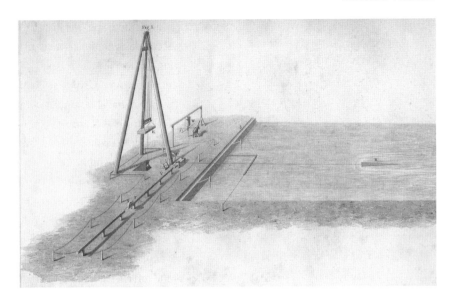

Beaufoy's Towing Apparatus

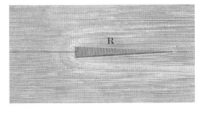

captured from the French. The new society would present a gold medal to anyone who could fully ascertain the laws of resistance to water.

More experimentation by Beaufoy followed: he carried out tests for six years at Greenland Dock on the south bank of the Thames near Greenwich, towing differently shaped wooden models through the water and comparing their speeds. His wife Margaretta, who was a mathematician and also his first cousin, provided invaluable assistance with the calculations. He had eloped with her to Gretna Green to marry without the consent of her father. The Beaufoys showed that resistance to movement of a solid through the water was reduced further if the length of the solid was increased by adding a cylinder in the middle, and they postulated that a floating solid with a triangular bottom will meet less resistance when moving in the direction of its longest axis. Seven years after Beaufoy's death in 1834, his son Henry published the experiments and established his father as the leading authority on the relationship of hull shape and size to frictional drag in water.

The advanced design of French ships was also noted in the United States. Following the signing of a treaty in 1778 between France and the United States in support of the Revolutionary War, a number of French frigates and luggers appeared in American waters. These luggers, of 150–200 tons, were similar to the ones used by the privateersmen of Brittany and were the fastest sailing vessels in their day; with the Bretons at the helm they could wreak havoc on the merchant ships of an enemy. At the earliest opportunity, the lines of the French frigates and luggers were carefully taken off by shipwrights in America, usually while in dry dock for cleaning or repairs. The first American frigates were designed from information gleaned from studying the French vessels.

The effect of hull shape on speed through the water fascinated Griffiths, who would sketch his designs on the drawing board and test the resistance of different solid objects in a water tank. Griffiths's aim was to design fast sailing ships that would exceed the known maximum speed of 13.5 knots. He knew that the hull shape below the waterline needed to be streamlined to give the least resistance as speed increased. Griffiths decided that a ship built for speed required a sharp flared hollow and concave bow, with the center of buoyancy in the ship's middle. As speed increased and the sharp bow rose up out of the water, it was important that the shape of the ship's stern would allow her to settle down comfortably in the water, with minimal drag. Thus, John Willis Griffiths conceived the revolutionary clipper ship design.

Griffiths's first clipper model was shown to American shipowners in 1841. It was long and narrow, with a knife-like concave overhanging bow; the hull gently widened into straight wall-like sides before narrowing again at the stern. Instead of upright masts, Griffiths's towering masts leaned backwards; these raking masts carried wide yards designed to spread a large area of sail that would lift the bow, as the ship gathered and maintained speed. The attractive lines, sleek hull, and towering rig gave the impression of a craft built for speed. Not everyone was impressed by Griffiths's design and model; some shipowners forecast that a ship with those lines would capsize in a stiff breeze.

Griffiths's streamlined hull design had some similarities to the fast double-ended longships that gave the Vikings control of the North Atlantic a thousand years earlier. The longships used for war were propelled by sail and oars, but the merchant version relied on sail only. These highly maneuverable craft had a single mast, stepped amidships, from where a large square sail was flown; the yard could swivel on the mast to allow the longship to sail with the wind from aft to as far forward as dead abeam.

Boats used on the River Thames had similar shaped hulls. Prince Frederick's

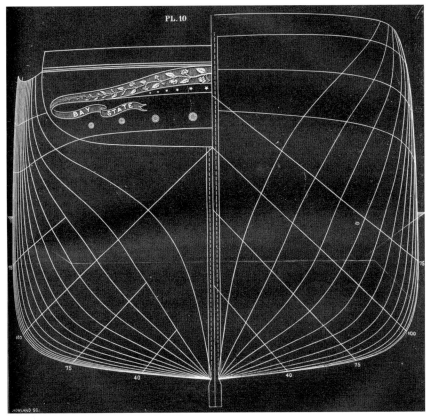

John Willis Griffiths

John Willis Griffiths

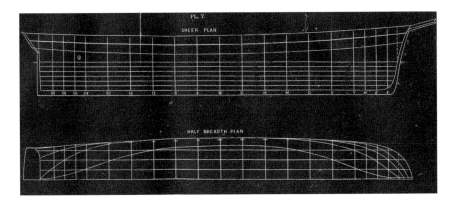

barge was built in 1732 by John Hall and designed by William Kent, the talented architect, landscape gardener, and artist to Frederick, Prince of Wales and eldest son of King George II. The narrow clinker built boat has a shallow concave entrance, with most of its width towards the high stern. Powered by eleven oars on each side, the 63-foot long barge saw service on the Thames for many years; it was last used to convey Prince Albert to the Coal Exchange in 1849. Prince Frederick's barge is currently an exhibit at the National Maritime Museum in Greenwich.

Royal Barge Passing London Bridge *(ILN)*

The origin of the term 'clipper' is uncertain: it possibly came from the Old Dutch word 'klepper,' meaning a fast horse. One of the earliest known uses of the word 'clip,' meaning to fly fast, was when John Dryden described the flight of the falcon:

> Some falcon stoops at what her eye designed,
> And, with her eagerness the quarry missed,
> Straight flies at check and clips it down the wind.
> John Dryden *Annus Mirabilis: The Year of Wonders, 1666*

'Clip' was freely used in New England in relation to speed obtained with a lightness of foot over the ground, in expressions such as 'to clip along' and 'to go at a good clip.' Its first nautical mention is with reference to the Baltimore Clippers, small privateers that dodged British warships during the Revolutionary War. They were called clippers because they clipped at speed over the waves and didn't plough through them.

Baltimore Clippers were long light vessels with markedly raked masts; look-outs on Royal Navy ships reported them as 'rakish vessels.' Most were Bermudan rigged, so-called because they carried fore-and-aft sails that were more efficient to windward than a square rig. Single-masted vessels were known as Bermudan sloops, a class of vessel that was in widespread use in the West Indies towards the end of the eighteenth century. At the time, Bermuda had the largest shipbuilding industry in American coastal waters, building what was then called the 'Jamaican sloop,' later the Bermudan sloop, a vessel of advanced design that was well ahead of other sailing craft. Some were up to 70 feet in length, quite long for a single-masted vessel.

Fast for its size, the Bermudan sloop suited the requirements of small mari-time traders at the time. But a large crew was required, and soon the more lightly sparred two-masted schooner began to replace the sloop as the classic Baltimore clipper. Baltimore clipper schooners were long sleek vessels, with extremely raked masts, stem and sternpost, and a low freeboard. Many of them were brig-schooners, as ships square-rigged on the foremast, and with fore-and-aft sails on the mainmast, were called. These fast vessels suited the requirements of traders and mariners; many of them were used for illegal activities such as smuggling and piracy in the West Indies, and a number were used as slavers.

As trade grew between the West Indies and the American Colonies, Britain rigidly enforced the Navigation Laws. Baltimore clippers could escape to wind-ward in strong winds, using their fore-and-aft sail arrangement, and avoid being overtaken by larger Royal Navy ships. They acquitted themselves well in the Anglo American War of 1812 in which they served as privateers.

* * *

The China tea trade was the catalyst for building fast clipper ships. Tea drinking was becoming popular and within a short time American clippers were compet-ing to bring tea from China to England and the United States. Tea could become moldy in the warm salt air of a long sea voyage, and the cargo of the first and swiftest sailing ship to return with the new season's finest tea would earn the highest price.

The Portuguese were the first European traders to reach China. In 1557 the Chinese allowed them to found a small settlement at Macao. In 1685 all Chinese ports were opened to foreign trade by the Manchu Emperor, but later he permit-ted the 'foreign devils' to trade only at Canton. China held the outside world in great disdain, and was virtually closed to outsiders until the end of the First Opium War in 1843. Until then, the East India Company had a monopoly of trade with China through Canton for a short time each year, when tea was ready for export. A limited number of merchants or their agents were allowed off the ships; on going ashore they were strictly supervised, and had to pay for tea with silver, as the Chinese had no wish to purchase foreign goods.

Britain, the United States, and to a lesser extent other European countries, were involved in shipping opium from India through unscrupulous Chinese merchants and corrupt officials to the market in China. Opium was shipped in fast 'Opium Clippers.' As early as 1831, three small British schooners, the fast *Jamesina, Lord Amherst,* and *Sylph,* were engaged in the extremely lucrative opium trade between India and China. As trade in opium increased, it attracted the Americans, whose fast schooners *Angola, Zephyr, Mazeppa,* and *Ariel,* ranging from 90 to 175 tons, carried opium to China in 1842 and 1843. Opium Clippers carried a variety of rigs, were not built to any particular design, and bore no relationship in hull shape or rig to the later clipper ships. Many of the captains and crews of the China tea clippers were reputed to have served on the Opium Clippers.

Opium Clipper *Wild Dayrell* (*ILN*)

Falcon

One of the more celebrated of the Opium Clippers was the full-rigged ship *Falcon*, measuring 352 tons. Previously the flagship of the Earl of Yarborough, commodore of the Royal Yacht Squadron, *Falcon* was built in 1824, regardless of expense, at the List yard in Wootton Creek on the Isle of Wight. *Falcon* was the only full-rigged ship among the Opium Clippers; she was generously sparred, with appropriately raked masts, and could generate the power required to drive a ship twice her size. Manned with naval discipline and efficiency, like an East Indiaman, she was kept in perfect condition.

For a number of years the 22-gun *Falcon* joined the cruise of the experimental squadron, when new Royal Navy ships were tested, mainly for speed; she was able to keep pace with the fastest of them. In October 1827 *Falcon* saw action in the Battle of Navarino in the Aegean Sea; she was in the thick of the action, with Yarborough flying his flag as Admiral of the Isle of Wight from the main, and his commodore's burgee from the fore. In 1836, *Falcon* was acquired by Jardine, Matheson & Co, who fitted her out for the opium trade. She carried three full watches; under sail she was fast, responsive, and dry, a delight to the crew who sailed her.

One of the smartest of Jardine Matheson's schooner-rigged opium clippers was the former tea and fruit carrier *Hellas*. In 1838 she arrived in Canton 124 days out from London, an impressive time for the 92-foot long, 209-ton brigantine.

Hellas

Hellas was built in 1832 at White's shipyard in Ferrybank, on the north bank of the River Suir at Waterford, for Charles Bewley of Dublin. A heavily sparred vessel, she spread a large amount of canvas, and was worked by a crew of 50. For six years she traded with China, before being acquired for the opium trade after her arrival in Canton in 1838. *Hellas* was the first ship to carry a cargo of tea directly to Ireland from China: on 1 March 1835 she arrived at Kingstown under the command of Captain A A Scanlan with 2,099 chests for Bewley's of Dublin, the East India Company's monopoly of the China tea trade having expired the previous year. In 1855 *Hellas* was lost without trace after leaving Leghorn, Italy.

Britain exerted tremendous pressure on China to open its ports to foreign trade. In 1839, the British authorities' response to the burning by the Chinese of opium, confiscated from British traders, was to send in warships and troops. This resulted in a number of skirmishes that became known as the 'Opium War,' a conflict that lasted until the Emperor Daoguang agreed to a treaty. The Treaty was signed on 29 August 1842 on board *HMS Cornwallis*, anchored mid-river on the Yangtze Kiang at Nanjing, following two weeks of negotiation between Sir Henry Pottinger representing the British Government, and Mandarin Qiyang on behalf of the Emperor. It was a humiliating defeat for the previously powerful

Chinese Empire; Huang Ti, known as the Yellow Emperor, founded Chinese civilization 3,500 years earlier, and he had developed a sophisticated system of government and introduced the art of writing.

The Treaty of Nanjing allowed the West to trade with the cities of Amoy, Canton, Foochow, Ningpo, and Shanghai, afterwards referred to as the five Treaty Ports; westerners could live in these cities with the privileges of diplomats. The island of Hong Kong was handed over to Britain in perpetuity; and the Chinese agreed to pay Britain $21 million compensation, mostly for opium that had been confiscated and burned. Payment was made in the form of 65 tons of silver, which was shipped to England and minted into coins. Other countries, particularly the United States, France, Germany, Japan, and Russia, benefited from the Treaty; the Stars and Stripes was the first foreign flag to fly in Shanghai after the Treaty was signed.

Tea was freely available to the British, Americans, and French from 1842, and American merchants were among the first to profit from the expanding market. In 1843, 1844, and 1845–1846 Captain Robert H 'Bully' Waterman sailed the 13-year-old Isaac Webb built former New Orleans packet *Natchez* in record time from China to New York with the new season's tea: 94 days from Canton in 1844, 78 days from Canton in 1845, and 83 days from Hong Kong in 1845–1846. Waterman's 78 days from Canton to New York was subsequently only improved on by one day, and it was within four days of the all-time record between a Chinese and American port; the all-time record was established within a few years by Waterman himself, when in command of one of the new clippers.

* * *

The keel of the first clipper ship, the famous *Rainbow* designed by Griffiths, was laid down in the shipyard of Smith & Dimon at the lower end of East 4th Street, New York, in 1843 for the shipping firm of Howland & Aspinwall. Experts studied her lines and sharp bow as she began to take shape, so different from the steep broad front of contemporary merchant ships; some predicted that she would plunge into the first big wave and not surface again. *Rainbow's* design and her lines elicited so much criticism that work on completing her was delayed by Howland & Aspinwall.

Meantime Nathaniel Brown (Nat) Palmer, a tall strong competent seafarer, and a captain on the China run, was considering ways of making faster voyages. Palmer, who was most knowledgeable about the design and construction of ships, and would later become known as the father of the American clipper ship captains, convinced the New York shipping merchants A A Low & Brother to build a ship based on a model he had carved. Lows commissioned the yard of Brown & Bell to build the 583-ton *Houqua*, named after an admired and highly respected Cantonese tea merchant and a close friend of William Low. Houqua, who had died the previous year and was of humble origins, had amassed a fortune of $26 million from honest and respectable business dealings with Western merchants. *Houqua* was launched in May 1844. Although not a true clipper ship, she had a long sleek hull and tall rig. On her maiden voyage she arrived in Hong Kong 85 days 17 hours out from New York; in 1850 the clipper ship *Oriental* would sail from New York to Hong Kong in 80 days 10 hours, an outbound record between those ports that would never be equalled by another sailing ship. *Houqua* returned to New York with tea in an impressive 90 days from Hong Kong.

Shipping merchants were impressed and Howland & Aspinwall decided to complete *Rainbow* without further delay. She was launched in January 1845, setting out on her maiden voyage on 1 February under the command of Captain John Land. Three days out of New York her three topgallant masts came down, and were repaired, sent back up, and stepped. The crew was on the point of mutiny on grounds of overwork when the passengers became involved and prevented trouble. *Rainbow's* time to Hong Kong was 108 days; the return to New York from Whampoa took 102 days; and a top speed of 14 knots was logged in the Atlantic north-east trades. Three subsequent homeward passages with tea were completed in 84, 86, and 88 days. *Rainbow* had proved to be an exceedingly fast ship. Captain William H Hayes succeeded Land, and on 17 March 1849 *Rainbow* set sail for Valparaiso and China. She was never heard of again and it is assumed that she foundered off Cape Horn.

Howland & Aspinwall asked Griffiths to design an even faster clipper for Waterman, who was one of their leading captains. Griffiths's second clipper, *Sea Witch*, was similar to *Rainbow*; she was launched from the Smith & Dimon yard on 6 December 1846. The 907-ton *Sea Witch* had a long hollow entrance, good 'deadrise,' and hardly any 'tumblehome,' as inward slope of the upper sides, or swell of the sides, was termed. Deadrise or 'rise of floor' was the angle the sides made with the keel: the base line was a line drawn at right angles to the keel; the greater the angle between the ship's side and this line, the bigger the deadrise. Extreme clippers with a V-shaped bottom were described as having large dead-rise, a shape associated with high speed. Although this was the accepted view at the time, the flatter-bottomed medium clippers that appeared later would prove to be almost as fast. Nat Palmer believed a flat bottom with little deadrise, as he had specified for *Houqua*, increased the speed of a ship.

Under way with all sail set, *Sea Witch* was a stunningly beautiful ship. Like many of the great Yankee clippers built later, she was heavily sparred with tall raking masts. She crossed three skysail yards, had royal studdingsails, a reef band in her topgallants, and four reef bands in her fore and main topsails. Her figure-head was a Chinese dragon. Her name *Sea Witch* was the suggestion of Waterman: his bride, Cordelia Sterling, had said that this great clipper was a witch that had come to take him away from her.

Robert Waterman lost his father, a ships master, at sea when he was eight, and went to sea himself when he left school in Fairfield, Connecticut, at the age of twelve. He was a tough captain to serve under; he paid and fed his crew well, but demanded total commitment to constant toil on deck and aloft in pursuit of speed, regardless of cost, severely punishing any sailor who failed in even the least of his duties. His uncompromising attitude to the crew earned him the designation 'Bully.'

In her time, *Sea Witch* was the swiftest ship that sailed the seas. In 1847, under Waterman's command, she returned from Canton to New York in 81 days. At the end of the same year, this beautiful and fast clipper left Canton on 29 December for New York, on what would be a record-breaking voyage: in one day *Sea Witch* logged 289 miles and on eight consecutive days *Sea Witch* sailed 2,200 miles in the north-east trades, an average of 275 miles in each 24 hours, arriving at her destination 77 days out from Canton, ahead of a fleet of over fifty other tea ships. It was an improvement of one day on the 78-day record that Waterman had achieved three years previously, when in command of the smaller packet *Natchez*. The following season, *Sea Witch* sailed from Whampoa on 9 January 1849, and arrived in New York 74 days 14 hours later, a time never again equalled by a ship sailing from China to the United States. During the voyage she logged 14,341 miles, including 358 miles in one 24-hour period.

Sea Witch was an extremely profitable investment, as shippers were able to charge a premium for using her to deliver the season's first cargo of tea from China. Waterman's reputation as one of the great American clipper captains was firmly established. A remarkable couple of round trips between New York, Valparaiso, Whampoa, and New York followed. *Sea Witch's* 24-hour run of 358 miles, an average speed of almost 15 knots through the water, was an incredible performance, considering that only a short time earlier the accepted maximum speed of a sailing ship was 13.5 knots.

The clipper bow could sail into a rising sea without suddenly being slowed down as happened in full-bowed ships, and this enabled clippers to carry on for longer in strong winds without having to reduce sail.

The success of *Rainbow* and *Sea Witch* in the China tea trade ushered in the great clipper ship era. Within two to three years, a whole fleet of American clippers was competing on the China run and, during the following decade, the Yankee Clippers, the most powerful sailing craft ever built up to that time, swept the seas.

Two other fast China clippers were built in New York for A A Low & Brother: the 957-ton *Samuel Russell* launched from the Brown & Bell yard in 1847; and the 1,003-ton *Oriental*, built in 1849 by Jacob Bell who had acquired his partner's share in the yard. *Oriental* cost $70,000 to build, including fitting-out. *Samuel Russell*, a heavily sparred and beautiful clipper, commanded by Captain Nat Palmer, reached New York 81 days out from Canton in 1848. Palmer was confidential adviser to Low's on all matters relating to ships, and had supervised the construction of *Samuel Russell*. Many of his suggestions were embodied in *Samuel Russell* and *Oriental*. An all round sportsman, with great enthusiasm and skill as a yachtsman, Palmer owned fifteen yachts in his lifetime and was one of the first members of the New York Yacht Club. The beautiful 70-ton schooner *Juliet* was his last yacht; he sailed her along the lovely New England coast for many summers before he died.

One of the smallest of the early clipper fleet was the 776-ton *Mandarin*, launched in June 1850 from the New York yard of Smith & Dimon for the firm of Goodhue & Co. *Mandarin's* beautiful appearance and fast passages soon earned her many admirers. She was built for the California trade, but her later voyages were mostly on the China run. In 1855, with the aid of favorable winds throughout a 13,000 mile voyage, she reached Melbourne 70 days out from New York, a time never again equalled by a ship sailing from an American East Coast port to Australia. In August 1864 this classic clipper struck a reef in the China Sea and sank without loss of life.

Clipper ships drew attention to themselves with their long sleek hulls and raked masts towering over the other ships and dockside warehouses, or as they sailed out into the ocean under a magnificent spread of canvas. They were classic full-rigged ships, with three masts, and square sails on each. Similar vessels, in which the foremast and mainmast were square-rigged, but the mizzenmast rigged fore-and-aft, were called 'clipper barques,' and considered by the seasoned clipper sailor to be inferior to the classic full-rigged ship, although a number of original clipper barques performed as well as their full-rigged counterparts. Barque rigs were sometimes converted from full-rigged because the sails could be handed by a smaller crew.

Clipper hulls were long and lean, with an average length/breadth ratio of 5:1. William L Crothers described the universal characteristics of a clipper hull: a stem raked forward in varying degrees and contours; sternposts that were upright; gently sweeping sheerlines low in the stern and noticeably higher at the bow; moderate to extreme deadrise at the mid-section; barely discernible to considerable tumblehome; varying degrees of flare in the bow; small counters; and well-rounded bilges.

Carefully selected pitch pine was used for the masts and yards of clippers; all except the lower masts were hewn from one length, and because of this were pole masts and pole yards. Each clipper mast was composed of three sections tapering upwards: lower mast, topmast and topgallant mast, stepped and firmly bound together where they overlapped. The upper part of the top-gallant was sometimes called the royal mast, although occasionally a short royal mast was stepped.

Lower masts were known as made masts because they were composed of parallel pieces of wood, about five in number, that were bolted together before being bound by up to 30 iron hoops, each over half-an-inch thick. The iron hoops were heated until they were red-hot, slipped onto and positioned on the mast, then they were rapidly cooled with water so that they contracted, tightly binding the wooden components together. Made masts were extremely heavy, weighing up to 33 tons, whereas the largest of the pole masts did not normally weigh more than seven tons.

Clipper ship masts were tall, reaching over 100 feet above the deck, with another 15-20 feet of mast extending from the keelson to deck level. Each mast was supported by strong ropes extending from deck level to the mastheads: forestays and backstays supported the mast in the longitudinal direction while the shrouds, extending from the ship's sides, provided lateral support. Each lower mast was stepped on the keelson, with its foot secured in an oak housing. Before the clipper era, the keelson consisted of a single band of oak extending the length of the ship, positioned on the floor parallel to the keel, binding the frames

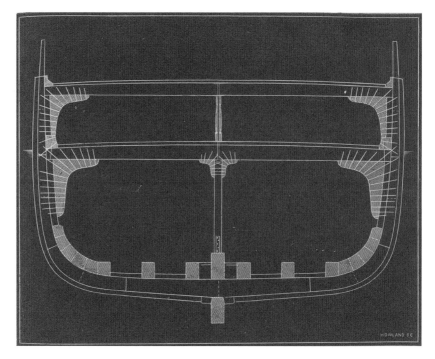

John Willis Griffiths

to the keel, and providing longitudinal stability to the hull. Clippers, with their increased length and larger size, required a stronger and more robust spine than the keel alone could provide. This potential weakness was overcome by adding longitudinal layers of oak that extended the full length of the ship, thus building the keelson into an extremely strong composite beam that provided strength and integrity to the frames and the hull.

The yards decreased in size the higher they were located on the mast. Their maximum diameter was at the center, from where they tapered outwards to the yardarms. The three lower masts were set with single fore, main and mizzen yards; the latter often called the crossjack. A clipper's main yard, weighing up to 15 tons and positioned about 50 feet above the deck, was about 80 feet or more in length, and extended well out over the sides of the ship when squared. The shorter and smaller topsail yards, one on each topmast, weighed 3–7 tons; on later clippers the single topsail was replaced by double topsails, each suspended from a yard. Topgallant masts carried the topgallant and royal yards, and sometimes skysail yards; moonraker sails, often referred to as moonsails, were carried on yards set above the skysails on a small number of the largest clippers.

The square sails bent on the lower yards and topsail yards were the largest sails carried. Those on the lower yards were called courses: foresail or fore-course, mainsail or main-course, and mizzen-course or crossjack. Clippers also carried a spanker on the mizzen mast, a relatively large fore-and-aft sail with a boom and gaff. When set, the spanker became known as the driver because it took advantage of the leading wind, and replaced the crossjack. In light airs, the spread of the spanker was increased by setting a ringtail, a type of studdingsail, rigged out on a sliding ringtail boom attached to the after end of the spanker boom.

Studdingsail booms were attached to the outer ends of the lower, topmast, topgallant, and sometimes the royal yards. They enabled the area of square canvas to be increased by sliding the booms out from the yardarms. Studdingsails were light fair-weather sails that were set in a moderate leading wind. In addition to the square sails, there were triangular staysails, set on stays between the masts, and as jibs on stays that extended from the bowsprit at about 45° to the foremast. Most clippers could set four jibs: the two foremost, the flying jib and the outer jib, were set in light weather with the heavy duty inner jib and foretopmast staysail (storm jib) almost always set.

A clipper ship's sails could generate as much as 3,000 horsepower in a fresh breeze. Square sails were normally set and trimmed from the deck. But sailors had to go aloft to work on the yards; standing on the footropes (horses) to loose, reef, and furl sail, and when rigging out or taking in the studdingsail booms. A complex array of over 200 ropes was attached to the sails and rigging, many of them coming down to the deck. In addition to the stays and shrouds that supported the masts, there were hoists, downhauls, outhauls, clew-lines, leech-lines, buntlines, gaskets, sheets, vangs, footropes, strops, ratlines, and braces.

* * *

In 1849 Britain repealed the Navigation Laws, laws that had prohibited foreign ships from trading with United Kingdom ports, unless they were conveying products from their own country. The laws were repealed when other nations, who wanted to trade freely without import or export duties, closed their ports to British ships and goods. Abolition of the Navigation Laws was a natural sequel to the repeal of the Corn Laws three years earlier, and the beginning of international free trade. The Navigation Laws were enacted by the Parliament of Oliver Cromwell in 1650 and 1651, and affirmed by King Charles II after the Restoration.

Repeal of the Navigation Laws immediately brought British merchant ships into direct competition with the ships of other nations, particularly the United States. The move was strenuously opposed in Parliament and the House of Lords, and by almost every shipbuilder and shipowner. Until then, Britain, in common with other European nations, paid scant attention to the changing pattern of seaborne trade and its increasing emphasis on speed. Fast voyages were of little concern to British and other European seafarers. Alexis de Tocqueville, writing earlier in the century, compared the rather relaxed attitude of the Europeans to that of the Americans:

> The European sailor navigates with prudence; he only sets sail when the weather is favourable; if an unfortunate accident befalls him, he puts into port; at night he furls a portion of his canvas; and when the white billows intimate the vicinity of land, he checks his way and takes an observation of the sun. But the American neglects these precautions and braves these dangers. He weighs anchor in the midst of tempestuous gales; by night and day he spreads his sheets to the winds; he repairs as he goes along such damage as his vessel may have sustained from the storm; and when at last he approaches the end of his voyage, he darts onward to the shore as if he already descried a port . . . The European touches several times at different ports in the course of a long voyage; he loses a good deal of precious time in making harbor, or in waiting for a favourable wind to leave it; and pays daily dues to be allowed to remain there. The American starts from Boston to purchase tea in Canton, stays there a few days and then returns . . . American ships fill the docks of Le Havre and Liverpool, while the number of English and French vessels in New York Harbour is comparatively small.
>
> Alexis de Tocqueville *Democracy in America*

Because of the lack of competition, British shipbuilders and owners did not have fast sailing ships capable of competing in the growing international trade in tea. Under the protection of the Navigation Laws, little consideration had been given to the Yankee Clipper until she captured the tea trade. By then, fast efficient ships mattered more than anything, and the China tea trade was the catalyst that would create the British clipper ship.

On 3 December 1850 the Jacob Bell built *Oriental* arrived in the West India

Oriental (*ILN*)

Docks with a load of tea from China, the first American clipper ship to enter the Thames, and the first non-British ship to carry a cargo of Chinese tea to England. She had arrived in a record 97 days from Whampoa. *Oriental* was commanded by Captain Theodore Palmer, the younger brother of Nat Palmer who had relinquished command of her earlier in the year to retire from seafaring.

The arrival of *Oriental* caused a sensation in the British shipping industry: it showed that British merchants abroad were willing to pay high freights to charter a superior American ship. Hong Kong merchants had willingly paid £6 per ton for the 1,600-ton tea cargo because of *Oriental's* known sailing qualities, at a time when other ships loading at Whampoa were only paid £3/10s per ton.

Oriental had covered 67,000 sea miles from the time she first set out on 14 September 1849. She sailed from Hong Kong to New York in 81 days on the return leg of her maiden voyage, and then returned to Hong Kong in a record-breaking 80 days 10 hours, reaching a speed of 16 knots. British traders in Hong Kong were so impressed with *Oriental's* performance that they wasted no time in chartering her to take tea to London.

> The trade with California and the repeal of the British navigation laws have together effected a revolution in the naval architecture of the United States ... Let our shipbuilders and their employers take warning

in time. There will always be an abundant supply of vessels, good enough and fast enough for short voyages. The coal trade can take care of itself, for it will ever be a refuge for the destitute. But we want fast vessels for the long voyages, which will otherwise fall into American hands. It is fortunate that the Navigation Laws have been repealed in time to destroy these false and unreasonable expectations, which might have lulled the ardour of British competition. We now all start together with a fair field and no favour. The American captain can call at London, and the British captain can pursue his voyage to New York.

The Times 5 December 1850

Large crowds gathered at the West India Docks to view the beautiful American clipper. No ship like her was ever seen in Britain until then. British shipbuilders and shipowners had ignored the clipper ships until *Oriental* and other American clippers arrived with full cargos of tea from China. The New York clipper made them acutely aware that they had nothing to compare with her for speed, beauty of model, rig, or construction. Arthur H Clark described *Oriental* as a triumph of the shipwrights and seamen's toil and skill:

> . . . every line of her long streamlined black hull oozed power and speed; her tall raking masts and skysail yards towered over the spars of all the other ships; her white cotton sails were neatly furled under bunt, quarter, and yardarm gaskets; her topmast, topgallant and royal stud-dingsail booms and long heavy lower studdingsail booms swung in along her rails, gave an idea of the enormous spread of canvas held in reserve for light and moderate leading winds; her blocks, standing and running rigging were neatly fitted to withstand great stress and strain. Everything on deck was there for a purpose: spare spars were brightly varnished, and neatly lashed along the waterways; the inner side of the bulwarks, the rails and the deck-houses were painted pure white; her hatch coamings, skylights, pin-rails, and companions were of Spanish mahogany; the narrow planks of her pine decks, with the gratings and ladders, were scrubbed and holystoned to the whiteness of cream; the brasswork on the wheel, binnacle, and skylights glittered brightly.

Arthur H Clark *The Clipper Ship Era*

In dry dock at the Blackwall Yard, home of the East Indiamen and the Blackwall Frigates, local surveyors and shipbuilders scrutinized *Oriental's* hull, and took her lines off; shortly afterwards they would take off the lines of the America's Cup winner, *America,* and the clipper *Challenge.*

The following December, another clipper ship from the Jacob Bell yard, the handsome 1,119-ton *White Squall* commanded by Captain Benoni Lockwood, arrived in London with a cargo of tea that netted her owners, William Platt & Sons of Philadelphia, $58,000. Her time of 104 days to the Downs from Whampoa was the best of the season, ahead of a number of other American clippers including the very fast California clipper *Surprise.* One week out of Whampoa, *White Squall* had had to sail against the south-west monsoon, anchor in light airs for two days off Anjar, and lose three days off Madagascar because the topmast came down.

Like many of the early clippers, *White Squall's* original rigging was no match for the elements: she lost her three topgallant masts two days out on her maiden voyage, and had to put into Rio de Janeiro for repairs. Her time to San Francisco from New York was 118 sailing days, for which her freight list earned her owners $74,000; *White Squall's* Philadelphia owners had paid $90,000 to have her built, including stores and provisions for one year. From San Francisco she had sailed to Whampoa, where she collected her lucrative cargo for London.

The following year, when under the command of Captain Samuel Kennedy, *White Squall* reached San Francisco 111 days out from New York, afterwards sailing to Whampoa, where she collected tea for New York. *White Squall's* life as a clipper ship was short: she was so badly damaged by the New York Harbor fire of 26 December 1853 that she was rebuilt as a barque with a single deck.

One of the largest and most well appointed clippers of the time was the 1,498-ton extreme clipper *Witch of the Wave,* launched from the yard of George Raynes at Portsmouth, New Hampshire, on 6 April 1851 for a consortium of two Boston companies and Captain John Bertram of Salem, Massachusetts, her home port. Cabins for captain, officers, and passengers were fitted out with mahogany, rosewood, maple, and satinwood, and upholstered with rich velvet. A fine library was supplied with 100 volumes. Martin Fernald was responsible for her standing rigging; he raked her masts at 1¼, 1½ and 1¾ inches to the foot from fore to mizzen. Unlike many of her sister ships, *Witch of the Wave* lost no spars on her maiden voyage circumnavigating the globe. Described by the Collector of the

Witch of the Waves (*ILN*)

Port of Salem, Ephraim F Miller, as the newest of the Salem Witches, her figure-head was a female figure in flowing white garments.

Witch of the Wave loaded for California at Boston, and set sail under the command of Captain J Hardy Millett on 20 May 1851 with 1,900 tons of general cargo. After a 123-day run, during which her best 24-hour distance was 300 miles and her top speed was 16 knots, she arrived in San Francisco. From there she sailed to Hong Kong in 40 days.

Witch of the Wave loaded 19,000 chests of first quality tea at Whampoa and set out for London on 5 January 1852. Shortly afterwards, she picked up the north-east monsoon and, with the benefit of the monsoon wind on her port side abaft the beam, progress was excellent: *Witch of the Wave* sped across the South China Sea, logging 338 miles in one 24-hour period; on 4 April, when 92 days out from Whampoa, she arrived at the East India Dock, a record time that would not be equalled by any other clipper ship from that port to London.

Her attributes were immediately recognized: *The Times* lauded the Salem Witch's 90-day passage to the Downs, informing its readers how she would have arrived several days earlier if she had not been headed by a strong easterly wind that required her to beat up the English Channel; the *London Shipping Gazette* described how she had worked up the Channel to windward of 400 sailing vessels, and not one of them could keep up with her; a lithograph in the *London Illustrated News* showed her under full sail, to royals, including studdingsails, accompanied by a report describing her bows as being similar to a large cutter yacht. Like *Oriental* and *White Squall, Witch of the Wave* attracted much interest when she was in dock.

This appears to have been the only tea cargo that *Witch of the Wave* carried from China while in American ownership. Eighteen days after arriving in London, she left for Boston where she arrived 23 days later. A 119-day voyage to San Francisco followed, under the command of Captain Benjamin Tay. From there she travelled to Hong Kong in 41 days. Shortly after leaving there for Calcutta she was in collision with the barque *Spartan*, and had to put into Singapore for repairs to her rudder. From Calcutta she sailed to Boston in 81 days, a record from Calcutta to any American port.

On 16 August 1853, *Witch of the Wave* left Boston under the command of Captain Lewis F Miller and arrived in San Francisco just ahead of five of the reputably fastest ships of the time. The six clippers arrived in port within 30 hours of each other during 10-11 December, turning in excellent times for their voyages across the Great Racecourse of the Ocean: *Witch of the Wave* 117 days; *Raven* 119 days; *Mandarin* and *Hurricane* 123 days; *Trade Wind* 125 days; and *Comet* 128 days.

In February 1855, *Witch of the Wave* arrived in Amsterdam with a cargo from Batavia. There she was chartered for a round trip to Batavia before being purchased by Van Eighen & Co of Amsterdam. Renamed *Electra*, she is known to have sailed under the Dutch flag for at least fifteen years.

Yankee Clippers dominated the British tea trade for a couple of years after *Witch of the Wave's* arrival in London. Twenty-two American ships arrived with Chinese tea in 1853, including ten clippers ships and three clipper barques.

CHAPTER 2

The Great Racecourse of the Ocean

Some of the most glorious trials of speed and prowess that the world ever witnessed have taken place over it. Here the modern clipper ship – the noblest work that has ever come from the hands of man – has been sent, guided by the lights of science, to contend with the elements, to outstrip steam, and astonish the world.

Matthew F Maury *The Physical Geography of the Sea*

The California Gold Rush could not have come at a better time for American ship designers, builders, and owners. By 1850 the rush to California had started in earnest: gold fever had taken hold and everyone wanted to go, they wanted to get there by sea, and in the shortest possible time. Fast ships that could charge the highest fares were in great demand; the clipper fleet was taking shape at precisely the right time.

In 1849, about 800 ships and boats of all types made it round Cape Horn to California; it is not known how many others set out but never arrived. *Rainbow,* the first extreme clipper ship ever built, was probably one of those lost off the Horn that year when she failed to arrive at Valparaiso as scheduled. The only clipper ship to sail to San Francisco prior to 1850 was *Memnon,* commanded by Captain Joseph R Gordon. She arrived there from New York on 28 July 1849 after a record passage of 120 days. A clipper of 1,000 tons designed by Griffiths with the intention of improving on *Sea Witch, Memnon* was launched from the New York yard of Smith & Dimon for Warren Delano; she was said to resemble Griffiths's masterpiece. *Memnon* sailed for Liverpool on her maiden voyage under the command of the veteran master mariner Captain Deliverance P Benjamin on 6 November 1848 and arrived off Port Lynas, Anglesey, 14 days 7 hours out from New York. When sailing at 13 knots under a spread of canvas she had overtaken the steamship *Europe*.

Eighteen-fifty was the first year that clippers sailed to California in any number; it was also the year of the first California Clipper Race. Seven clipper ships, racing against time, took part: *Celestial, Houqua, Mandarin, Memnon, Samuel Russell, Sea Witch,* and *Race Horse.* Each one had their supporters, and large sums of money were wagered on the outcome. *Sea Witch,* with an established reputation for speed, was the favorite.

The predictions that the four older ships *Houqua, Sea Witch, Samuel Russell,* and *Memnon* would be fastest, based on their previous performances, was confirmed when *Samuel Russell,* under the command of Captain Charles P Low, arrived in San Francisco on 6 May 1850 after a passage of 109 days, breaking *Memnon's* 120-day record. *Samuel Russell's* supporters and backers were confident that this passage would not be equalled by any of the other contenders. *Houqua* performed well, arriving on 23 July, 120 days out from New York.

Before setting out for San Francisco, *Sea Witch* had arrived back in New York from Canton in 85 days under Captain George W Fraser, a Scotsman who had earlier assumed command; Fraser had been *Sea Witch's* first mate under Waterman. By then Fraser, like his former skipper, had earned a reputation as a hard driver. *Sea Witch* sailed from New York on 14 April 1850 for San Francisco, arriving there 101 days later, having spent four days in Valparaiso, a record 97 sailing days. Already the holder of the all-time record from China to the United States, *Sea Witch* was the first ship to sail from Boston or New York to San Francisco in less than 100 days, breaking *Memnon's* record by 23 days, and completing the first California Clipper race eight days, twelve sailing days, ahead of her nearest rival *Samuel Russell.*

Sea Witch's performance was an astonishing one at the time. According to a contemporary report, seventeen ships left New York for California between 26 June and 28 July 1850, and arrived in San Francisco an average 157 days later. The previous year, when *Memnon* recorded her 120-day voyage, 23 vessels arrived in San Francisco during the first two weeks of September in 160-240 days, an average voyage time of 199 days. Ships setting sail in midsummer took longer on average to reach California than those leaving between the end of November and the beginning of March. According to the *New York Times,* the longest time was the 366 days taken by the sailing ship *Merchant,* reckoned to be a first-class vessel. By the time she arrived in San Francisco the underwriters assumed she was lost, and were already paying out insurance to shippers.

But *Sea Witch's* record did not last for long. Later in the year *Surprise,* a sharp clipper of just over 1,000 tons, was launched, fully rigged, from the East Boston yard of Samuel Hall on 5 October, for A A Low & Brother. *Surprise* was built under the supervision of her future commander, Captain Philip Dumaresq. Her owners were so pleased with her that they presented her builder with a bonus of $2,500. After part loading in Boston, *Surprise* was towed to New York where loading was completed. She crossed three skysails yards on thirteen-foot-long skysail masts stepped on her topgallant masts. *Surprise* looked magnificent under sail, dominated by large fore and main single topsails. On 13 December 1850, Dumaresq took her to sea and 96 days 15 hours later she arrived in San Francisco, the fastest passage over the Racecourse up to that time. In 1857, *Surprise,* then under the command of Captain Charles S Ranlett, reached New York 82 days out from Shanghai. Two years later, *Sword Fish* would improve on *Surprise's* time from Shanghai to New York by one day, when she arrived home in 81 days on 12 December 1859 and set the all-time record between the two cities.

Donald McKay, the builder of America's greatest sailing ships, raised the standard of shipbuilding in a relatively short time from small, clumsily-shaped, slow-moving craft to the largest, finest, and fastest merchant sailing vessels ever created. McKay's clippers, like his earlier transatlantic packets, were three-masted and full-rigged, the classic clipper rig. During the clipper era, Donald McKay's creations were the swiftest and most beautiful sailing ships in the world. McKay also created the first of the large cargo-carrying medium clippers that were to dominate the long distance ocean routes for over half a century.

McKay was primarily responsible for the emergence of three categories of clipper ship: extreme clipper, clipper, and medium clipper. Most of the early clippers were in the 'extreme' class, built with exceedingly fine lines to sail fast, while carrying a relatively small cargo; extreme clippers owed their success to their unique hull shape, large rigs, and their accomplished captains. 'Clippers' had fine lines, with greater cargo-carrying capacity than the extreme clippers; their streamlined hulls enabled them to make fast passages, sometimes as fast as those with the more extreme hulls. 'Medium' clippers, with their sharp clipper ends, were primarily built to carry large cargos; they had similar, but fuller, lines to the extreme clipper. Because of their large size, medium clippers were capable of fast passages when well laden and driven hard.

Clipper hulls were described according to their shape at the bow, amidships, and stern: the shape of the bow was described as the 'entrance,' the fullest part as 'mid-section,' and the shape of the stern as the 'run.' Yankee clippers were designed primarily for speed, and were 'fine-lined,' with the underwater part of the hull having a sharp entrance and run, with no abrupt curves to interrupt the smooth lines sweeping from stem to sternpost. The mid-section was the fullest part of the hull, about midway between the bow and stern, although in some ships it was slightly forward of this. It was the shape of the ship along the waterline, particularly the entrance and the run, that were important in the design of fast clippers.

The ideal hull was long and narrow, with a hollow concave bow forming a sharp streamlined entrance at the waterline, giving way to straight wall-like sides before tapering backwards and upwards to a shallow run. Clippers with long narrow hulls and large deadrise had potentially higher speeds.

Hull length played a major role in a clipper's speed: the longer the hull, the faster the ship was capable of travelling; the potential speed was directly related to waterline length. A mathematical formula provided an estimate of a sailing ship's optimum speed in knots: ships that attained speeds in excess of 1.4 times the square root of the waterline length in feet were fast.

In late 1850, Donald McKay launched *Stag Hound,* his first clipper, the first of the really great Californian Clippers, and a vessel that would establish his reputation as a master shipbuilder and creator of great ships. *Stag Hound,* an extreme clipper, was designed, modeled, and drafted by McKay at his Border Street yard in East Boston. Not only was *Stag Hound,* at 1,534 registered tons, the largest merchant ship ever built up to that time, but her model was a new idea in naval architecture. Her masts were each raked at 1¼ inches to the foot; her sails were of cotton duck, 22 inches wide in the cloth; and it was calculated that she would spread nearly 11,000 yards of canvas when under full sail. Built primarily for speed, the sharp outline, breadth of beam, and depth of hold were designed to aid stability. *Stag Hound* was built to the order of George B Upton and Sampson & Tappan, both of Boston and owners of a number of extreme clippers. Ten thousand people gathered on a bitterly cold day in December 1850 at McKay's Boston shipyard to witness the launch of *Stag Hound*.

Stag Hound created intense interest in New York when she arrived there shortly afterwards. Her loading berth was at the foot of Wall Street. No ship had ever been seen in New York that carried so many spars and so much sail, and her lines were sharper than those of any other ship. Because there was severe criticism of *Stag Hound* in some quarters, including suggestions that her sharp lines would bury her in heavy weather, marine underwriters charged an extra insurance premium for her maiden voyage. *Stag Hound* was critically examined by Walter R Jones, President of the Atlantic Mutual Insurance Company. Jones suggested to Captain Josiah Richardson that he must be nervous going on so long a voyage in so sharp a ship, so heavily sparred. Richardson replied that he would not go at all if he thought for a moment that she was going to be his coffin.

Stag Hound sailed from New York on 1 February 1851. Six days out, her main topmast came away in gale force winds, taking with it all three topgallant masts. Richardson continued the voyage without a main topsail for nine days and without topgallants for twelve days. During that time he and his crew salvaged the spars and set up a jury rig that took them round Cape Horn as far as Valparaiso. There, repairs to her rig were completed before she resumed her voyage to San Francisco. Richardson's skill as captain, his navigational ability, and his excellent judgment ensured that *Stag Hound* not only survived, but reached San Francisco 113 days out from New York, despite having had to sail for so long under jury rig, and having lost five days at Valparaiso. *Stag Hound* then sped across the Pacific to Manila, before going on to Whampoa to collect a cargo of tea, and sailing from there to New York, arriving back eleven months after leaving. During her first year at sea, *Stag Hound* frequently reached speeds of 16-17 knots and had a best day's run of 358 miles. As well as paying for herself in her first year, *Stag Hound* generated $8,000 extra profit.

In 1851 *Sea Witch* raced two other extreme clippers *Typhoon* and *Raven* on the Great Racecourse of the Ocean to San Francisco. *Typhoon*, built by Fernald & Pettigrew at Badger's Island, Portsmouth, New Hampshire for D & A Kingsland of New York, was the largest of the three, at 1,611 tons. She was rigged on the stocks, and crossed three skysail yards. On 18 February 1851, a large crowd of admirers gathered to see her launched onto the Piscataqua River, her rigging festooned with bunting. Under the command of Captain Charles H Salter, *Typhoon* arrived at Liverpool 13 days 22 hours out from New York on her maiden voyage, with runs of 313 and 346 miles on consecutive days, and having logged a maximum speed of 15.5 knots. *Raven,* 711 tons and with beautiful lines, was launched in July 1851 by James M Hood of Somerset, Massachusetts; she was first owned by Crocker & Sturgis of Boston, but soon passed into the hands of Crocker & Warren of New York.

The race was hard fought, with the three clippers changing position in the final leg as they raced neck and neck from 50°S in the Pacific to San Francisco. *Typhoon* was the winner, arriving on 18 November 1851, 108 days out from New York, a day ahead of *Raven* and two days ahead of *Sea Witch*. *Raven* was a much smaller clipper than *Typhoon,* and under the command of Captain William W Henry she performed admirably. *Sea Witch* was five years old, and that placed her at a disadvantage against the two newly built clippers.

* * *

The building of great American clipper ships commenced in earnest in the same year, 1851, spurred on by the exhilarating atmosphere of the early days of the California Gold Rush. The two largest, finest, and best known of the newly-built California clippers were *Flying Cloud,* built by Donald McKay in Boston, and *Challenge,* built by William Webb at his yard on New York's East River. By the time *Sea Witch, Typhoon,* and *Raven* finished their race, Donald McKay's *Flying Cloud* had stolen the limelight.

The flamboyant 22-year-old George Francis Train, nephew of Enoch Train, and then a partner in Enoch's White Diamond Line, commissioned McKay to build him a big ship, a clipper approaching 2,000 tons in size. 'I shall call her *Flying Cloud,*' said Train. The younger Train, who would go on to become one of the United States's greatest eccentrics, sold *Flying Cloud* to the New York shipping company of Grinnell, Minturn & Co while she was still on the stocks at McKay's East Boston Yard. Moses H Grinnell, partner of Robert Minturn, paid the asking price of $90,000 for *Flying Cloud,* earning the Trains 100 per cent profit. But it was a transaction they would deeply regret.

Within four months of finishing *Stag Hound,* McKay had built and launched *Flying Cloud,* an extreme clipper ship built for speed, that would become a legend in her lifetime. Thousands of Bostonians gathered on an April day in 1851 to watch *Flying Cloud* slide stern first down the launching ways into Boston Harbor. Donald McKay produced many magnificent vessels, but his shipyard never created another ship that captured the minds and hearts as completely as

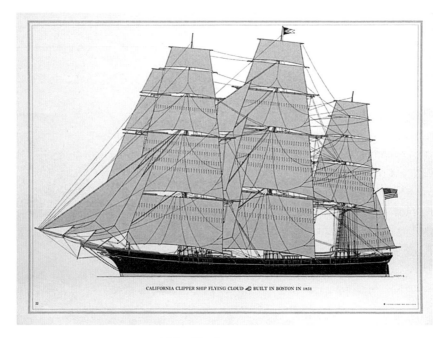

CALIFORNIA CLIPPER SHIP FLYING CLOUD ✦ BUILT IN BOSTON IN 1851

Flying Cloud (Currier & Ives)

Flying Cloud. She was a sharp sleek clipper, constructed of pine on oak, with an overall length of 229 feet and a relatively narrow beam of 41 feet, registering 1,782 tons; a few years earlier any ship over 130 feet in length was considered long. *Flying Cloud's* figurehead was an angel holding a trumpet to her mouth. Like many of the extreme clippers, she was over-sparred: her foremast was 113 feet high, main 127, and mizzen 102; her main yard was 82 feet long and, when squared, extended 20 feet out from her sides; she crossed three skysail yards and carried studdingsails on her royal yards; when set on the main yard, studdingsails extended to more than 40 feet from each side; there were four reef bands in the topsails and a single reef band in the topgallants. Like *Stag Hound,* her tall masts were raked alike at 1¼ inches per foot.

A month after *Stag Hound* arrived in California, *Flying Cloud* left New York on her maiden voyage with 37-year-old Captain Josiah Perkins Creesy in command. Creesy, who first commanded the China tea clipper *Oneida* when he was aged 23, originally went to sea on an East Indiaman, and worked his way up through the ranks. He sailed *Flying Cloud* fast, making her the most famous sailing ship of the clipper era. He paid particular attention to the recruitment and training of the crew, and like most other successful clipper captains worked them to the bone. Eleanor H Prentiss, whom Creesy had married ten years earlier, and who accompanied her husband on his many voyages, was an accomplished naviga-tor, an advocate of Maury's wind and current charts, and a competent nurse.

The Creesys were from the coastal town of Marblehead, Massachusetts. Eleanor learned pilotage and coastal navigation from her father, John Prentiss, who commanded a schooner. Her long sea voyages with her husband gave her the opportunity to further her interest in nautical astronomy and

Captain Josiah P Creesy

become an expert ocean navigator. She charted *Flying Cloud's* course over the Great Racecourse of the Ocean on the clipper's memorable maiden voyage.

On 3 June 1851 *Flying Cloud* swept out of New York in style, passing Sandy Hook under a cloud of white cotton, slicing through blue water before a fresh north-westerly breeze. Sandy Hook Lighthouse, located on the end of a long narrow spit at the north-east extremity of New Jersey, marked the entrance to New York Harbor, and the start and end of ocean voyages for ships travelling to and from the Southern Hemisphere.

Flying Cloud's cargo of assorted freight had the potential to earn $50,000 for Grinnell, Minturn & Co, and provide a handsome bonus for the Creesys; in addi-tion there were about a dozen relatively well-to-do paying passengers on board, bound for the booming new State of California.

The conventional route to Cape Horn was directly south, but Eleanor intended to follow Maury's recommended great circle route. *Flying Cloud* would take a wide sweep out into the North Atlantic, approach the doldrums mid way between the widest part of Africa and the Caribbean, give a fairly wide berth to Cape San Roque and keep about 300 miles off the coast of South America before passing to the west of the Falkland Islands.

Flying Cloud continued out into the ocean at an impressive pace under full sail to skysails and studdingsails. As the wind rose to nearly gale force, Creesy shortened sail by taking in the studdingsails and furling the skysails. It made little difference; powered by a large spread of canvas, McKay's creation continued to slice through heavy seas at speed with her lee rail almost constantly awash.

Three days out disaster struck: a sudden squall took away the main and mizzen topgallant masts, in addition to the main topsail yard, leaving much of the rigging amidships in a tangled mess. Sail was immediately reduced. *Flying Cloud* continued on course while Creesy directed the crew in their efforts to cut free the spars and get them safely on deck, before the flailing masts and yards had an opportunity to breach the integrity of the ship by holing the hull or deck. When the masts and yards were secure on deck, sail was reset and *Flying Cloud* surged ahead. Creesy drove the crew hard, refitting the topgallant masts that had come away, resetting the rigging, sending up and securing the repaired yards, and bending sail. The damage was made good, and Creesy had *Flying Cloud* racing ahead within 48 hours of her dismasting.

About a week later it was discovered that the lower mainmast had sprung near the top; presumably it had been damaged during the previous dismasting, and had opened up further from the load of the reset topmast yard and repaired topgallant mast and yards. The carpenter splinted the weak part of the mast with pieces of wood, positioned vertically, and bound them with strong rope, a poor substitute for the iron bands that had previously held the mast together; the three-foot diameter lower mainmast, weighing about 33 tons, extended 88 feet upwards from the keelson. Creesy had no option but to splint it, as he was unwilling to go into port and lose time having the mast taken out, properly repaired, and repositioned. He was taking a significant risk of dismasting if caught in a Cape Horn blast. But there was no way that he would sacrifice the opportunity of a lifetime: of sailing McKay's great clipper to California in record time.

Flying Cloud continued on a heading for Cape Horn. Like other ships bound for California, she would be rounding the Horn against the prevailing gale force winds and adverse current, with the likelihood of having to cope with extreme cold, fog, and the almost eternal darkness of the austral winter. Many a sailing ship rounding Cape Horn carrying an optimistic human cargo eager to get to California, with its opportunities, promise of a new life, and riches, failed to reach the Pacific Ocean and was never heard of again. Winter was not a pleasant time to round Cape Horn. June and July were, however, the months that offered the best chance of favorable east winds and Creesy was hoping that luck was on his side, and that he could sail *Flying Cloud* round the tip of South America running before a benign easterly breeze.

The jury rig was not significantly challenged until early July when *Flying Cloud* was hit by severe westerly squalls off the coast of Argentina; without a moment's delay Creesy had all hands on deck, sending them aloft to reduce sail. Under double-reefed topsails and staysails, Boston's pride and joy coped admirably with storm force winds, steep confused seas, thunder, lightning, and driving rain. The weather did not improve: big seas broke over the decks, and it became too dangerous to keep the fires lit in the stoves, with the result that there was no longer hot food for anyone. The wind then backed to the south-west, and Creesy had the remaining two reefs taken in, reducing *Flying Cloud's* canvas to close-reefed topsails and storm jib.

The damaged mainmast was then found to have sprung further, and Creesy had the main skysail, royal, and topgallant yards taken down to reduce weight; in addition he had the studdingsail booms removed from the remaining main yards. This dangerous work was achieved without injury or serious incident, the men going aloft and making their way out on the perilously swinging skysail yard, more than 100 feet above the deck, to secure the sails and lines before they could be lowered to the deck. A cold, wet, demanding, and particularly dangerous task for the crew had prevented a possible calamity. The reduced weight aloft made it less likely that the top of the lower mainmast would disintegrate and bring the topmast and topgallant masts crashing down.

No sooner had the storm abated than the main topsail halyard or tye, the heavy chain used for lifting the yard into position, parted. The yard immediately slipped down the mast sending the topsail dangerously out of control, with the yard threatening to fall onto the deck while the loose chain thrashed the mast uncontrollably. The crew quickly got the topsail stowed, and the yard lowered to its resting position, before removing the broken chain. A tye of new chain was then made and attached.

Shortly afterwards, attempted sabotage was discovered on board: two of the crew was found to have drilled through the floor under one of the forecastle berths. The two had signed on as sailors to get to California, but had become disgruntled by the harshness of life at sea and, blaming Creesy for what they perceived as his tough and demanding treatment of the crew, had created a hole through which water would leak into the hold and damage the cargo. Creesy had the two put in irons. Shortly afterwards he released them, and put them back to work with the prospect of being arrested and put on trial when the ship reached San Francisco.

As *Flying Cloud* approached Cape Horn, where the hours of darkness extended to 17 hours, a strong north-easterly gale was encountered, accompanied by freezing rain and extreme cold. Visibility was so poor that Creesy was unable to identify the landmarks leading to Le Maire Strait, a channel with strong tides that could only be negotiated with favorable winds in daylight. He was obliged to wear ship and retrace his course until visibility improved, losing two days as a consequence.

As Creesy guided *Flying Cloud* towards the entrance of the Strait for a second time, the gale-force wind veered easterly and visibility improved. Creesy was in luck. Running before a leading wind, *Flying Cloud* swept through the turbulent waters of the strait under a full spread of canvas on her fore and mizzen masts. The following day, only 50 days out from New York, she charged past the barren rock of Cape Horn, five miles away to the north, with the famous landmark clearly visible to the passengers on deck and the sailors in the rigging, as a dark silhouette against the backdrop of a snow-covered coastal landscape. *Flying Cloud* continued at speed, reaching 50°S in the Pacific on 26 July. She had 'doubled' the Horn, rounding it from east to west from 50°S in the Atlantic to 50°S in the Pacific, in a remarkable seven days, despite the two-day delay on the approach to Le Maire Strait.

After sailing sufficiently far west to clear the treacherous lee shore of the tip of South America, *Flying Cloud* changed course northwards as the wind veered to the south, bringing with it extremely cold air from the Antarctic ice cap. But a southerly wind was a favorable wind, and Creesy immediately ordered the yards and booms to be sent back up and re-rigged on the mainmast; the topgallant, royal, skysail, and studdingsails were then bent and set. Under full sail, *Flying Cloud* increased speed, on course for San Francisco.

Maury's recommended course north in the Pacific at all times of the year was a little to the west of what would have been a true great circle route. Eleanor plotted a course for *Flying Cloud* slightly west of north in the Southern Ocean westerlies, so as to follow a fairly wide concave sweep in a general north-westerly direction as far as the equator, and take full advantage of the south-east trades. *Flying Cloud* would cross the equator where the band of Pacific doldrums narrows, as it crosses from South America towards Micronesia. Advantage would then be taken of the north-east trades by continuing in a north-westerly direction, in the hope of picking up westerlies at about 30°N that would take *Flying Cloud* directly to her destination. Her course involved sailing well away from the landmass of America, passing about 2,500 miles west of Colombia. According to Maury, Pacific Ocean currents are weaker than those in the Atlantic, requiring less consideration by the navigator.

Heading north, *Flying Cloud* encountered fine weather and moderate winds off Chile, enabling her to make excellent progress under full sail, before squalls were encountered and Creesy had to take in the studding sails. When the wind strengthened to gale force, the royals were furled. *Flying Cloud* continued under an impressive spread of canvas, reveling in the conditions, and charging ahead even faster. A strong sea was running, showering the decks with spray as the sharp clipper bow ploughed through the waves. Earlier sailing ships would have had to reduce sail and slow down to enable their bows to rise over the waves. The price of this exhilarating experience for Creesy and his crew was a wet ship. *Flying Cloud's* sailing ability was remarkable: she travelled 374 miles in 24 hours from noon on 30 July, an average speed of 15.5 knots; the log on one occasion registered 18 knots, a speed and a record that would not be equalled for 23 years by an ocean-going steamship.

The winds increased further in strength, gusting storm force at times; the topgallants were taken in, and *Flying Cloud* continued at speed under full main topsail, and with the fore and mizzen topsails double-reefed; McKay's clipper was showing her true colors. Creesy was taking a calculated risk with the main topsail because of the weakened mainmast.

As the wind dropped, Creesy had the reefs shaken out of the topsails, and the topgallants set; he intended to continue to get the most out of his great ship while the wind direction remained favorable. Under a spread of canvas to topgallants, *Flying Cloud* gathered momentum and surged ahead until she was clipping along again. According to Eleanor's noon calculations on 1 August, *Flying Cloud* had logged 334 miles in the previous 24 hours, and 991 miles in three days.

Excellent progress was made during the following three days in moderate south-east trades. When *Flying Cloud* crossed the equator at 110°W on 12 August, she had sailed from 50°S in 17 days, a remarkable achievement that delighted the Creesys, who realized that if they could get through the doldrums without significant delay, and if the north-east trades favored them as they approached their destination, *Flying Cloud* would reach San Francisco in record time.

During the voyage north in the Pacific, Creesy dismissed his first mate Thomas

Austin from his post for neglect of duty, replacing him with Thomas Smith for the remainder of the voyage. This was a serious step for Creesy to take, but in the highly disciplined world of the United States Merchant Marine the captain's word was law, and there could be no questioning his decision aboard ship, although the owners, who had appointed the first mate, might express their concern at a later date. Creesy was considered in some quarters to be a hard taskmaster; he had become frustrated with Austin's less than enthusiastic response to his orders to continually drive the men and the ship, so that *Flying Cloud* could be sailed at the fastest possible speed in the prevailing conditions.

Flying Cloud encountered the Pacific Ocean doldrums just north of the equator; Maury's charts and sailing directions showed the band of calms and unpredictable winds moving north between March and September. The doldrums were soon cleared, and within three days *Flying Cloud* was benefiting from the north-east trades. A combination of Maury's predictions, Eleanor's navigational ability, Creesy's seamanship, and good luck had favored the new Boston-built clipper once again. There was a quiet confidence on board as *Flying Cloud* sailed briskly on a long starboard tack with the north-east trades on her beam as far as 130° W, before altering course and sailing on a port tack in the direction of San Francisco.

Eighty-four days out from New York *Flying Cloud* was on the final leg of her voyage, to the delight of all on board. But the wind dropped, and during the following three days progress was frustratingly slow. Then the weather changed. An approaching storm brought a brisk north-west wind with intermittent squalls, and soon *Flying Cloud* was charging towards the finish line: The Golden Gate. With the end of the voyage only a couple of days away, everyone relaxed. Then, suddenly and without warning, the fore topgallant mast came crashing down on deck, before going over the side, carrying with it a tangled mass of ropes, and sending the ship broadside to the wind.

Within hours the crew had the topgallant mast back on board, and the debris cleared from the water, enabling *Flying Cloud* to resume her course and make good progress. But Creesy was not going to allow *Flying Cloud* to be seen limping into port, even if she had arrived from New York in record time. He ordered the topgallant to be sent back up, replaced in its fid, and secured. The crew worked throughout the night, and within 24 hours *Flying Cloud* was again slicing through the sea under full sail, narrowing the gap between herself and the Californian coast. The following day, 31 August 1851, *Flying Cloud* arrived in San Francisco Harbor under sail, and dropped anchor just before noon. She had arrived 89 days

21 hours out from New York, improving on *Surprise's* record by six days. *Flying Cloud's* voyage was hailed as a spectacular success in both America and Europe.

From San Francisco *Flying Cloud* sailed to China, and despite being short-handed because many of the crew had 'gone off to the mines,' she again logged a 24-hour run of 374 miles. Returning from Canton, she reached New York in 94 days. Creesy, by now a national hero, received a tremendous welcome, and *Flying Cloud's* log was printed in gold on silk for distribution to the public. Orders poured into McKay's yard for copies of *Flying Cloud,* and bigger sharper clippers.

In 1854 *Flying Cloud,* still under the command of Creesy, broke the 90-day barrier a second time by arriving in San Francisco 89 days 8 hours out from New York. No other sailing ship ever equalled *Flying Cloud's* New York to San Francisco record of less than 90 days on two occasions.

The magnificent *Flying Cloud* performed best when she was under the command of Josiah Creesy, and guided by Eleanor, one of the most able navigators of the time. By the end of 1855, Creesy had commanded the famous clipper on five fast voyages to California, achieving an average time of just over 100 days. *Flying Cloud* continued to make fast passages between New York, California, and the Orient.

In 1863, *Flying Cloud* was purchased by James Baines of Liverpool for his Black Ball Line, and she sailed under the red ensign on the Liverpool to Brisbane run for the following decade. In 1874, while in the ownership of another British shipping firm, she was driven ashore in the Bay of Fundy at the entrance to the harbor of St John, New Brunswick, during a storm, and wrecked. The following year, the stranded wreck of *Flying Cloud* was deliberately set on fire on the instructions of the underwriters, so that her copper fastenings could be salvaged and sold.

The achievements of Donald McKay's renowned extreme clipper did not go unchallenged. Just ten days before *Flying Cloud* set sail on her maiden voyage from New York, *Challenge* was launched onto the East River from William Webb's New York yard amid feverish activity and great excitement. No expense was spared: *Challenge* was reputed to have cost $150,000 to build, three times more than *Flying Cloud.* She was built for the firm owned by the brothers Nathaniel and George Griswold, who already owned over 40 ships, including three early William Webb clippers. Webb was the leading shipbuilder in the United States at the time and the Griswold brothers asked him to build the sharpest and fastest clipper possible, with little regard to cost, stipulating that she must be the finest clipper and

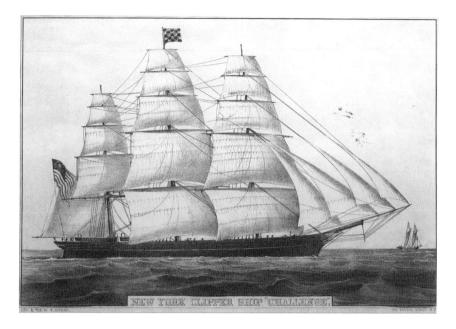

Challenge (Currier & Ives)

best sailing ship in the world. The result was *Challenge,* a 2,006-ton extreme clipper with three decks, and the finest-lined ship ever built by Webb.

Captain Robert Waterman, who had made his reputation on the China tea run, and was recognized as one of the most outstanding sailing ship captains of the time, was tempted out of retirement to take command of *Challenge,* with the promise of a $10,000 bonus if he reached San Francisco within 90 days. Waterman supervised her construction and fitting out. *Challenge* was built of the finest live oak, white oak, and hard pine, with every piece carefully selected for quality; only the best craftsmen were employed in her construction. Like other successful and daring clipper captains of the time, Waterman was convinced that flying a massive press of canvas was an essential factor in achieving fast passages. As soon as he took responsibility for *Challenge,* Waterman ordered longer masts and yards than those originally specified. *Challenge* was over-sparred as a result, with the mainmast an astonishing 230 feet high, not much different from her length of 224 feet; the height of the mainmast above the deck of a clipper was normally not greater than the distance between the foremast and the taffrail. Her masts were raked at ½, ⅝, and 1 inch to the foot. Challenge's hull was black with a gold stripe, her lower masts were also black, and her figurehead was a golden eagle on the wing with its eyes looking forward.

The clipper built to eclipse *Flying Cloud's* anticipated prowess on the Great Racecourse of the Ocean would carry 12,780 yards of canvas, a considerable spread of sail, but not as great as some commentators claimed. The amount of sail carried by sailing ships was not described by area, but by the measured running length in yards; sail canvas was produced in different widths, normally 24 inch, but also 18 inch and 22 inch. It was therefore not possible to calculate the precise area of sail that a ship carried from knowing the running length. *Challenge's* sails were made to order at a width of 16 inches, which explains why the total sail area was overestimated in some reports.

A fast and exciting voyage was anticipated as *Challenge* set sail for San Francisco on 13 July 1851 under the command of the redoubtable Waterman, who had every hope of making a record-breaking voyage. New Yorkers expected *Challenge* to beat all previous records, and bets were place that she would reach San Francisco in less time than *Flying Cloud*.

Experienced sailors were in very short supply in New York at the time, and getting together a suitable crew to man *Challenge* and other ships was one of the greatest difficulties faced by clipper captains. A life at sea appealed to few young Americans, compared to the many opportunities on offer with the opening up of the West. Shipowners, though they were making significant profits, refused to pay a reasonable wage, and actually drove the monthly salary for a seaman down from $10 per month at the beginning of the century to $8 in the 1850s, at a time when ships and skippers required experienced seafarers most.

Earlier in the 19th century, American merchant ships sailing to India and China were crewed mostly by Scandinavians, who were the best to sail before the mast, being well trained in sail-making and rigging work. The transatlantic sailing packets relied mainly on the Liverpool Irish: strong heavily built fearless sea warriors, whose bodies were extensively tattooed. They were at their best out on a topsail yardarm passing a weather reef-earing, wearing the Black Ball Shipping Line issue of caps, red shirts, and with trousers stowed in the legs of their sea boots, while the rigging was a mass of ice, and a blizzard howled in their ears as the ship jumped up and down on the Atlantic. Donning a coat or jacket in even the worst weather was regarded by them with derision. They were skilled at making and taking in sail, but had little interest in the finer points of seamanship such as rigging, sail-making, scraping paint, and keeping a vessel clean and shipshape. The transatlantic packet voyages were short and mainte-nance was carried out in port, with the ships always looking their best when hauled out of dry dock before setting sail again across the Western Ocean. In contrast, the China and California clippers looked their best after a long voyage, with the deck fittings clean and brightly polished, the masts perfectly raked, and all the yards square.

Californian clippers should have attracted seamen: the food was mostly good and the forecastle was a large house on deck between the foremast and main-mast, well lit and properly ventilated, divided fore and aft amidships by a bulk-head that facilitated separation of the watches. In most other sailing ships, the forecastle was in the forepeak beneath the deck, poorly lit and damp. For the clip-per sailors, there was a generous allowance of hot coffee day and night in bad weather.

As a result of the shortage of professional seamen, the forecastles of the clip-pers were filled with thugs, men who were unemployable elsewhere, misfits, ne'er-do-wells, and adventurers. Harsh discipline was necessary to keep these men under control: they were treated brutally by bucko mates on board ship, and dreadfully exploited ashore; 'bucko' was another word for bully. They were forced to labor for long periods under extremely demanding and dangerous conditions, for which they received little thanks. Low wages, sometimes medi-ocre or poor food, and harsh conditions aboard ship were unappealing to young men who might otherwise have been interested in life on the ocean wave. Sailing a fast handsome Yankee Clipper should have been a coveted occupation, but the poor reputation of seafaring meant that few young men wanted to go to sea. The lure of booming California did entice some of the Liverpool Irish to man Californian Clippers. They normally signed on in force, and having stayed in California for a short spell, had little trouble finding berths on outward-bound clippers.

> When the California clippers started, these packet rats, as they came to be called aboard the deep-water ships – men who had never before had the slightest idea of crossing the equator if they could help it, – were suddenly possessed with the desire to get to the California gold mines. They, with other adventurers, and blacklegs of the vilest sort, who were not sailors but who shipped as able seamen for the same reason, partly composed the crews of the clipper ships. The packet rats were

tough, roustabout sailormen and difficult to handle, so that it was sometimes a toss-up whether they or the captain and officers would have charge of the ship; yet to see these fellows laying out on an eighty-foot main-yard in a whistling gale off Cape Horn, fisting hold of a big No. 1 Colt's cotton canvas mainsail, heavy and stiff with sleet and snow, bellying, slatting, and thundering in the gear, and then to hear the wild, cheery shouts of these rugged, brawny sailormen, amid the fury of the storm, as inch by inch they fought on till the last gasket was fast, made it easy to forget their sins in admiration of their splendid courage.

Arthur H Clark *The Clipper Ship Era*

Larger ships, lower wages, and brutality, combined with corrupt boarding-house keepers, bar owners, and crimps, led to the exploitation of seamen and anyone else who was unfortunate enough to be caught in the web of waterfront corruption. Some clippers were sailed with potentially mutinous crews who had been dragged aboard in a drunken or drugged state by crimps, and woke up only to find that they had signed on for a long voyage. Crimps were thugs who shanghaied individuals to make up the shortfall in the crew; they were rewarded for their services with as much as $100 for each sailor delivered to the ship. The mate gave the crimp a receipt for each man; the fee paid included the sailor's first three months wages. Not only would the new 'recruit' lose three months pay, but he would be forced further into debt by having to purchase sea boots and foul weather gear from the ship at grossly inflated prices.

In New York, crimps operated from the hundreds of boarding houses, drinking dens, tattoo parlors, dance halls, and brothels that crammed the waterfront. It is said that many a young New Yorker, who had never been to sea, and who had no interest in seafaring, woke up after an alcoholic binge to find himself in the forecastle of a clipper heading for San Francisco by way of Cape Horn. Other victims were young farm boys who had come to New York to start a new life, and had gone to the waterfront to gaze in awe at the sailing ship wonders of the day. Crimps would befriend them, offer to show them around, ply them with alcohol, and, before they knew it, they had been signed on a Yankee Clipper bound for California.

One of the first crimps to operate in Boston was Maria Lee, a big black woman who operated during the 1830s and 1840s. She became known as 'Black Maria,' and would subdue up to six or eight drunken sailors at a time before delivering them to the ships. It was for her role in helping police arrest and escort drunken clients to jail that her name became synonymous with police wagons, earning her lasting fame.

The term 'shanghaied' originated from notorious San Francisco crimping practices. After arriving in San Francisco most of the sailors would take off for the goldfields. It was a particularly difficult place to find replacement crew, and many of the clippers sailed the Pacific below complement.

Sailors on board ships returning to New York were met by crimps, who would arrange boarding-house accommodation and introduce them to dance-hall 'hostesses' who would relieve them of everything they had, before they were dragged aboard another outbound ship.

Conditions on board some ships were harsh; there was hard labor, sweat, filthy accommodation, starvation, and flogging. Some captains and mates were described as 'shore saints' and 'sea devils' because of their contrasting behavior ashore and at sea. Discipline on board was maintained by the brutal bucko mate, who would beat the new men into submission if necessary; an iron belaying pin was the favorite weapon employed.

> The old-time bully Mates were undoubtedly brutal, more so on American than on British ships, but they got results. They did not mind being hated. They revelled in it. They welcomed trouble. It gave them a chance to show their superiority to the men they commanded. By establishing that superiority at the beginning of a voyage, with a few punishing examples, they cowed their crews into the obedience necessary for the discipline and safety of a ship.
>
> William H S Jones *The Cape Horn Breed*.

The California clippers recruited their carpenters, sailmakers, and boatswains from the shipyards spread along the waterfronts of New York's East River and East Boston. African Americans were often the cooks and stewards on board. Like the second mate they had a private cabin; a cook was also paid a comparable wage to the second mate. The equal pay received by black men working as deckhands aboard the packets sailing to and from Liverpool reinforced their claims for equality on other ships. But during the clipper era, sailors were paid at rates that were below the level required to raise a family, a situation made even worse when crews were hired through agents or crimps. As a result, few black sailors signed on as deckhands aboard the clippers, opting instead for the coastal trade and fishing, no different from other Americans for whom a career before the mast on ocean-going sailing ships had little or no attraction.

During the 1850s, racial segregation spread to seagoing ships. This brought an end to integrated crews, and from then on black and white sailors were required to live in separate quarters. Black men, who had a reputation for being among the best deckhands on sailing ships and firemen on steamers, and who might have been willing to accept the marginal pay and conditions available to seamen at the time, were excluded from many merchant ships. African Americans accounted for 14 per cent of the crews sailing from New York in 1835, but this had diminished to below 5 per cent by 1866; the number sailing from Boston went from 29 per cent in 1850 to 19 per cent in 1866. Because of segregation they preferred to sail as part of an all black crew. This resulted in clippers carrying all white or all black deckhands. Some captains filled the starboard watch with white sailors and the larboard (port) watch with black ones, hoping that racial rivalry would pressure each to outdo the other. The separate watches associated differently, and there was fierce competition between these 'checkerboard' crews.

It is difficult to establish how many American clippers were manned by African Americans, as crew lists kept by United States Customs did not include details of ethnic origin. *Adelaide,* a large medium clipper of 1,831 tons, built in New York and launched towards the end of 1854, is recorded to have had an all black crew of 26 able seamen on her third voyage from New York to San Francisco in 1857. In the same year *W Libby* sailed from Baltimore with a white crew, and at Liverpool took on an all black one. At Hong Kong a visiting American clipper was noted to have a checkerboard crew, while another had an all black crew.

It was customary for loaded ships leaving New York for San Francisco to drop down the East River and anchor off Battery Park, to await high water. Crowds gathered in Battery Park, then a fashionable resort, to witness the beautiful sight of a clipper ship getting under way, and listen to the sailors sing their shanties: sea songs sung with alternating solo and chorus.

Five to ten tons of gunpowder was often part of the cargo, and was taken on board when the ship was anchored. The gunpowder was then stowed in the main hatch, where it was easily accessible in case of fire. The 'tween decks was fitted with berths for the passengers to sleep in, and the hold was reserved for water and provisions. Any spare space was utilized for such freight as the passengers were able to ship, including what they most needed when they arrived in California, such as general provisions, household effects, lumbar, and other building material.

It was while at anchor that more crew were taken aboard, accompanied by the crimp and his runners. Many of *Challenge's* crew were drunk or drugged when they arrived on board, and were placed in forecastle berths, as they were in no fit state to work on deck or aloft. Longshoremen helped to get the ship under way because of the condition of many of the crew. As the flood tide began to slacken, the mate gave the order to man the windlass and heave short: the shantyman then burst into song, to be followed by the chorus as the anchor chain was shortened. Then, the more sober sailors were sent aloft to loosen and set the sails, while the crimp, runners, and longshoremen took to their boats. The windlass was manned again and, to the accompaniment of a shanty, the anchor was hauled up, enabling the great *Challenge* to fall off and gather headway. Those on shore were then treated to the spectacle of a beautiful clipper heading for Sandy Hook and the open sea under a cloud of sail.

With so many ships leaving for California in 1851, even the most successful clipper captains had to rely on these 'pressed' crews, often earning for themselves a reputation as bullies. Of the 48 men recruited as able seamen to crew *Challenge* on her maiden voyage, only two were American. Half of them had never been to sea before; many of the rest had minimal seafaring experience; only six had ever steered a ship; and seventeen were incapacitated by disease. Many had signed on to get to the goldfields. A search of *Challenge's* crew quarters produced so many pistols, knives, knuckledusters, and bottles of rum that Waterman, having replaced the mate who had recruited the crew, seriously considered returning to New York.

For some time after leaving New York, Waterman and his officers took the precaution of being armed when they came on deck. Later, when the crew seemed to have settled in, they stopped carrying guns. But the replacement first mate was bad tempered, and particularly rough with the inexperienced members of the crew. Friction between the mate and the crew led to an attempted mutiny off Rio de Janeiro, when he was attacked by four seamen, who intended to kill him. By the time Waterman came to his rescue the mate had been stabbed and badly beaten. Waterman, who realized that he would be the next target, attacked the mutineers with an iron belaying pin with such ferocity that two of them died from their injuries; he had eight others flogged. Waterman's action quelled the mutiny. Off Cape Horn, Waterman ordered the inexperienced recruits, who had only signed on as a means of getting to California, aloft and out on the yards with the other sailors. Three of them subsequently fell to their deaths from the mizzen topsail yard. Shortly afterwards four others died from dysentery.

During the voyage, Webb's *Challenge* performed well under favorable conditions but failed to live up to expectations. The passage took 108 days, much longer than the target of 90 days; and 19 days longer than her great rival, McKay's *Flying Cloud*. The performance of *Challenge*, the ship designed and built to be the finest and fastest clipper ship in the world, was completely eclipsed by her great rival's earlier record-breaking voyage. It was a bitterly disappointing outcome for *Challenge's* many backers.

After arriving in San Francisco, Waterman and the mate were attacked by a mob of sailors, incensed by reports of brutality on the voyage. They were saved from being lynched when the local Vigilance Committee came to their rescue. Waterman volunteered to be tried for murder. He was tried and acquitted, claiming the criticisms of him were unjustified, and that the severe measures he took to suppress the mutiny and punish the mutineers were necessary to maintain discipline. Paying passengers gave evidence on his behalf.

* * *

The great clipper race of 1851–1852 over the 16,000-mile Great Racecourse of the Ocean was between two extreme clippers: Donald McKay's 1,505-ton *Flying Fish*, and the 1,036-ton *Sword Fish*, built by William Webb for Barclay & Livingston of New York. There was great excitement, particularly in New York where many bets were placed on the outcome. *Flying Fish*, similar but slightly smaller than the 1,782-ton *Flying Cloud*, sailed from Boston on 11 November 1851 under the command of Captain Edward Nickels. *Sword Fish*, commanded by Captain David S Babcock, sailed from New York on the same day.

Flying Fish was in the lead by three days at the equator. *Sword Fish* caught up, and the two clippers raced round Cape Horn side by side; *Sword Fish* pulled ahead as they sailed north in the Pacific to arrive in San Francisco 91 days out, eight days ahead of McKay's *Flying Fish*. It was an excellent time for Webb's smaller *Sword Fish*, but *Flying Cloud's* record-breaking run remained unbeaten by a day.

After sailing to China from San Francisco *Flying Fish* returned to New York, arriving just in time to become a contestant in the most famous contest ever: the 1852–1853 race, in which fifteen fairly well matched ships took part. A description of the progress of four of the front runners, *Flying Fish, John Gilpin, Trade Wind*, and *Wild Pigeon*, was given by Matthew Maury.

He described how the four left New York between 11 October and 13 November, and raced against time. *Trade Wind*, an extreme clipper, was under the command of Captain Nathaniel Webber. She was built by Jacob Bell, who years earlier had recognized Donald McKay's talent and ability when he recommended him for the job of foreman in the Brooklyn Navy Yard. *John Gilpin*, a medium clipper with sharp ends, was designed and built by Samuel Hall in Boston for Pierce & Hunnewell, and commanded by Captain Justin Doane. *Wild Pigeon*, an extreme clipper built by George Raynes of Portsmouth, New Hampshire, was commanded by Captain George W Putnam; she was heavily sparred, crossed three skysail yards, and had masts raked at 1¼, 1⅜ and 1½ inches to the foot.

Flying Fish, again under the command of Nickels, and *John Gilpin* raced neck and neck from the equator in the Atlantic over the rest of the course, with *Wild Pigeon* joining them for part of it, the three rounding the Horn and crossing 51°S in the Pacific close together. The three ships crossed 35°S on 30 December, with *Flying Fish* leading the way, just ahead of *Wild Pigeon*, and with *John Gilpin* dropping behind. *Wild Pigeon* crossed the equator two hours behind *Flying Fish*, but fell behind when the winds failed on the course chosen by Putnam, enabling *Flying Fish* to get well ahead and win by reaching San Francisco in the shortest time. In the meantime *John Gilpin*, coming from two days behind *Wild Pigeon*, had a glorious 15-day day run to San Francisco to finish in 93 days 20 hours, compared to *Flying Fish's* 92 days 4 hours, anchor to anchor: excellent performances by the two Boston built clippers. *Trade Wind* had the next best time of 103 days, but *Wild Pigeon* took 118 days. This was the McKay-built *Flying Fish's* best time; her three subsequent passages to San Francisco took 100 days or more.

Eighteen-fifty-three was also the year of a race from Boston to San Francisco between two Medford, Massachusetts, built clippers, the 1,051-ton *Climax* and the 871-ton *Competitor*. Both were launched at the beginning of 1853: *Climax* by Hayden & Cudworth and *Competitor* by J O Curtis. *Climax's* construction was supervised by Captain William F Howes of Brewster, Massachusetts, who was to command her on her maiden voyage; he had her fitted with his patent double topsails. Howes's rig permitted *Climax* to be manned by a crew of fourteen men and two boys, about half the normal complement. *Climax* set sail from Boston on 28 March; *Competitor* followed a day later. *Competitor's* voyage nearly ended in disaster off Cape Horn when her stem split, and she began to leak badly. She was then sailed before the wind with her bows strapped together. Both clippers arrived in San Francisco after a passage time of 115 days, with *Competitor's* backers claiming victory by a few hours.

Eighteen-fifty-four saw a race to San Francisco between two of the most evenly matched clippers ever: the 1,782-ton McKay-built *Romance of the Seas,* launched towards the end of 1853, and the beautiful 1,717-ton extreme clipper *David Brown,* launched from the yard of Roosevelt & Joyce, formerly Brown & Bell, on 8 October 1853. *Romance of the Seas* was the last extreme clipper built by Donald McKay.

A A Low & Brother were so pleased with their clippers *Houqua, Samuel Russell,* and *Oriental,* that they named *David Brown* after one of the former owners of the Roosevelt & Joyce yard. Once again it would be Boston vying with New York.

David Brown, under the command of Captain George S Brewster, sailed from New York on 13 December 1853. Three days later *Romance of the Seas* left Boston with Captain Philip Dumaresq in command. Initially *David Brown* stretched her lead by one day, and crossed the equator four days ahead; but by the time they reached Cape Horn her lead was reduced to one day. *David Brown* crossed the Pacific equator still leading by a day; after which *Romance of the Seas* slowly gained until they both crossed the same latitude at noon on the same day, less than a week before their expected date of arrival. However, *Romance of the Seas* was 40 miles nearer by longitude. The clipper considered to be McKay's masterpiece continued gaining sea distance, and arrived at San Francisco 96 days 18 hours out from Boston, having logged 15,154 miles, a daily average of 156.6. *David Brown* arrived 99 days 20 hours out from New York, during which she logged 16,167 miles, a daily average of 161.6.

The two clippers had proved how closely matched they were, and when it was discovered that their next port of call was Hong Kong, a race from San Francisco was arranged and bets placed. *Romance of the Seas* was the favorite. They were towed to sea, both leaving at 3.30pm on 31 March 1854. They arrived in Hong Kong 45 days later, with *Romance of the Seas* one hour ahead of *David Brown.* They both loaded tea for London, where *Romance of the Seas* arrived 102 days after leaving Whampoa, and *David Brown* 111 days out from Shanghai.

In October 1860, *David Brown* took on a cargo of wheat and passengers at San Francisco, before setting sail for Liverpool under Captain John C Berry. In the South Atlantic, at about 45°S, she sprung a leak after being struck by particularly heavy seas during a gale. But Berry managed to continue sailing north by controlling the level of water with the pumps. In the Atlantic just north of 22°N, the leak became worse following a further encounter with strong winds and heavy seas, and on 6 January 1861 *David Brown* was abandoned. Berry took women and children, as well as eighteen crew, in his boat; the mate Daly took the male passengers and the remainder of the crew in the second boat. Three days later the boats got separated. Ten days after abandoning ship, the occupants of Berry's boat, by then suffering severely from thirst, hunger, and exposure, were picked up by the Spanish barque *Observador* and taken to Havana. At about the same time the barque *Sea Wave* found Daly's boat and occupants, who were also in a bad way, and took them to Liverpool.

Romance of the Seas made many distinguished passages across the oceans of the world. In one consecutive 16-day period she is reported to have sailed 4,172 miles. On 31 December 1862, she left Hong Kong bound for San Francisco and was never heard of again. She was posted missing in April 1863 with the loss of 33 lives. Insurance on *Romance of the Seas* and her cargo was $266,000.

A couple of months after launching *Challenge*, William Webb's next extreme clipper, the 1,851-ton *Comet*, took to the water. *Comet*, described as a particularly handsome ship, had her frame strengthened by diagonal iron latticework. She would prove to be one of the fastest sailing ships ever launched. Captain E C Gardner was placed in command, and would remain *Comet's* captain for nearly five years. Her first passage time to San Francisco from New York, leaving on 12 January 1852, was 103 days. From there she sailed to Hong Kong in a fast 37 days. At Whampoa, *Comet* loaded a valuable cargo of tea and silk, and reached New York in 97 days, a good run for the time of year.

Comet encountered prolonged spells of particularly adverse weather on her second voyage to San Francisco, reaching there 112 days out from New York. On her return voyage she left San Francisco on 12 February 1853 and raced *Flying Dutchman*, another Webb-built clipper that had left a day earlier. Both were in ballast. Thirty-two days out *Comet* overtook *Flying Dutchman*. They fell in together on 30 April and for a day neither one could get ahead, until the wind freshened and *Comet* pulled ahead. A couple of days later, *Comet's* mainsail split and *Flying Dutchman* got ahead during the night, after which they lost sight of each other. *Comet* arrived in New York on 7 May, a record 83 days and 18 hours out from San Francisco. *Flying Dutchman* arrived the following day, 85 days out. Maury reported on *Comet's* voyage: she logged 15,541 miles at an average of 185.5 miles each day, covering 1,238 miles in a consecutive four-day period, a daily average 309.5 miles.

Shortly afterwards a couple of splendidly matched clippers set sail from San Francisco: the 1,099-ton *Contest* left on 12 March 1853 bound for New York, and the following day *Northern Light* left for Boston. *Contest*, from the yard of Westervelt & Co of New York and commanded by Captain William Brewster, was a fast ship belonging to A A Low & Brother. *Northern Light*, a 1,021-ton Boston-built medium clipper, was designed by the well-known naval architect Samuel Harte Pook, built by Briggs Bros, owned by James Huckins, and commanded by Captain Freeman Hatch.

Westervelt & Co, owned by Jacob A Westervelt and his sons Daniel and Aaron, was previously known as Westervelt & Mackay, a company that built London and Le Havre packets. Jacob A Westervelt, whose father was a shipbuilder, was born in 1800 at Hackensack, New Jersey, and served before the mast before becoming an apprentice shipwright with Christian Bergh, with whom he secured a partnership. Their business prospered and Westervelt went on an extensive tour of Europe after he retired in 1837. Following his arrival back in the United States he returned to shipbuilding, founding Westervelt & Mackay. In 1854 Jacob A Westervelt became Mayor of New York.

By the time the two similar sized clippers reached Cape Horn, *Northern Light* had gained a day on her would-be rival. On coming level they exchanged signals, and a race was on. From then on, *Northern Light* led the way, arriving at Boston Light 76 days 6 hours out from San Francisco, three days before *Contest* arrived at Sandy Hook. *Northern Light's* time was the shortest ever recorded from San Francisco to any North Atlantic port by a sailing ship.

Comet's earlier 83 day 18 hour record had not stood for long. Shortly afterwards *Comet* made a valiant attempt to wrest the laurels from *Northern Light*. On her next return voyage, *Comet*, with Gardner in command, left San Francisco on 27 December 1853 and arrived in New York on 14 March 1854, a passage time of 76 days

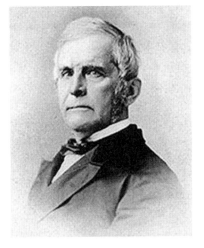

Jacob Aaron Westervelt

and 7 hours anchor to anchor, one hour outside *Northern Light's* record to Boston.

Contest's time was the fourth fastest ever from San Francisco to New York or Boston. Donald McKay's 1,703-ton *Bald Eagle* under Captain A H Caldwell, was the third fastest when she arrived in New York 78 days 22 hours out from San Francisco on 19 May 1854. The swift eastward voyages of *Northern Light, Comet, Bald Eagle,* and *Contest* would remain classics in the annals of commercial sailing. *Comet,* still under the command of Gardner, sailed from Liverpool on 17 June 1854 and arrived in Hong Kong a record 83 days 21 hours later.

Comet was renamed *Fiery Star* on becoming British-owned at the beginning of 1862, and was put on the Australia run. She left Brisbane on 1 April 1865 on the return leg of her second Australian voyage. Three weeks later a fire was discovered in the hold, and despite the crew's efforts to extinguish it with water, and seal the hold, it continued to burn. Eighty people, including all the passengers and some of the crew, took to the boats. The mate, a man named Sargeant, and seventeen of the crew elected to stay on board because there was not room for them in the boats. Captain W H Yale and the officers in charge of the three boats intended to stay near the ship, but the following morning were nowhere to be seen, and were never heard of again. As *Fiery Star* was about to sink, the barque *Dauntless* arrived on the scene and rescued those who had remained on board.

Bald Eagle, under the command of Captain Morris, left Hong Kong on 15 October 1861, bound for San Francisco with a cargo of rice, sugar, tea, plus $100,000 worth of treasure, and was never heard of again. She was assumed to have foundered in the China Sea with the loss of all hands in one of the severe typhoons that struck there at the time.

A small number of fast clippers were launched in 1857. One of the most attractive was the Mystic built 1,482-ton medium clipper *Twilight*. She received considerable attention from the crowds who went to view her at the foot of Wall Street where she was being loaded for her maiden voyage. Captain Gurdon Gates, who was one of her principal owners when she was launched from the yard of Charles Mallory on 6 October, was her commander. *Twilight* recorded many fast passages during her lifetime, ones that compared favorably with those of earlier fast extreme clippers. At noon on 5 January 1858 *Twilight* passed Sandy Hook, outward-bound for San Francisco. At latitude 45°S in the Atlantic, she fell in with the five-year-old medium clipper *Dashing Wave* from the yard of Fernald & Pettigrew of Portsmouth, New Hampshire, and commanded by Captain Herbert

Young. They agreed to race to San Francisco, probably the last clippers to race each other across the Great Racecourse. *Twilight* arrived in San Francisco 101 days out from New York, two days ahead of *Dashing Wave,* whose overall time from Boston was a respectable 107 days. *Dashing Wave* had her slowest voyage, 155 days to San Francisco when, in 1863, she spent 42 days off Cape Horn, during which time she was driven back through Le Maire Strait by westerly storms.

Captain Joseph Warren Holmes from Mystic became commander of *Twilight,* and took her to San Francisco twice. In 1863-1864 Holmes doubled the Horn in an excellent ten days, but encountered light winds throughout the remainder of the voyage, resulting in a 121-day passage. The following year *Twilight* was sold. Holmes had the distinction of rounding Cape Horn under sail a record 83 or 84 times.

By 1859 the days of the extreme clippers racing to San Francisco had come to an end. Eighty-five clippers set sail for California that year, some of them leaking, and many of them weakened by salt water and the almost constant battles with the elements. Only six reached San Francisco in less than 110 days.

However, at the end of 1859 one medium clipper excelled: *Andrew Jackson,* a 1,679-ton medium clipper built by Irons & Grinnell on the banks of the Mystic River in 1855 and owned by John H Brower & Co of New York. *Andrew Jackson* developed a reputation for fast passages that compared favorably with those of the earlier more extreme clippers; four consecutive passages from New York to San Francisco averaged an excellent 99 days. She was described as a handsome, well-designed ship, with a full-length statue of the seventh President of the United States as her figurehead.

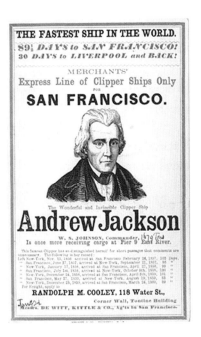

On 24 March 1860, when under the command of Captain John E Williams of Mystic, *Andrew Jackson* improved on *Flying Cloud's* 89 day 8 hour record-breaking voyage of 1854 by arriving in San Francisco 89 days 4 hours out from New York, having logged 13,700 miles, as against *Flying Cloud's* 15,091 miles. On his

return to New York, Williams was presented with a chronometer watch, with 89 days 4 hours engraved on it, by a grateful John Brower. Later in 1860 *Andrew Jackson* reduced the Liverpool to New York record to 15 days.

In 1868, when owned by H L Seligman of Glasgow, and under the command of Captain John McCallum, who had been her captain for five years, *Andrew Jackson* went aground in Gaspar Strait on 4 December and became a total loss. This clipper's excellent times and record-breaking run to San Francisco signaled the end of trials of speed under sail from one side of the United States to the other.

CHAPTER 3

The Golden Age of the Yankee Clipper

To see a clipper knife through the wind-swept seas and sprint from New York to San Francisco or between London and Hong Kong was to witness the quintessence of sailing. In winds that would cause others to reef sail, clipper captains flew every possible scrap of canvas until the masts quivered at breaking point. Clippers rode tempests like sea birds, reaching speeds as high as 21 knots, making some 400 miles a day and setting records that would last forever.

A B C Whipple *The Clipper Ships*

The 1850s was the golden era of the Yankee Clipper. These magnificent creations, the most powerful and fastest sailing ships ever built, swept the seas. Clipper ship building reached a peak in 1853 with the launching of at least 50 clippers from East Coast shipyards. Moored alongside in harbor, the long sleek Yankee Clippers towered above the dockside warehouses and other ships, making them instantly recognizable. They were to monopolize the China tea trade and dominate the oceans for most of the decade.

During the clipper era, ships at every stage of construction filled the shipyards of East Boston and New York's East River. Nearby were the workshops of the allied trades: sail-lofts, riggers-lofts, boat builders, pump-makers, painters, carvers, and gilders; makers of masts, spars, ropes, and blocks; blacksmiths and anchorsmiths, and those who fashioned ships' parts from brass and copper. Ships chandlers, stores that sold almost everything required aboard ship, were a prominent waterfront feature. The 'Captain's Room' in the ships chandlers was where the captains of ships from all over the world would congregate to drink coffee and tots of bourbon, and yarn about their experiences at sea.

One of the best known of the early American clippers was the 1,490-ton extreme clipper *N B Palmer*, owned by A A Low & Brother until 1873. She was the most famous ship built in the Westervelt yard, and was launched on 5 February

1851. *N B Palmer* was named after Nat Palmer, Low's renowned captain and ship designer. A fully rigged model of *N B Palmer* was one of over 13,000 exhibits at the Great Exhibition of 1851. Six million people attended the exhibition at the Crystal Palace, a massive structure of iron and glass in Hyde Park, London, and the model of the American Clipper attracted considerable attention.

During the 22 years she was owned by the Low firm of New York, *N B Palmer* was under the command of Captain Charles P Low, who occasionally handed over responsibility to someone else such as the first mate, if he were deemed capable of having his own command. Low's wife, Sarah, accompanied her husband on *N B Palmer's* voyages. Charles Porter Low was a brother of the New York shipping merchants. He was born in Salem in 1824 and moved with the family to New York when he was ten. Low was determined to be a sailor, much against the wishes of his parents, but they eventually relented. He first went to sea as a cabin boy; then he spent time as a seaman, progressing through third, second, and first mate on *Houqua,* before taking command of her at the age of 23. By then Low had served under the three Palmer brothers: Nathaniel B, Alexander, and Theodore D. Low was in command of the China tea clipper *Samuel Russell* on her first voyage to San Francisco in 1850, when she arrived there 109 days out from New York and established the record she held for 69 days before it was improved on by *Sea Witch* under Captain George Fraser.

N B Palmer's first three passages were to San Francisco. Then she was assigned to the China run, and sailed fifteen times to Hong Kong and twice to Shanghai. On her maiden voyage in 1851, Low took her to San Francisco in 107 days from New York; a two-day improvement on his record in *Samuel Russell* the previous year. The following year, when off Cape Horn, *N B Palmer* encountered continuous storms for 35 days: strong gales, rain, hail, snow, and very big seas. In addition to having to battle continuous storms off the Horn, Low was without assistance after two sailors attempted to murder his first and second mates; he was obliged to remain on deck for 18 days without any opportunity of going below to sleep until he put into Valparaiso to land the two mutineers. Most of the sailors deserted there, giving Low the opportunity to recruit a more reliable crew. *N B Palmer* arrived in San Francisco 41 days later, 130 out from New York, having lost four days diverting to Valparaiso.

Low was famous in San Francisco for performing a feat of seamanship that was never again equalled at the port: on 21 August 1851 he moored *N B Palmer* alongside her allocated wharf without the aid of a tug or other assistance. The pilot had brought her to anchor, but refused to bring her to the wharf as requested by the agents. Low assumed full responsibility for his ship, set sails to skysails, and hove anchor. On an ebb tide, and with a light wind on the beam, he sailed *N B Palmer* towards the wharf. As he closed on *N B Palmer's* allocated berth, Low backed the main yard, bringing the clipper to a stop, as she came alongside with an imperceptible bump. A great cheer went up from the onlookers who had gathered to witness the berthing of 2,500 tons of ship and cargo under sail. Low's skilful seamanship was remembered for a long time in the city.

Low was highly regarded as a navigator who took great pride in his ship: *N B Palmer* was the most popular vessel to trade with Hong Kong and Shanghai at the time. She was known as 'The Yacht' in the Chinese ports because of the nettings in the tops, gold stripe along the side, and the lavish entertainments provided by the Lows on the Fourth of July and George Washington's birthday. In 1853, when *N B Palmer* was at Hong Kong on the occasion of Queen Victoria's birthday celebrations, she was the most gaily decorated vessel in the harbor, covered in flags and bunting, and illuminated with lanterns in the evening. Six of *N B Palmer's* voyages to Hong Kong from New York were made in 100 days or less; her best runs were 88 days to Hong Kong when under the command of Captain James A Higham in 1858, and 93 days to Shanghai under Low in 1869.

Higham's return voyage from Shanghai to New York, arriving there on 18 January 1859, was a fast 82 days, equal to *Surprise's* record set two years earlier when under the command of Captain Charles A Ranlett; it was at the end of 1859 that *Sword Fish's* run of 81 days, when under Captain J W Cocker, set the all-time record from Shanghai to New York. And Higham, who was in his twenties, was quite unwell throughout the voyage, racked by weakness and persistent coughing from advanced tuberculosis. Five days after *N B Palmer's* triumphant arrival in New York, Higham, the captain who had guided her there at speed, succumbed to the deadly disease.

N B Palmer was nearly lost on 28 February 1853 when she struck the reef known as Broussa Shoal, near North Watcher Island in the Java Sea, as she travelled at eight knots. Low and his crew managed to get her off by kedging. But soon they discovered that the ship had been holed, and had developed a serious leak. As a result, water was filling the hold at the rate of seven inches an hour. This was controlled by the pumps and *N B Palmer* was taken to Batavia, where she was unloaded, repaired, and later reloaded. In dry dock a piece of coral, two feet in diameter, was found imbedded in the damaged area of the hull below the waterline. Had this come out at sea she would have rapidly filled with water and foundered. As *N B Palmer* was making her way to Batavia, Sarah gave birth to the first of the Lows' two children to be born at sea.

Shortly after leaving Hong Kong for New York in December 1864, *N B Palmer* was found to be leaking and had to return for repairs. On her arrival at New York, she was given a complete overhaul and almost completely rebuilt. The Lows sold their cherished clipper in 1873, and she spent the following nineteen years carrying oil from New York to Antwerp and Hamburg under the Norwegian flag, with Arendel as her port of registration. In January 1892, she developed a leak and was abandoned in mid North Atlantic at approximately 45°N 43°W.

Following the success of *Flying Cloud,* Donald McKay continued to build extreme clippers. In 1852 he built the 2,421-ton *Sovereign of the Seas* on his own account, to outsail *Flying Cloud.* Her solid frame was constructed entirely of seasoned white oak, while her planking and lower decks were of the best hard pine. At her launch in June, this magnificent clipper was considered the longest, sharpest, and most beautiful merchant ship afloat, designed to reach a speed of 20 knots in a strong breeze. Her overall length was 265 feet, her beam was 44 feet, and she spread 11,000-12,000 running yards of canvas; her cargo-carrying capacity was nearly 3,000 tons of measurement goods without drawing more than 20 feet of water.

Sovereign of the Seas (ILN)

Unlike *Stag Hound* and *Flying Cloud*, whose masts were raked alike at 1¼ inches to the foot, the masts of *Sovereign of the Seas* were raked ¾, ⅞ and 1⅛ inches to the foot. Her figurehead was a sea god, half man and half fish, with a conch shell raised to his mouth as if in the act of blowing.

Many pundits considered that McKay's decision to speculate on a clipper of such size was unwise, and predicted that he would be left with a white elephant on his hands. But shortly after she was launched, *Sovereign of the Seas* was bought by Andrew F Meinke of the New York ship-broking firm of Funch & Meinke.

Sovereign of the Seas loaded 2,954 tons of cargo in New York, before commencing her maiden voyage to San Francisco on 24 August 1852 under the command of Captain Lauchlan McKay, brother of Donald McKay. She carried a crew of over 100, including two carpenters, two boatswains, two sailmakers, two cooks, three stewards, eighty seamen, and ten boys before the mast. Lauchlan McKay had previously worked for four years in New York in the yard of Isaac Webb, after which he served as carpenter on board the United States frigate, *USS Constellation*. He then became involved in shipbuilding in Boston, and served as mate and captain on the Atlantic run. He was a quiet, mild-mannered, and even-tempered man with the innate qualities required to be a successful ship's captain.

On *Sovereign of the Seas*'s maiden voyage, McKay showed more consideration for the crew than they would have received from most other commanders: he provided good food, encouraged them in their efforts to dry their clothes, and tried not to endanger their lives unnecessarily. He dismissed the mate twenty days out of New York for swearing and bullying the crew, and for insubordination; the mate had mistakenly assumed that McKay was afraid of him and a weak captain because of McKay's mild manner.

A strong south-westerly wind with big seas was encountered off the Falkland Islands and it was a beat all the way to Cape Horn. McKay pushed on under a press of canvas that had the topmasts and the topgallants bending and quivering fearfully. The large clipper coped admirably with the adverse conditions, never missing stays. In order to get round Cape Horn against the adverse current while being headed by strong gales, McKay had to push his ship to the limit. *Sovereign of the Seas* rounded the Horn 51 days out from New York, without any of the crew becoming sick or disabled.

During a storm off Valparaiso, while carrying the usual large spread of canvas, *Sovereign of the Seas*'s main topmast, fore topmast, 80-foot-long foreyard, and mizzen topgallant mast came crashing down. This could have been disastrous, but McKay rallied the crew, and with great skill and effort they cleared the wreckage and retrieved the spars from the water, a dangerous and time-consuming task. It was normal practice to cut away the spars and rigging that were in the water because of the damage the broken masts and yards could do to the hull, including the possibility of holing the ship below the waterline. If McKay had cut the wreckage away, and not salvaged them as he did, he would have been short of spars, and unable to re-rig his ship.

Within a day of the dismasting, *Sovereign of the Seas* was under way, reaching 12 knots under mainsail, crossjack, and mizzen topsail. After twelve days of intense activity repairing spars, stays, and sails, the ship was again fully rigged. *Sovereign of the Seas* then charged ahead as though nothing had happened, arriving in San Francisco 103 days out from New York, and beating every vessel that sailed within a month of her. Before McKay set sail, Matthew Maury had given him a copy of his wind and current charts and predicted with great accuracy that *Sovereign of the Seas* would reach San Francisco in 103 days. McKay's action in re-rigging so efficiently was recognized by the underwriters in New York who presented him with a silver tea service; Boston underwriters gave him a silver pitcher, and presented his wife with a gold bracelet.

From San Francisco, *Sovereign of the Seas* sailed to Honolulu, where she took on a cargo of 8,000 barrels of whale-oil. With the crew reduced to 34 men before the mast, and despite a sprung fore topmast and jury fore topgallant mast, *Sovereign of the Seas* set sail from Honolulu on 2 February 1853. She arrived in New York a record 82 days later, a time between the two ports that would only be equalled once more. According to Maury, *Sovereign of the Seas* encountered trade-like west winds after crossing the 40th parallel, and aided by the westerlies, travelled from 48°S in the Pacific to 35°S in the Atlantic in 22 days, logging 5,391 miles during that time, an incredible daily average of 245 miles; on 18 March, when running before a south-westerly on the way to Cape Horn, *Sovereign of the Seas* logged 411 miles in 24 hours, the first ship to exceed 400 miles in one day. Like all the clippers built by Donald Mackay, *Sovereign of the Seas* took the Roaring Forties in her stride, speeding along before a leading gale and big following seas, reaching speeds of up to 19 knots, and covering a formidable 3,144 miles in ten days.

Sovereign of the Seas earned $200,000 in her first eleven months, more than justifying the resources invested in her. But she was considered too big for the San Francisco and China trades by New York shippers, and in May 1853 she was loaded for Liverpool, where she was destined to become part of the Australian emigration boom. In June she took 13 days, 22 hours, and 50 minutes to cross the Atlantic, from leaving the dock in New York to the time she anchored in the River Mersey, arriving well ahead of the Cunard steamer *Canada. Sovereign of the Seas* had logged 340 miles in 24 hours on June 30 when she passed the Fastnet Rock at sunrise, with all sail set to royal studdingsails and skysails. Donald Mackay and his wife were on board for the voyage; McKay spent much of the time keenly watching every aspect of his ship's behavior under sail, an experience that helped him to further enhance the success of his later creations. In Liverpool, Lauchlan McKay relinquished his command, and the McKays returned to Boston to supervise the building of the giant clipper barque, *Great Republic.*

Boston declared a public holiday on 4 October 1853 for the launching of McKay's four-masted barque *Great Republic,* the largest timber clipper ever built. An estimated 60,000 people witnessed the launching, many of them having arrived by special trains from all over Massachusetts and from outside the state. *Great Republic,* the largest merchant sailing ship ever built in the United States, was 335 feet long, registered 4,555 tons, and was designed and built as an extreme clipper with a cargo capacity of 6,000 tons. She had four decks, with a height 'tween decks of eight feet. Her mainmast towered to over 170 feet above the deck, and she flew 15,653 yards of canvas. All accommodation was on the upper 'tween decks, including luxurious staterooms for passengers, and a library for the crew. One-and-a-half million feet of hard pine, 3,500 tons of white oak, 326 tons of iron, and 56 tons of copper were used in her construction.

> Built for freight, and yet for speed,
> A beautiful and gallant craft;
> Broad on the beam, that the stress of the blast,
> Pressing down upon sail and mast,
> Might not the sharp bows overwhelm;
> Broad on the beam, but sloping aft
> With graceful curve and slow degrees,
> That she might be docile to the helm,
> And that the currents of parted seas,
> Closing behind, with mighty force,
> Might aid and not impede her course.
>
> Henry Wadsworth Longfellow *The Building of the ship*

After fitting out, *Great Republic* went to New York to load for Liverpool. A crew of 100 men and 30 boys was recruited to sail her under the command of Lauchlan McKay. By late December she was fully loaded, and ready for sea. But on 26 December a big fire broke out in a nearby street, and the wind carried blazing debris to the waterfront where *Great Republic* was moored alongside. The giant clipper caught fire almost immediately, and before long she sank in the shallow water and burned to the waterline. *Great Republic* was insured for $180,000 and her cargo for $275,000.

Great Republic (ILN)

It was the same inferno that almost completely destroyed the three-year-old *White Squall*. She was cut adrift, but not until the flames had taken hold; she then drifted down the East River before grounding and burning to the waterline. *White Squall* was rebuilt to much reduced specifications as a barque.

Great Republic never had an opportunity to justify her creator's dream, of her towering over all other clippers on the high seas. The severely damaged hulk was bought by A A Low & Brother, and rebuilt in New York under the supervision of Captain Nat Palmer. Her masts and yards were reduced in size, and her upper deck was not rebuilt. During the following seventeen years, the reduced *Great Republic* carried a variety of freight across the oceans of the world until she sank in 1872 after encountering a storm at 32°N in the Atlantic, when on a voyage from Rio de Janeiro in ballast to collect timber at Saint John. There was no loss of life and the crew reached Bermuda safely.

Even under her greatly reduced spread of canvas, *Great Republic* made excellent passages. On 12 December 1856, when five days out from New York under the command of Captain Joseph Limeburner and bound for San Francisco, she logged 413 miles, to join an elite band of clippers that exceeded 400 miles in a 24-hour period. The following year Limeburner took her from New York to San Francisco in 92 days.

* * *

By the early 1850s, shipyards outside New York and Boston were launching state-of-the-art clipper ships. One of the most interesting was the 1,066-ton *Nightingale*, designed and built by Samuel Hanscomb Jr at Portsmouth, New Hampshire, and said to be the most beautiful clipper in America when she was lunched onto the Piscataqua River in 1851. She had a long, varied, interesting, and at times infamous career: a record-breaking tea clipper, a pioneer on the Australian run, a California clipper, a warship, a slaver, and a lumbar-carrying Norwegian barque. An extreme clipper with sharp ends, considerable deadrise and beautifully propor-tioned spars, her masts were raked at 1¼, 1½ and 1¾ inches to the foot. As her figurehead, *Nightingale* had a bust of Jenny Lind, the famous Swedish-born opera singer she was named after; on her stern there was a representation of Jenny in a reclining position with a nightingale perched on her finger.

While still on the stocks, excursion tickets for return transatlantic trips on the new clipper to the Great Exhibition in London were being advertised. But the launching of *Nightingale*, with accommodation for 250 passengers, was marred by financial difficulties. Having lain alongside her wharf in Boston for six weeks, it was decided to auction her. The brokers who had advanced the money to build her bought her, before selling her on to Sampson & Tappin, who were to own her for many years.

On 17 October 1851 *Nightingale*, commanded by the experienced Captain John H Fiske, left Boston for Australia, but was delayed by adverse winds on the way and arrived in Sydney a disappointing 90 days out. Shortly afterwards she obtained a cargo of tea at Shanghai. After leaving Shanghai, *Nightingale* encoun-tered adverse weather in the China Sea, the worst for years, and it took her 61 days to clear the Sunda Strait, separating the Indonesian islands of Sumatra and Java;

Nightingale

followed by a further 72 days to London. *Nightingale's* maiden voyage was such a great disappointment for Fiske that he left her after arriving in London. Sampson & Tappin then sent Captain Samuel W Mather to take command. The following year *Nightingale* had an uneventful round trip between London and Shanghai. But it was during a transatlantic voyage from London to Boston that the North Atlantic winter took its toll: *Nightingale* arrived at the Boston Light during a snow-storm on 24 February 1854 with only four of her crew fit for duty.

The following year was *Nightingale's* golden year as a tea clipper. Still under the command of Mather, she arrived in London 90 days 18 hours out from Shanghai, the shortest time ever recorded between the two ports, and by a margin of eight days. The next fastest time from Shanghai was the medium clipper *Florence,* built by Samuel Hall and commanded by Captain Philip Dumaresq; she arrived in London 99 days out from Shanghai on 4 April 1859. *Florence* was carrying vegetable oil as part of her cargo. It had been collected from Nagasaki before she sailed to Shanghai, and was the first cargo to be shipped from Japan to Britain. The following year *Nightingale* had an excellent 88-day passage from New York to Shanghai.

For most of 1860 *Nightingale's* movements were a mystery: she is known to have been involved in the slave trade, and likely to have been owned and commanded by Captain Francis Bowen, described as the 'Prince of Slavers.' Bowen had been to the African coast previously when in command of the slave ship, *Sultana*. After leaving New York in early February 1860, *Nightingale* probably sailed to the African coast before shipping slaves to South America. In April, she was seen by an American steamer captain clearing the African coast at speed with a cargo of 2,000 slaves. On a number of occasions, *Nightingale* was stopped on the high seas by the United States Navy, but no slaves were found on board, and her papers were in order. In late 1860 *Nightingale* loaded grain at New York for Liverpool. Having unloaded at Liverpool she took on freight valued at $21,000 for St Thomas. Shortly afterwards *The Times* described her as a slave ship.

On 22 April 1861 *Nightingale* was seized by *USS Saratoga* under Commander Alfred Taylor, as she was loading slaves on the coast of Africa. A prize crew was put on board under the command of Lieutenant John J Guthrie. He permitted Bowen and Valentino Cortina, who claimed to be in command of *Nightingale*, to escape. Guthrie, a Southerner, was himself a slave holder from North Carolina. Two weeks later the freed slaves were landed in Monrovia, Liberia, and put into the care of the Reverend John Sayes, who was the agent responsible for receiving and providing for African slaves recaptured by United States warships. Of the original 961 captives, only 801 were repatriated, the remainder having died from African Fever, a particularly virulent form of malaria that was rampant among the half-starved occupants of *Nightinglale's* crowded hold. Members of the prize crew, including Guthrie, contacted the disease; and two subsequently succumbed to it.

In July 1861, *Nightingale* was purchased by the United States Government after she had been condemned and confiscated by the district court. She was then converted into an armed merchantman for service with the Gulf Blockading Squadron; the American Civil War had started in April of that year. In early October, *Nightingale* was nearly lost when she went aground and stuck fast in the mud, north of the bar at the Southwest Pass of the Mississippi. It proved impossible to move her, even after unloading her cargo of coal and pig iron over the side. The crew was preparing to abandon and set fire to her on spotting a rebel flotilla approach from upriver. But the Confederate steamer *Ivy* turned around having approached to within ten miles of the immobilized *Nightingale*, and the clipper with a checkered history was spared and successfully pulled off the mudbank at a later date.

The Civil War halted commercial traffic on the Mississippi, and the river with its many shallows and other hazards was left without pilots. One of those whose career came to an end as a result was Samuel Langhorne Clemens, a pilot who was licensed on the Mississippi in 1859. Clemens made a new career for himself as the highly acclaimed author writing under the pen name Mark Twain. 'Mark twain' is what the lead man on a ship would call for a depth of two (twain) fathom.

During most of 1862, *Nightingale* was a supply and store ship to the Eastern Gulf Blockading Squadron, and during 1863 she served as an ordinance vessel at Pensacola, Florida. She was ordered to proceed to Boston in May 1864, as she was suspected of being infected with yellow fever. There she was sold at auction the following February. In October 1865, *Nightingale,* now back in trade, set out for San Francisco under the command of Captain D E Mayo with a freight list valued at $21,107, and arrived there 119 days out from Boston. Not long after her arrival she was purchased by the Western Union Telegraph Company. The company was exploring a proposed telegraph link between the Old and New World by a cable crossing the Bering Strait. *Nightingale,* under the command of Captain Charles M Scammon, showed her sailing qualities by making fast runs between San Francisco and Petropaulovsky, and San Francisco and Plover Bay.

In September 1868, *Nightingale* arrived back in New York having left San Francisco in January; en route she had sprung a leak and was forced to put into Valparaiso for extensive repairs. On arrival in New York, she was purchased by the Boston firm of Samuel G Reed & Co, and for the following eight years plied her trade between New York, San Francisco, and China. In 1871, *Nightingale* was forced to put into the Falkland Islands as she was leaking and had a mutinous crew; the mate, Edward B Hunt, had died from a knife wound. She returned to Rio de Janeiro, where she spent two weeks before setting sail again for San Francisco.

From 1876, *Nightingale* sailed under the Norwegian flag from Kragerø, her new home port. Re-rigged as a barque, and retaining her original name, she was mostly involved in the North Atlantic lumbar trade. On 17 April 1893, when sailing from Liverpool to Halifax she sprang a leak, and Captain Christiaan Ingebritsen and his crew were forced to abandon the 42-year-old former clipper. They were rescued by a passing vessel.

According to some experts the sharpest, and potentially the fastest, of the American clippers was *Hurricane*. So sharp was she that when fully laden her cargo weight only approached her registered tonnage of 1,608. She was heavily sparred, and had the distinction of being one of only a small number of sailing ships to cross moonsail yards on the fore and main masts. *Hurricane* was launched onto the Hudson River from the yard of Isaac C Smith of Hoboken, New Jersey, on 25 October 1851 for C W & H Thomas of New York. For most of her career flying the Stars and Stripes, *Hurricane* was under the command of Captain Samuel Very. She was fitted with Cunningham's patent roller reefing topsails, enabling the sail to be unspooled and spooled as the yard was raised or lowered. She was the only Yankee clipper known to have carried roller reefing topsails. The famous Canadian-built clipper, *Marco Polo,* was also fitted with Cunningham's roller reefing topsails.

Hurricane proved a fast sailer: on her maiden voyage from New York to San Francisco she reached speeds of 18 knots. When off the coast of South America she was hit by a 'pampero,' lost her fore and mizzen topmasts and had to go into Rio de Janeiro for repairs. As a result, she arrived at San Francisco 120 days out from New York, 108 sailing days. Pampero is the name given to the fiercely cold penetrating wind that starts in the Andes and gathers speed as it crosses the South American pampas on its way to the Patagonian coast. The wind creates an opaque mist with spray torn from the top of waves, a mist that can suddenly engulf a ship in a 'white squall.'

In 1854, *Hurricane's* third voyage to San Francisco from New York was extremely fast. Despite encountering light winds and calms, she was within a thousand miles of San Francisco 85 days out, with the prospect of a 90-day passage, when she was headed by northerly winds and calms and took another fifteen days to reach her destination. The following year, 1855, *Hurricane* took freight from London to Calcutta, setting a record of 83 days from the Needles, on the western end of the Isle of Wight, to the mouth of the Hooghly River. In 1860 *Hurricane,* after some lean times, was sold at Singapore and re-registered as *Shaw-Allum* of that port.

Two of the most long-lived and successful Yankee clippers, *David Crockett* and *Young America,* were launched in 1853. *David Crockett,* at 215 feet long and with a registered tonnage of 1,679, had a cargo capacity of 2,800 tons. She cost $93,000, and was launched from the Mystic yard of Greenman & Co on 18 October. The Mystic-built clipper had a working life of 37 years, making her one of the longest-lived of the American clippers in addition to being a phenomenal commercial success: she made a fortune of $500,000 clear profit for her owners during her lifetime, and cost her underwriters nothing. She was noted for her combination of cargo-carrying capacity and speed; her hull shape below the waterline was extremely efficient. Driven hard, *David Crockett* made fast passages, even after she passed the 25-year-old mark, evidence of the high quality of her construction. A life-size figurehead of the famous backwoodsman with his long rifle was carried on board, but never mounted.

> The palm for the fastest average passages both to and from San Francisco belongs, without question, to the David Crockett.
>
> *New York Times* 7 September 1890

During 1854, *David Crockett* operated as a packet between New York and Liverpool for the Handy & Everett Line. In January 1855 she left Liverpool for India, returned to Liverpool, and then crossed to New York. After that she served on the California run, much of the time carrying general cargo from New York, and grain from San Francisco to Liverpool.

On her way to San Francisco in 1857, *David Crockett* battled for fifteen days against severe gales off Cape Horn; rogue waves washed away her boats, the deck-house, and other deck fittings. Despite this, she arrived in San Francisco 122 days out from New York. Her longest outward voyage was 131 days in 1859, when she encountered persistently severe weather. Otherwise, *David Crockett* made consistently good times on the 25 occasions that she sailed on the Great Racecourse from New York to San Francisco, nearly all in less than 120 days, registering 103 days on one occasion. Her times from San Francisco to Liverpool and New York were equally impressive.

In 1860, Captain John A Burgess of Somerset, Massachusetts, became commander of *David Crockett,* and remained with her for fourteen years. Burgess had been educated at Brown University, and went to sea for health reasons. Before taking over *David Crockett,* he had commanded *Governor Morton* and *Monarch of the Seas,* and established a reputation as an outstanding navigator. Under Burgess's command, *David Crockett* made fast passages, carrying grain to Liverpool from San Francisco in 98, 100, 107, 108 and 114 days. Many of the crew were from Liverpool, and *David Crockett* and her captain are remembered there to this day:

Farewell to Prince's Landing Stage
River Mersey, fare thee well
I am bound for California
A place I know right well

Chorus:
So fare thee well, my own true love
When I return united we will be
It's not the leaving of Liverpool that's grieving me
But my darling when I think of thee

I'm bound off for California
By the way of stormy Cape Horn
And I'm bound to write you a letter, love
When I am homeward bound
Chorus:

I have signed on a Yankee Clipper ship
Davy Crockett is her name
And Burgess is the Captain of her
And they say she's a floating hell
Chorus:

I have shipped with Burgess once before
And I think I know him well
If a man's a seaman, he can get along
If not, then he's sure in hell
Chorus:

In June 1874, Burgess, having decided to retire from the sea, was homeward bound off the River Plate when he was washed overboard from the deck and drowned as he tried to release tackle that had jammed. The first mate, Jack Anderson, took over and remained in command of *David Crockett* until the end of her days as a clipper.

In 1890, the fast ocean voyages of *David Crockett* came to an end when she was sold and towed to Philadelphia to be converted into a barge. It was an ignominious end to the illustrious career of one of the most renowned of the American clippers. *David Crockett* was considered a perfect example of a successful Yankee Clipper.

> The David Crockett still flies our flag . . . Within a day or two, however, the writer has learned that this pride of the California fleet has been sold, and is to be converted into a coal barge. Divested of her tall masts and spars very likely, fitted with three stump masts and leg-of-mutton sails, she will carry coal for Eastern ports between Gay Head and Cape Elizabeth, to any port where there is water enough to float her. She will earn her future livelihood with the matter-of-fact assistance of a steam tug at all times. Her sailing days are ended.
>
> *New York Times,* 7 September 1890

William H Webb built over 100 sailing ships in New York during the shipbuilding boom, the most commercially successful of which was *Young America,* launched in April 1853, two years after *Challenge,* also Webb-built, had slid down the ways with such great excitement and promise. *Young America,* an extreme clipper, was the last clipper ship built by Webb. Like *Challenge,* no expense was spared: *Young America* cost $140,000, had three complete decks, and was considered by some to have the finest lines and the most beautiful appearance of any American clipper. At 1,961 tons, she had capacity to carry a fairly large cargo and became popular with American shipping merchants because of her fast passages.

William H Webb

Young America was heavily sparred, crossing skysails on her three masts; the large mainsail, bent on a 104-foot long yard, dominated the square sails, and she carried large single topsails on the fore and main masts; five jibs flew from her bowsprit when fully canvassed. She was worked by a crew of 75, including four mates.

During her 30-year career, *Young America* spent much of her time carrying freight between New York and San Francisco, establishing herself as an effi-

Young America

cient passage maker: her average time for the run was 118 days. When she was nearly 30 years old she recorded a 103-day run. She made three excellent runs from Liverpool to San Francisco of 99, 111 and 117 days; her 99 days was a record that was never again equalled by a sailing ship. *Young America's* six runs from San Francisco to Liverpool averaged 108 days, including one of 125. On her best run, 103 days, she swept through St Georges Channel and the Irish Sea in June 1874 passing 38 other ships, although one large clipper did keep up with her for 36 hours. In June 1876, *Young America* doubled the Horn, sailing from 50°S in the Atlantic to 50°S in the Pacific in six days, a record that would stand for over 60 years.

Young America's reputation and successful passage-making enabled her to command lucrative freight rates: $86,400 for her maiden voyage from New York to San Francisco, $50,442 for a voyage in 1866, and $40,000 for one of her runs from San Francisco to Liverpool. She also carried passengers. Friends and admirers wagered money on her prowess, and nearly always won.

Young America had few mishaps during the 30 years she sailed under the Stars and Stripes. She was hit by hurricane force winds and partly dismasted in the North Atlantic at 32°N 9°W in October 1862; she had to make for Plymouth,

Cornwall, in distress. In December 1868, she was struck by a pampero while off the coast of Argentina and was taken aback; she lost her main topgallant, mizzen topgallant, and fore royal masts, and ended up on her beam ends with water leaking into the hold. Fortunately, *Young America's* cargo of railway iron was well stowed and didn't shift. Passengers helped the crew to pump water out of the hold. A jury rig was set up on the remains of the mizzen mast. Ten days later, the repaired main topgallant mast was sent up, stepped, and fidded, before the yards were sent up and secured and new sail bent. Despite the delay, *Young America* arrived in San Francisco 117 days out from New York. Her commander, Captain George Cummings, was rewarded with a purse of $1,000 in gold by the underwriters for carrying out running repairs and not putting them to the huge expense and delay of putting into Rio de Janeiro. In 1870, *Young America* ran onto a reef near Cape San Roque, but came off four hours later, having sustained only minor damage.

In 1883, her last voyage west took her 100 miles up the Great Columbia River to Portland which was then emerging as a major grain outlet in the Pacific Northwest. On her return to New York she was sold for $13,000. For the following five years, she sailed under the flag of Austria as *Miroslav*. In 1888, she left Philadelphia bound for Europe and was never heard of again.

* * *

Nearly all the Yankee Clipper captains were from New York and New England. They established a reputation for reaching top speeds under sail by throwing caution to the wind and flying a mass of towering canvas in gale force winds. Even when they failed to get away with it, by losing masts and spars in fierce storms, they sailed under jury rigs, set up new masts, and continued to break records. Tremendous ability, toughness, great skill, stamina, and outstanding leadership were the hallmarks of a successful clipper captain. The ship's master had sole responsibility for the ship, its crew, passengers, and cargo on a fast non-stop voyage of over 15,000 miles out of the sight of land. With only the wind for power, and guided by the sun, moon, and stars, the master would have to cope with the changing moods of the great oceans, and bring his ship safely into harbor at the end of a challenging voyage, a feat that could only be consistently achieved by really great seamanship and true leadership. Clipper captains would weather unpredicted storms, and pilot their ships through calms, fog, shallows, currents, and adverse winds. Voyages took them round the unpredictable Cape

Horn, where ships could disappear without trace, overwhelmed by huge seas, blizzards or ice, and never be heard of again. This lonely isolated and cold stretch of ocean was one of the most inhospitable places on earth; but it was the best way to get from one side of the United States to the other.

Cape Horn clipper captains were highly regarded in social circles. It was customary for captains to change their clothes at eight o'clock in the evening and at the same time in the morning, except perhaps in stormy weather or when there was poor visibility. The officers and men of the watch below were expected to come on deck at a moment's notice to make or to shorten sail. The captain could appear on deck at any time, day or night; this required the officers to maintain a high state of alertness at all times.

To be a successful clipper captain required courage, physical strength, and strong nerves to drive a ship continuously, day and night, in all weathers with rigging and sail strained to breaking point. A ship and her crew were in great peril if the captain was unfortunate enough to become incapacitated or die during a voyage.

In January 1852, Captain Josiah Richardson, after completing his first round trip in *Stag Hound,* was given command of *Staffordshire,* an 1,800-ton Atlantic packet launched in June 1851. *Staffordshire* was named after the English Potteries from where her owners Enoch Train & Co conveyed and imported freight. She had earned the title 'The Queen Clipper of the Atlantic' under the command of Captain Albert H Brown, who had started his sailing life as an ordinary seaman before the mast and was regarded as one of Boston's most capable packet masters. *Staffordshire's* powerful yards were painted black, her lower masts white, and her royal mastheads were crowned with gilded balls and spires.

Enoch Train decided to put *Staffordshire* on the California run. Richardson took her from Boston to San Francisco in 102 days, before continuing on to Singapore. She went from there to Calcutta, before returning to Boston, arriving there in April 1853. *Staffordshire* then resumed her role as an Atlantic packet.

On 9 December 1853, *Staffordshire* left Liverpool for Boston, carrying passengers and crew totaling 214. After crossing the Grand Banks of Newfoundland a storm developed, and she sprung her rudderhead. Four days later, the bowsprit was carried away, the foremast came crashing down and the temporary rudder was carried away. While the wreckage was being cleared away to prevent it from holing the bow, Richardson climbed the fore rigging. From there he fell about 35 feet to the deck and was seriously injured. He was taken to his cabin where he was treated by the ship's surgeon. The following day the wind moderated slightly. That night *Staffordshire* struck Blonde Rock, four miles from Seal Island, near Cape Sable at the southern tip of Nova Scotia, and foundered. Richardson, by now seriously ill, refused to leave, and went down with his ship; 169 of those on board lost their lives, and 44 were saved.

The sea area off Cape Sable was particularly dangerous for seafarers. Sable Island, a crescent-shaped island sandbank about 100 miles south-east of Nova Scotia, was one of the most feared hazards in the North Atlantic; hundreds of vessels were wrecked there. Sable Island is exposed to the full fury of local storms, regardless of wind direction. There is a shelf of shallows extending for miles offshore, creating dangerous cross seas and breaking waves. Gales, strong currents, shoals, and frequent fog combine to make this a dangerous place for sailors. Storms there are often accompanied by coastal erosion; on one occasion 100 feet of the island was washed away. At the end of the 19th century, Sable Island was 1.5 miles wide and 20 miles long, 20 miles shorter than a hundred years earlier.

Eleanor Creesy and Sarah Low were not the only spouses to go to sea during the clipper ship era; other wives accompanied their captain husbands on long voyages, assisting with navigation or helping manage some aspects of the ship, and often providing nursing care to the crew. Captain Babcock was accompanied by his wife Charlotte, on board *Sword Fish,* when he drove the Webb clipper from New York to San Francisco in 91 days and attained victory in the clipper race of 1851-1852. Captain Edgar Wakeman, who commanded the large medium clipper *Adelaide,* built by A C Bell, son of Jacob Bell, was always accompanied by his wife, Mary Eliza. Two Wakeman children were born on board; the first-born was named Adelaide Seaborn Wakeman. Captains' wives were made welcome in foreign ports; in China, husbands and wives were lavishly entertained by the tea merchants.

On 19 December 1853, a rakish 1,853-ton extreme clipper named *Challenger,* designed by Samuel Pook, was launched from the East Boston yard of Robert E Jackson. Two years earlier, almost to the day, a British tea clipper named *Challenger* was launched in London, the first clipper to be built on the banks of the Thames. On the Yankee *Challenger's* second voyage, Captain William H Burgess was in command, and accompanied by his wife Hannah. Previously he had been in command of the smaller extreme clipper *Whirlwind.*

William and Hannah had married when *Whirlwind* was on the stocks at the Medford yard of James O Curtis. *Whirlwind's* figurehead was the 'Goddess of the Winds' with a torch grasped in her left hand, leading the way. Hannah had missed her husband so much when he took *Whirlwind* to San Francisco in 119 days from Boston on her maiden voyage that she joined him on the next run to San Francisco in 1854. As soon as they got to sea, Hannah began to study navigation and learn its practical applications from her husband. She quickly mastered her brief, and is said to have been taking sights and making the necessary calculations to establish the ship's position and plot a course within a couple of months. Hannah soon became *Whirlwind's* navigator. *Whirlwind*, headed by severe storms, was 22 days off Cape Horn. According to her journal, Hannah was undaunted by the elements and witnessed the extremes of the Cape Horn at first hand by spending time on deck lashed to the rigging. Having been delayed at Cape Horn, *Whirlwind* arrived in San Francisco after a passage of 129 days. After the return leg of *Whirlwind's* voyage, Burgess was given command of *Challenger*.

On 2 June 1855, *Challenger* set out from Boston with Burgess in command, and Hannah as navigator. Headwinds and calms were encountered nearly all the way and the voyage lasted 134 days. *Challenger* sailed from San Francisco on 9 November, bound for Hong Kong, arriving there on 19 December. Getting freight for the return voyage to the United States was slow. Finally, on 31 July, *Challenger* set sail from Shanghai with the most valuable cargo ever loaded onto a ship up to that time: $2,000,000 worth of tea and silk. *Challenger* hadn't even left the river when she went aground, and stuck hard and fast on a mudbank. Fortunately, she came off undamaged without too much delay and the homeward voyage was resumed.

Details of the start of *Challenger's* next voyage from New York are not available, but it is known that on 22 November 1856 when *Challenger* was somewhere off the tip of South America, Burgess became seriously ill and had to stay in bed. Following some discussion with the first mate, Hannah assumed command. She also continued as navigator, as well as nurse to her sick husband. It was also decided to make for Valparaiso. On 15 December Hannah Burgess sailed her clipper into port. Her husband, William, had died on board a few days earlier when *Challenger* was in sight of the Juan Fernandez Islands.

Hannah was not the first woman to assume command of a Californian clipper. A month earlier, on 15 November, a pregnant 20-year-old sailed a 1,616-ton clipper into San Francisco, having assumed command on the approaches to

Cape Horn during a particularly stormy season in the infamous waters off the southern tip of America.

In April 1853, the attractive 16-year-old Mary Ann Brown married the handsome 26-year-old Captain Joshua Adams Patten in Boston. Eighteen months later, Patten, who hailed from Maine, was given command of *Neptune's Car*, an extreme clipper that was built in 1853 to a William Webb design and launched from the yard of Page & Allen onto the Elizabeth River at Portsmouth, Virginia, for Foster & Nickerson of New York. *Neptune's Car* is the only clipper ship known to have been built in the State of Virginia.

In January 1855, Mary Patten joined her husband on *Neptune's Car* in New York for a voyage to California, arriving in San Francisco 101 days later, an excellent time that would have been even shorter had they not been virtually becalmed for eight days when crossing the Pacific doldrums. Earlier, in the south-east trades, *Neptune's Car* had 24-hour runs of 310, 310, and 313 miles on three consecutive days, in addition to frequently logging 16 knots. From San Francisco, *Neptune's Car* sailed to Hong Kong, again making excellent time and beating the Donald McKay clipper *Westward Ho* by eleven days; *Westward Ho*, under the command of Captain Samuel B Hussey, had beaten *Neptune's Car* by a mere five hours on the New York to San Francisco run. British merchants in Hong Kong were impressed with *Neptune's Car*, and she was chartered to take tea from Foochow to London.

The United States' maritime achievements under sail were at their zenith in 1855, with no other nation profiting from such a large share of world commerce. That year, twelve of the finest and fastest American clippers landed tea from China in London: *Courser, Flying Dutchman, Nabob, Neptune's Car, Neptune's Favorite, Nightingale, Romance of the Seas, Sovereign of the Seas, Spitfire, Stag Hound, Storm King,* and *Wild Pigeon.* Following the arrival in London of *Neptune's Car*, Mary Ann Patten's English relatives made her and her husband welcome, entertaining them for the duration of their stay. When the Pattens arrived back in Boston they were guests at a succession of parties.

From the moment she first set foot on *Neptune's Car*, Mary Patten became intensely interested in her husband's work as she watched him compute the ship's course and position. She took advantage of periods of calm in the Pacific to teach herself navigation, and before long was competent in the art and science of navigation, and knowledgeable in the workings of the ship and its rig. She also studied medical procedures, learning skills that came in useful when the ship was struck by lightning during the Atlantic crossing from London to New York when several of the crew were injured. At the end of her first extended voyage, Patten stated that his wife would easily pass the examination for a master mariner certificate.

Neptune's Car set sail again from New York on 1 July 1856 bound for San Francisco. Two other fast clippers, the 1,173-ton *Intrepid* and *Romance of the Seas,* left New York on the same day and bets were placed as to which ship would get to San Francisco first. The handsome William Webb built *Intrepid* was commanded by Captain Gardner, who had previously commanded *Celestial* and *Comet.* Donald McKay's *Romance of the Seas* was commanded by Captain William W Henry.

Mary Ann Brown Patten had no idea what the voyage held in store for her. By the time *Neptune's Car* reached San Francisco, she would be a hero and an icon for the newly founded Women's Rights Movement, and cited as a classical example of women's ability to compete successfully with men in the workplace, although Mary herself declined an invitation to join the organization.

On the way to Cape Horn, Captain Patten became aware that there was likely to be trouble: he had discovered that the ship's first mate, Keeler, was abusive, insubordinate, neglectful of his duties, sleeping on watch, and not adjusting the sail trim as required for the changing wind and sea conditions. After repeated warnings had been ignored, Patten suspended Keeler, and confined him to his cabin for the duration of the trip. He promoted the second mate, Hare, to take Keeler's place. Mary, now pregnant, became *Neptune's Car's* navigator.

To makes matters worse, Patten, now with the added burden of the mate's duties, was becoming unwell, and before long found it difficult to continue in command. Rounding Cape Horn was never easy; but *Neptune's Car* was rounding the Horn from east to west during the austral winter, and 1856 was particularly cold and stormy. The clipper *Rapid,* which left New York a month before *Neptune's Car,* was beaten back from the Horn and had to retreat to Rio de Janeiro after spending weeks battling to get round Cape Horn.

As Patten guided *Neptune's Car* through Le Maire Strait, he became increasingly fatigued, and then delirious and lapsed into a coma, from what was likely to have been tuberculous meningitis. He was unable to continue in command and Mary Ann Patten, aged twenty, had no option but to assume command of *Neptune's Car* four days after arriving off Cape Horn. Hare, the first mate, was good at his job, but was illiterate, and had no knowledge of navigation. Keeler, still confined to his cabin sent a message to Mary warning her of the responsibilities of command and the dangers of completing the voyage; he offered to return to work and take

Neptune's Car into Valparaiso. She refused the offer, as she knew that her husband did not trust Keeler. He threatened to incite mutiny but Mary, supported by Hare, obtained the unanimous support of the crew.

The young commander slept little as she cared for her husband and commanded her ship. Her crew were beset by the usual problems of rounding the Horn from east to west against almost continuous gales, adverse seas, and towering waves. *Neptune's Car* spent two weeks battling the storms off Cape Horn. During one 48-hour period, Mary Patten, clad in oilskins to protect her from the almost constant spray, never left the poop as she waited patiently for even the slightest easing of the wind and change in wind direction that would allow her to let out a little more sail, and set a more favorable course. And when the break came it proved to be a hard beat to windward under reefed topsails and storm jib. The skies were cloudy and overcast all the time, so it was impossible for Mary to get a position fix with the sextant; instead she had to rely on dead reckoning. After rounding Cape Horn, a north-north-west course was set to take *Neptune's Carr* to San Francisco. With a fair wind and a generous press of canvas, *Neptune's Car* surged ahead, logging over 300 miles in one day.

Joshua Patten's condition improved slightly and he developed lucid spells. Seeing how exhausted his wife had become, he decided to give Keeler another chance but discharged him again soon afterwards and sent him back to his quarters when he discovered that Keeler had set a new course for Valparaiso. Patten's condition deteriorated again and he became blind when *Neptune's Car* was off Chile.

Encountering calms and storms, *Neptune's Car* sailed on, and made it safely to San Francisco, 52 days after Mary had assumed command, and 136 days out from New York. *Neptune's Car* is reported to have entered harbor looking extremely smart. Mary Ann Patten was presented with a cheque for $1,000 by the Committee of New York Insurance Officers for bringing her husband's ship and its cargo safely into port.

Romance of the Seas and *Intrepid,* the clippers that had set out with *Neptune's Car* from New York, made it to San Francisco in 113 days and 146 days respectively. *Romance of the Seas,* in her battle with Cape Horn, had her figurehead carried away, one of her boats smashed, her steering gear damaged, and her decks flooded. *Intrepid,* on her maiden voyage, was so badly damaged off Cape Horn that Captain Gardner had no option but to put back to Rio de Janeiro for repairs, and 146 days after leaving New York, *Intrepid* arrived in San Francisco.

Able commander though he (Patten) was, few shipmasters then living could have excelled his wife, in seamanship or as a navigator, as Captain Gardner of the *Intrepid* and formerly of the magnificent clipper *Comet*, could justify.

Carl C Cutler, *Greyhounds of the Sea*

Mary Patten continued to care for her husband, but Joshua never recovered and died less than a year later in Boston. A son was born to Mary in March 1857, four months before her husband died. On 17 March 1861, the brave, talented, and beautiful Mary Ann Patten, who as a 20-year old had commanded a clipper ship round Cape Horn, died from the dreaded tuberculosis, a sad ending to her short but remarkable life.

* * *

Donald McKay was an unusual combination of an artist and scientist, of idealist and practical man of business. With dark hair curling back from a high, intellectual forehead, powerful Roman nose, inscrutable brown eyes, and firm lips, he was as fair to look on as his ships. His serene and beautiful character won him the respect and the affection of his employees and made the atmosphere of his shipbuilding yard that of a happy and loyal family. His ships were alive to him and when permitted to name them himself by a wise owner, he invariably chose something fitting and beautiful.

S E Morrison *The Maritime History of Massachusetts*

Henry Wadsworth Longfellow completed his highly acclaimed narrative poem *Song of Hiawatha,* based on a legendary Native American chief of miraculous birth in 1855. Donald McKay, a friend of Longfellow, named the medium clipper, *Minnehaha,* after the arrow-maker's daughter who was the subject of Hiawatha's wooing. A finely carved figurehead of the Indian maiden adorned the bow.

> At the doorway of the wigwam
> Sat the ancient Arrow-maker,
> In the land of the Dacotahs,
> Making arrow-heads of jasper,
> Arrow-heads of chalcedony.

> At his side, in all her beauty,
> Sat the lovely Minnehaha.
>
> Henry W Longfellow, *Song of Hiawatha*

Longfellow and his sons, Charles and Ernest, were present on the occasion of the launching of the 1,698-ton *Minnehaha* at noon on 22 March 1856. Described as a handsome ship in every way and a fast sailer, the three-deck *Minnehaha* was built for Messrs Kendall & Plympton of Boston and operated successfully between New York and the Far East. She was commanded by Captain Isaac Beauchamp on her maiden voyage to Australia, and on later trips by Captain Charles Hopkins and Captain David Bursley. On 3 December 1867, *Minnehaha* was moored at Baker Island in the Pacific when a storm blew up, driving her onto a reef. Within 24 hours she was a total wreck. But no lives were lost as the crew got ashore in time.

A railroad crossing the 55-mile Isthmus of Panama was completed in 1855, making it easier and quicker for people and goods to get to California. Constructing the railway cost the lives of thousands of African, Chinese, and Irish workers, mostly from disease. The new railway would have been stiff competition for clipper ships, but there was a slump in the California trade in the 1860s and business from transporting goods to California declined. The gold had been extracted from the mines and the diggings, and there were far fewer opportunities for adventure. In addition, California had become much more self-sufficient. Enough fast clippers were already available for the lucrative trade between England and Australia, and Donald McKay turned his attention to building the beamier medium clipper, with its less ambitious sail area, and a hull shape that retained the sharp clipper bow while permitting large cargos to be conveyed at speed.

The American Civil War ended the dominance of the Yankee clipper. The American clipper ship building program could probably have survived its first trade slump, but the Civil War and the emergence of the British iron and steel clippers ended the international dominance of the American sailing ship. During the Civil War, Confederacy raiding ships attacked merchant ships of the Union with such devastating consequences for the American merchant fleet that it would take years to recover. By the first decade of the twentieth century, the tonnage of merchant ships sailing under the flag of the United States was only getting back to the level it had been in 1860.

Clippers sailing under the Stars and Stripes were subject to unexpected attack by Confederate privateers, even when far from home. On 21 August 1863, the medium clipper *Anglo Saxon*, under the command of Captain John M Cavarly, was four days out of Liverpool with a cargo of coal for New York when she was captured and burned by the Confederate privateer *Florida*, under Lieutenant-Commander John Newland Maffitt, off the Old Head of Kinsale, County Cork. At approximately the same location, twelve miles south of the Old Head of Kinsale, on 8 May 1915 the Cunard Steamship Company's *Royal Mail Steamer (RMS) Lusitania*, under the command of Captain William Turner, bound for Liverpool from New York with 1,959 passengers and crew was hit by a single torpedo fired by the u-Boat *U-20*, Kapitänleutnant Walther Schwieger. *Lusitania*, holder of the Blue Riband of the Atlantic, sank in eighteen minutes with the loss of 1,198 lives. The ship that was the pride of the Cunard fleet had carried many distinguished passengers during her relatively short life. In 1911, after attending the coronation of King George V the famous Japanese Admiral and victor of the Battle of Tsushima Strait, Heihachiro Togo OM, travelled to the United States on board *Lusitania*.

On 15 October 1863, the renowned clipper, *Contest*, set out from Yokohama homeward bound for New York under the command of Captain Frederic G Lucas. On the morning of 11 November, as she approached the Sunda Strait, a steamer was observed on her beam, bearing down on her. After a short interval, the steamer hoisted the Stars and Stripes as her ensign. Lucas replied by running up his ensign and holding his course. A blank shot was fired by the steamer, after which she hauled her ensign down, and ran up the Confederate flag. The steamer was subsequently identified as the Confederate privateer *Alabama*, commanded by Captain Raphael Semmes. Further shots were fired from the privateer, and a chase ensued. With the help of a 14-knot wind, *Contest* gained ground on *Alabama*, now under sail and steam. But the wind died to about six knots, and there was no escape for Lucas, who was forced to surrender. He and *Contest's* crew were taken off, and later transferred to the British ship *Avalanche*. *Contest* was then fired. On the previous day, *Alabama* had captured and fired the beautiful Boston clipper *Winged Racer*, commanded by Captain George Cummings, who with his crew were set free in the boats. Semmes accounted for 64 of the over 200 Union merchant ships destroyed by Confederate raiders when in command of the privateers *Sumter* in 1861 and *Alabama* from 1862. His actions alone were a significant contribution to the demise of the great Yankee Clipper fleet.

Snow Squall, a fast extreme clipper of 742 tons, built by Alfred Butler in Cape

Elizabeth, Maine, was under the command of Captain James S Dillingham Jr when she had a narrow escape from capture by the Confederate privateer *Tuscaloosa* near the Cape of Good Hope in mid 1863, while on a voyage from Penang to New York. Described as Butler's masterpiece, she had beaten *Romance of the Seas* by two days when they raced to New York from Shanghai in 1859. *Snow Squall*, then under the command of Captain G W Lloyd took 91 days, the seventh best time between those ports.

Tuscaloosa, on coming alongside *Snow Squall*, fired a shot and broke the Confederate flag. *Snow Squall*, whose wind had initially been taken by the privateer, managed to get ahead and fill her sails. She was a sharp clipper with fine lines and a good turn of speed, and it was not long before she distanced herself from her adversary and escaped. Dillingham was awarded a purse of $1,375 in appreciation of his action in saving *Snow Squall* and her cargo from capture. Less than a year later, she went aground in Le Maire Strait, but Dillingham managed to get her afloat, and sail her, leaking and damaged, to Port Stanley. There it was discovered that *Snow Squall* was not worth repairing, and she was abandoned after her cargo was removed.

Glory of the Seas, a medium clipper and the last clipper ship built by Donald McKay, was launched the month the Suez Canal opened. The market for bulk freight continued and *Glory of the Seas* remained in commission for 54 years. There was a slump in shipbuilding when she was launched in 1869 and few merchants would invest in new ships. McKay built *Glory of the Seas* on his own account and operated her himself. Registered at 2,102 tons, and capable of carrying double that amount of freight, she was 250 feet long, with three full decks. Under a press of canvas, *Glory of the Seas* was a true clipper with graceful lines, splendidly sparred, and with a magnificent suit of sails.

She was one of a select group of sailing ships to make the passage from a North American Atlantic port to San Francisco in less than 100 days. On 18 January 1874, she arrived at San Francisco 94 days out from New York. *Glory of the Seas* traded almost exclusively between the United States and British Ports from 1870 to 1885, frequently conveying wheat from San Francisco to Liverpool.

McKay's clipper narrowly escaped being wrecked at the end of a long 120-day voyage from California to Ireland in 1880 with a cargo of wheat. Arriving in Dublin Bay at the height of a sudden gale, *Glory of the Seas* was unable to cross the bar and enter the port because she was drawing 25 feet. She sought shelter at nearby Kingstown, which was built as a 'refuge harbor' earlier in the century and the largest man-made harbor in the world at the time. The Port of Dublin was extremely hazardous during storms, and many ships were lost in Dublin Bay before a harbor was built at Kingstown that could offer refuge to ships in adverse weather.

Glory of the Seas made it safely into Kingstown and dropped anchor. The huge seas running into the harbor, combined with severe onshore winds of storm force, drove her aground at low water after one of the huge cables holding her parted. She was soon refloated by powerful tugs, and after discharging some of her cargo to make her lighter she was able to cross the bar and enter the River Liffey.

After 1885, this magnificent medium clipper ceased crossing the oceans, and was engaged in various trades on the Pacific coast, at one time carrying coal from Puget Sound to San Francisco and making the occasional trip to Alaska. *Glory of the Seas* was then used for a while as a floating cannery and, following increasingly long periods of inactivity, she took on her final role as a cold storage plant at Tacoma. When *Glory of the Seas* was no longer required she was beached at Endolyne, five miles from Seattle, and on 13 May 1923 she was set on fire to yield her iron, copper, and any other metal of value; an ignominious end for such a fine sailing ship.

During the Civil War, McKay built ships for the United States Government. They included *Nausett*, the ironclad *Moniter*, the wooden gunboats *Trefoil* and *Yucca*, and the armed sloop *Adams*. In 1877 Donald McKay retired to his farm in Hamilton, Massachusetts, where, three years later on 20 September 1880 he died from tuberculosis. McKay married twice. After the death of his first wife Albenia he married Mary Cressy Litchfield.

CHAPTER 4

Australian Clippers

The first ship to shorten the journey between England and Australia was the famous *Marco Polo*, generally spoken of as the pioneer ship of the Black Ball Line.

Basil Lubbock The Colonial Clippers

In 1851 gold was discovered in Australia, creating an even greater demand for fast sailing ships. The largest, finest, and fastest sailing ships that were owned and chartered by British shippers between the years 1850 and 1857 were built in the shipyards on the East Coast of the United States and Canada. But it did not take British shipbuilders long to start building fast clippers for the China tea trade, and for the developing Australia run.

Just as the requirement for fast passages to San Francisco from Boston and New York was the catalyst for the extreme clipper during the Californian Gold Rush, it was the discovery of gold in Australia in 1851 that created the demand for the less extreme but equally fast and beautiful 'Australian Clippers.' As a result of the enterprise of the local shipowners, Liverpool became the starting point of the rush for Australian gold, and also the great emigration port of Britain. Two prominent firms, great rivals on the Liverpool to Australia run, were the Black Ball Line of James Baines, and the White Star Line of John Pilkington and Henry Threlfall Wilson. The two companies successfully contracted to carry mail between Australia and Britain.

Voyages to and from Australia involved circumnavigating the globe on the route suggested by Matthew Maury and John Towson. Having set out from Liverpool, the Australian clippers followed a great circle route through the North and South Atlantic, before joining the Roaring Forties below the Cape of Good Hope, in order to make a direct run to Melbourne on the south coast of Australia. In Melbourne, passengers, mail, and cargo were discharged; then the ship reloaded and headed south a short distance to rejoin the Roaring Forties, bound for Liverpool by way of Cape Horn, the Atlantic, the Western Approaches, St Georges Channel, and the Irish Sea.

Crew and passengers on the Australian Clippers were the first people on record to circumnavigate the globe with any degree of regularity. The American clipper ships, with their fine hulls, stout rigging, and elegant spread of canvas were at their very best on the Australia run; they sailed at speeds that were considered impossible a short time previously, and they did it with panache and few mishaps.

During the boom in shipbuilding, many fine clipper ships were built outside Boston and New York, in shipyards all along the north-east coast of the United States, as well as in Canada's New Brunswick and Nova Scotia, particularly around St John and other ports in the Bay of Fundy. One of the most famous ships to come from there was *Marco Polo*, a ship of 1,625 tons built by James Smith in 1851. She would afterwards be described as one of the ugliest clippers ever built. But despite her appearance she distinguished herself in service between Liverpool and Australia.

Marco Polo's launching was a dramatic event that nearly ended in disaster for the new ship. She was built at a place called Marshy Creek in Courtney Bay, St John, a muddy area with little water at low tide. *Marco Polo* was the largest ship ever built there, and it was decided to launch her on the flood as high water approached during a spring tide. The launching party lost control and failed to stop her after she entered the water; the hull of the large clipper careered across to the other side of the creek, ploughed into the mud, and became stuck. As the tide ebbed, she fell onto her side and became firmly embedded. Recriminations followed between the builder and the local shareholders who had invested in the project and been party to the decision to build her there. But it was soon realized that unless the hull was floated the ship would be lost. Extensive excavation was carried out around the hull, and two weeks later *Marco Polo* was floated off on another high tide.

The hull was slightly distorted as a result of the mishap: the weight of each end of the ship on the keel resulted in it being hogged, curved upwards in the middle, by about six inches. Hogging, as opposed to sagging, occurred in older wooden vessels following a long life, and was considered a problem. In *Marco Polo's* case, it was afterwards claimed that this slight upward curve in her keel accounted for her remarkable speed.

Her first voyage was to Liverpool with a cargo of timber. From there she sailed to Mobile, where she loaded cotton for Liverpool. In Liverpool, she was bought by James Baines for his Black Ball Line at what he considered to be a bargain price. Baines had earlier studied *Marco Polo's* lines when she was in dry dock and came to the conclusion that she was a really powerful ship, ideally suited for the Australia run: her cumbersome shape above the waterline would enable her to continue to carry a spread of canvas in strong winds for much longer than other clippers, while her fine underwater lines would give her speed. A handsome figurehead of her namesake, the renowned Venetian explorer and traveller, adorned her bow.

James Baines ordered a refit to a high standard for the emigrant trade that would provide three well appointed passenger decks. Above the waterline, *Marco Polo* resembled the older transatlantic packets, enhanced by a line of painted ports with black squares on a white strake. In previous times, these false gun-ports were painted along the sides of merchant ships trading with the East, to give the impression that the ship was armed and dissuade pirates from attacking. Ports were painted on some clippers because they looked stylish. *Marco Polo* was ship-rigged, crossed skysail yards, and had Cunningham's self-reefing topsails on each mast. On one occasion, sail was reduced from royals to double-reefed topsails in twenty minutes. On 23 May 1851, Henry Duncan Preston Cunningham, pay-master of the Royal Navy, patented a self-reefing system whereby a sail could be unwound or wound on a yard, as it was raised or lowered.

Marco Polo set sail for Melbourne on Sunday 4 July 1852 under the command of Captain James Nicoll 'Bully' Forbes with a crew of 30 experienced seamen, supplemented by another 30 who were working their passage to Australia. Forbes could also rely on passengers to work ropes such as halyards and braces from the deck, enabling him to wait until the last moment to reduce sail. A total of 930 carefully selected emigrants travelled as passengers; married couples were berthed amidships, with single men forward and single women aft. Two doctors staffed sickbay.

On the evening before departure, a farewell dinner was served on the poop under an awning. There were speeches, starting with James Baines and finishing with Captain Forbes who boasted that he would have *Marco Polo* back in the Mersey within six months, a boast that was greeted with skeptical good humor.

After an excellent voyage from Liverpool, *Marco Polo* arrived inside Port Philip Heads on the morning of 18 September, a record 68 days after leaving Liverpool, and a week faster than the steamer *Australia*. When running before westerlies in the Southern Ocean *Marco Polo* covered 1,344 miles in four days, an impressive 24-hour average of 336. On his arrival at Melbourne, Forbes found that nearly

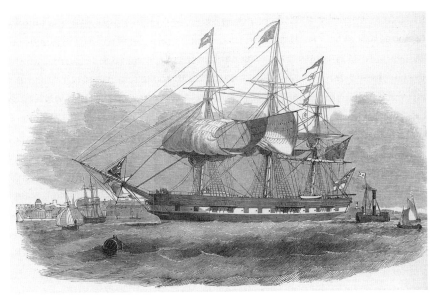

Marco Polo (ILN)

50 ships were waiting to sail, delayed because of a shortage of crews. To ensure that his crew would not abscond to the gold diggings, he trumped up charges of insubordination against his regular crew, and had them imprisoned until they were required for the return voyage.

Marco Polo left Melbourne on 11 October bound for Liverpool by way of Cape Horn, and arrived in the Mersey after a record 76-day voyage from Australia. Forbes had completed the round trip in 5 months 21 days, to the astonishment of the shipping world. According to a contemporary report, James Baines was informed by a waterman that *Marco Polo* was coming up the Mersey. Baines is said to have replied that she had probably not yet completed her outward voyage.

Before taking *Marco Polo* on her ground-breaking circumnavigation of the globe, Forbes was advised by John Towson to follow a great circle route, and take advantage of the prevailing winds and currents as advocated by Matthew Maury. Forbes was the first Liverpool clipper commander to follow the new route. Towson, who considered Forbes to be one of the great navigators of the time, would afterwards offer advice to other Liverpool sea captains on the best routes to take across the oceans.

Liverpool was proud of their ship *Marco Polo*. Crowds, including people who had travelled from all parts of England, flocked to see her at Salthouse Dock where she lay alongside, with a banner slung between the fore and main masts declaring her 'The Fastest Ship in the World.' *Marco Polo* and her skilled commander are rightly credited with setting the pace over this new Round the World Racecourse: to Australia and back. On *Marco Polo's* second voyage, Forbes was unable to match his earlier success. He took 75 days for the outward passage; on the return voyage, *Marco Polo* encountered ice thirteen days out from Melbourne at 60°S, and had to slow down. Despite being delayed, Forbes was back in Liverpool exactly six months after leaving, to yet another enthusiastic welcome.

Despite his reputation for toughness, Forbes, who was born in Aberdeen in 1821, was a hero among British sailors, and a match for the celebrated Yankee Clipper captains. He was fearless: he once crawled, hand over hand, across the top of the rigging from the spanker boom to the shark's fin on the jib boom; not such a difficult feat for an extremely fit young sailor, but an unusual one for a ship's master. The saying 'Hell or Melbourne' is credited to him; it is said that this was his reply to a deputation of frightened passengers who requested him to reduce sail when he was driving his ship hard, running before a strong gale. At the beginning of *Marco Polo's* second passage to Australia, Forbes boasted to the passengers: 'Ladies and gentlemen, last trip I astonished the world with the sailing of this ship. This trip I intend to astonish Almighty God.' He was a tough and tremendously skilled sailor with boundless initiative, who gained his reputation by making fast passages in ships that were not regarded as having the qualities required for sailing at speed. He had taken command of the Quebec-built *Wilson Kennedy* in 1849 at the age of 28, and of *Marco Polo* when he was thirty-one.

Marco Polo remained a favorite with passengers on the Australia run under Forbes, and afterwards when commanded by Captain Charles McDonnell who had been chief officer under Forbes. *Marco Polo* sailed from Liverpool in November 1853 under McDonnell's command. On arrival at Melbourne, the passengers subscribed to a splendid service of silver, to be presented to the captain on his return to England. It bore the following inscription: 'Presented to Captain McDonnell, of the ship *Marco Polo*, as a testimonial of respect from his passengers, 666 in number, for his uniform kindness and attention during his first voyage, when his ship ran from Liverpool to Port Philip Heads in 72 days 12 hours, and from land to land in 69 days.'

On 7 January 1854, *Marco Polo* logged a record 438 miles in 24 hours. The record stood for less than a year before it was improved on by *Champion of the Seas*.

It remains, however, the second fastest 24-hour run of a sailing ship; and McDonnell would be the only person to command clippers with runs in excess of 400 miles a day on as many as four separate occasions. No steamship of the time could come within a hundred miles of *Marco Polo's* 438-mile-passage in 24 hours; it would be nearly 30 years before an ocean steamship exceeded *Marco Polo's* best day's run.

On 4 March 1861, *Marco Polo* collided with an iceberg in the Southern Ocean and was badly damaged: her bow was stove in, she developed a severe leak, started to sink, and was nearly abandoned; in addition her bowsprit was carried away and her foremast sprung. A month later, during which time the crew had to man the pumps, she limped into Valparaiso for repairs, eventually reaching Liverpool 183 days out from Melbourne. *Marco Polo's* condition deteriorated as her hull became water soaked and strained. In her final days, under another flag, and almost falling apart, she was caught in a gale in the Gulf of St Lawrence, and after a lifespan of 32 years *Marco Polo* was driven ashore at Cape Cavendish, Prince Edward Island.

* * *

There was great interest in *Sovereign of the Seas* following her arrival at Liverpool in July 1853 under the command of Laughlin McKay, and with Donald McKay as a passenger. She was immediately chartered by the Black Ball line, who offered to carry freight at £7 a ton to Melbourne, with the promise of £2 a ton refund in the event of a faster passage being made by a steamer on the same berth. *Sovereign of the Seas* set sail for Australia under the command of Captain Henry Warner on 7 September 1853 with 65 passengers, and loaded down to 23.5 feet with a cargo valued at $1,000,000. Warner described it as a long and tedious passage, with *Sovereign of the Seas* arriving in Melbourne 77 days out from Liverpool, having been hampered by light and contrary winds, but ahead of the ships that set sail with her.

Sovereign of the Seas's homeward voyage with mail, passengers, and over four tons of gold dust, was completed in an excellent 68 days. It was an eventful voyage: some of the crew mutinied, hoping to seize the ship and steal the gold, but Warner dealt with the mutineers in a decisive and firm manner; the mutiny was suppressed without loss of life, and the mutineers were arrested and put in irons. Following her first round trip to Australia, *Sovereign of the Seas* was acquired by the Hamburg firm of J C Godeffroy. For a number of years *Sovereign of the Seas* sailed between Europe, Australia, and China, before she was wrecked on Pyramid Shoal in the Straits of Malacca on 6 August 1859.

Lauchlan McKay subsequently commanded the British ship *Nagasaki* on a voyage from Liverpool to Australia. When in Sydney he successfully raised a large ship that had sunk, after others had spent a month trying to do so without success. On the same voyage he went to the rescue of a ship in distress, took the crew off, and with his carpenter saved the ship from sinking. The prize crew he placed on board then took the ship to a port in India. McKay was rewarded by the underwriters and complimented by the British Board of Trade for his prompt and decisive action.

The success of *Sovereign of the Seas's* single round trip to Australia, and the experience of Liverpool shippers with *Marco Polo,* resulted in further orders for United States and Canadian ships. Before Donald McKay left Liverpool, James Baines commissioned him to build four large clipper ships that were to become famous: *Lightning, Champion of the Seas, James Baines,* and *Donald McKay.*

Lightning, 2,000 tons, was the first clipper built for Baines's Black Ball Line by Donald McKay. Her bow was formed into a 16-inch concavity that made her entrance the hollowest of all American built clippers.

> No timid hand or hesitating brain gave form and dimension to the Lightning. Very great stability, acute extremities, full, short mid ship body, comparatively small deadrise, and the longest end forward, are points in the excellence of this ship.
>
> John Willis Griffiths *Boston Daily Atlas 31 January 1854*

Forbes, who was then the favorite skipper of James Baines, was sent to Boston to take command of *Lightning.* He and Laughlin McKay became friends and Laughlin accompanied Forbes back to Liverpool. *Lightning,* under Forbes command, left Boston on 18 February 1854 and arrived in Liverpool 13 days 9 hours and 30 minutes later; on 1 March *Lightning* logged 436 miles in 24 hours, an average of 18 knots, and very close to the record set by *Marco Polo* three months earlier.

'Melbourne or Hell in sixty days' was Forbes's slogan as he set out with *Lightning* for Australia on 14 May. But the 15,000 mile outward trip took 77 days. The return trip to Liverpool with a cargo of gold dust valued at £1,000,000 only took 63 days, beating the previous record by five days. *Lightning's* round trip to Australia took her round the world in a record 5 months 9 days, a time that would never be equalled by another sailing ship. James Baines & Co, concerned with the hollowness of *Lightning's* entrance, had the concave area of bow filled in with planking shortly after her delivery from Boston. On her outward voyage to Australia, one side of her false bow was washed away and Forbes had the one on the other side removed in Melbourne. *Lightning* had two further 24-hour runs of over 400 miles: 421 miles in November 1854 with Forbes again in command, and, three years later, 430 miles when running her easting down to Melbourne during a 69-day voyage under Captain Anthony Enright, who took command in 1855. Enright, born in Austria in 1816 and certified as a master mariner in Aberdeen, had established his reputation as commander of the British China tea clippers *Reindeer* and *Chrysolite*. *Lightning's* sailing exploits earned her the title 'the swiftest ship that ever sailed the seas.' Clipper voyages between Liverpool and Melbourne were out of the sight of land and non-stop over the longest distance between two ports at the time.

> Landfall and Departure mark the rhythmical swing of a seaman's life
> and of a ship's career. From land to land is the most concise definition
> of a ship's earthly fate.
>
> Joseph Conrad, *Mirror of the Sea*

Commanding a great Australian clipper was not only prestigious; it was also highly remunerative. Enright, as captain of *Lightning*, was paid the unprecedented salary of £1,000 per annum. *Lightning* continued to make fast passages and was one of the most popular passenger ships on the Australia run. This great clipper was about to leave Melbourne in October 1869 with a cargo of wool, copper ore, tallow, and leather, when she caught fire and sank at Geelong, bringing to an end *Lightning's* illustrious career as one of the Greyhounds of the Ocean.

Following the success of *Marco Polo*, numerous other ships were built in New Brunswick and Nova Scotia for Liverpool shipowners. The main rival of James Baines & Co's Black Ball Line in the Australia trade was the White Star Line of Pilkington and Wilson, later managed by Ismay, Imrie & Co. Pilkington and Wilson hoped to improve on *Marco Polo's* records by having a number of ships built at St John, including the 1,420-ton *Ben Nevis*, the 2,012-ton *Guiding Star*, and the 1,065-ton *Hibernia*. As time passed it became ever more apparent that *Marco Polo* was a remarkable ship, and her high speed voyages were credited to her exceptional commanders.

Star of the East was an impressive Canadian-built clipper and a worthy competitor to *Marco Polo*. Immediately after arriving in Liverpool, the 1,219-ton *Star of the East* was acquired by the well known and respected local shipowner James Beazley, who spent £22,683 on purchasing the ship and fitting her out for the Australia run. Under the command of Captain William Christian, *Star of the East* reached Melbourne in 76 days. Beazley also acquired the clipper *Merry England,* the largest wooden sailing ship ever built in Ireland. *Merry England* was launched from White's Waterford yard in 1856, and made many voyages from Liverpool to Melbourne, returning to Liverpool from Sydney.

The White Star Line chartered impressive ships in 1854 to compete with their rival: Black Ball Line's four McKay clippers. They chartered *Chariot of Fame, Blue Jacket* and *Red Jacket. Lightning's* great rival would be *Red Jacket,* a fine ship of 2,460 tons register, 3,500 tons burden, 260 feet long, and very sharp in bow and stern. An extreme clipper celebrated for her graceful lines, and perfectly proportioned spars and rigging, *Red Jacket* slid down the ways into the harbor at Rockland, Maine, from George Thomas's yard on 2 November 1853. A week later she was towed to New York, where she was fitted out with spars and rigging. Designed by Samuel H Pook, and built for Seacomb & Taylor of Boston, *Red Jacket* was considered the handsomest of the larger clipper ships built in America. She was named after Chief Sagoyewatha of the Wolf clan, who during the American Revolutionary War espoused the British cause and was conspicuous by wearing a brilliant red jacket which was a present from a British Army officer. *Red Jacket's* figurehead was a full-length representation of the Chief, showing him in his magnificent regalia, including red jacket, feather head-dress, and beaded buckskins.

Red Jacket set sail on her maiden voyage from New York to Liverpool under the command of Captain Asa Eldridge on the morning of 11 January 1854. It was not long before strong south-west to west-south-west gales, with big seas, rain, sleet and snow, typical of the North Atlantic winter, were encountered. The strength of the gale required *Red Jacket* to run dead before the wind at times. Eldridge had a reputation as a great sailor and navigator. He was one of three brothers who were sailing ship commanders; his brothers, John and Oliver, commanded Western Ocean packets. *Red Jacket* arrived in Liverpool in a record 13 days 1 hour and 25 minutes, eight hours faster than *Lightning*. Her longest 24-hour run was reported as 413 miles, but according to Eldridge's abstract log it was actually 417 miles. *Red Jacket* had covered an astonishing 2,083 miles in six consecutive days on the final leg of the transatlantic voyage.

A summary of *Red Jacket's* voyage was published in *The Times* on Friday 26 January. The following day a letter was published doubting the likelihood of a sailing ship achieving the 24-hour distances logged, because it was faster than could be achieved by a steamship. The writer also questioned why *Red Jacket* needed to travel 3,600 miles with a following wind, when the transatlantic distance over the same route for a steamer would be 3,084 miles. On the Monday a letter was published from an indignant American, pointing out that *Sovereign of the Seas, Flying Cloud,* and *White Squall* had already exceeded *Red Jacket's* reported 413 mile day's run, the former between New York and Liverpool. Eldridge then had a letter published, accompanied by his abstract log of the voyage:

" To avoid any further mistake, I beg leave to refer you to an abstract log of my daily runs, setting forth the winds, courses, and distance sailed.—Left New York, Jan. 10, at 7 o'clock a.m.,—

Jan.	Lat.	Lon.	Dis.	Wind.	Course.	Remarks.
11	40 33	71 45	103	S. by E.	E. ½ N.	Rainy, unpleasant weather.
12	41 03	68 30	150	Ditto	E. by S.	Rain, hail, & snow.
13	42 19	62 41	265	S.S.E.	E. by N. ½ N.	Ditto.
14	44 25	58 20	232	S.E. by E.	N.E. by E.	Ditto.
15	46 35	54 15	210	Ditto	N.E. ½ E.	Rain.
16	46 13	51 52	106	S.S.E.	E. by S.	Snowy & hailing.
17	45 55	49 03	119	Ditto	E. ⅜ S.	Ditto.
18	50 39	47 00	300	E. by S.	N. by E. ½ E.	Ditto.
19	51 58	35 55	417	W. by S. ½ S.	E. by N.	Ditto, terrific gale, and high sea.
20	50 39	27 00	364	Ditto	E. by S. ½ S.	Ditto, and gale.
21	49 27	18 35	342	Ditto	E. by S.	Ditto, fresh gales.
22	51 07	11 21	300	W.S.W.	E. by N. ½ N.	Snow, strong wind, & heavy squalls.
23	53 27	4 11	360	South	Up Channel	Ditto, and squally, dirty weather.

I am, Sir, your obedient servant,
A. ELDRIDGE,
Commander of the ship Red Jacket.
Liverpool, Jan. 28.

The log extract of the *Red Jacket, The Times,* 31 January 1854 © The Times Digital Archive

Red Jacket received favorable attention in Liverpool and was immediately chartered by the White Star Line. She set sail for Melbourne on 4 May 1854 under the command of Captain Samuel Reid, and having logged 13,880 miles, including a 24-hour run of 400 miles on July 6, arrived out in 69 days 11 hours. *Red Jacket* remained in port for only 12 days, before leaving with a cargo of 45,000 ounces of gold and sovereigns valued at £208,044, bound for Liverpool. Reid was determined to find wind, and shorten the homeward distance by using the great circle route to best advantage. He sailed well into the southern latitudes as he guided *Red Jacket* towards Cape Horn on as short a route as possible. He got wind initially, with *Red Jacket* logging 17 to 18 knots in fresh winds and reaching an amazing 14 to 15 knots when close-hauled. It was the middle of winter in the southern hemisphere and it became extremely cold, with ice extending in every direction on the sea. Then the wind moderated. Before long, frozen spindrift covered the ship in an icy mantle to the mainmast, and soon *Red Jacket* was down in the bow. Sailing cautiously under topsails on a flat calm sea with light winds, Reid had to force a passage through dense masses of ice, while taking care to avoid icebergs.

Red Jacket was further delayed in the Atlantic, where she spent a week getting through the doldrums, and encountered more calms and light headwinds further north. Despite these delays, *Red Jacket* arrived in Liverpool having covered 14,863 miles in 73 days on the leg from Melbourne, an average of 202.25 miles daily; her best day was 376 miles. *Red Jacket* had arrived back 5 months and 11 days after leaving Liverpool, within two days of *Lightning's* record. Like *Lightning,* she was one of only three clippers that logged 400 miles or more in 24 hours on more than one occasion. Shortly afterwards the White Star Line bought *Red Jacket* outright.

> No racing yachts have ever been handled with greater care and skill than these clipper ships.
>
> Arthur H Clark, *The Clipper Ship Era*

Donald McKay perfected the design and strength he had used in *Lightning* when he built *Champion of the Seas* and *James Baines,* each with three decks, and about 2,500 tons register. They were built in 1854 for the Black Ball Line's Liverpool to Melbourne run. *James Baines* was 266 feet in length and her mainyard was 100 feet long; her rig and sail plan were increased shortly after she went into service. She crossed three skysail yards, a main moonsail yard, and could fly studdingsails to skysails, probably the only clipper ever to be so heavily rigged.

James Baines broke a number of *Lightning's* individual records. On her maiden voyage, under the command of *Marco Polo's* former captain, Charles McDonnell, *James Baines's* time from Boston Light to Liverpool's Rock Light in September 1854 was 12 days 6 hours, logging 20 knots at times, and beating *Red Jacket's* record by 18 hours. *James Baines,* still under the command of McDonnell, reached Melbourne in just over 63 days, having left Liverpool on 10 December 1854, an

James Baines (*ILN*)

improvement of five days on *Marco Polo's* record. With all sail set to moonsail and studding sails, *James Baines* had a day's run of 423 miles on 6 February 1855; ten days earlier a day's run of 407 miles was achieved. *James Baines* returned from Melbourne to Liverpool in 69 days 12 hours. On 28 May 1856, *James Baines* broke the 400 mile barrier for the third time with a 24-hour run of 404 miles; and within a month, on 18 June, McDonnell established the accepted all-time top speed recorded by a sailing ship: *James Baines* reached 21 knots as she stormed ahead in the Roaring Forties under a full spread of canvas. It would be 30 years before a steamship logged 21 knots: the City of Dublin Steam Packet Company's side-paddle steamer *RMS Ireland*, recorded 21 knots during her maiden cross-channel voyage between Holyhead and Kingstown in October 1885. In 1898 the Norddeutscher Lloyd line's 15,000-ton *Kaiser Wilhelm der Grosse* won the Blue Riband of the Atlantic for a westbound crossing averaging 22.29 knots; her furnaces consumed 22 tons of coal per hour to maintain her record-breaking speed.

Twenty-one knots is unlikely to have been the actual top speed achieved by a clipper. According to a report in the Sydney newspaper *The Empire, James Baines's* sister clipper *Sovereign of the Seas,* while owned by Godeffroy of Hamburg and

RMS Ireland (ILN)

commanded by Captain J J G F Müller, logged 22 knots on a number of occasions in the Roaring Forties before her arrival at Sydney on 22 October 1854. But evidence from the abstract log to credit him with the record of 22 knots under sail is not available. Müller is also recognized as achieving a day's run of 410 miles with *Sovereign of the Seas*.

The record for the fastest speed logged by a sailing ship was further challenged by the narrative of Captain Joshua N Taylor of Orleans, Massachusetts, who was sailing master under Captain James White on board the beautiful *Blue Jacket* during a 63-day voyage to London in 1865. Taylor claimed that at times *Blue Jacket's* patent log registered 23 knots during a rollercoaster from Lyttleton New Zealand to Cape Horn, running before a south-westerly gale that enabled her to average 384 miles a day all the way to the Horn, '. . . beating all records ever made by a sailing ship up to that time.' Captain White had a reputation for carrying sail, boasting that he had never taken a topsail off the lovely clipper while at sea. *Blue Jacket*, built by Robert E Jackson at Boston in 1854, was equipped with powerful steering gear and double wheels.

In February 1869, when off the Falkland Islands on another voyage from Lyttleton, *Blue Jacket's* cargo of flax and other goods caught fire; the flames spread rapidly, and the crew were forced to abandon ship. Eleven days later, exhausted, hungry, dehydrated, and suffering from exposure, they were rescued by the barque *Pyrmont*.

McKay's *Champion of the Seas*, a popular passenger and freight carrier that made repeatedly good but not particularly fast passages, holds the record for the best day's run of any sailing ship. In December 1854, when on a voyage from London to Melbourne under the command of Captain Alexander Newlands, she made a noon-to-noon run of 465 miles, a staggering average of almost 19.4 knots and equivalent to 535 statute miles or 862 kilometers. *Champion of the Seas* was described as the most perfect ship built by Donald McKay. Newlands had been sent from Liverpool to superintend her construction: he designed her interior and decided on how she was to be rigged; the masts of the 2,448-ton extreme clipper were raked ½, ⅝ and 1 inch to the foot, and her sails were made from 12,000 yards of 18-inch wide canvas.

Lightning, James Baines, Sovereign of the Seas, Red Jacket, Champion of the Seas, Blue Jacket, and *Donald McKay* were among the fastest sailing ships ever built, attaining overall average speeds of 10–12 knots throughout their working lives on the oceans of the world. Sail held the record for speed and the best day runs for many years after the last American clipper ship was launched.

> The art untouched by softness, all that line
> Drawn ringing hard to stand the test of brine;
> That nobleness and grandeur, all that beauty
> Born of a manly life and bitter duty;
> That splendour of fine bows which yet could stand
> The shock of rollers never checked by land.
> That art of masts, sail-crowded, fit to break,
> Yet stayed to strength, and back-stayed into rake,
> The life demanded by that art, the keen
> Eye-puckered, hard-case seamen, silent, lean,
> They are grander things than all the art of towns,
> Their tests are tempests, and the sea that drowns.
> They are my country's line, her great art done
> By strong brains labouring on the thought unwon,
> They mark our passage as a race of men
> Earth will not see such ships as these again.
>
> John Masefield, *The Emigrant Ships*

On 10 March 1855 the 2,598-ton *Donald McKay*, the last of the four great McKay clippers built for the Black Ball Line, was delivered to Liverpool by Captain

Warner, who had previously commanded *Sovereign of the Seas*. On the sixth day out of Boston, *Donald McKay* logged a 24-hour run of 421 miles in a strong north-westerly gale that reached hurricane force at times. Donald McKay was on board, and afterwards expressed satisfaction with her performance.

Donald McKay's figurehead was a Scottish Highlander dressed in the famous McKay tartan. The clipper that bore her builder's name had three decks and a weight-carrying capacity slightly in excess of *Great Republic*. *Donald McKay* was the largest clipper ship afloat at the time; two years later, the 2,800-ton Danish-built *Cimber* took to the water. For the next twelve years, *Donald McKay* was a popular Black Ball packet, making consistently good passages on the Australia run, before spending time as a troop carrier. In 1879, *Donald McKay* was sold to a German firm and Bremerhaven became her home port.

Donald McKay was fitted with Howes double topsails, the greatest improvement ever in the rig of a square-rigged ship. Captain Robert Bennett Forbes, a former ships captain, successful businessman, and shipbuilder in Boston had devised double topsails in 1844. He did not patent his invention, pointing out that Daniel Tonge of Liverpool had already invented a double topsail rig in 1824. Forbes double topsails were fitted to the clippers *Reindeer* in 1849 and *Flying Childers* in 1852. But it was after Captain William F Howes refined, patented, and fitted them to *Climax* in 1853, before sailing the Medford-built clipper on her maiden voyage, that they became widely used. After 1855, most ships had Howes double topsails fitted, and they became standard rig for the remainder of the sailing ship era. Soon afterwards sailing ships undergoing a refit would have their single topsails replaced by doubles.

Before double topsails the crew would have to go aloft onto the topsail yard, to reef or stow the sail in heavy weather; it was a slow, dangerous and time-consuming task that was eliminated when lower and upper topsails were fitted. The lower topsail, the size of a close-reefed topsail, could be set entirely by the sheets. The foot of the upper topsail was attached to the lower topsail yard so that little wind could escape between them; the upper topsail could be lowered to a position in front of the lower topsail when not in use, and this could be done by the crew on deck. When canvas needed to be reduced further, the lower topsail could be stowed from the deck. This type of rig enabled sailors to reduce sail in heavy weather without going aloft.

Black Ball and White Star Australian clippers could carry a full press of canvas longer than other ships, without damaging their rigging or having spars carried away, a common occurrence with the earlier American clippers, and also a problem with early British iron clippers. A lot was learned from the dismasting, constant loss of spars, and heavy casualties aloft that occurred with such frequency on board the earlier Californian clippers. Clipper ship builders over- came the inherent weaknesses of the earlier rigs, and fitted the six famous Black Ball and White Star clippers with wooden spars and hemp rigging of consider- able strength. Their masts and yards were of a greater diameter than on earlier clippers; rope used for the standing rigging was of immense thickness. *Lightning's* lower rigging, forestays, backstays, and main stays were made of 11.5 inch thick Russian hemp.

The relatively high sides and shorter load waterline of the Australian clippers, a result of the relatively lighter weight of 400–500 passengers, meant they were buoyant and dry. They were incredibly steady and without a tendency to roll quickly and heavily in a seaway. According to the logs, the decks were so steady that the passengers frequently enjoyed dancing on the poop, as the clippers ran before gales and big seas at speeds approaching 16 knots. On 16 June 1856, *James Baines* logged 17 knots in the Roaring Forties under a press of canvas to main skysail and passed a smaller clipper that was under double-reefed topsails. Two days later, having added starboard studding sails in a freshening breeze, *James Baines* logged her record 21 knots.

Donald McKay created many of the finest and fastest of the clipper ships. Six of the nine clippers credited with 24-hour runs of 400 miles or more were designed and built by him: *Lightning* 436, 430, and 421; *James Baines* 423, 407, and 404; *Sovereign of the Seas* 411 and 410; *Donald McKay* 421; the cut-down *Great Republic* 413; and the fastest of all, *Champion of the Seas's* record-breaking 465 miles on 12 December 1854 when under the command of Alexander Newlands. The other clippers to break the 400 mile barrier for a day's run were *Marco Polo, Red Jacket,* and the Glasgow-built iron clipper *Lord of the Isles.* The large and beautiful *Red Jacket,* designed by Samuel Pook, logged 24-hour runs of 417 and 400 miles in 1854. The reported 24-hour runs of over 400 miles by *Flying Cloud* and *White Squall,* mentioned in the letter to *The Times* on 30 January 1854, cannot be confirmed.

The 438-mile run by *Marco Polo,* the pathfinder of the Australian Clippers, in addition to being the second longest 24-hour run, was the first of four 24-hour runs in excess of 400 miles recorded by the captain, Charles McDonnell; the other three were during his time as commander of *James Baines*. These achievements and the record 21 knots, achieved by *James Baines's* when under his command, mark McDonnell out as one of the most successful and consistently fast master mariners in the Age of Sail.

A great clipper ship charging past under full sail was an awesome sight to behold. Seeing one of these tall ships clipping along under full sail was enjoyed by few people, as the spectacle nearly always took place on the wide ocean, well out of the sight of land.

> Notwithstanding all that has been said about the beauty of a ship under full sail, there are very few who have ever seen a ship, literally under all her sail. A ship going in or out of port, with her ordinary sails, and perhaps two or three studding-sails, is commonly said to be under full sail; but a ship never has all her sail upon her except when she has a light steady breeze, very nearly, but not quite, dead aft, and so regular that it can be trusted and is likely to last for some time. Then with all her sails, light and heavy, and studding-sails, on each side, alow and aloft she is the most glorious and moving object in the world. Such a sight, very few, even some who have been at sea a good deal, have never beheld; for from the deck of your own vessel you cannot see her as you would a separate object.
>
> Richard Henry Dana, *Two Years Before the Mast*

The Bass Strait between the Australian mainland and Tasmania was a place where land bordered one of the great sailing routes, and where clippers could be viewed passing through the strait on their way to Cape Horn. At a later time, Alan Villiers would describe the great full-rigged clipper carriers charging past under full sail, as viewed from Tasmanian soil.

Most people rely on artists to convey the majesty and beauty of a great clipper under full sail. Anton Otto Fisher's fine painting of *Lightning*, beautifully reproduced in Richard McKay's book, *Some Famous Sailing Ships and Their Builder Donald McKay*, conveys the true grandeur of a remarkable ship under sail: one of the swiftest ships ever to sail the seven seas clips along with her lee rail awash and lee rigging slack; she is held well down in the water by a full cargo and with all sail perfectly set and filled from a quartering wind; the bowsprit leads the way with the figurehead of a carved female in flowing robes decorating the underside of the junction of bowsprit and stem; *Lightning's* hollow knife-like clipper bow carves a clean path through the uneven blue water as turbulent foaming white crests hit the bow; four fore-and-aft jibs lead the fourteen billowing squares of canvas, diminishing in size with their increasing height above the deck, the large foresail and mainsail just above the deck, with the large topsails immediately above and above them the topgallants, royals, and skysails, all carried on three raked masts; fore-and-aft staysails catch the wind in between, while the large gaff-rigged spanker on the mizzen mast extends out over the stern. What a thrill it must have been to have had the wheel of this great ship as she sped quietly through the waters of the ocean, her motive power generated solely from the wind. Another artist who captured the tremendous power of a clipper ship was A G Green when he depicted *James Baines* under full sail to main moonraker and starboard skysail studdingsails.

Sailing ships capable of carrying large bulk cargos continued to have a role; the medium clipper was designed for this purpose. Donald McKay was again in the forefront; he is credited with creating the medium clipper, a vessel that would prolong the role of the sailing ship as a 'merchantman.' Medium clippers were designed and built to carry large cargos, rather than to attain high speeds. Once again California created the demand for the new medium clippers: growing and harvesting wheat had become as profitable as gold mining and San Francisco began exporting the Californian grain.

Commodore Perry and *Japan*, each 1,964 tons, were the last McKay ships built for James Baines's Australia run, and the first medium clippers to sail the high seas. McKay designed them with the emphasis on buoyancy and stability; their great wide floors facilitated the carrying of large cargos. They were fine sailing ships with towering masts and spars. *Commodore Perry*, in ballast on her delivery trip from Boston to Liverpool in 1855, outsailed the ships in company with her. She then made a fast passage from Liverpool to Sydney, thus confirming McKay's theory that a flat bottom was superior to deadrise.

Baines's success was meteoric: he bought his first ship in 1851, and by 1860 his Black Ball Line had 86 ships, sailed by approximately 300 officers and 3,000 seamen. (It is not known how James Baines managed to get the house flag of the prominent New York Black Ball line.) But 1860 was the year Baines's fortune began to decline: his softwood clippers were becoming increasingly expensive to maintain as the hulls were deteriorating from the ingression of water, a venture into steam had been unsuccessful, and in 1866 James Baines went bankrupt. He ended his days impoverished, depending on charity from friends.

* * *

During the 1850s, British shipbuilders, mostly in Scotland at shipyards in Aberdeen and on the Clyde, began building clippers, usually with hardwood or iron hulls. One of the few British ships built as a direct rival to the big Yankee Clippers was *Schomberg*. Donald McKay recognized her as the only real British competitor to his great clipper ships. Launched from the Aberdeen yard of Alexander Hall & Sons on 5 April 1855 for James Baines's Black Ball Line, *Schomberg* was an extreme clipper of 2,284 tons. She was 262 feet in length, 45 feet in breadth, and 29 feet in depth with a long sharp entrance, and considerable deadrise; her long yards provided space for a large area of sail. *Schomberg* was the largest wooden-hulled merchant ship ever built in Britain, one of only two larger than 1,500 tons launched during the 1850s. During the same period, 72 ships of over 1,500 tons were launched in the United States; thirteen of them over 2,000 tons.

Schomberg's hull was constructed of Scottish larch, consisting of six inch thick longitudinal planks on the outside, tightly screwed to a layer of two two-and-a-half inch thick diagonally worked sheets laid at 90° to each other and 45° to the keel, on an inner layer of longitudinal planking; layers of felt and tar were sandwiched between the four layers of larch. Screw trenails, patented by William Hall, were used to bind all layers of the larch hull tightly together. Trenails, also called treenails, were hardwood nails used to fasten layers of timber sheathing together. Hall's screw trenails were made from African oak; each had a screw thread, a square head, and was 1⅜ inches in diameter. The trenails were screwed into threaded holes that had been skillfully bored in the hull at one foot intervals along each strake of planking; it required the strength of two men using a long-handled key to screw each trenail home. Iron was used for the deck supports and hold pillars.

Schomberg had three decks, with passenger accommodation provided on all three: the main deck provided 60 staterooms for first-class passengers as well as second-class accommodation. The first-class dining saloon, the ladies cabin, the library, and the smoking room were on the upper 'tween deck; steerage passengers were accommodated on the lower 'tween deck. There was room on board for about 1,000 passengers. The crew numbered 130, including captain, officers, seamen, cooks, and stewards. *Schomberg* was greatly admired when she arrived in

Schomberg (ILN)

Liverpool to load, and it was generally believed that she would prove faster than her American rivals, especially as Captain Forbes, of *Marco Polo* and *Lightning* fame, and by then Commodore of the Black Ball Line, had been appointed to command the magnificent Aberdeen-built clipper.

After setting out from Liverpool on 6 October 1855, adverse winds and light airs delayed *Schomberg* on her way to the Cape of Good Hope. This was disappointing for Forbes, who was looking forward to a fast voyage. After rounding the Cape, *Schomberg* benefited from the westerlies of the Roaring Forties as far as the coast of Australia, reaching a speed of 15.5 knots, and recording a day's run of 368 miles.

East winds then delayed *Schomberg* off the coast of South Australia. *Lightning* and *James Baines* were also delayed, and arrived in Melbourne 81 and 85 days out from Liverpool. But Forbes was able to make little progress with *Schomberg.* On Christmas Day, land was sighted at Cape Bridgewater on the coast of Victoria, about 35 miles west of Cape Otway, itself less than 100 miles from Melbourne. By the afternoon a fresh east-south-east wind was driving the ship north; during the night and the following day the wind continued from the same point, requiring Forbes to tack frequently. When within five miles of the shore on December 27, the wind died and *Schomberg* was becalmed. That evening Forbes ordered ' 'bout ship.' At first *Schomberg* began to come round slowly, but she refused to answer the helm. Forbes then tried to wear ship but a westward flowing current of three to four knots, of which he was unaware, and of which there was no mention on the chart, rendered the attempts unsuccessful. Without warning, the current set *Schomberg* onto an uncharted sandbank.

Schomberg became firmly stuck and all efforts to move her failed. The passengers and crew were rescued the following morning by the steamer *Queen*, under the command of Captain Doran. *Schomberg* eventually broke up, after attempts to refloat her failed. The greatest wooden-hulled clipper ship ever built in Britain had set out from Liverpool with tremendous pomp, ceremony, and great promise on her maiden voyage, but failed to complete it. Instead she foundered on a sandbank in a calm, within a day's sailing distance of her destination. It was a sad ending for this magnificent ship and for those whose expertise had made her possible.

It was claimed afterwards that *Schomberg* was overloaded and was drawing over 25 feet of water when she left Liverpool; her cargo was mostly iron and plant for the Geelong railway. At the Court of Inquiry, Forbes and the third mate Saxby were charged with negligence for not letting go an anchor to prevent the ship from immediate loss. Forbes's case was supported by an expert court witness: Captain Matthews testified against anchoring, as the vessel was heading away from land when it got stuck, and there were no rocks or breakers marked on the chart. Even though he was exonerated by the Court of Inquiry, Forbes, who had an enviable reputation as a master mariner when he took *Schomberg* out of Liverpool a short time earlier, was never given another command by the Black Ball Line of James Baines.

Alexander Hall also designed and built the wooden-hulled Australian clipper packet *Sobraon,* the largest composite sailing ship ever built. Built in 1866 at a cost of £43,965, *Sobraon* registered 2,130 tons, had a cargo-carrying capacity of about 3,500 tons, and was 317 feet in length. Only the finest Malabar teak was used, giving her hull considerable strength; her three lower masts were of wrought iron while her lower yards and topmasts were of steel. She was finished to very high specifications. Her three decks were devoted to 250 passengers. The accommodation was fitted out to the highest standard, with the first-class saloon occupying most of the main deck, and second-class passengers occupying the 'tween decks. The loftily rigged *Sobraon* crossed skysails on fidded royal masts and carried double topsails; her main topgallant was fitted with roller-reefing gear, and she spread two acres of canvas with all sail set.

Shaw, Lowther & Maxton of London, the owners of the famous China tea clipper, *Ariel,* bought her from Hall's. *Sobraon* never went on the China run, as her loading agents Devitt & Moore chartered her right away for their Australian service and loaded her for Sydney at the West India Docks. In 1872, Devitt & Moore bought her outright and put her on their Melbourne service, where she spent the rest of her sailing career, and established a reputation as a famous passenger carrier between England and Australia.

Captain John Kyle commanded *Sobraon* on her maiden voyage to Sydney; she arrived there 75 days out from London and returned in 88 days via the Cape of Good Hope. Kyle was followed by Captain James A Elmslie from Sydney who remained in command of *Sobraon* for 22 years. Shortly after taking command, Elmslie dispensed with the skysails, having decided that the skyscrapers provided

Sobraon *(ILN)*

121

no real advantage. In 1883, he had the single topgallant sails replaced with doubles on the fore and main masts, but retained the deep single mizzen topgallant.

Sobraon's crew normally numbered 69, and during the time Elmslie was in command of this giant clipper he had the full confidence of the crew, with many of the officers and men serving under him for long periods. There was keen competition to serve on Sobraon. The crew consisted of four mates, eight apprentices, a surgeon, carpenter, sailmaker, boatswain and two boatswain's mates, donkey man, chief steward, chief cook, butcher and butcher's mate, twelve cooks and stewards, two stewardesses, thirty seamen, and two boys. James Cameron, the carpenter, had been the foreman shipwright during Sobraon's construction, and joined her at the time of her maiden voyage; he stayed as carpenter for the 25 years of the composite clipper's seafaring career. Thomas Willoughby was another long-serving crew member. He had served under Elmslie on Cospatrick and moved with him to Sobraon as butcher, later becoming chief steward and continuing in that role until 1891. Elmslie's son, A G, served for eleven years under his father aboard Sobraon, during which time he advanced from apprentice to chief officer.

Fresh food was served on board. Meat was provided from the menagerie of farm animals carried on board: a few bullocks, nearly a hundred sheep, about fifty pigs, and hundreds of fowl. Three cows provided fresh milk during the voyage. The animals were kept in pens and henhouses built on deck. A large amount of fodder, including hay, corn, pollard, bran, parsnips, and turnips, was stored in the boats and provided the animals with plenty to eat; an adequate supply of straw and grit was carried for bedding. For two days before departing from the West India Docks, Sobraon's deck resembled a farmyard. Carts carrying sheep, pigs, and cattle would arrive alongside to be hoisted on board, while other carts delivered crates of live poultry. The animals came from the farm of the partner, Joseph Moore, in Cornwall, who preferred to have his own farm-hands drive the livestock overland and deliver them safely to the ship. Occasionally sheep, pigs, and cattle were brought by rail and transferred at the railway dock to barges that brought them alongside.

Elmslie achieved relatively fast voyages without sustaining serious loss of spars. He did so by paying due attention to the weather conditions and not pushing his ship too hard. One round trip was made each year. Departure from London was in late September and from Australia at the beginning of February. On her return voyages from Sydney, Sobraon made scheduled stops at Cape

Town and St Helena. Although she made her reputation as a passenger ship, her large cargo-carrying capacity created considerable revenue. She made excellent passages throughout her career although she was never sailed as hard as the great Black Ball and White Star clippers. *Sobraon* sailed equally well in light breezes and strong winds, sometimes exceeding 16 knots in strong leading winds or moderate gales in the Roaring Forties. It was said that no other sailing ship passed her when she sailed before the wind. *Sobraon* covered over 1,000 miles in one three-day period, and over 2,000 miles in one week; 24-hour runs of 300 miles were common, logging 340 miles on one occasion. *Sobraon's* fastest passage from London to Melbourne was an excellent 68 days.

A young female passenger, who was travelling first-class, was lost overboard in November 1883 when *Sobraon,* with all sail set, was running before a strong quartering wind at a steady 13 knots in the South Atlantic. Just after four bells, ten o'clock at night, the quartermaster, who had just taken the wheel, saw a young woman arrive on the poop, walk aft, and seat herself on the wheel-box grating behind him. A few minutes later he noticed that she was nowhere to be seen and, assuming that she had gone overboard, he raised the alarm and ran to the stern. The third mate, A G Elmslie, was in charge of the watch, and he quickly joined the quartermaster. They found the girl clinging to the outside of the lower rail; they tried to grab her, but before they could do so she fell into the sea. An apprentice threw lifebuoys over the rail.

When the quartermaster let go of the wheel the ship came up into the wind, checking *Sobraon's* headway. Third mate Elmslie ordered the royal and topgallant yards to be lowered, followed by the upper topsail yards. By this time Captain Elmslie and all hands were on deck. Within four minutes of the alarm being raised, the fourth mate had a boat and crew launched. This rapid response was possible because of the large number of crew carried and because they were practiced at getting the lifeboat away.

The boat retraced *Sobraon's* track; it was reckoned that she had travelled a half mile in the four minutes. The night was pitch dark and big seas were running. No trace of the woman or the lifebuoys was found, despite a four-hour search. Some time later the lifebuoys were picked up by another ship. The young passenger was travelling alone, and there was no explanation for why she had gone overboard.

On another occasion a cadet fell overboard. It happened one morning when *Sobraon* was sailing in the tropics at a leisurely five knots. The lifeboat was launched, and it reached the young man shortly afterwards. The crew found him rather relaxed, happily swimming around with his heavy boots slung round his neck, he having unlaced them and slipped them off.

Following her arrival at Melbourne in 1891, *Sobraon* was sold to the New South Wales Government for £12,500. They converted her into a reformatory and had her towed to Sydney Harbor where she was moored off Cockatoo Island. During the following twenty years she housed 400 boys at a time. In 1911, she was acquired by the Australian Government for £1,500 and converted, at a cost of £7,000, into a training ship for boys entering the Royal Australian Navy and renamed *HMAS Tingara*. A survey at the time showed that the hull was in near perfect condition. But *Tingara* did not go to sea; instead she lay at her mooring in Rose Bay, where, during the following sixteen years, about 3,000 young men received their preliminary naval training on board. In 1927 she was sold, and spent most of the following fourteen years moored in Berry's Bay, before being broken up in 1941. Her finest timbers were reclaimed and used to build the yacht named *Sobraon*.

Sobraon was the largest and most comfortable of all the Devitt & Moore's ships, noted for her ease of handling and her dry decks. She is believed to have been the only sailing ship where a game of cricket was played while running her easting down.

Thomas Henry Devitt and Joseph Moore were ship and insurance brokers who set up a successful business partnership in London; they managed ships for clients as well as owning vessels of their own. In 1836 they were appointed loading brokers for eleven ships. Duncan Dunbar, the leading shipowner in London at the time, gave his work to the new firm. Thomas Lane Devitt acquired his father's share of the business at the age of 21, following his father's death in 1860, and the partnership became Devitt & Moore. In 1863, Devitt & Moore acquired ownership of two of Duncan Dunbar's Australian clippers: *Viaiera* and *La Hogue*. They specialized in providing a first-class passenger sailing service with excellent accommodation on the Australia run, a service that continued for twenty years after steamer services commenced on the route.

Devitt & Moore owned 29 clipper ships and two steamships during their 55 years as shipowners. Their experience with steam was short-lived. Within a year of entering service, *Queen of the Thames* was wrecked off Cape Agullias, South Africa, with the loss of four seamen and the purser, who had returned to the wreck to save the ship's papers. From 1875 to 1880 they owned the 1,318-ton steamer *Glenelg*. After their short experience with steam, they decided that they would acquire no more 'steam kettles.'

Devitt & Moore's passenger ships were fair weather sailers, rarely encountering winter weather during their voyages. They set sail from London in the summer and from Australia during the Austral summer, with stops at Plymouth, Cape Town, St Helena, Adelaide, Melbourne, and Sydney. These fine clippers were under no pressure to sail hard, and avoided Cape Horn by returning to London via the Cape of Good Hope. At the end of the nineteenth century, Devitt & Moore ran a highly regarded training scheme for cadets aboard their Australian clippers, and in 1917 they founded the Nautical College at Pangbourne that continued to operate until 1931.

The first ship specifically built for Devitt & Moore's Australian service was the handsome passenger and cargo composite clipper, *City of Adelaide*. She was launched from the Sunderland yard of William Pile Jr on 7 May 1864 for the service between London and Adelaide. Like other composite clippers, her wooden hull below the waterline was protected from fouling by a layer of Muntz-metal sheeting, a form of brass, consisting of 60 per cent copper and 40 per cent zinc that had been patented by George Frederick Muntz of Birmingham. *City of Adelaide* carried Cunningham patent roller reefing single topsails. In addition to carrying passengers, *City of Adelaide* regularly collected a cargo of wool at Port Augusta, at the head of Spencer Gulf, for the homeward voyage.

She was owned by Messers Martin & Harold in association with the clipper's first commander, David Bruce, who owned a quarter share. Bruce, the son of a Perth weaver, first went to sea at the age of ten. He was followed as commander by his son John in 1867. Under John Bruce's command, *City of Adelaide* achieved a time of 65 days from London to Adelaide, pilot to pilot, a record she held jointly with *Yatala* for a number of years; it was subsequently improved on by another renowned passenger carrier on the London to Adelaide run, the large composite clipper *Torrens*, on which the author Joseph Conrad served as chief officer. John Bruce was followed as commander by Captain Llewellyn Bowen in 1873. He commanded her for two years before Alexander Bruce, another of David's sons and a brother of John, took over. *City of Adelaide's* last commander under the management of Devitt & Moore was Captain Edward D Alston, who commanded the clipper from 1876 to 1887.

On 24 August 1874, *City of Adelaide* had almost reached her destination after a 91-day passage from London when she went aground on Kirkcaldy Beach near

Adelaide. Fortunately, it was a sheltered place and tugs helped the crew put out anchors astern in order to kedge the clipper off the beach. When this failed, part of her cargo was unloaded and her topgallant masts and yards were sent down. Eventually, on 4 September, *City of Adelaide* was refloated.

Between 1887 and 1889 *City of Adelaide* was confined to the coastal trade: carrying coal from Newcastle-upon-Tyne to Dover. In 1889 ownership was transferred to Dixon's of Belfast, who reduced her sail plan to barque rig. During the following five years, *City of Adelaide,* commanded in turn by Captains Patrick Crengle, John Gibson McMurtry, and John Brown, was involved in the North Atlantic timber trade. Afterwards, McMurtry took command of the ill-fated Belfast four-master *Lord Downshire* that went missing in 1894; she probably foundered after colliding with another vessel off the coast of Brazil.

Carrying timber provided *City of Adelaide* with her last role as a commercial sailing ship. In 1893 she was purchased by Southampton Corporation for £1,750, and moored on the River Test off Millbrook where she served as an Isolation Hospital following an outbreak of cholera in the city. Although *City of Adelaide* survived for a further century in a number of capacities, she never sailed again.

Other European maritime countries built fine clipper ships. In April 1858, *The Illustrated London News* reported and illustrated the magnificent Danish clipper *Cimber,* commanded and owned by Captain Jørgen Bruhn, as she was discharging cargo at the East India Docks. *Cimber,* built by Bruhn at his Kalvø yard, was constructed throughout with Danish-grown oak; she was 280 feet long and registered 2,800 tons. She was bigger and more impressive than most of the American clippers, exceeding the celebrated *Sovereign of the Seas* by ten feet in length. Bruhn's masterpiece was one of the fastest clippers afloat at the time, setting a Liverpool to San Francisco record of 104 days, an improvement of twelve days on the previous record; *Young America* subsequently reduced the record to 99 days.

One of the most attractive clippers ever was the Dutch ship *De Noach,* built and owned by Fop Smit, the first of six clippers to bear the same name. The fine-lined *De Noach,* a medium clipper of 892 tons, carried tall raked masts, an enormous bowsprit, a very long jib-boom, and a figurehead of Noah. She was the first Dutch ship to have iron-wire standing rigging, made by the London firm of Newall & Co. Iron-wire was first introduced into British shipyards in 1850.

De Noach carried passengers, attracted by her comfortable and luxurious

Cimber (ILN)

accommodation, and freight. This magnificent clipper achieved fast voyages when under the command of Captain P Wierilex: her best homeward run from Batavia to Brouwershonen was 71 days in 1863 with a troop of soldiers as passengers, and ore and sugar as cargo. *De Noach's* voyage to Australia in 1859 was marred by a storm that brought down her foremast, and tore away her jib-boom and much of her copper sheathing, forcing her into Port Jackson for repairs. In 1877 she was reduced to a barque rig, and in 1884 she was broken up. Parts of *De Noach* and much of her timber were used in the construction of *Trovbecke*, the last clipper ship to be built in the Netherlands.

* * *

An Australian clipper, *Hampshire*, was used by the Royal Navy for sail-training. Many Royal Navy cadets completed their training by gaining practical experience of seamanship and navigation aboard her. When *Hampshire* set sail for Australia in February 1875 the future Admiral of the Imperial Japanese Fleet and victor in the Battle of Tsushimi Strait, Heihachiro Togo, was on board.

Togo was the oldest of twelve young Japanese men, who, as cadets in the Imperial Japanese Navy, arrived in Britain by steamer during the spring of 1871 to train with the Royal Navy. While *en route* to England, on the morning of 25 May,

Heihachiro Togo

the Japanese arrived on the bridge at dawn dressed in traditional Japanese clothes. They had turned out to see Cape Trafalgar on the Spanish coast where Nelson's decisive victory had taken place. Togo, who was interested in all things related to the sea, was a life-long devotee of the famous British admiral; in October 1873, when training on board *HMS Victory*, Togo stood to attention with the other cadets on the anniversary of the Battle of Trafalgar as Nelson's famous signal was hoisted. After they arrived in England, the cadets were fitted out in traditional naval uniform; shortly after they returned home, the Japanese Navy adopted a uniform modeled on that of the Royal Navy.

After completing two years training, Togo joined the full-rigged 1,200-ton sail-training ship *Hampshire*. In February 1875, *Hampshire* set sail for Australia with Togo and other cadets from the Thames-based Nautical Training College *HMS Worcester*.

Hampshire arrived in Melbourne after a 70-day voyage. One aspect of the voyage failed to impress Togo: the diet of salted meat and ships' biscuits. Following *Hampshire's* arrival in Melbourne, Togo went to the nearest restaurant and had a meal of fresh food, consisting mostly of vegetables. The two months in Melbourne was a vacation for the cadets, and they amused themselves in boats, on foot, and exploring the countryside on horseback. During an excursion inland, Togo was surprised to find that Australia was so beautiful and so well developed. It was a continent relatively near to his own country, but he had never heard of Australia before leaving home. *Hampshire* sailed from Melbourne on 11 July 1875, and rounded Cape Horn on 11 August, leaving the bleak rock 70 miles to port. After his 30,000 mile Round-the-World sailing voyage, Togo went to Cambridge University and studied mathematics, before returning to Japan in 1878. Commander John Henderson-Smith, Captain-Superintendent of the Nautical Training College at the time, afterwards described Togo as one of the best cadets that had been through *Worcester*.

In 1905, Tsushima Strait, between the Tsushima islands and the Korean Peninsula was the location of one of the most decisive victories in naval history. Russia's powerful Baltic Fleet commanded by Admiral Zivony Rozhestvensky and consisting of 49 ships including 17 battleships, had travelled half-way round the world only to be routed by the Imperial Japanese Navy led by Admiral Heihachiro Togo in his flagship *HIJMS Mikasa*. When the 15,200-ton *Mikasa* was commissioned by Vickers at Barrow-in-Furness on 1 March 1902, she was the largest warship afloat and the most powerful battleship in the world.

As the powerful battle squadron of the Imperial Russian Navy emerged out of the early morning mist on 27 May, Togo hoisted the signal that was to become

HIJMS Mikasa (ILN)

famous: 'The fate of our Empire hangs upon this battle. Everyone must exert himself to the utmost.' The Russian fleet was no match for the Japanese who had been training for months: Togo's warships were much more accurate with their guns, and at night the Russian ships were easy targets for fast Japanese torpedo boats. About 4,545 Russian officers and men died, 6,106 were taken prisoner, and the Baltic fleet was almost completely destroyed. The Japanese lost 117 men and three torpedo boats.

It was a humiliating defeat for the Imperial Russian Navy, with enormous consequences for the ruling Romanovs. Mutiny and revolution followed. The crew of the Black Sea Fleet battleship *Potemkin* mutinied less than three weeks later, the mutineers including in their demands an end to the Russo-Japanese War. Tsar Nicholas II agreed to peace talks, and the Russo-Japanese war ended with the signing of the Treaty of Portsmouth, New Hampshire, on 5 September 1905.

Britain was an ally of Japan and Captain Pakenham, later Admiral Sir William Christopher Pakenham, was British Naval Attaché to the Imperial Court in Tokyo. Pakenham accompanied Togo on board *Mikasa* and witnessed the Battle of Tsushima Strait at close quarters. Emperor Mutsuhito afterwards bestowed the Order of the Rising Sun for services to the Imperial Japanese Navy on Pakenham; and on John P Holland, the former Irish Christian Brother who invented the modern submarine. Holland's submarines had been acquired by the Japanese Navy and were undergoing trials in Tokyo Bay when the Russo-Japanese War ended.

Togo became Japan's greatest naval hero following the victory of the Japanese Fleet in Tsushima Strait. He was made a Count, and in 1913 was appointed Admiral of the Fleet of the Imperial Japanese Navy. King Edward VII bestowed the Order of Merit (OM) on Togo, and a lock of Nelson's hair arrived from Britain with a request for a lock of Togo's in return. In 1911 Togo, in full uniform, attended the coronation of King George V, in attendance to Prince and Princess Higashifushimi. A small bust of Horatio Nelson, carved out of wood and copper from *HMS Victory,* was presented to Togo by his many British friends, in recognition of his victory at Tsushima. He was also the guest of honor at the annual dinner of the *Worcester* Association.

The decisive victory at Tsushima established Japan as a world power. Three years later a powerful United States Navy task force of sixteen new battleships, the 'Great White Fleet,' was sent around the world by President Theodore Roosevelt to show the flag, the first such voyage by a United States naval squadron. At the time of Tojo's death, Japan was striving to achieve naval parity with Britain and the United States, then the world's two greatest sea powers.

* * *

New Zealand, situated nearer to Cape Horn than Australia, began exporting frozen mutton by clipper ship to Britain during the 1880's. The first cargo of frozen meat ever imported into Britain arrived from Australia on board *Strathleven* in 1881. Shortly afterwards the P&O steamer *Orient* carried frozen beef from Sydney to London.

Cold air refrigeration provided the low temperature that was required to keep the meat frozen. This dry air refrigeration was pioneered by Sir Alfred Searle Haslam, engineer and politician, who in 1880 had acquired the patents of the Bell-Coleman cold air machine. Haslam had foreseen the benefits of refrigeration and for most of the following twenty years equipment made at his factory, the Union Foundry in Derby, dominated the frozen meat trade. By the end of the 19th century, refrigeration was being used to enable the transportation of fish, milk, vegetables, fruit, and other perishable foods from Australia, New Zealand, South America, and North America to Europe. In 1891, Haslam invited Queen Victoria to lay the foundation stone of the new Derbyshire Royal Infirmary. At the end of her visit the Queen knighted Haslam.

New Zealand's first cargo of frozen meat, a cargo of lamb, arrived in London on board Shaw, Savill & Co's refrigeration clipper ship *Lady Jocelyn* in 1882. Cold air refrigeration equipment was powered by a small steam engine. In the early days of the frozen meat trade, freshly slaughtered carcasses were frozen on board ship because of the absence of freezing facilities ashore. Cape Horn sailing ships dominated the New Zealand frozen meat trade until the beginning of the 20th century.

CHAPTER 5

Tea Clippers

They were all beautiful vessels of an entirely original type with nothing about them to remind one of the American clippers; for they had considerably less sheer, much less freeboard, and lower bulwarks, and their comparatively small breadth gave them a slim, graceful appearance.

Arthur H Clark *The Clipper Ship Era*

By the early 1850s the Aberdeen shipyards of Alexander Hall, Walter Hood, and Alexander and John Duthie, had built a number of clipper ships with the Aberdeen bow for the China tea trade. Hood designed and built famous ships for George Thompson of Aberdeen, whose White Star Line operated services to Australia and China. Among them was the 470-ton *John Bunyan*, launched in 1848. In the spring of 1850, *John Bunyan* arrived at Deal 101 days out from Shanghai, a fast passage that was overshadowed by the American clipper *Oriental's* 97 days over the shorter distance from Whampoa later in the year.

Another Aberdeen clipper matched *Oriental's* 1850 performance. The 328-ton *Reindeer,* built by Alexander Hall and launched in 1848, was the first vessel to bring the new season's tea from China in 1850, arriving in Liverpool on 19 January, 106 days out from Whampoa. The owners were so pleased with the performance of the little clipper that they presented her master, Captain Anthony Enright, with a chronometer. The following season, *Reindeer* arrived home in an equally good time of 107 days from Hong Kong.

Hall's yard launched *Stornoway* (506 tons) and *Chrysolite* (471 tons) in 1851, the first British clippers specifically built for the China tea trade. Aberdeen-built tea clippers were designed to cope with the tricky China Sea and were smaller than their American counterparts. *Stornoway* was owned by Jardine, Matheson & Co of London and China, and named after Stornoway Castle on Lewis, one of the islands comprising the Outer Hebrides. Sir James Matheson owned Stornoway

Castle and retired there after a long and successful career as a merchant in the China trade. *Chrysolite* was built for Taylor & Potter of Liverpool.

Hall's Aberdeen yard continued to build fast clippers with knife-like bows and fine lines, rigged to fly picturesque billowing canvas when under way. Among Hall's most famous clippers were *Black Prince*, *Flying Spur*, and *Thermopylae*. Many other fine clippers, including *Ariel*, *Crest of the Wave*, *High Flyer*, *Sir Lancelot*, *Spirit of the Age*, *Star of China*, *Taeping*, and *Wild Deer*, were built by British yards. Some owners, although not regular China traders, built and owned tea clippers for the pleasure of owning a recognized thoroughbred of the seas. Baring Brothers treated their clipper *Normancourt* as their private yacht, and spent any amount necessary to keep her looking shipshape. *Thermopylae* and *Cutty Sark* were really fine clippers, built just before the opening of the Suez Canal and the end of the China clipper ship-building programme.

The East India Company had a monopoly of trade with China until their charter expired in 1834. Up to then, tea, silk, and other goods were carried in slow moving East Indiamen. Canton retained dominance of the tea trade until the early 1850s, with ships collecting tea cargos at Whampoa on the Pearl River, ten miles below Canton and 60 miles inland from Hong Kong. Then Shanghai, located on the Whangpoo River, twelve miles upriver from Woosung in the Yangtze Kiang Estuary, became an important port for loading tea, and remained so until Foochow became the dominant tea port. With the Whangpoo River navigable by ships under sail in favorable winds, Shanghai was a very busy port, handling a variety of cargos in addition to tea. Clippers loading there complemented their tea cargo with 4,000-5,000 bales of raw silk.

British China tea clippers sailed out and back by the Cape of Good Hope. Many of the Americans did the same, although some preferred to return by going south to the Southern Ocean, and then rounding Cape Horn into the Atlantic. To bring the new season's tea to the London market, the clippers would sail a distance of up to 16,000 miles out, and 16,000 miles back: they crossed the equator four times, travelled through the Sunda Strait, before and after negotiating the China Sea each way, crossed the Indian Ocean twice, rounded the Cape of Good Hope in both directions, sailed the whole length of the Atlantic at the start and end of each voyage. Navigation wasn't easy with typhoons, calms, and shallow uncharted reefs in the China Sea.

Richard 'Dickey' Green, of Richard and Henry Green's Blackwall Yard on the

Thames was one of the few people involved in British shipping to support the repeal of the Navigation Laws. In 1851 he spoke at an important dinner in the City of London. He followed the secretary of the American Legation, who had made the usual complimentary remarks. Dickey Green drew attention to the pessimism then present in business circles about the future of British shipping; he ended his speech:

> . . . the British shipowners, have at last sat down to fair play and open game with the Americans, and, by jove, we'll trump them.
>
> Basil Lubbock *The China Clippers*

And, true to his word, it was not long before a sailing vessel with a sharp Aberdeen style bow began taking shape in Blackwall. *Challenger*, the first London built clipper ship, was launched onto the River Thames on 23 December 1851, in time to sail to China for that season's tea. *Challenger*, a small clipper of 699 tons owned by W S Lindsay of London, then raced the New York-built *Challenge*, a clipper twice her size, back to London.

After loading tea at Shanghai *Challenger* set sail. *Challenge*, having loaded tea at Canton also set sail. The two almost identically named clippers fell in with each other in the Sunda Strait off Anjer, and an informal race to London began. News of the race was telegraphed to London where high stakes were wagered on which clipper would arrive in London first. *Challenger*, under the command of Captain James Killick, had a fast run and docked two days ahead of *Challenge*. *Challenger's* overall time from Shanghai to Deal was 113 days, compared to *Challenge's* 105 days from Canton to Deal. Dickey Green won a large amount of money on the bets he had placed on *Challenger*, and is reputed to have bought *Challenge* with the proceeds.

Challenger further enhanced her reputation the following year: she left Woosung on the same tide as the American clipper *Nightingale*, and arrived at Deal two days ahead; in 1855 *Nightingale* had an exceedingly fast 91-day passage from London to Shanghai. *Challenger* traded exclusively between Shanghai and London for fifteen years. Her fastest passage home was 105 days; her best outward passage to China was 101 days in 1856. Before her return voyage she was delayed for a month in China: she left Woosung with a cargo of tea and silk valued at £500,000, but almost immediately ran aground and lay on her side, before being refloated and repaired.

Dickey Green, the older of the two brothers, and the senior partner, was widely known and respected in shipping circles. The Greens were a prominent shipping family, who built and owned the famous Blackwall Frigates. The Blackwall Yard was the first shipyard to be located on the banks of the Thames.

The main purpose of the yard was to build ships for the East India Company; in their day the East Indiamen were the largest merchant vessels afloat. The year 1611 saw the launch of the first East Indiaman from the Blackwall Yard by its founder, the shipbuilder Henry Johnson. As well as East Indiamen, Johnson built two third-rates for Oliver Cromwell and four for Charles II. Johnson was knighted by Charles II. East Indiamen were replaced on the routes to India and the East by the equally large and impressive Blackwall Frigates. The ships of the Blackwall Line were known for their strength; they were superbly built of the finest hardwood, English oak and Malabar teak, and never wore out. The last Blackwall Frigate was launched from the yard in 1875. The introduction of iron into shipbuilding hastened the end of the famous Blackwall Line of East London. Dickey Green was determined not to build iron ships at the Blackwall Yard. In 1875, after his death, the yard launched one of the finest iron clippers of the time: *Melbourne*.

To be the captain of a Blackwall Frigate was to have reached the pinnacle of success in the British Merchant Navy. The navigation skills required were well in

A Blackwall Frigate

advance of those required by other sea captains, and they were paid salaries of £5,000 per annum. An officer assuming command of a Blackball Frigate could use the lunar distance method with ease, and navigate by the stars, when many captains of other ships would often make do with a meridian altitude. Blackwall Frigates were mostly crewed by cockneys, traditionally people born within hearing of the bells of the church of St Mary-Le-Bow, the 'Bow Bells,' in East London. They were some of the finest sailors in the world, with a tradition going back before the East India Company was formed. Naval-type training, expertise, and order were hallmarks of the Blackwallers. Orders were followed to the tune of the boatswain's whistle. There was frequent sail drill, with crew members assigned to regular stations, so that there would be no confusion concerning which sail had to be handed.

Blackwall frigates sailing to and from India normally called at Calcutta and Madras, as well as Cape Town and St Helena. Many magnificent sailing ships took part in the Calcutta jute trade. Among them were Corry's beautiful iron clippers from Belfast. But none was a match for the the magnificent teak Blackwall frigates with everything shipshape, their masts and yards perfectly raked and aligned, and manned by a large, well organized crew.

The Green family was highly regarded in Poplar, because of the employment they provided, and their charitable and philanthropic work. Dickey continued to support the good works of his father George who had established Almshouses, Green's Sailors Home, The Trinity Schools, Trinity Chapel, and made other

Dickey Green

significant contributions to London's East End. George Green, who was born in 1767 in Chelsea, had started work as an apprentice shipwright at the Blackwall Yard. The comfort of the officers and men was more important to Dickey Green than the balance sheet. After he died in 1863, a bronze statue of him was erected beside the East India Dock Road, a testament to how highly he was regarded in the locality.

Sir Robert Wigram, who founded the Wigram fortunes, was a great entrepreneur in his time. He and two of his sons acquired the Blackwall Yard in 1813. Wigram was the son of John Wigram of Bristol, a sailor and commander of the privateer *Boyne*. In 1742 John set sail for Malaga from Bristol, but had to put into Wexford. There he met Mary Clifford of Ballyhally. Not long afterwards *Boyne* again put into Wexford, where Wigram renewed his friendship with Mary and they married. John Wigram was lost at sea when Robert, his son, was about two, and the young Wigram was reared by his mother and his maternal uncle who was a doctor. In 1762 his mother gave Robert £200, a letter of introduction to a Dr Allan, and sent him to London to train to be a doctor. After two years as an apprentice he became a surgeon in 1764, and shortly afterwards joined the East India Company as a ship's surgeon. Wigram contacted ophthalmia in China eight years later, resulting in permanent damage to his eyesight, and he was forced to abandon his career with the company.

During his time with the East India Company, Robert Wigram became knowledgeable about trade with India and China. He later put this to use by becoming an importer of pharmaceuticals with premises in Cornhill, London. His business flourished, and in 1782 Wigram moved his premises to Crosby Square, Bishopgate. In addition he bought into a number of other businesses, acquired shares in East India Company ships, and was the leader of a group of shipowners who put pressure on the government to establish the East India Docks at Blackwall for the company's ships.

The East India Dock Company was formed in 1803. Wigram was a member of the committee responsible for the construction of the docks; he chaired the company from 1810, and became a director in 1815. Part of the nearby Blackwall Yard was acquired for the new East India Docks, and by 1813 Wigram was also the owner of the Yard itself. He managed the yard with two of his sons, and in 1819 sold it to them and George Green; the Blackwall Yard then became Wigrams & Green. The partnership lasted until 1843 when George's sons, Dickey and Henry took it over, and it became the R & H Green Yard.

Like the Greens, Wigram was a generous benefactor as well being prominent in public affairs. He became Member of Parliament for Fowey in 1802 and for Wexford in 1806; he was bestowed with a baronetcy in 1805. In 1772 he married Catherine Broadhurst, with whom he had two sons and two daughters. A year after her death he married Eleanor, widow of Captain Agnew and daughter of John Watts of Southampton, with whom he had thirteen sons and four daughters. Sir Robert Wigram died at his home, Walthamstow House, in November 1830.

*

China tea clippers were used to take general cargo to Australia, and there they would load with coal for Chinese ports. After unloading the coal, they waited for the tea cargos. The captains were men of considerable ability, who handled their ships and sailors with skill and good judgment; and some of them accumulated considerable fortunes in the process. Like the East Indiamen and the Blackwall Frigates before them, the tea clippers were manned by first-class sailors, many of whom had served in the Royal Navy. According to Arthur Clark there was no smarter sailor afloat, whether aloft, or with a marlinspike, palm and needle, or watch-tackle.

The tea was ready for loading in May or June; the new season's growth was ready in Foochow earlier than anywhere else, and after 1854 this became the favorite port for fast clippers to load tea. Foochow lies roughly midway between Shanghai in the north and Hong Kong in the south, about 450 miles from each. Tea was loaded at Pagoda Anchorage, an extensive expanse of water surrounded by beautiful scenery that lies off Pagoda Island on the Min River, 11 miles below the town of Foochow, and 24 miles upriver from the outer bar.

Tea was conveyed from the inland plantations to the warehouses at Foochow by sampan. After agreeing a price, each hong (merchant house) sent chops by lighter downriver to the anchored clippers; chop was the name given to a number of boxes of the same quality tea, usually the product of one garden. A lighter had capacity for a hundred chests of tea. The arrival of the first tea at the anchorage signaled the beginning of the race to get the new season's tea to England. Loading started immediately. Each ship's hold would have already been meticulously cleaned, ready for the cargo of tea.

> Cargo junks and lorchers were being warped alongside at all hours of the day and night; double gangs of good-natured, chattering coolies were on board each ship ready to stow the matted chests of tea as they came alongside; comfortable sampans worked by merry barefooted Chinese women sailed or rowed in haste between the ships and the shore; slender six-oared gigs with crews of stalwart Chinamen in white duck uniforms darted about the harbor; while dignified master mariners, dressed in white linen or straw-coloured pongee silk, with pipe-clayed shoes and broad pith hats, impatiently handled the yoke lines.
>
> On shore the tyepans and their clerks hurried about in sedan chairs

carried on the shoulders of perspiring coolies, with quick firm step to the rhythm of their mild but energetic 'woo ho–woo-ho–woo-ho.' The broad cool veranda of the clubhouse was almost deserted; in the great hongs of Adamson, Bell; Gillman & Co; Jardine, Matheson & Co; Gibb, Livingstone; and Sassoon; the gentry of Foochow toiled by candle-light over manifests and bills of lading and exchange, sustained far into the night by slowly swinging punkahs, iced tea, and the fragrant Manilla cheroot.

Arthur H Clark The Clipper Ship Era

Loading of the clippers would continue day and night, until the ship's hold was full. Tea was lighter than other cargos, and the clippers carried 200-300 tons of clean shingle ballast, laid beautifully smooth and even onto which the chests of tea were placed. The square boxes of tea were packed carefully into the hold with dunnage wood placed in empty spaces between them to keep the cargo firmly in position. Chinese stevedores were highly regarded, and considered by many of the clipper captains to be the best in the world. After the holds were filled to capacity, they were hermetically sealed. For example, *Taeping*, a clipper of 767 tons register, carried 1,234 tons of tea occupying 50 cubic feet per ton.

Taeping, a magnificent clipper, was one of a number of celebrated tea clippers built at the Greenock yard of Robert Steele & Co and designed by Robert's brother William. She was the first composite clipper to come from the yard when launched onto the River Clyde on 23 December 1863. Her hull was constructed of greenheart and teak planking, secured to the frame by phosphorated screw bolts; greenheart is a South American wood known for its resistance to marine borers.

When loading was complete, the clippers would make their way down the Min River. The Min was hazardous to negotiate, with its gorges, submerged rocks, and treacherous currents; the narrow gorges, with sheer cliffs on either side, created currents that sometimes reached a speed of seven knots, and ships navigating downriver loaded with tea would be propelled to a speed approaching 20 knots. The most treacherous gorge was the seven-mile-long Mingan Pass, and there many ships were wrecked. Clippers could come to grief during inward or outward passages in the gorge. If they touched the bank they would quickly swing round in the fast current; within minutes control would be lost, and the vessel would heel over and become partly submerged. Local fishermen or pirates would descend on the stranded clipper, invite the crew to leave, and strip the wreck of all valuable parts as quickly and as efficiently as any of the wreckers or looters on the coast of Britain in earlier times.

Many clippers were lost in the Mingan Pass, including the famous *Oriental* in 1853 and *Vision* in 1857. The Hall-built *Vision*, belonging to James Beazley of Liverpool, was considered to have tremendous potential when she was launched onto the River Dee in 1854. Her first tea-carrying passage from Whampoa to Liverpool was accomplished in 103 days and therefore she could earn £6 per ton of tea the following year. But *Vision* failed to live up to expectations: her time from Foochow in 1855 was 139 days; and in 1856 it took her 129 days to reach Liverpool. Her life as a tea clipper was short. In 1857 she hit the bank of the Min, was capsized by the strong current, and became a total wreck.

In November 1858, the McKay-built *Flying Fish*, the winner of the famous California Clipper Race of 1852–1853, loaded tea at Foochow and proceeded down the Min towards the sea. At the mouth of the river, she was headed by the wind and had to tack. On the third tack she misstayed; Captain Nickels tried to anchor, but the anchors fouled and *Flying Fish* drifted onto a sandbank. It took two days to float her off, by which time she was badly damaged. Her tea cargo was salvaged, and she was sold as a wreck to a Manila firm who had her rebuilt at Whampoa. For a number of years, she sailed between Manila and Spain as *El Bueno Suceso*, before foundering in the China Sea.

Childers, a really fine tea clipper of 1,016 tons from the Blackwall Yard and commanded by Captain Enright, arrived in London on 12 August 1864, 104 days out from Foochow on the return leg of her maiden voyage. On 30 May the following year, while being towed downriver with tea insured for $800,000, she struck the North Sand Bank at the mouth of the Min, two miles outside Sharp Peak, and was wrecked. *Childers* was the last tea clipper to be built by Greens.

Chinese and European pilots were engaged to guide the clippers along the rivers, and into and out of port. At Foochow, Chinese pilots guided the clippers on the Min River; they were dropped off or taken on board at the river mouth. Deep-water pilots were then responsible for guiding ships across the outside bar as far as the White Dogs, three islands off the estuary, where outward bound clippers would set sail on the first leg of the 16,000 mile voyage to London.

Conrad described the person representing ships chandlers who would board the incoming clipper at ports in the East:

He was spotlessly neat, apparelled in immaculate white from shoes to hat, and in the various Eastern ports where he got his living as ship-chandler's water-clerk he was very popular. A water-clerk need not pass an examination in anything under the sun, but he must have Ability in the abstract and demonstrate it practically. His work consists in working under sail, steam, or oars against other water-clerks for any ship about to anchor, greeting her captain cheerily, forcing upon him a card—the business card of the ship-chandler—and on his first visit on shore piloting him firmly but without ostentation to a vast, cavern-like shop which is full of things that are eaten and drunk on board ship; where you can get everything to make her seaworthy and beautiful, from a set of chain-hooks for her cable to a book of gold-leaf for the carvings on her stern; and where her commander is received like a brother by a ship-chandler he has never seen before. There is a cool parlour, easy-chairs, bottles, cigars, writing implements, a copy of harbour regulations, and a warmth of welcome that melts the salt of a three month's passage out of a seaman's heart. The connection thus begun is kept up as long as the ship remains in harbour, by the daily visits of the water-clerk.

Joseph Conrad, Lord Jim

For clippers leaving the Min estuary with their tea cargos, the first 2,800 miles was through the treacherous China and Java Seas. It was always a race to get to London first, often without any idea where the other competing clippers were. The tea clippers sailed south through the Formosa Strait and the South China Sea off the Cochin-China coast, before entering the Indian Ocean by passing through the Sunda Strait.

> The China seas north and south are narrow seas. They are seas full of everyday, eloquent facts, such as islands, sand-banks, reefs, swift and changeable currents–tangled facts that nevertheless speak to a seaman in clear and definite language.
>
> Joseph Conrad, Typhoon

The China Sea, with its large number of shoals and reefs, as well as unpredictably strong currents, was poorly charted; many of the shoals and reefs bore the names of ships that sank, after their hulls were ripped open on the jagged

Chinese Pirate Boat (*ILN*)

coral reefs; Fiery Cross Reef was one such. There was a particularly notorious reef off the Island of Banca in the Java Sea that claimed a number of fine clippers. Many years earlier the Dutch had surveyed the South China Sea when they were establishing themselves in the region, but they kept their charts in great secrecy. However, one tea clipper captain is reported to have been using a set of Dutch charts as late as 1870.

Piracy was an ever-present offshore danger in the South China Sea; pirates infested the coast of China. It was particularly risky for a tea clipper to be becalmed or stranded on a reef at night, as pirates were likely to use it as an opportunity to arrive in their lorchas, and attack the crew under cover of darkness. The clipper crews were heavily armed and many captains would stay on deck until they were clear of the South China Sea. The penalties for piracy in China were severe: immediate public execution for those caught.

After sailing across the Indian Ocean, the tea clippers rounded the Cape of Good Hope, and began the long haul north through the South and North

Atlantic to the English Channel, where they often found themselves in company with ships they had not seen since they left China. British tea clippers preferred moderate winds, whereas most American clippers, designed for crossing oceans and rounding Cape Horn, liked to be driven hard before strong winds. *Stornoway* and *Chrysolite* were good passage makers, but they did have a tendency to push their bows down into the sea if they were driven too hard. Anthony Enright, who afterwards commanded the great American-built Australian clipper *Lightning*, established his reputation as commander of *Chrysolite*.

Captain Anthony Enright

The advantage of smaller-sized clippers for the China tea run was shown by the 471-ton *Chrysolite* in 1851. As the unloading of *Chrysolite* was nearing completion at Whampoa, *Memnon* went past on her way downriver with a cargo of tea, bound for London. A number of people, including *Memnon's* agents and the American consul, were on board *Chrysolite* at the time, and bets were placed as to which of the two clippers would make the best time to London. Enright adopted his usual practice of not placing a bet, as he was opposed to gambling.

Three days later, *Chrysolite* was fully loaded, at £4/4s per ton, and ready to sail. But there was a dispute by members of the crew who realized it would be a demanding voyage, and Enright discharged six of them. He promised the remaining sixteen that he would divide the wages of the six among them if they would sail *Chrysolite* shorthanded, and they agreed. He reminded them that they were in a race with the American ship, and that the honor of their country was at stake; they agreed to give of their best, and *Chrysolite* was soon under way.

Twenty-three days out a large ship was sighted during the afternoon; it was close to the Island of Banca and inside the coral reef. Enright, assuming that the ship ahead was *Memnon*, decided to follow her, despite the risk: the channel across the reef was narrow with a strong adverse current. Enright took the wheel himself and guided his ship along the channel; about half way through both bilges brushed against the reef, but there was deep water under the keel and *Chrysolite*

Chrysolite (ILN)

got through. Shortly afterwards she came alongside *Memnon*. Captain Gordon hailed Enright and asked him if he intended to take *Chrysolite* through the Macclesfield Strait, between Banca and Pulo Leat. Enright said: "Yes."

The Macclesfield Strait was a favorite short cut for clippers racing home with tea cargos. Navigating the strait was difficult and dangerous, particularly at night, because of 'Discovery Rock' that lay just below the surface in the center of the channel. And that night there was a strong headwind from the south-west that obliged both ships to beat. *Chrysolite* went ahead, slowly pulling away from *Memnon,* and then losing sight of her in a severe squall. The squall drove *Memnon* into shallow water, and Gordon immediately let out both anchors; it was too late: *Memnon* hit the hard coral seabed, and was holed as she went aground. She held fast. There was a depth of eight fathom under the bow which gave Gordon hope that he would get her off the reef. But water rushed into the hold.

The following morning, the stranded *Memnon* was boarded by Malay fishermen and, assisted by a number of locals who had signed on as crew at Macao, they plundered *Memnon.* Gordon had no option but to abandon ship and take to the boats with his wife, her maid, the officers, and crew. They made it to Gaspar

Island, where they set up camp. Gordon returned to *Memnon* but found it had been stripped bare. Six days later he and his group were rescued by the barque *Jeremiah Garratt*, and shortly afterwards transferred to the brigantine, *J M Casselly*, then on her way to Singapore. *Memnon* was wrecked by the same notorious reef off the Island of Banca that would also claim *Lammermuir*. It was a sad end to *Memnon*, the first clipper to complete the Great Ocean Racecourse to California.

Off Mauritius, in an area of the Indian Ocean subject to typhoons, *Chrysolite* had to weather an electrical storm that lasted three days: intense flashes of lightning brightened an otherwise constantly black sky, and the ship shook like a leaf during tremendous thunder claps, as rain bucketed from the heavens. On reaching the South Atlantic, the south-east trades were generous to Enright, and *Chrysolite* sped along logging 3,641 miles in just fifteen days; an average of 243 miles for each 24 hours; in one 24-hour period *Chrysolite* covered 320 miles, reaching 14 knots on a couple of occasions.

North of the equator, *Chrysolite* fell in with the frigate *HMS Havannah* and the clipper *Fly*. The three sailed in company for the following eighteen days, Enright's clipper holding station two to five miles ahead. During a calm, Enright dined aboard *Havannah* and the officers told him that never before had there been a ship that could keep up with them. When Enright was leaving they gave him letters to post, assuming that he would arrive in England first.

Near the Azores, *Chrysolite's* three topgallant masts came down after she was hit by a squall. The captain of another sailing ship then in company with *Chrysolite* refused to lend Enright any of his spare spars, but Enright refitted the upper masts as best he could. *Chrysolite* arrived in the Prince's Dock, Liverpool, on 1 December 1851 at the end of her maiden voyage, 103 days out from Whampoa. It was a remarkable performance for the new tea clipper and her captain; *Chrysolite* had logged 29,837 miles in 206 days. The owners were delighted, and Enright was given a gratuity of £50.

Giuseppe Garibaldi, the revolutionary leader best known as a popular Italian statesman and a heroic figure of the 19th century, was a sailor by profession. He went to sea aged fifteen, was a master mariner by the age of 26, and returned to a life at sea after unsuccessful military campaigns. In June 1852, Captain Garibaldi was commander of the 400-ton Peruvian barque *Carmen*, then taking on tea at Whampoa at the same time as *Chrysolite*. *Carmen*, belonging to Lima resident Signor Pietro Denegri, had arrived in Canton 93 days out from Calleo with guano from the Chincha Islands. Garibaldi and Enright became acquainted, and discovered that as a boy Garibaldi had sailed on a vessel belonging to Enright's uncle. Garibaldi and Enright became good friends.

Stornoway was loading tea alongside *Chrysolite* in 1852. They left together on 9 July and were in sight of each other for 21 days in the South China Sea. Enright described in his personal log how he stayed on deck in a bamboo chair secured to the deck, nodding off occasionally, but otherwise closely following his course, and keeping an eye on the wind and sails. But there was no way that *Chrysolite* could get ahead. The two clippers remained together for 45 days. Then the winds favored *Chrysolite* and she went ahead, arriving in Liverpool 104 days out from Whampoa at nine on the morning of Saturday 22 October, the first ship to land the new season's tea that year. By evening much of the tea had been unloaded, duty paid, and was for sale in Liverpool, as well as being dispatched to other parts of the country. The owners again awarded Enright a gratuity. Three days later, *Stornoway* arrived at the Downs 107 days out. The rate for tea freight in 1852 was £8 per ton, the highest ever.

A new clipper was built at Hall's Aberdeen yard during the winter of 1852–1853, and fitted out in time for the 1853 tea season: *Cairngorm,* at 1,000 tons equivalent to 1,250 tons American register, was larger than the previous Aberdeen clippers. This fine-lined vessel had iron deck beams, a mode of construction that provided relatively more cargo space in the hold. Jardine, Matheson bought *Cairngorm* while she was still on the stocks at the suggestion of Captain John Robertson who became a part owner with sixteen shares. Robertson had a reputation as a keen racer and had been *Stornoway's* commander. On the return leg of her maiden voyage, *Cairngorm* was the fastest tea clipper from Shanghai, arriving home in 110 days at the beginning of December, ahead of *Challenger,* and the American clipper *Nightingale.* About £4,000 in bets was won by *Cairngorm's* winning voyage.

But the real star of the 1853 tea carriers was the little Baltimore clipper *Architect.* Built by Nye, Parkin & Co in 1847, the 520-ton full-rigger was not as sharp as the later clippers and was not recognized as a true clipper, which explains why her voyage from New Orleans to San Francisco in 1849 is not included in the clipper annals. On that voyage the only crew member paid for serving before the mast was the Scotsman, Major William Downie; afterwards he was prominent in the development of Northern California and the town of Downieville was named after him.

Architect was an excellent passage-maker. In May 1853, while in Hong Kong, she managed to get a tea cargo for London. Under the command of Captain George A Potter, *Architect* arrived in the Downs on 21 July, 107 days out from Whampoa. (Later that year the Webb-built clipper *Celestial* had a fast run from Foochow: 96 days to Liverpool). As a result of her performance, *Architect* was able to charge the highest freight, £2 per ton extra, the following season. *Cairngorm* made the fastest passage from Shanghai in 1854; the new clipper *Crest of the Wave*, from the yard of John Pile of Sunderland, took only a couple of days longer.

Chrysolite and *Stornoway*, with a record of many fine passages, became slower as their hulls became water-soaked. Their place was taken by a number of new clippers that continued the tradition of fast passages, before they too slowed down.

One of the first tea clippers constructed entirely of iron was the 691-ton Clyde-built *Lord of the Isles,* launched in 1853 for the Australia run. She performed admirably on her maiden voyage to Sydney under the command of her celebrated skipper-owner, Captain Peter Maxton. According to Arthur Clark, Maxton was in command in 1855 when *Lord of the Isles* arrived off Lizard Point 87 days out from Shanghai, having come through the north-east monsoon. Her 87 days was a very fast time, probably an all-time record for a clipper ship from Shanghai, although it is not recorded as such: credit instead going to Samuel Hanscomb's beautiful *Nightingale,* under the command of Captain Samuel W Mather, for a 90-day run the same year. According to Carl Cutler the second fastest time from Shanghai to London was 99 days, achieved by the 1,045-ton *Florence* in 1858 under the command of Captain Philip Dumaresq.

Clippers racing from Foochow to London hoping to be the first to land the new season's tea generated tremendous interest among the public. In 1856 £1 per ton premium was offered to the first ship to land tea. There was a close race between the American *Maury,* a 600-ton barque with a reputation for speed, and Maxton's *Lord of the Isles. Lord of the Isles* finished loading first and left on 10 June, four days ahead of *Maury,* then commanded by Captain Charles E Fletcher. Fletcher guided his barque across the Indian Ocean at speed, logging an average of 272 miles a day over 12 days, including an astonishing one-day run of 370 miles. Both vessels were in company on several occasions as they headed for London. *Maury* arrived at Gravesend about ten minutes ahead of *Lord of the Isles,* then 127 days out. Maxton got the better tug, arrived in dock and came alongside first, to win the prize for landing the first tea. It was an exceptional performance by the little barque *Maury.*

A beautiful barque, *Spirit of the Age* from the John Pile yard in Sunderland, was

Spirit of the Age

fastest from Whampoa in 1856, arriving in the Downs 100 days out. *Spirit of the Age* had earlier been driven hard on the voyage from London to Sydney, arriving out in an excellent time of 73 days.

A new type of clipper appeared in Britain in 1859. The first such was *Falcon*, of 937 tons register, built by Robert Steele for Shaw, Lowther, Maxton & Co. A number of others, each less than 1,000 tons, were built during the following three years: *Min* and *Serica*, also from Steele's yard; *Kelso* by William Pile of Sunderland on the River Wear; and *Belted Will* by Feel & Co of Workington on the River Derwent in Cumbria. These vessels were slim sleek sailing craft; their rails, deck-houses, bulwarks, companionways, hatch-combings, and skylights were of varnished Indian teak; the teak decks were holystoned; extra spars were lashed amidships; and with their highly polished brasswork they had the appearance of large smart well maintained yachts. Built to be fast even in light and moderate winds, they were specifically for the China tea trade, and were not designed to cope with the rigors of Cape Horn and the Roaring Forties. Less than thirty vessels were built.

In the mid 1860s competition to be first to get the new season's tea to the London market was as intense as ever; the fresher the crop the more the traders were prepared to pay. In 1865 there was a close and exciting race between *Fiery Cross* and *Serica*, both all-wooden ships sheathed with copper. *Fiery Cross* was built by Chaloner & Co of Liverpool in 1860, and *Serica*, launched in 1863 by Robert

Cairngorm (ILN)

Steele, was similar to Steele's *Falcon*. These were slim and elegant yacht-like clippers with little sheer, a low freeboard, and narrower on the beam than previous clippers.

Fiery Cross and *Serica* left Foochow together on 28 May 1865. It was a close race throughout: they sighted each other several times and arrived off the Isle of Wight, signaling St Catherine's Lighthouse at almost the same time, 106 days after leaving Foochow. Running before a westerly breeze they sailed up the Channel with *Serica* two miles ahead, until they were both taken in tow off Beachy Head. But *Fiery Cross* had the more powerful tug. She docked one tide ahead, winning the premium of 10 shillings per ton of tea.

Fiery Cross, commanded by Captain Richard Robinson, had previously won the premium for being the first ship home with the tea in 1861, 1862, and 1863; and in 1864 *Fiery Cross* finished a day behind the winner *Serica*.

* * *

British merchant sailing ships reached the pinnacle of perfection in the China Tea Clippers. Their beautiful streamlined appearance, strength, carrying capacity, and speed, were remarkable. Composite construction, wooden planking on iron frames, was considered by British ship designers, builders, and owners to be

149

superior to the traditional all-timber construction. This method of shipbuilding, described as a basic skeleton of iron with a wooden skin, was very strong and required less wood. The composite method was favored by those shipbuilders who continued to build wooden sailing ships; nearly all the British tea clippers built after 1862 were of composite construction. An iron framework increased the strength of the hull, and made it easier to fasten on copper sheathing and prevent fouling. In 1863 *Taeping, Eliza Shaw, Yang-tze,* and *Black Prince* were built using this method.

Sir Lancelot, built for James McCunn of Greenock in 1865, regardless of cost, and her sister ship *Ariel,* were almost identical composite clippers, each capable of delivering 1,432 tons of tea on a mean draft of 18 feet 8 inches. *Ariel* and *Sir Lancelot* were beautiful nautical creations; *Sir Lancelot* became known as the 'Yacht of the Indian Ocean.' Her figurehead was a knight in armor with plumed helmet, his visor open, and his right hand about to draw his sword. They were among the first tea clippers to carry double topsails: *Ariel* carried double topsails on her three masts; *Sir Lancelot* carried them on her fore and main, with a single roller-reefing topsail on the mizzen. Like all sharp clippers, these were wet ships in rough seas.

Ariel (ILN)

The first patent for composite construction was granted to William Watson of Dublin in 1839. He proposed using a frame of iron T-bars, to which wooden planking would be secured by bolts or rivets. That year the 450-ton steamer, *Assam,* was constructed in India by the composite method. John Jordan, of the Liverpool shipbuilding firm of Jordan & Getty, perfected the technique when he built the schooner *Excelsior* in 1850 and the barque *Marion Macintyre* the following year. In 1853 *Marion Macintyre* was probably the first composite ship to carry tea from China. Jordan & Getty built three more composite ships, but otherwise the method was not widely adopted in Britain, although shipyards in Nantes and Bordeaux were building composite ships at the time. The method of composite construction, as recommended by Lloyds, was displayed at the Paris International Exhibition of 1857: a cage or skeleton of iron, complete in every way except for keeping out water, became a ship by planking it with wood.

Eighteen-sixty-six is remembered as the year of The Great Tea Race, when sixteen of the finest and fastest sailing ships in the world assembled at Foochow in early May to await the new season's tea. *Taeping,* built by Robert Steele in 1863, was there, as were three other clippers of composite construction: *Ada* built by Alexander Hall in Aberdeen; *Taitsing* by Charles Connell & Co of Glasgow; and *Ariel,* also from the Steele yard. The new composite clippers were expected to be among the leaders.

> The contest of 1866 was one of the grandest ocean races ever sailed, partly on account of the number of evenly matched vessels engaged in it, but chiefly by reason of the splendid manner in which it was contested and the close, exciting finish.
>
> Arthur H Clark *The Clipper Ship Era*

There was a carnival atmosphere at the Pagoda Anchorage while the clippers waited for the tea to arrive. Each clipper had a unique color scheme: hulls were mostly black or green and the masts and spars were a mixture of green, pink, white, and varnish. Apprentices ferried captains and officers to other ships and ashore. A one-day regatta was held with boats from different ships racing each other; the crews were extremely competitive and often words were exchanged and fights developed.

On 24 May the first chop-boats arrived with tea, and loading commenced amid great excitement. The stevedores, supervised by the mates, packed the thin-sided wooden tea chests into the holds of the clippers, working day and night, including weekends. Because *Ariel* was favored by the tea merchants, she got loaded first and was anchored in deep water with the aid of a tug, ready to leave at first light. Early the following morning, she was taken in tow for the short voyage down the Min River to the sea. *Fiery Cross, Taeping, Serica,* and *Taitsing* all completed loading within about twelve hours and were not far behind. *Ariel* was forced to anchor downriver after colliding with her tug. Soon she was overtaken by *Fiery Cross,* whose crew lined the rail and gave three mocking cheers of farewell to the hapless *Ariel. Taeping* and *Serica* also passed *Ariel,* and with *Fiery Cross* reached the sea that day. When *Ariel* and *Taitsing* got to sea the following day, the race was on.

Each ship followed an individual course across the South China Sea, and crossed the Indian Ocean under a press of canvas, driven by the south-east trades. At Mauritius, *Ariel* and *Taeping* were neck and neck, a couple of days behind *Fiery Cross,* and a day ahead of *Serica* and *Taitsing.* The five leaders rounded the Cape of Good Hope and turned north into the Atlantic where *Serica* and *Taitsing* fell further behind. But when they passed the Azores, *Serica* was within hours of the three in front and *Taitsing,* having previously trailed the others by a week, was only two days behind.

At daybreak on 5 September, *Ariel* and *Taeping* arrived off the Bishop Rock lighthouse with about five miles separating them. A strong southerly wind, well abaft the starboard beam, filled their clouds of white cotton canvas as they charged through the English Channel at about 15 knots on a relatively smooth sea. After passing Lizard Point the wind moderated: one would gain an advantage and then the other. They arrived off Dungeness pilot station and requested pilots at the same time. *Ariel* got a pilot first and went ahead; *Taeping* subsequently got a more powerful tug, and entered the Thames well ahead, but had to anchor at Gravesend, allowing *Ariel* to overtake her again. The next day, 6 September, *Ariel* was delayed by the tide as she tried to get alongside at the East India Docks; *Taeping* came alongside in the London Docks thirty minutes earlier than *Ariel. Serica* was not far behind. When they arrived together off the Kent coast and were about to pick up pilots and engage tugs, the captains of *Ariel* and *Taeping* had agreed to share the premium of 10 shillings per ton and the £100 prize. The following day *Fiery Cross* and *Taitsing* docked.

The first three clippers home in The Great Tea Race of 1866 were from the Clyde yard of Robert Steele. It was a remarkable ending to one of the greatest ocean races in the history of sail. *Sir Lancelot* had loaded with tea at £7 per ton at

Ariel and *Taeping* off the Lizard (*ILN*)

Hankow but was involved in a collision with a tug there, and missed taking part in the famous race from China to London.

Ariel, owned by Shaw, Lowther, Maxton & Co was commanded by Captain John Keay, from Anstruther in Fife. *Taeping,* owned by Roger & Co was commanded by Captain Donald McKinnon, who came from the island of Tiree in the Inner Hebrides. After the race all the captains dined together at the Ship and Turtle Tavern in Leadenhall Street.

The dramatic finish, with *Ariel* and *Taeping* racing neck and neck at top speed under full sail to skysails before a leading wind off Lizard Point, was captured in a lithograph that occupied a full page of the *Illustrated London News* two weeks later; *Taeping* is shown in the foreground with *Ariel* in the distance, identified by her double topsails. *Ariel* and *Taeping's* legendary finish in the Great Tea Race of 1866 remains a popular subject for marine artists.

In 1867 *Maitland* was the first clipper home with tea, followed by *Serica, Taeping,* and *Falcon; Taitsing* came in last of the eleven ships that took part that year.

The two fastest clippers in the 1868 Tea Race were *Ariel* and the new 899-ton *Spindrift* which was designed and built by Charles Connell, and the finest clipper ever built by him. Launched in July 1867, she was fitted with double topsails on

Spindrift (*ILN*)

her fore and main masts, and a roller reefing topsail on her mizzen. *Spindrift's*
owner, James Findlay of Greenock, already owned *Serica,* winner of the 1864 race.
Ariel, Taeping, and *Sir Lancelot* set sail from Foochow on 28 May 1868 with *Spindrift*
leaving on the following day, and *Lahloo,* another Robert Steele beauty, a day later.
Ariel was the first to arrive off Deal with *Spindrift* close behind, both 97 days out
from Foochow, followed by *Sir Lancelot* at 98 days, *Lahloo* at 100 days, and *Taeping*
at 102 days. *Spindrift,* whose time was fourteen hours less than *Ariel's,* was
declared the winner.

About 100 British sailing ships carried tea from China to England and
America in 1869, the year the Suez Canal opened. No premium was declared on
the first tea landed that year. Although there would be no race, *Spindrift* was
expected to perform well, and set out from the Thames bound for Shanghai on
20 November with a crew of 35 and freight valued at £200,000. The following
day, during a winter storm, she was driven ashore at Dungeness on the south-east
corner of England and wrecked. Her cargo was not insured. *Spindrift* had been in
the water for less than three years.

Serica and *Taeping* foundered in the China Sea after striking reefs. On 22
September 1871, while on a voyage from Amoy to New York, *Taeping* went
aground on Ladd's Reef and was wrecked. No loss of life was reported. On 3

November 1872, a day after leaving Hong Kong for Montevideo, *Serica* was wrecked on the Paracel Islands, a group of islands and coral reefs off Hainan Island; one of the crew survived.

*

Twelve new clippers, including *Caliph, Cutty Sark, Sobraon,* and *Thermopylae,* all of composite construction, were built shortly after the Great Tea Race of 1866. British shipyards were then using imported hardwoods such as teak and mahogany on iron framing for their composite sailing ships. This made them expensive; but they were strong, and remained in sound condition without deterioration of the hull, thus retaining the ability to sail fast for years and years. In America there was a plentiful supply of timber at low prices, but it was nearly all softwood such as pine and larch, and sometimes not sufficiently seasoned. These softer woods absorbed water and were likely to become sodden and make the ship sluggish. Over time, movement developed between the planks, creating gaps and allowing leaks to develop that could damage the cargo.

From 1866 onwards, the new Liverpool steamers, owned by Alfred Holt, provided strong competition for the China tea clippers because they could travel from London to Mauritius without refueling. But steamers were expensive to

Caliph (*ILN*)

operate, so the clippers managed to retain their role in the China tea trade until the opening of the Suez Canal in November 1869.

The fastest of the newer tea clippers were capable of about 15 knots, although they rarely exceeded 300 miles in a 24-hour period. They could make way even in light winds and have reasonably fast passages. They differed from the large American-built clippers that performed well in strong winds, achieving speeds of up to 21 knots, and covering distances of over 400 miles in a day.

Caliph, launched from Hall's Aberdeen yard in 1869 for Alex Hector of London, was designed to be fast, particularly in light winds. Duthies considered her a superior model to either *Cutty Sark* or *Thermopylae*, and likely to be the fastest of the British tea clippers. *Caliph* was 215 feet long, with a registered tonnage of 914, and looked magnificent under sail; she had double topsails, and crossed skysails on her three masts. She carried a small 8hp engine which drove two small screw propellers that could be lowered overboard to drive her at 2.5 knots in calm weather.

In October 1869 *Caliph* sailed to Foochow on her maiden voyage. There, she was loaded with tea for New York. She was one of the last of the tea clippers to leave, and she was never heard of again. The weather was fine and there were no reports of typhoons when she was crossing the China Sea where she went missing. It was assumed that the crew were overwhelmed by pirates during a calm.

> Of the three hundred grant but three,
> To make a new Thermophylae!
>
> Lord Byron, *Don Juan*

The composite clipper *Thermopylae*, registering 948 tons, was launched in 1868 from Walter Hood's Aberdeen yard for Thompson's Aberdeen White Star Line, to join their fleet of ships in the Australian trade. The planking from keel to topsides was of rock elm, with East India teak above; the deck was of four inch yellow pine, and the poop house decking was of New Zealand Kauri. *Thermopylae* was designed by the accomplished naval architect Bernard Weymouth, who for many years was the secretary to the Lloyd's Registrar of Shipping. When *Thermopylae* was fitted out she represented the high point in wooden clipper ship design and construction: her deck was well appointed with the appropriate amount of varnished teak and polished brass; her picturesque standing rigging was mostly painted white; and her tapered wooden spars were brightly varnished. *Thermopylae's* mainmast was 145 feet high, and her main yard was 80 feet in

Stern view of *Thermopylae* (ILN)

length. Like the other Thompson ships, her hull was painted sea-green. Her figurehead, carved from a solid block of wood, represented the young King Leonidas, with a shield on his left arm and a sword in his extended right arm; with 300 Spartans he defended the pass at Thermopylae against the Persian army of Xerxes in 480 BC.

In November 1868, three months after she was launched, *Thermopylae* set out from the Thames; 60 days and 15,000 miles after dropping the pilot at Gravesend, her captain signaled for a pilot off Port Phillip Heads at Melbourne. This was a three-day gain on *James Baines* 63 days from Liverpool to Melbourne; no steamship could match this, and no sailing ship ever did.

Thermopylae then sailed to Newcastle, New South Wales where she was loaded with coal and set off for Shanghai, sailing there in 28 days, a record time between the two ports. She went on to Foochow to load the new season's tea and created great excitement by joining the tea clippers for their last race to London before the opening of the Suez Canal. *Sir Lancelot,* carrying a cargo of 1,430 tons of tea and under the command of the experienced and energetic Captain Richard Robinson, set out from Foochow on 17 July 1869 and arrived at Deal 89 days later, having lost four days in the English Channel because of light variable winds. It had been an excellent voyage for *Sir Lancelot* during which she had set a 24-hour record for a wooden-hulled tea clipper by attaining 354 miles in the Indian Ocean, driven by the south-east trades. *Thermopylae*, having set out on 3 July, arrived at Deal 91 days later, an excellent time considering that her nearest rivals were the previous top performers *Ariel, Taeping,* and *Leander,* all of whom had left within days of her, and took 102 days or more.

Thermopylae did not take long to establish a reputation; she quickly became a legend because of her beautiful lines and exceptional passage-making ability, averaging 67 days for ten passages from London to Melbourne alone. Her ability to ghost in light winds, and make good progress on all points of sailing ensured good average speeds on long voyages. *Thermopylae*, with *Sobroan* and *Cutty Sark*, then under construction, would carry cargo for many years.

The small round stern with slight overhang, favored by many British tea clippers, was attractive looking but lacked buoyancy. In 1872 *Ariel* disappeared without trace; she had created a sensation in the greatest China Tea Clipper race of all time when she charged up the English Channel to a photo finish with *Taeping*. On a number of previous occasions *Ariel* was pooped, and this was blamed on a lack of buoyancy in her stern; her lines gave a clean run that extended above the waterline and continued well forward, making it possible for a big following sea to engulf the stern before it could rise quickly enough on the front of a big wave. It seems likely that *Ariel's* loss resulted from a large following sea that came over her stern during a storm and washed away the helmsman. This would have caused her to broach, thrown her on her beam ends, and she would be swamped.

Really fast passages were only achieved by constant attention to detail, day and night, by the clipper captains. The tea clippers were finely-tuned racing machines, and only captains of considerable ability were given command of these prestigious sailing ships. It was an exceedingly demanding job; they had to be courageous, tough, experienced seafarers and competent navigators who handled their ships with great skill. Commanding a tea clipper was well paid: captains were paid a basic wage of £20 per month, and there was commission on cargo and bonuses for fast passages; they were sometimes part owners of the ships they commanded and could profit further by carrying a small amount of freight on their own account.

A common seaman's lot was quite different. He was paid £4 a month, and had to provide his own clothing. The crew were divided into two watches, four hours on and four hours off, day and night. The early evening watch was divided into two two-hour stretches, so that the watches alternated daily. Even when off watch they could be roused at a moments notice by the call 'all hands on deck.' Living conditions in a cramped and often wet forecastle were poor; they had to sleep in narrow bunks arranged along the sides, one on top of the other. Their diet consisted mostly of hard biscuit, salt meat, salt fish, dried peas and beans, with a daily allowance of 1–2 pints of fresh drinking water. It was an unhealthy diet and many of the seamen developed scurvy. On British ships, there was some improvement in the food ration issued to seamen following the Merchant Shipping Act of 1854, when lime juice was added to the diet to prevent scurvy.

CHAPTER 6

The Rigging Takes the Strain

Her cutty sark, o' Paisley harn,
That while a lassie she had worn,
In longitude tho' solely scanty,
It was her best, and she was vuantie.

Now, wha this tale o' truth shall read,
Each man and mother's son take heed;
Whene'er to drink you are inclin'd,
Or cutty-sarks rin in your mind,
Think! Ye may buy the joys o'er dear;
Remember Tam o' Shanter's mare.

Robert Burns, *Tam o' Shanter*

In 1869 John Willis, a London sailing shipowner who took great pride in his ships, had the 921-ton composite clipper *Cutty Sark* built. Willis had little faith in the French-built Suez Canal becoming an established short cut to the East; he assumed that fast wind-powered sailing ships would continue in the China tea trade for years to come. In his opinion the Suez Canal would cave in, silt up, or if it functioned it would be taken over by the Egyptians and become unusable. Like Willis, others in the British sailing ship industry remained optimistic about a future for clipper ships. Full-rigged ships launched from United Kingdom shipyards that year included *Ambassador, Blackadder, Caliph, City of Hankow, Doune Castle, Duke of Abercorn, Normancourt, Oberon* and *Wylo*.

According to Basil Lubbock in the *Last of the Windjammers*, there were 25,663 sailing ships afloat in 1860, amounting to a net tonnage of over four million, compared to 2,006 steamers of net tonnage 400,000. By 1868, sail had reached its zenith with a net tonnage of almost five million, compared to the tonnage under steam of less than a million.

A year later, The Suez Canal opened, connecting the Mediterranean with the Red Sea and referred to as the 'dirty ditch' by an enthusiastic sailing apprentice. It was one of the great engineering feats of the 19th century, and a personal triumph for the Frenchman Ferdinand de Lesseps, who oversaw the project. A hundred miles in length, the canal reduced the distance between Britain and ports in India by more than 3,500 miles. Four years after it opened, steamship tonnage had risen to over one-and-a-half million and the tonnage under sail had dropped to four million.

Willis was involved in the China tea trade, and owned a number of clippers including *Lammermuir* and *The Tweed*. He appointed Captain George Moodie to take command of *Cutty Sark,* and supervise her construction. Designed by Hercules Linton, *Cutty Sark* was built to exacting specifications at the Scott & Linton yard in Dumbarton and launched onto the River Leven, a tributary of the Clyde. John Rennie, chief draughtsman at Scott & Linton, designed *Cutty Sark's* sail plan. Like other clippers she was built for speed; but 'Old White Hat,' as Willis was known because of his white silk hat, also wanted to give his new ship the best chance of survival. When Linton visited London, Willis took him to see *The Tweed,* and it was decided that *Cutty Sark* would have a more powerful stern than earlier tea clippers. *The Tweed* was then under the command of Captain William Stuart:

> Our captain was a man famous for the quick passages he had been used to make in the old *Tweed,* a ship famous the world over for her speed ... it was he in a sense who completed my training.
>
> Joseph Conrad, *The Mirror of the Sea*

The very best timber was used in *Cutty Sark*: seven-inch-thick teak planking for the hull. Moodie examined every piece, rejecting any plank that had knots or other flaws. The cost of building the new clipper to such high specifications eventually drove Scott & Linton out of business, but by then they had built a ship with a perfect hull. *Cutty Sark* was finished and fitted out at another yard.

Many British clippers were built with a fine shallow stern, but *Cutty Sark* had a powerful stern that might restrict her speed slightly, but would lift her up in a swell, and make her less likely to be swamped by a big following sea. A huge wall of water crashing onto the stern was particularly dangerous for a ship running before storm-force winds. The poop was the nerve center of a sailing ship: she was steered from there by the helmsman who would be lashed to the wheel in strong winds and big following seas; the ship's compass was there, housed in the

John Rennie

Cutty Sark's sail plan

binnacle; and it was the station of the officer of the watch. Being pooped could spell disaster. Willis was determined that his new clipper would have the best chance of lifting when running before a treacherously big sea.

When Willis took delivery of *Cutty Sark* in January 1870, she was considered by many to be the finest clipper ship ever built. Alan Villiers described *Cutty Sark* as 'the ultimate expression of that wonderful ship-form, the deep-sea, square-rigged racer – a beautiful thoroughbred of a ship if ever there was one.'

Cutty Sark got her name from *Tam o' Shanter*, one of Robert Burns best known poems. It relates the story of a farmer, Tam, who was heading home on a wet and windy night on his fine grey mare Meg, when he encountered a dance of witches and was pursued by a young witch Nannie, clad only in her cutty sark (short shift). Cutty and sark are Scottish and Northern English words: cutty means short, while sark means chemise, a smock or undergarment hanging straight from the shoulders, sometimes referred to as a shift. *Cutty Sark's* figurehead was a beautifully carved version of the buxom witch Nannie, scantily clad in her cutty sark, her outstretched arm holding a fistful of Meg's tail, which she grasped when attempting to get a grip on Meg and bring Tam to ground. The carving was done by George Hellyer, a member of a long-established family of master wood carvers, whose workshop was at the Wigram yard in Blackwall. In addition, Hellyer carved a string of naked nymphs along each bow; these were subse-

Cutty Sark

quently removed for fear of offending the good burghers of Sydney when *Cutty Sark* was about to become engaged in the Australian wool trade. Tam was shown on Meg, riding furiously towards the stern, where more of Hellyer's graphic scroll-work adorned the clipper's quarters.

Willis intended *Cutty Sark* to outsail *Thermopylae,* and claimed that she was capable of sailing to Melbourne in 55 days. Moodie, an experienced Scottish seaman and a first-rate clipper captain, who had already commanded two tea clippers, took *Cutty Sark* on her maiden voyage from London to Shanghai. The voyage did not prove as successful as Willis had anticipated; *Cutty Sark* took 104 days to reach Shanghai. The passage times of *Sir Lancelot, Lahloo,* and *Taeping* were shorter. *Thermopylae* had an excellent passage to Melbourne, before sailing on to China. It took time for Moodie, an expert rigger, to get *Cutty Sark's* rigging fully functioning and finely tuned.

Cutty Sark's real test would be the homeward voyage with the new season's tea. There was no chance that she would be the first home with tea, as steamers would reach London before any of the clippers. In the short time that the Suez Canal had been operating, the new waterway had proved a great success, as it reduced considerably the time required for steamers to travel to Europe from

Australia, the Far East, and Southeast Asia. The Suez Canal was not an option for clipper ships: there was a lack of wind in the Red Sea, intense heat bearing down on the crew, fees to pay for using the canal, and sailing ships would have to pay a tug to tow them through.

The sailing ship fraternity forecast that the heat in the Red Sea would be a problem for steamers, as the firemen, already hot from tending the furnaces, would drop dead. There was even concern among steamship owners themselves about the effect the intense heat would have on the men firing the furnaces. In an attempt to cope with this, they took on stokers from the coast of Benin in West Africa, a particularly hardy group of surf-boatmen. They collapsed in front of the furnaces because of the intensity of the heat, and had to be relieved at frequent intervals. Chinese workers were recruited, but they were unable and unwilling to work in such tremendous heat. It was Liverpool Irishmen, considered be the strongest and toughest sailors at the time, who were up to the task of stoking the boilers in the intense heat of the Red Sea. They gained repute, like their fathers had done when handling sail aloft in the stormy North Atlantic or rounding Cape Horn in a Hooley.

In 1870 three steamers, coming via the Suez Canal, brought tea to London in less than 60 days. *Cutty Sark's* homeward journey with tea took 109 days, longer than was envisaged; strong headwinds, calms, and lack of favorable wind in the China Sea and Indian Ocean delayed her. Nearing home, *Cutty Sark* charged up the channel, driven by a south-westerly gale, to complete what was a good run. It was the best passage for a clipper that year, outpacing the other clippers that had sailed from Shanghai. *Thermopylae*, sailing from Foochow a month later, made it in 105 days, but the voyages were not comparable.

Willis was disappointed with *Cutty Sark's* performance, but remained optimistic about her chances for the following year. His optimism was justified. Steamships were favored by the merchants in 1871 and took most of the tea cargos; clippers were offered the remainder at a low freight. Seven American clippers loaded tea; in their case there was little competition from steamers because the distance to New York was far longer.

Cutty Sark and *Thermopylae* were berthed beside each other in Shanghai, each anticipating an exciting race to London, when *Cutty Sark's* agents refused £3 per ton of tea and sent her to Foochow. There she could not even get the £3 rate and returned to Shanghai, where she was lucky to pick up a cargo. She raced the great *Ariel* to London and arrived a week ahead. Her performance against *Thermopylae* was inconclusive: *Cutty Sark's* 107 days was one day longer than *Thermopylae's* 106, but Willis's clipper set sail months later than her rival. Another lovely tea clipper from the Greenock yard of Robert Steele was well ahead of the field that year: *Titania,* under the command of Captain Joseph Dowdy, was the first clipper to reach London with tea; she arrived there 93 days out from Foochow.

In 1872 a proper race was planned between the two well-matched clippers; many claimed that it would be the clipper race of the century. Captain Robert Kemball of *Thermopylae* and his crew were determined to win, and so was Moodie and his crew aboard *Cutty Sark.* They left Shanghai on 17 June and hoisted sail on the same tide as they cleared the Woosung Bar at the mouth of the Yangtze River. It promised to be a well-matched and fair race.

But there were problems from the outset. Almost immediately both clippers became enveloped in dense fog that lasted three days. Then they got going, sailing neck and neck through the East China Sea with nothing to indicate which clipper was fastest. What a magnificent sight to behold as they carved their way through the turquoise sea propelled by the brisk north-east trades, each under a full press of canvas, studding sails to port and starboard.

There was great excitement amongst the crews, and the captains rarely left the deck as they urged on their charges, as knights of old urged on their steeds. Kemball on *Thermopylae* and Moodie on *Cutty Sark* stood beside the helmsman giving instructions for minor alterations in course, in order to get the very best speed from even the slightest change in the wind. They would cast their eyes aloft to observe the sails every few minutes and also listened intently for any sound of extra strain on the rigging. The crews were pleased to see the constant slack on the lee shrouds as the deck heeled to leeward and the occasional sea washed over the rail before draining through the scuppers. Kemball and Moodie were at the high point of their careers and loved stretching to the limit two of the finest sailing ships ever created.

Owners and friends ashore were unable to witness this exciting display of speed under sail on the high seas, but the captains and crews would treasure the memories. Chinese traders in picturesque junks, sailing gently under fully battened lugsails, and Hakka fishermen in their sampans had a grandstand view. They must have gazed in awe at the spectacle of these magnificent wind-driven machines from the Western world charging past in a cloud of sail. Pirate lorchas lurking inshore, hoping for easy prey, were shown a clean wake.

British built clippers suited the weather conditions in the China Sea; their narrow beam provided a smaller surface in contact with the water than on an American clipper, and this combined with the smooth copper bottom on the tea clipper lowered resistance. The bigger American Cape Horn clippers had longer and sharper ends and greater beam in relation to length, making them more stable and buoyant: factors that enabled them to carry more sail in strong gales and heavy seas, and attain greater speeds.

Cutty Sark pulled ahead, benefiting from a leading wind in the Indian Ocean, and was 400 miles in front of *Thermoplyae* by 7 August. Disaster struck a week later when *Cutty Sark* lost her rudder during a severe gale, after a huge wave crashed into the stern. This was serious, as the hapless ship could not be steered without a rudder. Moodie and his men were undaunted. They made a temporary rudder and continued sailing; this too was carried away and they had to set about making another one.

Two stowaways, discovered on board soon after leaving Shanghai, proved surprisingly useful in fashioning the new temporary rudder. One was a blacksmith who set up a temporary forge on deck, the other a shipwright. Fitting the rudder, a difficult task even in calm weather, was incredibly difficult in a ship that was pitching about on a stormy sea. The crew persisted and succeeded in fitting a jury rudder. Robert Willis, the owner's brother, was a passenger; he was a sullen antagonistic critic of Moodie's handling of the ship after she was disabled by rudder failure, even suggesting that Moodie should alter course and put into port for repairs. Moodie, though a first-class sailor and commander, was unable to get the optimum performance from the repaired ship and sailed the remaining 8,000 miles under easy sail, steered by a jury rudder.

The wounded *Cutty Sark* arrived in the Downs under full sail and docked in London on 19 October, seven days after *Thermopylae*. It was an incredible performance for *Cutty Sark;* she had lost an estimated thirteen days as a result of losing her rudder. There was no agreement on the outcome, as each captain and crew claimed to have won. By the unusual misfortune of losing her rudder, *Cutty Sark* had lost an opportunity to prove that she was the faster of the two great clippers. Moodie had done a magnificent job, but stung by Robert Willis's criticism, he relinquished command of *Cutty Sark* and became a steamship captain. The loss of Moodie greatly concerned Old White Hat, as good sailing ships captains were not easy to find.

No more tea clippers were built, and within ten years of the opening of the Suez Canal sailing ships were virtually eliminated from the China tea trade. *Cutty*

Sark, built as a China tea clipper, carried a few more tea cargos. While the new season's tea was being prepared she did short runs in the China Sea, sometimes carrying rice from Bangkok to Hong Kong.

Captain Frederick W Moore took command of *Cutty Sark* after Moodie left. Moore, an experienced captain with an excellent reputation, had seen many damaged ships in his role as marine superintendent for Willis. He was a cautious commander and reluctant to put *Cutty Sark's* standing rigging under the strain required to get the ultimate performance from her. Alan Villiers described how the clipper he admired so much would have felt on being restrained by her new captain:

> So the *Cutty Sark* rarely did her best for him. She needed driving. The spirit of the wanton witch could cope with gales and high winds, and did not like lying down to them. The scream of the gale was music in Nannie's ears, and she would tear along as if she really were after her man, rigged down to her 'cutty sark' and ready for action. Snugged down she sulked a little though she would not allow any other ship to pass her. She did not like the sedate hand of Captain Moore.
>
> Alan J Villiers, *The Cutty Sark: Last of a Glorious Era*

In 1873 Moore collected tea in Shanghai alongside *Sir Lancelot, Thermopylae,* and *Titania. Cutty Sark* and the other three clippers left Shanghai at the same time but were delayed in the East China Sea as they battled strong head winds, rain, poor visibility, and short steep seas. *Cutty Sark* then encountered a typhoon off Formosa. Her homeward voyage lasted 117 days, twelve days longer than *Thermopylae.*

The following year, Captain William Edward Tiptaft took *Cutty Sark* to Australia with freight and then collected a cargo of coal at Newcastle, NSW, for Shanghai. By now, clippers were profiting from carrying Australian coal to Chinese ports for bunkering steamships. There was no tea for *Cutty Sark* at Shanghai that year, and it was fortunate that her China agents, Jardine Matheson, secured a cargo of tea for her at Hankow, 600 miles inland on the Yangtze Kiang or Eternal River (Chang Jiang), as it was frequently referred to by the Chinese. It was a long, and at times, dangerous journey with fast unpredictable currents, mudbanks, and hidden rocks.

The ports on the Yanktze opened to foreign trade in 1861, in accordance with the Tientsin Treaty of 1858, following the second Anglo-Chinese War. The Yangtze was an incredibly busy waterway, 3,964 miles in length and navigable by junks from the Woosung Bar to the city of Yibin, almost half its total length. Hankow, located 586 miles inland from Shanghai, was a major port where the Han River, its largest tributary, joins the Yangtze at the center of a vast network of canals extending throughout much of China.

A long and expensive four to six day tow was required to negotiate the river. In 1866, the tow line to the clipper *Guinevere* snapped after she was sent ahead of the tug's stern, when caught by a sudden swift current; an anchor was thrown out but to no avail, the current swept her on to the rocks and she sank. Five of the seven ships that collected tea at Hankow in 1866 had collisions or groundings, one of which was *Guinevere*. The level of the river at Hankow was about 45 feet higher in summer than in winter; it was soon realized that the threat of sudden and rapid currents made it necessary for the tea clippers to be lashed to the tug as they were maneuvered alongside. Underwriters charged 2 per cent extra insurance on tea cargos from Hankow.

As *Cutty Sark* was towed upriver, she would have mingled with sampans and junks of all sizes, each with its own unique color scheme, as they plied their trade on a river that gave a livelihood, in one way or another, to about a third of the people of China. *Cutty Sark* loaded her cargo at Hankow and set out with the new season's tea downriver to the sea. It took her nearly four months to get to London that year, two weeks longer than her rival *Thermopylae*.

Willis, believing that he owned a ship that was the fastest China tea clipper, was becoming frustrated. *Cutty Sark*, though sailing well and making times faster than nearly all other clippers, was always being beaten by *Thermopylae*. Her captains were excellent, but they were cautious, and commanders who failed to push this icon of the clipper era to the limit would not get from her the optimum performance that had been envisaged and planned for by her designer, builders, and owner. Kemball, the captain of *Thermopylae*, had all the qualities required to successfully command a clipper on the China tea run. He did not hesitate to push his ship to the limit by following the shortest, if more hazardous, routes in the China Sea in order to save time. And he gained maximum speed by letting the rigging take the strain in strong winds and gales.

Strong rivalry continued between the two fastest sailing ships ever built in Britain. In London there was intense support for the locally owned *Cutty Sark* rather than the George Thompson of Aberdeen owned *Thermopylae*. In 1876 *Cutty Sark*, commanded by Tiptaft, picked up a cargo of tea at Hankow and made an excellent passage home, for the first time beating *Thermopylae* by a week; the latter was no longer under the command of Kemball.

The China Tea Clippers were by then competing with more efficient and competitive steamers. And contrary to Willis's and others' predictions the Suez Canal was proving a great success; the Canal Company was thriving and maintaining the waterway in excellent condition. Eighteen-seventy-seven was the last year that *Cutty Sark* carried tea from China, when she collected it once more from Hankow on the Yangtze.

The following year was not a good one for *Cutty Sark:* on two occasions she tried to get a load of tea, but without success. She took a cargo to Japan the first time, and was forced to sail to Sydney in ballast afterwards.

In 1879, Willis's tea clipper was nearly wrecked in the English Channel during a severe November storm that sank other ships and caused much loss of life. *Cutty Sark* was saved by being taken in tow by a couple of tugs, and had to return to London for repairs, before sailing to Australia. She reached Sydney in an excellent 72 days. *Thermopylae* took two days longer to get to Melbourne at about the same time.

Thermopylae established records that neither *Cutty Sark* nor any other clipper could match: 60 days out to Melbourne, and 91 days from China to London with tea. It was proving difficult to get cargos, and *Cutty Sark* had a lean, difficult and demoralizing time during the following six years. But the pride of Willis's fleet would have opportunities to race and defeat *Thermopylae* on the racecourse from Australia to London.

* * *

There was a boom in Australian wool at the time, and soon *Cutty Sark* would achieve the glory that had eluded her in the China tea trade; as she sailed from Australia round Cape Horn to London with valuable cargos of wool. She was designed for the China tea trade, but could cope better with the Southern Ocean and stormy Cape Horn than other tea clippers because of her solid hull, powerful high stern, and sturdy rigging.

During the 19th century wool, tallow, hides, and wheat were the main Australian exports to the United Kingdom. Their wool was in great demand because it was longer, softer, and silkier than the best Europe could produce. Demand had developed in the early part of the century, and by 1850 wool from Australia and New Zealand had overtaken European wool on the British market in both quantity and quality. Fast clippers were in demand to transport wool to the London Wool Sales, which took place during the first three months of the year. Like tea, the new season's wool was in great demand, and the highest prices were paid for the first cargos to arrive.

> Fare you well, you Sydney girls, time for us to go!
> The Peter's at the fore truck, and five thousand bales below,
> We've a dozen shellbacks forrard, and a skipper hard as nails,
> And we're bound for old England and the January sales!
>
> C Fox Smith, *The Return of the 'Cutty Sark'*

Wool was loaded and dispatched from Sydney, an exciting port for clipper crews. A dozen or more clippers would berth at Circular Quay, waiting for the wool-laden horse-drawn wagons. As soon as they arrived, the wool would be loaded aboard with all possible speed. Bales of wool were packed as tightly as possible: when the hold was full to capacity the captain would insist on further bales being screwed in, with not an inch of space remaining. Tightly packed wool was unlikely to ignite by internal combustion; the risk of fire was greater if loosely packed wool became damp. Wool was lightweight and an ideal cargo because clippers fully loaded with it were not down to the Plimsoll line. When loading was complete, and the cargo secured, the clippers departed under sail through Sydney Heads bound for London by way of Cape Horn.

The opportunity of a new lease of life offered to *Cutty Sark* by the lucrative Australian wool trade was secured by the truly excellent leadership and seamanship skills of Captain Richard J Woodget, a man who had previously commanded another of Willis's sailing ships. Born into a Norfolk farming family, Woodget developed an interest in the sea from an early age and learned his sailing skills in the coastal trade. He started his career as a cabin boy in a billyboy belonging to Bullard, King & Co that carried glass bottles between Sunderland and London. Having served in any and every capacity on schooners, brigantines, barques, scows, and ships, Woodget became first mate on board *Copenhagen* in 1874. Six years later he became captain of *Cold Stream*, his first command after 30 years at sea. For four years he cared for the 40-year-old *Cold Stream*, a frigate style ship that leaked badly but provided him with interesting and useful experiences.

Woodget did a magnificent job as commander of *Cutty Sark* for a legendary ten years from 1885; he sailed her as hard as possible by pushing the crew and ship to the limit, but not over it; he respected and looked after his crew, half of whom were unpaid apprentices: loyal, reliable, and reputedly as good as ordinary seamen. He was a fearless sailor who eschewed alcohol and tobacco; under him *Cutty Sark* made outstandingly fast passages to and from Australia; she never sailed as well for anyone else. As a master mariner, jester, and philosopher, Woodget was in a class of his own. He was devoted to animals, particularly the collie dogs that accompanied him on voyages, and became a feature of life on board.

Woodget's first voyage in command of *Cutty Sark* started on 2 April 1885 when he set out for Sydney at the same time as a fleet of other fast clippers. Under him, the gallant clipper gave a splendid performance and arrived in Sydney ahead of the

Captain Richard J Woodget

fleet, 73 days out from London; *Samuel Plimsoll*, the next fastest, arrived a day later. There, *Cutty Sark* waited to load the new season's Australian wool for the London January Sales alongside nine other clippers, including *Thermopylae*. This would be Woodget's first passage round Cape Horn. While other clipper captains were light-heartedly telling him that he would lose his way, he was quietly assuring his third mate that *Cutty Sark* would outsail *Thermopylae* on the home run.

The wool clippers left Sydney and Newcastle during October; *Thermopylae* set sail from Sydney two days after *Cutty Sark*. Five days out from Sydney, *Cutty Sark* came perilously close to foundering when sailing at high speed in the low latitudes of the Roaring Forties while under a generous spread of canvas. She had logged 306 miles the previous 24 hours and was running before gale-force winds, accompanied by snow and hail, when she was hit by a particularly strong squall that caused her to broach, and a number of her sails were shredded. Her deck on the lee side was immediately engulfed by water which caused considerable damage, including the loss of two boats. Without heaving-to, Woodget sent the crew aloft in the dark, where they stood on the footropes of the swaying yards with the wind howling and showering them with hail as they bent new sails.

Cutty Sark rounded Cape Horn 23 days out from Sydney having gained nine days on the first wool clipper to leave. Woodget drove *Cutty Sark* relentlessly, reaching the equator in record time and arriving off Ushant, 67 days after leaving Sydney. From there, he was dogged by headwinds and it took five days to cover 305 miles in the English Channel. *Cutty Sark* anchored in the Downs during a raging blizzard on the sixth day, 73 days after leaving Sydney. Having outpaced all her rivals, *Cutty Sark* was the first clipper to land wool that year, docking at least a week ahead of the next arrival, and seven days faster than her main rival, *Thermopylae*. The other seven wool clippers took 8–24 days longer than *Cutty Sark*.

Willis was delighted to be the proud owner of *Cutty Sark*, the first wool clipper to arrive home that year, having made the fastest passage and convincingly beaten her fierce rival *Thermopylae*. As an emblem of victory, Willis presented the ship with a two-foot nine-inch-high golden cutty sark carved in metal, gilded, and with a channel for a vane through its center. The emblem was fitted on the upper masthead by the third mate.

Thomas William Selby joined *Cutty Sark* as second mate on her next voyage and remained with her until 1891. Selby was aged 22, extremely competent, and considered to be the finest sailor that served under Woodget. Selby's father was manager of Bullivants, the wire rope makers, and the younger Selby was skilled at working and splicing wire rope. He willingly taught his skills to the crew and they held him in high regard because of his energy, professionalism, and strong sense of duty. Selby was strict and expected perfection in others be they fellow officers, apprentices or crew.

Cutty Sark was kept in shipshape condition when Selby served as mate. In port he would take one of the boats out to view the rigging, checking that the masts were perfectly aligned and raked, and that the yards were dead square; on deck the brass, varnish, and paintwork shone, everywhere was spotless; below deck the bilges were kept clean, and the iron framework was maintained in excellent condition by chipping off rust and applying red lead to exposed areas.

> For a ship with her sails furled on her squared yards, and reflected from truck to water-line in the smooth gleaming sheet of land-locked harbour, seems, indeed to a seaman's eye the most perfect picture of slumbering repose.
>
> Joseph Conrad *The Mirror of the Sea*

Cutty Sark's next voyage was a long and frustrating one for the crew. She set sail from London with a mixed cargo in February 1886, arriving four months later in

Shanghai. There she waited in vain for over three months for a cargo of tea. Only three other clippers went to China that year as, by then, the steamers had established a monopoly of the tea trade: *Wylo* returned with a mixed cargo from Shanghai, while *Hallowe'en* and *Leander* obtained tea cargos at Foochow. *Cutty Sark* managed to get a late wool cargo in Sydney, two months after Thompson's famous Aberdeen White Star clippers *Thermopylae, Salamis,* and *Patriarch* finished the race with the new season's wool; they had arrived in London during the third week of January within four days of each other.

Cutty Sark left Sydney at the end of March 1887. Woodget was not afraid of going well south to shorten the distance and, not surprisingly, he encountered a month of heavy weather as he headed for Cape Horn during the approach of the austral winter. He flew generous amounts of canvas to benefit from the leading gales, and drove his *Cutty Sark* as fast as possible. A maze of ice was encountered, through which he had to sail. In his log, Woodget reported passing numerous icebergs, including one he estimated to be 250 feet high and three miles long. After rounding Cape Horn, he continued to sail his clipper to the limit, arriving off Lizard Point 70 days out from Sydney, by far the best passage from Australia that year, and an improvement on his winning passage of the previous year by a day.

Soon after midnight on 22 October 1887, *Cutty Sark* was dismasted while outward bound to Australia: the fore topgallant backstay gave way during a severe squall in the Southern Ocean, bringing down the fore topgallant mast and main topmast, with their yards, and sending them over the side. The sturdy clipper did not stop. Woodget refused to cut away any gear, instead salvaging the wreckage that was being dragged alongside, and using it for running repairs at sea. *Cutty Sark* logged over 200 miles on four of the five days following the dismasting, including 280 miles one day, while essential repairs were carried out by the crew. Woodget managed to re-rig the main topmast during a short spell of calmer weather. Under jury rig he continued on to Australia, logging over 300 miles a day on a couple of occasions.

By now Woodget had established *Cutty Sark's* reputation as a fast clipper and her agents no longer had trouble obtaining freight for her. She loaded wool at Newcastle as soon as her outward cargo was discharged, and set sail at 5pm on December 28. It was then full speed for London, sailing well below the 60° southern limit recommended by the Board of Trade, avoiding icebergs below 62°S, and reaching 64°50'S, before altering course for Cape Horn. *Cutty Sark* reached the English Channel in 69 days, beating the other twelve wool clippers by 12–59 days. Under Woodget's command, *Cutty Sark's* first three homeward runs with wool from Australia, made in 69, 70, and 71 days to the English Channel, was a record that would never be approached by another clipper. The famous clipper made outstanding passages to and from Australia under Woodget; her valiant commander and his band of warriors had enabled her to show her true colours, as one of the fastest of the British clipper ships.

The following year, 1888, *Cutty Sark* left Sydney with wool on 26 October. Tragedy struck three days out: one of the apprentices was washed overboard and drowned by a rogue wave that broke over the lee side of the deck. On the home run that year *Cutty Sark* took 80 days, equalled by *Star of Italy*, and faster than the other wool clippers.

At about that time, Woodget became interested in photography, a challenging hobby to pursue at sea. His apprentices had the unpopular task of filling the skipper's bath with water for use as a developing tank. Woodget took excellent photographs of other clippers under full sail, icebergs in the Southern Ocean, Cape Horn, ocean wildlife, and his lovely sable collies that sailed the oceans with him; he took numerous pictures of his own elegant clipper at anchor in various ports. Only occasionally did he manage to photograph *Cutty Sark* under full sail: when the sea was calm with little wind he would go a short distance off in one of the ship's boats. Bicycling was a skill that was becoming popular, and Woodget developed his cycling skills 'tween decks.

Another opportunity for the feisty clipper to show her prowess arose the following year, while sailing in moderate winds off the Australian coast. The new Peninsular and Oriental (P&O) RMS *Britannia* left Melbourne for Sydney on Saturday 25 July 1889, six hours ahead of *Cutty Sark*. As the two ships were rounding Gabo Island the following evening in excellent visibility, the officers on *Britannia's* bridge observed *Cutty Sark's* lights astern. It was not long before the wind-powered clipper caught up with *Britannia*, then steaming at 15.5–16 knots, before passing her at an estimated 17 knots powered by a brisk southerly wind. *Britannia's* passengers were delighted: they lined the rails cheering *Cutty Sark* as she gained on the steamer. On Monday when *Britannia* steamed into Sydney Harbor, *Cutty Sark* was already at anchor with most of her sails furled. A great cheer went up from the crowd on *Britannia's* deck, and was reciprocated from the main yard, where the mate and all hands were standing on the footropes, carefully stowing the main-course. *Cutty Sark's* performance was celebrated in Sydney, and her crew fêted.

Richard J Woodget

Cutty Sark distinguished herself again in 1890 by outsailing three particularly fast clippers on the outward voyage to Port Jackson: *Salamis, Cimbera,* and *Aristides.* During the voyage, Willis's clipper logged 7,678 miles in 30 days.

Exceptionally heavy weather was encountered by *Cutty Sark* on her outward voyage to Sydney in 1891. She was hit by a massive rogue wave that nearly sank her when a following sea, a huge wall of water of such height that it threatened to completely engulf her, approached from astern. She rose to it and for a moment balanced on the crest of this giant wave, before it broke on board with tremendous force, swamping the ship, and smashing everything in its path. The gallant little *Cutty Sark* then slid down the slope of this great wave at an alarming angle. No significant damage was done, and she survived by rising on the following sea. Willis's *Cutty Sark* had come close to being lost with all hands. Woodget was on deck lashed to the wheel with the helmsman. The rest of the crew, on seeing the giant wave approach fled for cover. Anyone unlucky enough to have been on deck when the wave struck would have been washed overboard, or smashed against the bulwark.

Cutty Sark carried seven wool cargos from Australia to London under Woodget, always drawing large crowds as she waited to load her cargo at Sydney. Woodget had the skill and nerve to drive *Cutty Sark* at maximum speed, beating all her rivals in the race home with wool. Only once did another clipper come near

175

to outpacing *Cutty Sark* on the home run, and that was when *Cimbera* equalled her 75 days in 1889-1890. On her wool passages from Australia, *Cutty Sark's* times were far better than those of any other ship, with an average 77 days port to port. Woodget could judge precisely the optimum amount of canvas to fly for the prevailing conditions, enabling him to gain the fastest possible speed. He was a tireless worker, a skilled navigator, and considered by those who served with him to be the finest seaman they had ever worked with. An officer who served with Woodget on board *Cutty Sark* is quoted by Basil Lubbock in his *Log of the Cutty Sark*:

> It was a pleasure to see the 'old man' in dirty weather. He fairly revelled in it. With one side of his moustache jammed into his mouth, and hanging on to the weather rigging, I can see him now, his sturdy figure in yellow oilskins and long leather sea boots, watching aloft and hanging on until the last minute. He gave his crew complete confidence in him and I never remember seeing him anything but calm in dirty weather.

Woodget commanded great loyalty from his crew. The cook, an old sailor who went by the name of Toby Robson, was Chinese. Many years earlier, as a baby, he was rescued by the crew of a homeward bound tea clipper who found him drifting alone in a small boat in the China Sea. He was well nourished and could not have been adrift for long. The captain's wife adopted him, and brought him up as her son. When he was old enough he went to sea and became a first-class sailor. He was leading seaman on *The Tweed*, before becoming the ship's cook in 1882. Robson transferred to *Cutty Sark* in 1885 at the same time as Woodget. During the sailing ship era the galley was mostly reserved for reliable sailors who were getting old, and no longer limber enough to continue working on deck and aloft. Robson served *Cutty Sark* as cook and night watchman for many years, while at the same time Woodget also relied on his seamanship skills as a spare boatswain and back-up sailmaker. As watchman Robson was required to remain on deck during the hours of darkness when the ship was in port to prevent theft. He was a great storyteller and popular as the ship's cook.

Woodget was an excellent teacher and tutored his apprentices, some as young as 12 or 13, in the art of seamanship and navigation. Many of them went on to gain commands of their own in steamship companies, while others developed successful careers ashore. An apprenticeship with Woodget on board *Cutty Sark* was an excellent recommendation for a position as a junior officer in one of the leading steamship companies such as P&O.

It was becoming difficult for sailing ships to get freights because of increasing competition from steamships. In June 1894, *Cutty Sark* set sail for Australia in the hope of getting a cargo of wool, arriving in Brisbane 77 days after passing Lizard Point, a respectable performance considering that she was due for an overhaul, particularly to the hull below the waterline. In Brisbane, Woodget screwed a record 5,303 bales of wool into the hold, before leaving Australian waters for the last time. On her voyage home, *Cutty Sark* caught up with a large number of homeward bound ships, and passed them all, arriving in London on 26 March 1895. Woodget then learned that the clipper that he had driven to glory was up for sale.

* * *

Sobraon, Thermopylae, Cutty Sark, and *Torrens* were among a relatively small number of original wooden-hulled clipper ships that, in the latter part of the 19th century, continued the great sailing ship tradition started by the Yankee clippers. By then most of the original clippers had been replaced by the iron and steel clipper carriers and steamships. The four composite clippers were beautiful ships, particularly when making way under a spread of canvas; when well driven they attained great speeds, travelling between distant parts in record time. On her voyage from London to Sydney at the end of 1875, *Cutty Sark,* when under the command of Tiptaft, ran 2,163 miles in six consecutive days in the Roaring Forties, an average of 360 nautical miles per day, at times logging just over 17 knots. *Thermopylae,* sailing a week behind her, charged along at an even faster speed of 370 miles a day. These were incredible speeds, and compared favorably with the record set by the much larger *James Baines,* when she reached 21 knots, attesting to the tremendous achievements of the much smaller Scottish-built clippers. The great Australian clipper packets that plied from Liverpool, such as *Marco Polo, Champion of the Seas, Lightning, James Baines, Red Jacket,* and *Blue Jacket* were larger and carried passengers instead of cargo 'tween decks, giving them much more freeboard and a smaller percentage of hull that needed to be driven through the water.

In 1890 *Thermopylae, Cutty Sark's* famous rival, was sold to a Canadian company and spent the following five years in the Pacific, transporting rice from the Far East to British Columbia, before being bought by the Portuguese Government for use as a sail training ship at the mouth of the Tagus. In 1907, when she was of no further use, *Thermopylae* was towed out to sea for use as target practice and sent to the ocean floor by a torpedo; a sad end to one of the finest sailing ships ever to take to the seven seas.

As the end of the 19th century approached, cargo-carrying steamers drove the older clippers out of business. By then, British shippers and shipowners were only interested in steamships. In the 1890's the Portuguese, whose forefathers pioneered ocean sailing, picked up many old clipper ships at bargain prices. Willis was forced to sell his favorite ship, the remarkable *Cutty Sark*, for the meager sum of £2,100 to the Ferreira brothers of Lisbon. She was renamed *Ferreira* before she sailed from Gravesend for the last time, bound for Oporto. During the following 25 years, the cargo-carrying *Ferreira* was admirably sailed by the Portuguese, mostly between Lisbon, Rio de Janeiro, New Orleans, Oporto, Angola, Mozambique, the Cape Verde Islands, and Britain. The seafarers who sailed her under the Portuguese flag continued to care for her, alluding to her former name and figurehead by referring to her as *El Piquina Camisola* (the short petticoat).

There was little interest in what happened to *Cutty Sark* during her first 20 years under the Portuguese flag, with the exception of some local interest when she docked at Cardiff in 1905. Nine years later, British interest in the famous wool clipper increased following reports of her demise in the West Indies. During a hurricane she had been driven ashore and lost her rudder, but was otherwise undamaged, a tribute to the strength of her hull nearly forty years after she was built. A new rudder was fitted in Key West, and she was off to sea again. Shortly afterwards in June 1914, there was great excitement when *Ferreira* sailed into the River Mersey with a cargo of whalebone and oil. As news spread of her sudden and unexpected appearance in Liverpool, the true worth of this ageing greyhound of the ocean began to be recognized. Almost instantly *Ferreira* became the focus of attention in the newspapers, and an attraction for tourists who flocked to see her.

Following her stay in Liverpool she sailed for West Africa. From then on, her every movement was followed: interest in the former *Cutty Sark* became widespread following an account of her in Basil Lubbock's *The China Clippers*. Lubbock received letters from *Cutty Sark* enthusiasts throughout the world, including soldiers in the trenches on the Western Front; Lubbock served in France and India during the Great War and was awarded the Military Cross (MC) for gallantry.

Ferreira visited Liverpool again in 1915. Portugal declared war on Germany that year, and *Ferreira* was fortunate to escape the attention of the u-Boats that sent many a sailing ship to Davy Jones Locker. In 1916 *Ferreira* was dismasted, and lost her masts, off South Africa; her original ones having survived for 47 years. *Ferreira's* masthead cutty sark emblem, awarded by Willis in 1886, also went over the side, but was retrieved. The damaged clipper put into Cape Town for repairs. There was a shortage of suitable timber there because of the war, and *Ferreira* was re-rigged as a barquentine. She continued to carry freight, calling at London, Swansea, and Newcastle during the following three years.

By the time she arrived in the Thames towards the end of 1921, the former *Cutty Sark* had celebrity status. Her ownership changed in 1922 when she was acquired by Campanhia Nacional de Navegacao and renamed *Maria do Anparo*. Shortly afterwards her new Portuguese owners, realizing that the ship they had bought and overhauled at considerable cost would never make a profit, made it known that she was for sale. A syndicate of admirers in London tried to buy her, but could not afford the asking price.

But by the end of 1923 *Cutty Sark* was again flying the red duster, the colloquial name for the red ensign, as she had been acquired by Captain Wilfred Dowman of Falmouth for the considerable sum of £3,750. Dowman reconverted *Cutty Sark* to her original full rig, after which she looked her old magnificent self as she lay at her moorings in Carrick Roads, where Dowman used her for sail training. In 1924 she was towed to nearby Fowey for the annual regatta, with the indomitable Captain Richard Woodget at the wheel, after a 30-year break spent in retirement on his Norfolk farm.

Dowman intended to fit her with a full suit of sail and send her out on the ocean. But he died in 1936 before he could do so, and Catherine, his widow, donated *Cutty Sark* to the Thames Nautical Training College. In 1938 the clipper was towed from Falmouth to the Thames, where she became an auxiliary training vessel to *HMS Worcester* at Greenhithe.

London, the city she had loyally served for so many years, would be *Cutty Sark's* final resting place. Having survived the rigors of the oceans for over half a century, the conflict at sea during the Great War, and the threat of the breakers yard, this sturdy ship endured the threat of instant death as she lay moored on the Thames throughout World War II, minus her topgallant masts and yards as they were housed ashore. During the Blitz, *Cutty Sark* was silhouetted against the night sky by the red glow from the burning buildings ashore, as the Luftwaffe's high-explosive and incendiary bombs fell around her.

In 1951, *Cutty Sark* was dry-docked at Millwall and her hull was found to be in sound condition. The following year she was acquired by the then newly formed Cutty Sark Preservation Society, restored to her former glory with hull, deck, and rigging intact, and placed in dry dock on the south bank of the Thames at Greenwich, her final resting place.

CLIPPER CARRIERS

Preceding page: *Herzogin Cecilie*   A S Herring

CHAPTER 7

Iron and Steel Clippers

I must go down to the sea again, to the lonely sea and the sky,
And all I ask is a tall ship and a star to steer her by,
And the wheel's kick and the wind's song and the white sails shaking,
And a grey mist on the sea's face and a grey dawn breaking.

John Masefield, Sea-Fever

By the time sail reached its zenith in 1868 more iron square-rigged sailing ships were being launched, sailing vessels that would continue the clipper legacy. High-quality steel became available in the 1880s, and soon afterwards steel replaced iron as the material of choice for constructing ships. Britain led the way in iron and steel shipbuilding, and during the shipping boom of 1888–1893 a significant number of steel-hulled sailing ships were launched from British shipyards.

Iron and steel proved ideal for the construction of large ships, and by the turn of the 20th century, full-rigged iron and steel ships and barques dominated the long-distance cargo routes of the world. Large four-masted barques, many launched from British shipyards, had become popular with shipowners; the sail plan of these powerful ocean carriers was similar to the three-masted fully-rigged sailing clippers, with square sails on the three forward masts as well as fore-and-aft sails on the mizzenmast. A few ships with five masts were also built. These mighty ships, using a combination of size, power, and speed could clip along under a press of canvas with cargoes of four, five, six, or even eight thousand tons, a truly magnificent sight for anyone fortunate enough to see them sailing briskly through the water before a leading wind, or rounding the Horn against wind and current.

From records dating back to antiquity, wood was an essential component in the construction of boats and ships. That changed when large quantities of high quality iron and steel became available during the Industrial Revolution. The plentiful supply of local timber that had permitted the rapid development and expansion of shipbuilding on the North American East Coast during the clipper boom was not available to British shipbuilders. They had to import timber, and that was expensive, so the easy availability of iron and later steel was welcomed by the shipyards, and the suitability of these metals for the fabrication of ships' hulls was appreciated.

Britain took the lead in the building of iron sailing ships. Iron hulls were first used in canal boats, when they were introduced as passenger craft at about the turn of the 19th century. Each craft was drawn along the canal by two horses, and could transport passengers at speeds of up to ten miles per hour. Travel by canal boat was the favored mode of mass transport until the advent of the railways.

Steamships were the first vessels to be constructed of iron instead of wood. In 1824 the steamer *Aaron Manby* was built at an inland town and brought in sections to London, where it was assembled at a dockyard before being launched onto the Thames. From there, the iron steamship was piloted through the Thames Estuary to the sea, and then navigated across the Dover Strait to Le Havre before steaming upriver on the Seine to Paris. Shortly afterwards, a small iron steamer was delivered to the River Shannon in Ireland. But it was Isambard Kingdom Brunel's great auxiliary steam clipper *SS Great Britain*, of just less than 3,500 tons and launched in 1843 at Bristol, that was the catalyst for the building of large iron-hulled ships.

During the 1850s iron began to replace wood in the construction of clipper ships; iron was also in use for fabricating the frames of composite clippers. The advantages of iron were its strength, relative lightness, and durability; qualities that would enable longer and extremely sharp-ended ships to be built. These ships had a greater cargo capacity; the relative space available for cargo was increased by the use of smaller and stronger iron frames, compared to the wide timber frames in wooden ships. Other European countries were slow to follow Britain's lead in iron ship construction; France was the exception where iron was used for building composite sailing ships. In the United States, iron was not widely used for building sailing ships because timber was freely available and iron was highly taxed.

Ironsides was the first sailing vessel to be constructed of iron; it was built at Liverpool by Messrs Jackson, Gordon & Co in 1838. The first iron clipper ship is likely to have been *Three Bells*, launched in 1850 on the River Clyde from the Dunbarton yard of William Denny, and named after her Scottish owners, the Bell brothers. *Three Bells* had beautiful clipper lines and was relatively small at 649 tons. She was built for the Australia run with capacity to carry 250 passengers, and was the first iron ship to visit there. *Three Bells* reached a maximum speed of 12 knots, and her longest day's run was 273 nautical miles.

Some of the better known iron clippers built in the 1850s were *Typhoon, Tayleur, Evangeline, Hurricane, Ellen Bates, Gauntlet,* and *Lord of the Isles*. Iron clippers were longer ships, narrower in the beam, and they had less freeboard for their length than those of wooden or composite construction. But they were no less attractive, as the bow and stern were beautifully shaped, the yards were squarer and there was no need for studding sails. Beautifully turned deck fittings of varnished teak and polished brass reflected the ambient light, and engendered in the crew a feeling of pride in their ship as she was berthed alongside, ready to take to the ocean under full sail.

There were some disadvantages to the use of iron: the varying quality of iron, the tendency to severe fouling of the hull, and problems of compass deviation; the latter caused by complex, and permanent, magnetic fields due to hammering and vibrations during the construction of iron ships. Compass deviation resulting from these magnetic fields would vary according to the point of sail, and significant compass errors were the cause of a number of shipping disasters until the problem was recognized and rectified. The errors in deviation could be neutralized by placing small soft iron spheres and bars around the compass. Any residual small degrees of deviation that persisted at different points of the compass could be recorded on a deviation card and made available to the officer of the watch and the quartermaster at the wheel.

Iron clippers were 'wet ships': less buoyant because they were constantly swept by stormy seas. The steel clippers that followed would have the same problem. Some older sailors avoided these new sailing ships.

Scotland, with its coalfields, iron ore deposits, and ironworks located adjacent to the shipyards, was where most iron sailing ships were built. Some 70 of the 90 iron and steel clipper ships and barques registered in Sweden between 1875 and 1942 were built at Scottish yards.

Typhoon was built in 1852 on the Clyde at Govan by Alexander Stephens & Sons for the Australia service of Potter & Wilson. The latter immediately ordered another iron ship, the 979-ton *Hurricane*, a clipper with particularly fine lines. *Hurricane* was completed early in 1853; she had twelve to fifteen staterooms in the poop and accommodation for 250 more passengers 'tween decks. *Typhoon* and

Hurricane were built under cover in the Stephens yard. *Hurricane's* masts and spars were added and the rigging completed after she was launched. Her maiden voyage to Melbourne took 83 days, not a particularly outstanding performance for a ship with a potential speed of 18 knots. She performed better on the following outward voyage, arriving at Port Phillip Heads 75 days after passing the Tuskar Rock.

The Tuskar Rock and its lighthouse, located off the Wexford coast at the south-east corner of Ireland, was the accepted starting point for calculating the passage time of ships setting out under sail from Liverpool or Glasgow.

> In the grey of the coming on of night
> She dropped her tug at the Tuskar light,
> 'N the topsails went to the topmast head
> To a chorus that fairly awoke the dead.
> She trimmed her yards and slanted South
> With her royals set and a bone in her mouth.
>
> John Masefield, *The Yarn of Loch Achray*

Hurricane had a short life as a sailing clipper: following her second round trip, she was hauled out and spent a couple of years on the slip having engines installed; meanwhile the company who had overstretched to buy her went bankrupt. Little more is known except that she was still afloat in 1867.

A number of other iron ships of extreme clipper design were built in 1853 for the Australia trade. Cargo-carrying capacity was not a priority as revenue was generated mostly from outward-bound emigrants, and from carrying gold on the home run. *Lord of the Isles*, registering 691 tons, had very fine lines, similar to Donald McKay's extreme clippers. She was rigged to carry a generous area of plain sail, including large staysails; her topsails were fitted with Cunningham's roller reefing gear, and there were other labor-saving devices for handling sails and spars at deck level. *Lord of the Isles* was built by Scott & Co at Greenock.

Under sail and driven hard by the experienced commander Peter Maxton, *Lord of the Isles*, described as a most beautiful ship, was an impressive performer on her maiden voyage to Sydney. She made excellent time, traveling from the Tuskar Rock to Sydney in 72 days, despite having to beat through the Bass Strait. Her time from the Tuskar to Cape Otway, the south-west tip of Victoria at the western entrance to the Bass Strait, was among the fastest on record. On arrival at Sydney, a passenger described how the *Lord of the Isles* travelled at 8–9 knots with scarcely any wind, reaching 18 knots in a strong breeze, logging between 360 and 400 miles on several days, passing every other ship and leaving them astern and out of sight within 5–6 hours. One day she logged 428 miles, an average of just under 18 knots, while just maintaining her maximum speed for a few hours. This was an astonishing achievement when compared to the all-time 24-hour record of 465 miles by the much larger clipper ship *Champion of the Seas,* and *Lightning's* two 24-hour runs of 430 and 436 miles.

Shortly afterwards *Lord of the Isles* was transferred to the China tea trade, where she continued to make fast passages, including a record 87 days land to land from Shanghai to Lizard Point in 1855.

* * *

The finest iron clipper and the largest British merchant sailing ship of her time was *Tayleur,* registering 1,979 tons. Launched on 27 September 1853, she was one of only three clipper ships of over 1,500 tons built in Britain during the 1850s. Commissioned by Charles Moore & Co of Liverpool, *Tayleur* was built by Charles Tayleur & Co at their Bank Quay Foundry in Warrington on the River Mersey, about 18 miles inland from Liverpool. Designed to sail on the Liverpool to Melbourne run, where she would be competing with the powerful American-built clippers, no expense was spared in fitting her out. There were three decks with room for 680 passengers on the main deck.

Tayleur set sail from the River Mersey on Thursday 19 January 1854 under the command of Captain Noble, bound for Australia with a full complement of passengers, most of them emigrants and many of them Irish; it was estimated that the number of people on board, including crew, came to almost 700. At the time, Ireland was beginning to recover from the ravages of the Great Famine, and emigration was one of the few ways many people had of escaping abject poverty.

William Carley was on board, bound for Australia for the second time. Thirteen years earlier, Carley was sentenced to ten years transportation at Rutland Assizes in the English Midlands for sheep slaughtering. At the time he was planning to marry his pregnant girlfriend. Painful scenes were witnessed by those in court as his young wife to be, expecting him to be acquitted, clung desperately to her man in a vain effort to prevent him from being taken away. She heard no more from Carley. Twelve years later, while travelling on business by train in Rutland, she changed seats to avoid the attention of one of the male

Tayleur (ILN)

passengers; catching her eye again, the man exclaimed: 'I'm the man,' and it was then that she recognized her former boyfriend, William Carley. The couple married shortly afterwards, and Carley, who had done well as a gold-digger after he was released from the penal colony, persuaded her to go to Australia with him.

Tayleur was towed out into the channel by the steam tug *Vanguard*. Then all sail was set. According to the pilot who took *Tayleur* out of Liverpool, she was the fastest ship afloat, sailing beautifully and answering the helm with ease as she gathered momentum in a fresh breeze, reaching a speed of 13–14 knots; *Vanguard* dropped astern because of the danger of being run down by *Tayleur*, and then came alongside to take off clerks from the shipping office and people who were on board seeing off their friends. In the confusion of noise and commotion that occurred when visitors were being taken off, a passenger jumped aboard *Vanguard* by mistake. Shortly afterwards he made it known that he wanted to go to Melbourne. The tug immediately put about to catch up with *Tayleur* and get the man back on board. But the new clipper was already speeding ahead under a billowing cloud of canvas, and *Vanguard* soon gave up the chase. Instead, *Tayleur's* disappointed passenger had to return to Liverpool.

Tayleur made good progress for some hours, driven by a fair wind. When she was off Holyhead the wind veered from south-east to the south-west, and increased in strength. Soon the big clipper was struggling against an adverse gale, and the captain ordered sail to be shortened. It quickly became obvious to some of the passengers that the ship was shorthanded and that the crew were inexperienced and didn't know the ropes. A further complication was the inability of the mainly Chinese and Lascar (Indian) crew to cope with the cold winter weather; many had the added disadvantage of not being able to understand the English language. The mate could not get anyone to go out on the yards to shorten sail, so the ship struggled at the mercy of wind and wave and three hours was spent taking in the mizzen topsail and the fore topsail.

Passengers began airing their concerns between each other, fearing that they would never reach the end of the voyage. One passenger afterwards complained that the main topsail and lower sails could not be taken in, and were left flapping and beating all night. The boatswain and the third mate managed to shorten sail the following morning. *Tayleur,* sailing close hauled, made little progress south while off Holyhead on Friday, as she struggled against gale force winds. The captain then altered course in a northerly direction.

The wind moderated on Friday night. The passengers' confidence in the crew was diminishing by the minute, though they were full of admiration for the splendid ship, stating that she was the most beautiful ship that had ever sailed the seas. One passenger was critical of the captain for setting the lower sails, topsails, and topgallants, as the crew were deemed not capable of taking them in, in an emergency. As dawn broke, visibility was poor, the wind speed had increased to gale force again, and big seas were running.

To complicate matters further, it was discovered that there was a difference of almost two points, 24° degrees, between the compass of the helmsman and the one at the front of the poop deck. Not knowing which compass was in error, the captain incorrectly, as it later transpired, assumed that the one near the wheel was correct. A third compass, located in the skylight between the other two, was sluggish and totally unreliable.

In order to cope with the strengthening wind, sail was again shortened, mostly to reefed topsails. By eleven on the Saturday morning, *Tayleur* was on a long tack with the purpose of avoiding a lee shore, when suddenly land loomed up directly ahead. It was Lambay Island, off north County Dublin. The captain tried to wear ship but was unable to do so: *Tayleur* was drifting, out of control, towards the rocky shore. Passengers rushed on deck adding further to the confusion and making it even more difficult for the crew. The two anchors were released, momentarily slowing this mighty iron ship's drift towards her doom. As soon as the anchors took hold on the seabed their chains snapped like glass.

Just after midday on Saturday 21 January, less than 48 hours after leaving the River Mersey, *Tayleur*, now drifting helplessly, struck a reef that ran out from a creek on the east side of Lambay Island. The impact shook the great ship from stem to stern, but *Tayleur's* iron hull was not seriously damaged. She rose on the crest of the next wave and was carried broadside onto the reef; as the water receded, *Tayleur* came crashing down on the sharp rocks and was badly holed below the waterline. She stayed in this position, perilously perched on the reef, for a short time.

As water rushed in through the breach in her hull, everyone instinctively knew that the ship was in great peril and unlikely to survive for long. A man jumped from the stern towards the shore but failed to make it. He struck his head on the rocks, struggled for a short time, and was drowned. The next person to jump was the cook's mate, a black man named Archibald Jack; he got a good footing, and was quickly followed by two Chinese and two Indian crew members. A rope was thrown ashore and made fast. This proved a lifeline for many of the passengers and crew, who used it to haul themselves ashore, aided by the exhortations of young male passengers. Three women were saved in this way. A number of passengers, mostly women, fell from the rope; many got half way, and unable to get further would lose their grip from the pressure of those coming behind. Of those who fell into the water, about five were saved. Two men, with children strapped on, made it to the shore by the rope. The third mate managed to get a plank to reach the rocks, and others reached safety that way.

Those who jumped from the bow were dashed against the rocks. Among them was the ship's surgeon Doctor Cunningham. He made valiant, but unsuccessful, efforts to save the lives of his wife and child; the child was some distance away and perished in the unforgiving sea as did Cunningham as he endeavored to rescue her.

Within 30 minutes of striking the reef, *Tayleur*, having taken water through the breach in her hull, suddenly lurched, slid backwards, and sank to the bottom in seven fathoms of water. The rope snapped throwing those who were clinging to it into the sea. Passengers and crew on deck rushed forward as the stern went under; they were washed overboard and pounded on the rocks; only five made it safely to the shore; the cries of those who perished in the water were harrowing. More than 200 people were lost within sight and almost within reach of land. The ship settled on the bottom in an upright position with her masts above the water. Two men climbed the mast and remained above water. One was rescued by the local coastguards who had been alerted by Archibald Jack. Fourteen hours later, in the early hours of Sunday morning, the second man was found asleep in the rigging and saved.

Those who got ashore safely were soon suffering from exposure and hunger. Communication with the mainland was made the following day: on Sunday morning, 22 January, three passengers were conveyed aboard a fishing boat to the mainland. There they boarded a train to Dublin and raised the alarm. The City of Dublin Steam Packet Company's vessel *Prince* sailed from Kingstown and arrived at Lambay Island on Sunday evening to take off the survivors. A total of 296 people survived including the captain, first mate and third mate. Of the 200 women and 50 children who were on board, only three women and a small number of children were saved. Carley and his wife were among those who survived.

Two month's later, the Board of Trade investigation, carried out by Captain Walker, reported. Three major failings had contributed to the disaster: *Tayleur* was insufficiently manned, there had been no sea trials before her maiden voyage, and the steering compass error had contributed significantly to the disaster. Noble was also criticized for not taking soundings with a lead line on Saturday morning when he was uncertain about his position. The Admiralty chart of the Irish Sea had depths marked on it, and a number of packet captains used soundings to navigate across the channel between Liverpool and Dublin.

Walker, though in agreement that no expense was spared in the building and fitting-out of the ship, was highly critical of the failure to swing the compasses and make the necessary adjustments for compass deviation immediately before the voyage when all the equipment, cargo, and stores were aboard. The compasses were swung two months before the voyage, but further deviation should have been anticipated following the final stages of equipping and loading. More care should have been given to the subject of compass error, and Captain Noble should not have proceeded to the Southern Ocean without ascertaining compass accuracy and the degree of deviation. Walker's report finished by stating that all iron ships should have compasses adjusted and deviation ascertained, with errors listed on a deviation card, before proceeding to sea.

* * *

The 1860s was a period of transition. While many composite clippers were being built for the China tea trade, an increasing number of iron sailing ships were launched. In 1860 over 800 sailing ships were built, of which 32 were iron; five years later this had climbed to 116; in 1875 a total of 193 iron sailing ships were built. Of the 316 sailing ships built in 1880, all, with the exception of 36 small wooden craft, were iron. Sail was helped by the flourishing Australian wool trade, and the increasing amount of grain being grown in the American Northwest.

In addition, the new transatlantic telegraph cables and the development of the national and international telegraph during the latter part of the nineteenth century enhanced the efficiency and commercial value of the long-distance merchant sailing fleets. Ships' masters would receive details of their next voyage as soon as they arrived in distant ports, or on their arrival off the European coast at places like Falmouth or Queenstown, where they would receive 'orders' for their port of discharge.

In 1860 the first Belfast-built iron ship, the 953-ton clipper *Jane Porter*, was launched from the new Harland & Wolff shipyard on Queen's Island. *Jane Porter* was the fifth ship to be built at the yard, and the first of many iron square-riggers.

Edward J Harland was born in Scarborough in 1831. Instead of becoming a barrister, as his father had wished, he served an apprenticeship with the Newcastle-upon-Tyne locomotive and railway engineering firm of Robert Stephenson & Co, that had been created in 1823 by George Stephenson, the 'Father of the Modern Railway,' and others. Robert Stephenson, George's son, later joined the firm. Robert's greatest engineering triumph was the Britannia Railway Bridge over the Menai Strait in North Wales. When it opened in 1850 it completed the London to Holyhead rail link that would carry mail and passengers on the 'Irish Mail' train to and from the Irish Sea packets at Holyhead for more than a hundred years.

Harland afterwards worked for the Clyde shipbuilding firm of J G Thomson, before going to Belfast to work for Robert Hickson's fledgling shipbuilding firm. In 1859 Hickson sold the yard to Harland. The shipyard was on Queens Island, a mudflat in the estuary of the River Lagan, and that become the center of the Belfast shipbuilding industry during the second half of the nineteenth century. Harland, later Sir Edward Harland, was an engineering genius who made Belfast the great shipbuilding center it became. Gustav Wilhelm Wolff was born in Hamburg and studied at Liverpool University. In 1860 he joined the Harland yard to take charge of the drawing office. Seven years later, Wolff became a partner and the firm of Harland & Wolff was created.

Fleets of Colonial Clippers were operated by Belfast owners engaged in the cargo and passenger trade with America, Australia, India, the Far East, and the West Indies. They mostly operated from the home ports of Liverpool and London, and many of the larger clippers were registered in Liverpool. *Jane Porter* was the first of the 'Irish Stars', as Irish owned clipper ships became known, and the first of a fleet of thirteen beautiful iron clippers to be owned and operated by J P Corry & Co of Belfast; twelve of Corry's thirteen sturdy ships were built by Harland & Wolff. At the time, other shipyards were stepping their masts up-right, but ships built by Harland & Wolff had their masts raked an inch to the foot, greatly enhancing their appearance and performance. Most Belfast-built clippers crossed stout royal yards, but rarely crossed skysail yards.

Corry's clippers were engaged mostly in the Indian jute trade, and had a reputation for good passage making. A particularly fast sailer was the beautiful *Star of Erin,* launched by Harland & Wolff in 1862. *Star of Erin* performed well under Captain John Simpson, who afterwards commanded *Star of Persia*. In 1873, when under the command of Captain James Mill, *Star of Erin* sailed from London to Calcutta in a remarkably short time of 80 days. Mill had previously commanded *Star of Albion* and *Queen of the West.*

The Calcutta jute trade was at its peak in the early 1860s. However, in October 1864, Calcutta was hit by a severe cyclone that swept through the anchorage on the Hooghly River. In the space of three to four hours, all except six of two hundred vessels were ripped from their moorings, many of them capsizing, or being driven aground. There was tremendous loss of life, part of the city was left in ruins, and it took many years to repair the damage. The opening of the Suez Canal five years later put paid to the Calcutta jute clippers.

The largest of Corry's iron clippers was the 1,027-ton *Star of Russia*, built in 1874. This was a ship with a reputation for fast passages on the Australian and New Zealand emigrant run, and she continued to carry passengers even when steamers later came to monopolize the trade. *Star of Russia's* fastest voyage from London to Melbourne was 77 days. In 1898 she was bought by Shaw Savill who sold her to Alaska Packers three years later. She was renamed *Star of Peru*. In 1926, with her iron hull in good condition, she was sold to French owners at Nouméa, New Caledonia, and they renamed her *Bougainville*. Shortly afterwards she carried a cargo of lumber from Vancouver to Fiji, and later she went into use as a storage hulk at Nouméa, where, in 1972, she was reported to be intact. The former *Star of Russia* now lies in 35 metres of water in Port Vila, Vanuatu, with her hull apparently intact.

The last two Harland & Wolff ships to sail under the Corry flag were *Star of Italy* and *Star of France,* both launched in 1877. They carried very tall rigs, with their lower masts and topmasts cast in one piece. During their 21 years with Corry's they put in good passages, mostly sailing between London and Calcutta, and London and Melbourne.

Another impressive fleet was operated by the Belfast firm of Thomas Dixon & Son. Dixon's early ships were Canadian built barques that operated mostly in the Canadian lumbar trade. Dixon's first iron clipper, built in 1877 at the Harland & Wolff yard, was the first of the 'Irish Lords,' the 1,372-ton *Lord Cairns*. Cairns was a prominent Belfast personality who served in Benjamin Disraeli's government as Chancellor of the Exchequer. On her maiden voyage, *Lord Cairns* was under the command of one of the most highly regarded of the master mariners sailing out of Belfast: Captain James B Dunn. Dunn was from Rush, County Dublin. He spent fifty years with Dixon's and commanded a number of their ships. Under his command, *Lord Cairns* had a 99-day passage from San Francisco. In 1882, *Lord Cairns* passed into Welsh ownership, and later she was bought by a Liverpool company. In 1903 she went under the Italian flag, serving her Italian owners as *Spica,* until she went to the breaker's yard.

Dunn later commanded the large 2,263-ton four-masted barque *Lord Downshire,* the first of a number of four-masted barques to be built at the Harland & Wolff yard for Dixon's. This large clipper barque proved very fast in strong winds, particularly on the California run. For a number of years, *Lord Downshire* was under the command of Captain John Newcombe, who like Dunn, hailed from Rush, County Dublin.

> Many famous seamen came from the little ports of Rush, Skerries and Balbriggan, men from these towns were to be found in command of ships all over the world during the nineteenth century.
> Ernest B Anderson *Sailing Ships of Ireland*

In 1894, when under the command of Captain John Gibson McMurtry from Carrickfergus, *Lord Downshire* loaded nitrate at Caleta Buena, Chile, before setting sail for Europe. She never arrived, and was posted as lost with all hands. It is believed that she was in collision with the Liverpool registered *Prince Oscar* off the coast of Brazil, just south of Cape San Roque. The collision occurred at night, and according to crew members of *Prince Oscar* who survived, their ship collided with an unidentified sailing vessel. Both ships were lost. There were no survivors from the other vessel, whereas all but six of those on board *Prince Oscar* survived.

The inquiry into the loss of *Prince Oscar* heard how she was sailing close hauled on a starboard tack in the south-east trades when the navigation light of another vessel was seen ahead. *Prince Oscar* stood on, expecting the approaching vessel to give way in accordance with the Regulations for Preventing Collisions at Sea. As the vessels closed on each other, the crew of *Prince Oscar* discovered that their green starboard navigation light was extinguished, making them invisible to the unidentified ship in the darkness. By then it was too late: the two ships collided with a tremendous impact and sank. The crew of the second vessel would have been unaware of the danger, and totally unprepared for the collision. Later, when she was posted as missing, *Lord Downshire* was assumed to have been the unidentified ship that collided with *Prince Oscar*.

The Belfast shipping firm, Messrs David Grainger & Son, were the owners of a very large fleet of ships. From the 1860s, their fleet included a number of fine clippers of over 1,000 tons. Grainger's ships were nearly all engaged in the American cotton trade, and the Australia passenger run. Belfast-owned ships were prominent carriers of cotton from New Orleans to Liverpool, a trade that had begun in small barques of between 200 and 300 tons. One such was *Aurora*, built in Quebec in 1833.

Riverdale, an 1,847-ton vessel belonging to Graingers, was commanded on a number of voyages by the famous Captain Charles McDonnell, who, when in command of the Australian clippers *Marco Polo* and *James Baines*, logged four 24-hour passages of over 400 miles, and set the all-time accepted record for the top speed of a sailing ship at 21 knots through the water. McDonnell was from Glenariff, not far from Cushendall, a fishing village on the Antrim coast.

One of the finest iron clippers ever built, and one of the most consistently fast sailing ships ever to come from a British yard was *Melbourne*, later named *MacQuarie*. A full-rigged ship, this celebrated beauty was built by Green's at their Blackwall yard from surplus iron plates that remained following the building of a warship there. *Melbourne*, 1,965 tons and 270 feet long, was built, fitted out and furnished, regardless of expense, for the princely sum of £42,000. The 69-foot-long poop deck had a stern cabin with large windows, similar to those of an East Indiamen. She was launched onto the Thames in 1875, and sold to Devitt & Moore by R & H Green in 1887. *Melbourne* was the last of the Blackwall Frigates.

In 1875, when under the command of Captain Frederick Delabene Marsden,

Melbourne sailed from London to Melbourne in 74 days; she logged 5,100 miles in seventeen days, an average of 300 miles per day, and during her best 24-hour run she averaged 15.5 knots. Devitt & Moore sailed *MacQuarie* as a passenger ship on the Australia run for the following twenty years. Later she went into use for sail training cadets at the Nautical College at Pangbourne, Berkshire. In the early 1900s, *MacQuarie* was in Norwegian ownership under the name *Fortuna* and later ended up in Sydney Harbor as a hulk. When she was broken up fifty years later, the iron plating was in excellent condition.

* * *

The renowned author Joseph Conrad had a career as a harbor pilot and master mariner, and honed his seamanship skills on some of the great clipper ships of the time. He was born Józef Teodor Konrad Korzeniowski to Polish parents in Berdyczów, Ukraine, on 5 December 1857, at a time when Berdyczów was part of Poland. His father, Apollo Korzeniowski, came from a landowning and patriotic soldiering family; he fell in love and married the beautiful Ewelina Bobrowski, whose wealthy family remained aloof from the nationalist politics of the time. Both of Konrad's parents died of tuberculosis, his mother when he was three, and his father when he was fourteen. Konrad's uncle, Tadeusz Bobrowski, a wise and influential landowner, became his guardian and acted as his mentor, as well as providing him with financial support for many years. The young Konrad Korzeniowski, keenly interested in literature and far-off places, dreamed of exploring foreign lands. In the autumn of 1871, despite always having lived far from the sea, Konrad made known his wish to become a sailor.

Three years later, the sixteen-year-old Konrad, by then fluent in French, went to live in Marseilles where he became a lifelong admirer of the 'Cradle of Sailing,' the Mediterranean Sea. He was introduced to the art of sailing by harbor pilots, whom he accompanied when they boarded and piloted incoming and outbound vessels. Konrad himself became proficient enough to pilot boats unaided, and he developed an admiration for the pilot's crucial role in guiding ships through confined and confusing harbors and narrow river channels:

> He resembled a pilot, which to a seaman is trustworthiness personified.
>
> Joseph Conrad, *Heart of Darkness*

Konrad spent his first sea voyage as a passenger on board the barque, *Mont-Blanc,* which was owned by Jean-Baptiste Delestang, a Royalist whose wife's salon was a focus for local supporters of the Bourbon restoration. *Mont-Blanc* left Marseilles on 15 December 1874 for Martinique under Captain Sever Ournier. Konrad was no longer a passenger on the return voyage, but a member of the crew. The following year Konrad joined *Mont-Blanc* as an apprentice under Captain Jean-Prosper Duteil for another voyage to Martinique and St Thomas, and arrived back in Le Havre on 23 December. Konrad signed off and returned to Marseilles, spending a few days in Paris on the way.

Six months later Konrad went to sea again, as a steward on board the 432-ton barque *Saint-Antoine,* under the command of Captain Antoine Escarras. The mate was the Corsican, Dominique Cervoni, who features in Conrad's *Nostromo.* During the voyage, *Saint-Antoine* visited Martinique, St Thomas, and Haiti, and returned to Marseilles in mid February 1877 with a cargo of logwood and sugar. For the following twelve months Konrad stayed in Marseilles, living on an allowance from Uncle Tadeusz.

Tadeusz Bobrowski arrived in Marseilles in March 1878, having been summoned urgently. He found his nephew almost completely recovered after an attempt to take his own life. Bobrowski stayed a couple of weeks, during which time he settled Konrad's debts and assured himself all was well again with his beloved nephew.

The cause of Konrad's despair was twofold: his plan to take up a berth aboard *Saint-Antoine* that Escarras had offered him did not materialize, and he had lost money. The Bureau l'Inscription forbade him to sign on because Konrad was a 21-year-old alien who was under obligation to serve in the Tsar's Army; they had discovered that he had not obtained permission from the Russian Consul to work in France. The Inspector of the Port of Marseilles, who had previously registered the existence of such a permit, was severely reprimanded and nearly lost his job.

It was bad news for Konrad: the affair was widely known about, and despite the best endeavors of shipowner Delestang and Captain Escarras, Konrad was obliged to stay behind when *Saint-Antoine* set sail. There was no hope of him getting a berth on a French merchant vessel, and neither had he any wish to return to Poland, where he would have been conscripted into the Imperial Russian Army.

This was not the only catastrophe to befall the aspiring sailor. Konrad had been persuaded by Duteil, his captain on *Mont-Blanc*, to invest money in an enterprise on the Spanish coast, probably involving contraband and arms smuggling. Initially the enterprise realised a profit, but next time Konrad lost all of his investment of a couple of thousand francs that he had received from Bobrowski. When he returned to Marseilles, and discovered that he was ineligible to serve on *Saint-Antoine*, he attempted to take his own life with a revolver, but the bullet passed through his chest missing his heart and major blood vessels. The precise details of the wound are not known; it may be that the bullet entered and exited through the outer chest wall as described by Babrowski: *'durch und durch'* (through and through).

Uncle Tadeusz was impressed by the sailing skills his nephew had acquired, and by his ambition to reach the highest levels in the merchant marine: on two occasions during Babrowski's stay in Marseilles, Konrad received requests to pilot vessels into port, and received a fee of 100 francs on each occasion for doing so. A number of Konrad's friends advised him that he should join the British Merchant Navy if he wished to continue his career as a seafarer. Following further discussions with his uncle, Konrad decided to move to England, although he didn't know anybody there or speak the language.

On 24 April 1878, Konrad left Marseilles on board the small British steamer *Mavis*, probably as an unofficial apprentice. *Mavis* followed a circuitous route to England: she first sailed east, passing through the Dardenelles, with a stop at Constantinople, before proceeding through the Bosphorous Strait to the Black Sea and the Strait of Kerch, with stops at Kerch and Yeysk on the Sea of Azov in the Crimea; *Mavis* then returned to the Mediterranean, where she stopped at Malta, before setting out on the final leg of her voyage to Lowestoft, where Konrad Korzenowski set foot on English soil for the first time on 10 June 1878.

From Lowestoft, Konrad travelled to London and, during the following month, used up much of his ready cash. On 11 July, he returned to Lowestoft and signed on the coastal schooner *Skimmer of the Sea* as ordinary seaman, Conrad de Korzenowski. *Skimmer of the Sea* had a crew of seven, all from around Lowestoft. Years later, Conrad said that he would never forget the kindness shown to him by the people of Lowestoft: he learned the duties of a schooner sailor, English nautical terminology, and his first words in English from the crew of the schooner.

Conrad was determined to master the new language. He started by reading the daily papers and buying a copy of the *Complete Works of Shakespeare*. He also obtained copies of the *King James Bible* that were distributed to sailors in English ports, later saying that he had always accepted these free copies so that he could use the pages for rolling cigarettes, having read them first. Conrad made three voyages to Newcastle-Upon-Tyne, from where *Skimmer of the Sea* returned with cargoes of coal. During his two-and-a-half months in the coastal trade, Conrad gained a basic understanding of his third language, English.

On 12 October 1878, Conrad signed on as an ordinary seaman to become one of the 23 crew members of the beautiful 1,047-ton Australian wool clipper *Duke of Sutherland,* commanded by Captain John McKay. Three days later she departed from the East India Docks, taking Conrad on his first long trip across the oceans, a voyage that would take him round the world. Beset by adverse and light winds, it was a 107-day voyage that ended on 31 January 1879 in Sydney Harbor. During much of the following four months, *Duke of Sutherland* was moored at Circular Quay, and Conrad was the clipper's night watchman; many of the crew had left the ship after her arrival in Sydney. Having loaded her cargo of wool, *Duke of Sutherland* left Sydney on 6 July on a heading for Cape Horn and the Atlantic Ocean, and arrived in London on 19 October.

In December, Conrad joined the steamer *Europa* as an able seaman on a short voyage to the Mediterranean, calling at Genoa, Naples, Palermo, and Patras, before arriving back in London at the end of January 1880. Conrad next attended the East London navigation school of John Newton to prepare for the second mate's examination. And on 28 May he satisfied the examiner, Captain John Rankin, of his suitability, and was awarded the certificate.

It was not until 21 August that Conrad got his next berth, as third mate on *Loch Etive,* an attractive iron wool clipper highly regarded in Sydney. Third mate was an anomalous rank on British sailing ships, more akin to being a senior able seaman than one of the officers. Time served as third mate, without charge of a watch, did not count towards the year's experience as second mate that was required before taking the examination for a first mate's certificate.

Loch Etive's captain, 48-year-old William Stuart, had commanded John Willis's *The Tweed* for eleven years from 1863. Stuart was a first-class master mariner; *The Tweed* gained a reputation for fast sailings under his command, making her the most famous ship in the fleet, until Willis's even more famous *Cutty Sark* set a blistering pace on the Australia wool run under Captain Richard Woodget. *Loch Etive* left London on 22 August and arrived in Sydney on 24 November. There was a delay before her wool cargo was loaded, and on 11 January 1881 *Loch Etive* set sail for London, outsailing several other wool clippers on a not particularly fast voyage of 103 days. Conrad was impressed and inspired by Stuart's professionalism, afterwards describing his experiences during the voyage in his book, *The Mirror of the Sea*.

Conrad did not get another berth until September, when he signed on as second mate aboard the small barque *Palestine* for a voyage to Bangkok. It proved to be an eventful, dangerous, and long drawn-out adventure, with the ship needing almost constant repair. Sailing north from London to collect her cargo of 557 tons of coal at Newcastle-upon-Tyne took 22 days because of headwinds. After leaving Newcastle at the end of November, *Palestine* encountered strong winter gales in the English Channel that caused her to lose a mast and develop a leak, making it necessary for her to put into Falmouth for repairs. Many of the crew refused to work as they were unhappy with the state of the ship, and they left the vessel at Falmouth. Conrad's motivation for remaining with the ship was his requirement for a certificate of service as second mate, a position that was not easy to come by. While waiting at Falmouth, Conrad had an opportunity to explore the beautiful Cornish coast and to read. During a trip to London he bought a volume of Lord Byron's poetry.

Palestine, operated by a new crew, finally left Falmouth for Bangkok on 17 September 1882. The time taken for repairs and overhaul was prolonged because her London owner, John Wilson, was wrangling over the cost of the work. The crew taken on at Falmouth included five Cornishmen, and a man from each of the following countries: Australia, Ireland, Netherlands, Norway, and Antilles in the Caribbean.

It was a slow passage with an eventful ending: the cargo of coal caught fire by spontaneous combustion when *Palestine* was sailing through the East Bangka Strait on 11 March 1883. Initially the fire was contained, but four days later the crew abandoned ship and took to the boats before the ship became engulfed in flames. Twenty-four-hours later, they reached Muntok on Bangka Island, off Sumatra. Conrad later described 'waking up in an open boat in my first Eastern port and seeing the East looking at me.'

By then Conrad had served nearly 18 months as second mate on *Palestine*. But he had spent only nine-and-a-half months of the time in charge of a watch, and although he was given credit for an extra month, he was still short of the full year required to take his next examination. He had acquitted himself well as second mate: *Palestine's* first mate, an Irishman named H Mahon, described him as 'a capital chap, a good officer, and the best second mate he had ever shipped with.' Conrad spent a month in Singapore before returning to London as a passenger on a steamer, arriving there at the end of May 1883.

Shortly afterwards, Conrad met with uncle Tadeusz, their first meeting in five years. Little is known about their two-month sojourn at the Spa town of Marienbad, and Teplice in Bohemia. We do know that Bobrowski, by then an elderly recluse, was encouraging his nephew to prepare for and take the chief officer's examination. On parting, he paid Conrad's expenses for the trip, gave him £25 to cover the cost of naturalization in Britain, and promised to send him £350 to buy a share in a London shipping firm.

In September 1883, Conrad became second mate on the 1,490-ton clipper *Riversdale*, crewed predominantly by Scandinavians, on a voyage to Madras. Captain Lawrence Brown McDonald, described as a conceited despot who was not highly regarded by his officers, had his wife and sons on board. He dismissed Conrad after *Riversdale* arrived in Madras. Conrad was dismissed because of what ensued when he had been sent ashore to fetch a doctor for the captain who had become ill. He was accompanied by the captain of a steamer who was a friend of McDonald. On being asked by Dr Daniel Thompson what he thought was wrong with his Captain, Conrad said that he thought he was drunk. This, and the letter from Captain McDonald's wife, convinced Thompson that the patient he was going to see was someone who was the worst for drink, an opinion that was not borne out when he saw McDonald. Captain McDonald dismissed his second mate after he was made aware by his steamer captain friend of what Conrad had said to Dr Thompson. Conrad subsequently withdrew the accusation and apologized, but to no avail.

He quickly found another ship: *Narcissus*. The 1,336-ton clipper had arrived from Penarth, South Wales, without a second mate. *Narcissus* arrived at Dunkirk on 16 October 1884 and Conrad, having now completed the required time as second mate, signed off. On 17 November Conrad was unsuccessful at passing, at his first attempt, the examination for his chief officer's certificate. He failed on 'Day's Work,' the 24-hour entries in the logbook recording the ship's position, course, speed, distance logged, wind direction, wind strength, and barometric pressure. Two weeks later, having benefited from attending a crammer, he was examined by Captain P Thompson and passed the examination.

Postings were becoming more difficult to obtain as the tonnage of British sailing ships was diminishing, and Conrad had to work hard in the search for his next job. He found a vacancy on the 1,517-ton clipper *Tilkhurst*, the largest sailing ship on which he would serve. He joined her as second mate on 24 April 1885 at Hull. After taking on a cargo of coal at Penarth, *Tilkhurst* set sail for Singapore and arrived there on 22 September. *Tilkhurst* was a happy ship, and only one crew member left at Singapore. Conrad enjoyed working under Captain Edwin John Blake, the well-educated and highly informed son of a physician. Conrad considered him an excellent commander.

After unloading at Singapore, *Tilkhurst* sailed to Calcutta to load jute, and in early January began her homeward voyage. She arrived in Dundee on 16 June 1886. Uncle Tadeusz had been urging his nephew to apply for British nationality so that he would no longer be a subject of the Tsar, living illegally abroad. On 19 August, when Conrad was 29, he learned that his application to be a British National was granted. Later in the year he was able to inform Babrowski that he had qualified as a master mariner, news that was eagerly awaited by his uncle. Conrad had passed the examination at his second attempt on 10 November. He had initially taken it in July, but failed in arithmetic and log book entries. His inadequate knowledge of English at the time and lack of a systematic education in mathematics, were the likely contributing factors to the failure of this highly motivated and not unintelligent sailor to reach the required standard at the first attempt.

The following February, Conrad obtained his first berth as chief mate when he signed on the 1,040-ton iron barque *Highland Forest*, then lying in Amsterdam. Her commander was the 34-year-old Irishman, Captain John McWhir, who afterwards became the much older ship's captain, McWhirr in Conrad's book *Typhoon*. *Highland Forest's* chief officer would afterwards use his experiences in writing *The Mirror of the Sea*. One of Conrad's responsibilities was to take charge of the apprentices; he was afterwards remembered by one of them as being particularly kind and caring. On *Highland Forest's* voyage to Semarang, Java, Conrad sustained an injury from a falling spar. He was not seriously hurt, but he did require hospital treatment in Singapore.

In August 1887, he became first mate on the small 206-ton steamer *Vidar*, commanded by Captain James Craig, and owned by the Singapore merchant Syed Mohsin Bin Salleh Al Joffree. *Vidar* made round trips to ports on the Malay Archipelago, Makassar Strait, and Celebes Sea.

On January 1888, Conrad signed off *Vidar* at Singapore, and two weeks later was engaged to take temporary command of the 346-ton Australian iron barque

Otago, as the captain had died at sea. Captain Korzeniowski assumed command of *Otago* in Bangkok, and sailed her to Sydney with a cargo of teak. In Sydney, *Otago's* owners decided to sign him on as her permanent captain; Conrad had now reached the highest echelon of the mercantile marine.

Conrad remained in command of *Otago* for nearly a year. During that time the small barque conveyed a variety of cargoes: wheat from Melbourne to Sydney; fertilizer, soap, and tallow to Mauritius; sugar to Melbourne; and wheat to Port Adelaide from Spencer Gulf. He gave a tea party on board in Port Arthur for the wives of local farmers. *The Secret Sharer* is based on Conrad's time in command of *Otago.* He resigned his command at the end of March 1889 in order to visit Europe and meet with Uncle Tadeusz. The owners of *Otago,* the Black Diamond Line of Henry Simpson & Sons, Port Adelaide, were extremely complimentary in their letter responding to the 31-year-old Polish captain's resignation.

He loved the unique solitude of the ocean:

> The true peace of God begins at any spot a thousand miles from the nearest land.
>
> Joseph Conrad *The Secret Sharer*

During the long periods at sea he became bored, and decided to try his hand at writing. His experiences under sail, those he sailed with, and the many exotic places he visited as a sailor, provided Conrad with material for his books. In the autumn of 1889, after returning to London, and while living in Bessborough Gardens beside the River Thames at Pimlico, Conrad started writing *Almayer's Folly,* while continuing his quest for another command.

In 1890 he travelled to Warsaw and Lubin to meet with relatives. On 16 February he arrived at the snow-covered Ukrainian village of Kazimierówska, where he stayed with Uncle Tadeusz for two months, meeting many relatives, as well as Babrowski's neighbors and friends. In late April, Conrad travelled from Poland to Brussels, where he visited the Belgian Society for Commerce in the Upper Congo, with whom he had had discussions before his visit to Poland. The company offered him immediate command of their steamship, *Florida,* which he accepted, news having just reached them that her Danish captain had been murdered by local tribesmen.

On 10 May Conrad embarked on *Ville de Maceio* at Bordeaux. His voyage was a tortuous one, and unlikely to have been a good experience. A fellow passenger,

Prosper Harou, described a rather dismal picture of expatriate life in the Upper Congo: only seven per cent of those recruited by the company completed the three-year contract; about 60 per cent resigned within six months, and the remainder died from disease, heat exhaustion, or were sent back to Europe because they were unable to cope with the climate of Equitorial Africa.

Conrad spent less than a year in the Congo Free State; he returned to Europe because of ill health. For him the climate, tropical diseases, and witnessing the exploitation of the native Congolese was a nightmarish experience. Conrad afterwards supported the campaign started by the distinguished journalist Edmund Dene Morel and Roger Casement against the cruel treatment of Africans by Belgian colonists. The experience provided Conrad with the material for *Heart of Darkness*, acclaimed as his finest work. The successful film *Apocalypse Now*, directed by Francis Ford Coppola, is reputed to be an adaptation of Conrad's *Heart of Darkness*.

The 1890s provided Conrad with fewer opportunities to continue as a ship's master. Sail was giving way to steam. Conrad did two round trips to Australia as first mate aboard the highly reputable passenger clipper *Torrens*, commanded by Captain W H Cope.

Torrens, at 1,276 tons, was the largest ever and the last composite clipper ship built. She was launched onto the River Wear at Sunderland in October 1875 from the yard of James Laing. The construction was supervised by her first captain, Henry Robert Angel, who had a substantial interest in her; Angel's son, Falkland, became her commander in 1896. Reputed to have been Joseph Conrad's favorite ship, *Torrens* was beautifully designed; she had excellent sailing qualities, reaching a speed of 18 knots at times, and logged 365 miles in one 24-hour run when under full sail. She carried six boats. Basil Lubbock considered her the finest of the composite clippers; and she was also a favorite of Harold Underhill. *Torrens* was the flagship of the Elder Line and sailed between Plymouth and Port Adelaide, carrying mostly emigrants out and wool back. In 1899 *Torrens* collided with an iceberg near the French Crozet Islands, located at 46°S in the Indian Ocean, and lost her foremast, bowsprit, jib boom, and figurehead. Repairs were carried out after she was dry-docked in Adelaide. In 1903, she was sold to Italian owners and in 1910 was broken up and her timber sold for firewood.

In March 1893, on the return leg of Conrad's second voyage to Australia, *Torrens's* first officer befriended a number of passengers. One was John Galsworthy of *Forsyte Saga* fame, whom Conrad regaled with accounts of his voyages and travels in many parts of the world. Unlike Conrad, who was already writing although he intended continuing with his seafaring career, Galsworthy, who was keenly interested in literature, had not considered the idea of making writing his career. He had studied law at Oxford, but had no wish to become a barrister. He was returning from Samoa, where he had hoped to visit Robert Louis Stevenson, but to no avail.

Galsworthy was impressed by Conrad's abilities as a seaman, and this voyage from Australia in the last days of the wind driven passenger ships with their unique crews, is reputed to have prompted Galsworthy to take up a literary career. In his first work, *The Doldrums,* the first mate, Armand, was modeled on the future great fiction writer he had befriended. Much later, shortly after Conrad's death, Galsworthy penned reminiscences of his short voyage from Sydney to Cape Town aboard *Torrens:*

> He was a good seaman, watchful of the weather, quick in handling the ship; considerate with the apprentices—we had a long, unhappy Belgian youth among them, who took unhandily to the sea and dreaded going aloft; Conrad compassionately spared him all he could. With the crew he was very popular; they were individuals to him, not a mere gang; and long after he would talk of this or that among them, especially of old Andy the sail-maker: 'I liked that old fellow, you know.' . . .
>
> For Conrad had commanded ships, and his subordinate position on *Torrens* was only due to the fact that he was still convalescent from the Congo experience which nearly killed him. Many evening watches in fine weather we spent on the poop. Ever the great teller of a tale, he had already nearly twenty years of tales to tell. Tales of ships and storms, of Polish revolution, of his youthful Carlist gun-running adventure, of the Malay seas, and the Congo; and of men and men; all to a listener who had the insatiability of a twenty-five-year-old.
>
> At Cape Town, on my last evening he asked me to his cabin, and I remember feeling that he outweighed for me all the other experiences of the voyage. Fascination was Conrad's greatest characteristic—the fascination of vivid expressiveness and zest, of his deeply affectionate heart, and his far-ranging subtle mind.

It was the sea that gave Conrad to the English language, it had been enshrined for him, as a boy in Poland by Charles Dickens, Captain Marryat, Captain Cook and Franklin the Arctic explorer.

I first re-encountered Conrad some months after that voyage when we paid a visit together to *Carmen* at Covent Garden Opera. *Carmen* was a vice for both of us. It was already his fourteenth time of seeing that really dramatic opera. The blare of Wagner left him as cold as it leaves me; but he shared with my own father a curious fancy for Meyerbeer.

John Galsworthy, *Reminiscences of Conrad*

Following his voyages on *Torrens*, Conrad's professional sailing career came to an end. Uncle Tadensz Bobrowski died on 10 February 1894, bequeathing Conrad 15,000 roubles, a legacy that enabled him to devote his time to writing.

The poet and novelist John Masefield was also enchanted by the sea and the great sailing ships of the day. John Edward Masefield, the third of six children, left Warwick School with the intention of becoming an officer in the merchant navy and enrolled on the training ship *HMS Conway* at Liverpool. At the age of sixteen he joined the four-masted barque, *Gilcruix*, on a voyage round Cape Horn to Chile. During the voyage, Masefield became aware that being a sailing ship apprentice was not for him; he was prone to debilitating seasickness and was sent home DBS, the acronym for Distressed British Seaman.

Shortly afterwards Masefield undertook another voyage across the Atlantic but on arrival he jumped ship. After travelling rough around the United States, he returned to New York where he worked as a bartender in Greenwich Village, and afterwards in a factory at Yonkers. During his time in New York he read avidly. He returned to England in July 1897, intending to write poetry. Back in London he obtained work as a clerk and began writing.

In 1900 Masefield met the poet William Butler Yeats. Yeats introduced him to fellow Irishman, the author and playwright John Millington Synge, and other literati. Masefield gave up his job to write full-time in 1901. His collections, *Salt Water Ballads* published in 1902 and *Ballads* in 1903, quickly became popular and established his reputation as a poet.

* * *

Advances in steel-making were taking place at the time. The Siemens process of 1863 meant that large-scale production of consistently high quality steel suitable for shipbuilding became a reality. Cast iron had a high carbon content whereas wrought iron had practically none. Steel, with moderate carbon content, had the hardness of cast iron combined with the malleability of wrought iron. The main shortcoming of the Bessemer process, the method of producing large quantities of steel at low cost devised by Sir Henry Bessemer in 1852, was the difficulty in ensuring a consistently high quality metal because of the rapid manufacturing process.

Sir (Charles) William Siemens, who developed the regenerative furnace, had left Germany as Karl Wilhelm Siemens to come to England as agent for the Berlin firm of Siemens & Halske. In 1847, Siemens & Halske started a small factory at Millbank, not far from the Palace of Westminster. Afterwards, William moved its operations to a six-acre site at Charlton in Kent where, with his brothers Werner and Karl Heinrick, he founded the famous engineering firm of Siemens and employed 2,000 workers. They were later joined by Alexander Siemens, an electrical engineer and son of a cousin of the Siemens Brothers; Alexander had been wounded during the Franco-Prussian War of 1870–1871 and was awarded the Iron Cross for bravery.

Sir William, an electrical engineer, inventor, metallurgist, and very successful businessman, came from a German family of scientists and engineers: his brother Ernest Werner von Siemens created the Berlin electrical engineering firm of Siemens, and developed and pioneered the electromagnetic generator, electric traction, and electroplating; Heinrich applied the open-hearth furnace principle to glass-making and partnered William in creating the regenerative furnace, where products of combustion were led from the furnace through a chamber lined with refractory brickwork; the heat was transferred to the bricks instead of passing directly to the chimney; when the chamber became sufficiently hot the stream of combustion products was switched off, and the air supply to the furnace was drawn through it so that the air was hot when it reached the fuel in the furnace. A continuous process was established by using two chambers alternately. The process was further refined by using gas as fuel and bringing it through the chamber so that it too arrived for combustion at a very high temperature. Siemens' regenerative furnace was first used in 1857 for processing steel. In time, it was used for a number of manufacturing processes, particularly glass making. A modification of the regenerative process was used in blast furnaces.

Steel production was revolutionized by William Siemens, by both the 'Siemens-Martin' method of melting a mixture of wrought iron and cast iron on an open hearth, and his 'Siemens' process of making steel from iron ore. The latter was first used in the mid 1860s and, within twenty years, millions of tons of high quality Siemens steel was being produced throughout the world.

Sir William made a number of other significant contributions to scientific and industrial developments, including the laying of telegraph cables across the Atlantic and to India, the latter in conjunction with Werner's Berlin firm. He designed an advanced electric generator and was one of the first to suggest the transfer of electrical energy by transmission. He pioneered the use of electricity in locomotion with the building of the Portrush Railway in 1883. Sir William took out more than 150 British patents during his life. He was elected FRS in 1862, and was President of the British Association in 1882.

The Chinese were the original inventors of high quality steel. The process that they devised two thousand years before was similar to the Siemens method; they mixed wrought iron and cast iron, and subjected the combination to very high temperatures in a furnace; the cast iron melted first and penetrated the wrought iron, the two eventually blending to produce uniform steel suitable for sickle and saber blades.

The combined strength and malleability of steel made it an ideal material for the construction of ships: it was lighter than iron, thus enabling larger cargoes to be carried; steel ships were more likely to survive if they collided with other ships, or went aground, because steel would distort rather than fracture. The net tonnage of a ship with an iron hull was 50 per cent of the gross tonnage, whereas a steel vessel's net tonnage was 40 per cent.

In Britain steel had almost completely replaced iron for shipbuilding by 1880. Steel sailing ships increased steadily in size. Steel masts, yards, and stays increased the strength of the standing rigging, and this in turn improved the sailing potential of clipper ships and clipper barques. During the shipping boom of the early 1890s, large steel vessels, the great sailing juggernauts of the ocean, were launched, and continued to be built into the early years of the 20th century. They were magnificent sailing vessels with steel hulls, masts, and yards. These ocean carriers, laden with cargoes of up to eight thousand tons, clipped along before the wind.

European iron and steel clipper carriers dominated the long distance ocean routes in the early years of the 20th century, trading mostly in grain, coal, iron, nitrate, and nickel ore. The tonnage registered in Liverpool alone amounted to three times the overseas tonnage of the United States; France was operating a large number of 'Long Couriers;' and large German four and five masters were dominating the Cape Horn route to Chile and Peru. German shipyards were slow to adopt iron for the building of sailing ships, although they afterwards built a number of really impressive steel clipper barques. France was originally slow to start building metal sailing ships, but, by the turn of the 20th century, significant steel sailing ship production was taking place, mostly at the Brittany port of Nantes on the Loire.

> . . . and even I, looking at the high masts, saw or imagined, the geography which had been scantily dosed to me at school gradually taking substance under my eyes.
>
> James Joyce, *Dubliners*

The largest fleet of iron and steel ocean carriers registered in Dublin was owned by Messrs Richard Martin & Co. Sir Richard Martin, the company's managing director, purchased his first ship in 1881. Martins' ships were mostly engaged in the Californian and Australian trades. The fastest, finest, and most beautiful clipper ship owned by the Martin family was *Dunboyne*.

> In July, 1926, I was sailing across from Hamble to Ryde in order to race. It was a beautiful day and a nice southerly breeze was blowing. To my astonishment I noticed a white painted full-rigged running up the west channel under full sail. She passed the Thorn Knoll Buoy and it was not until she was abreast of the North Thorn that she made any attempt to take in sail, although she would shortly have to round the Calshot lightship and head up the narrow channel of the Southampton Water.
>
> Suddenly, as I was looking, a crowd of black figures appeared in her rigging, and as they swarmed aloft her royal, topgallant and topsail halyards were let go, and the sails hauled up by the spilling lines. In another moment her yards were black with men, and, as it seemed to me watching, in less than five minutes her upper sails were furled, her courses hauled up, and she was all ready to receive the hawser of an attendant tug.
>
> Basil Lubbock *The Last of the Windjammers*

The sailing ship encountered by Lubbock in the Solent on that July day was the Swedish Navy's magnificent sail training ship *af Chapman*, once Martins' treasured *Dunboyne*.

Dunboyne, an iron-hulled three-masted clipper ship, was built at the small harbor of Whitehaven in Cumbria. The keel was laid down in 1885 according to the shipbuilder's account, as a means of keeping the yard open during a slack period, to provide work for key craftsmen and apprentices. She had been on the stocks for three years when she was purchased by Charles Martin and named *Dunboyne* at her launching on 28 February 1888. Martins' paid £14,995 for their new clipper; she was 1,350 tons register and 243 feet long. On Good Friday 1889, *Dunboyne* set sail on her maiden voyage to Portland, Oregon, with a cargo of Workington steel rails for the American railroads.

Captain John O'Neill, a Dubliner, assumed command of *Dunboyne* at the time of her launching, and commanded her until 1904. Under O'Neill's command, *Dunboyne* was an excellent passage maker, logging 16 knots at times: on her second outward voyage in 1889, she reached Sydney 84 days out from Liverpool, and in 1891 reached Port Pirie 84 days out from Sunderland. *Dunboyne* made a number of passages from ports in the American Northwest to Europe in just over 100 days. O'Neill married Kathleen O'Flaherty shortly before he assumed command of *Dunboyne* and she accompanied him on his voyages. Their first child was born on board but died when en route to Sydney in 1891 and was buried at sea. Their other children were born on board and spent much of their early years at sea.

At the turn of the twentieth century *Dunboyne's* grain-carrying capacity of 2,070 tons was considered uneconomical in the trade, and, twenty years after she was launched, she was sold for £3,625 to Leif Gundersen of Porsgrund, Norway. During his ownership, *Dunboyne* was commanded by Captain L O Hamre, and retained her original name. In 1915 she was acquired by Götenburg's Swedish Rederiaklieb Transatlantic Company for £7,500 and renamed *G D Kennedy*. During the following eight years she carried cargo while also acting as a cadet training ship; the company operated ocean-going steamships and acquired the former *Dunboyne* to train their future officers. In addition to the normal crew, *G D Kennedy* took 30 boys and instructors on voyages round the world, sailing a total of 200,000 miles on ten voyages, and logging 15 knots at times.

In November 1923, *G D Kennedy* was purchased by the Royal Swedish Navy for 128,000 kroner and named *af Chapman*, after the well-known Swedish naval

af Chapman formerly *G D Kennedy* (Allan C Green)

architect, Frederick Henrick af Chapman. As a sail training vessel, she provided accommodation for 200 naval cadets and embarked on a number of blue water cruises that took them to many of the world's major ports. The Navy's *af Chapman*, with her attractive clipper rig, her shapely white hull, and her smart shipshape appearance, attracted favorable attention wherever she went. After about twelve years her hull begun to leak and in 1937 she was laid up.

During World War II, *af Chapman* served as a training barracks for naval personnel. In 1947, she was saved from the breaker's yard when the City of Stockholm bought her. Since then, this beautiful sailing vessel, one of a few surviving clipper ships and the finest Irish-owned sailing ship, is the sole survivor of thousands of sailing craft built on the Cumberland coast; she remains afloat in Stockholm harbor, acting as a youth hostel.

Martins' largest vessel was the 2,510-ton steel four-masted barque *Fingal*, built by Harland & Wolff, and launched onto the River Lagan in 1883. *Fingal,* the flagship of Martins' fleet, was referred to as a 'floating warehouse' with a capacity for carrying 4,000 tons of grain. From 1908 to 1910 *Fingal* was under the command of Captain O'Neill. In 1910 *Fingal* was sold to a Norwegian shipping firm. She changed hands again in 1916 when she became the Swedish *Hugo Hamilton*. Not long afterwards, on 9 December, 1916, she sailed from Caleto Buena, about 25 miles north of Iquique, Chile, under the command of Captain Henric Henricsson, with 3,800 tons of nitrate bound for Götenburg, by way of the Panama Canal. In the North Atlantic, about 100 miles north-west of Ireland's Malin Head at 55°45'N 12°10'W, *Hugo Hamilton* was sunk by u-Boat *U-81,* and became one of the very many sailing ship casualties of the Great War.

Martins' owned another fine clipper ship, *Antrim.* During her six years with the company, *Antrim* was commanded by Captain R F Martin. She then passed into German hands and was renamed *Emelie,* before going under the Norwegian flag. She later sailed under the Russian flag, as *Asia.* In 1915 *Asia* went missing without trace.

CHAPTER 8

Grain, Nitrate and Nickel Ore

> There must be few more thrilling sights than a large square-rigged ship in full sail. These magnificent vessels, almost seeming alive, engineless working ships carrying heavy bulk cargoes of nitrate, coal, guano or grain, battling the storms off Cape Horn, fighting the midwinter gales of the North Atlantic, or just gliding gently in and out of harbour in a light breeze, commanded admiration, perhaps at their best almost reverence.
>
> Alan Villiers, *Voyaging with the Wind*

There was a lull in Cape Horn shipping when gold fever subsided. Later, Europe began importing grain from Northwest America and South Australia, and fertilizers such as nitrate and guano from Chile and Peru. By the end of the 19th century, industrialized Europe was importing large quantities of wheat, as well as products to increase its own food production. In addition, the French territory of New Caledonia in the South Pacific possessed huge deposits of nickel ore, a commodity highly prized by Europe's developing industries.

American wheat was exported mostly from San Francisco, Portland in Oregon, and Seattle and Tacoma on Puget Sound. Australian wheat was shipped from Spencer Gulf, a long inlet on the south coast of Australia, just east of the Great Australian Bight.

Portland in Oregon is located a hundred miles inland from the Pacific Coast of North America. Incoming ships have to negotiate the notorious Columbia River Bar, one of the most dangerous and demanding harbor or river entrances in the world, in order to get to the safe sheltered waters of the river estuary at Astoria. From there they make their way upriver. Their captains rely on the knowledge and skill of the Columbia Bar Pilots to bring them safely across the bar.

In the days of the clippers, tugs towed the ships across the bar in good weather; in stormy weather, when the winds were the prevailing westerlies, the clippers would sail across under topsails, with two men on the wheel and lookouts in the rigging, all under the supervision of a pilot and with the ship's master stationed in the mizzen rigging. Having safely crossed the bar, the clipper would anchor or moor alongside overnight. Next day the ship would be towed upriver by one of the Portland River sternwheelers, of which the tug *Oklahoma* was the most famous.

> Whites came to the Columbia very, very late.
> William Dietrich *Northwest Passage: The Great Columbia River.*

It is estimated that Native Americans lived along the Columbia River for up to eleven thousand years before the waterway was discovered by Europeans. The existence of the mighty Columbia River was unknown to American Colonists and Europeans alike until after the American Declaration of Independence. Because of its great distance from Europe, the American Northwest was one of the last coastal regions in the world to be explored, surveyed, and charted.

In 1592, Juan de Fuca, originally from the Greek island of Cephalonia, noted the break in the coastline, and in the years that followed it became known as the mythical Strait of Fuca. In 1774, Spain's Juan Perez surveyed the coast, and missed the river. On 17 August of the following year, Bruno Heceta suspected that he had found the mouth of a big river, because the water was a different color and there were strong local currents. He was unable to explore it further because his crew were too weakened by scurvy to man a longboat. Heceta named the unseen river *Rio San Roque,* and Spain laid claim to it. A couple of years later, the great English explorer Captain James Cook and his small squadron of ships sailed past the Strait of Fuca in both directions without finding, or suspecting, the presence of a river. According to William Dennison Lyman, many other British, French, and Russian expeditions missed this great river.

In 1788, by which time *Rio San Roque* appeared on Spanish charts, British trader, John Meares, assumed that the line of broken surf on the bar was the shore and expressed his disappointment, stating that no such river existed. Meares named the bay Deception Bay, and its northern rocky boundary Cape Disappointment, a name it retains to this day. Captain George Vancouver, who had served under Cook, and who in 1792 carefully explored and surveyed the coast of Northwest America in an attempt to find the Northwest Passage, also ignored the significant change in the color of the water and the surf. Vancouver, with a good ship, excellent surveying equipment, and an experienced crew, continued north and discovered Puget Sound and the large island that bears his name, Vancouver Island. He charted the inside passage that lies between the island and the mainland where the capital city of British Columbia now stands.

As Vancouver meticulously surveyed his newfound territories, he was blissfully unaware that he had made a big error by not investigating the Strait of Fuca, Meares's Cape Disappointment, and Heceta's *Rio San Roque* more thoroughly. Vancouver's sloop *Discovery* was accompanied by the armed tender *Chatham,* under the command of Lieutenant William Broughton; *Chatham* was the best equipped survey ship ever to have sailed along the coast.

Columbia Rediviva

Vancouver met Captain Robert Gray, commander of *Columbia Rediviva* of Boston, and they discussed their exploits. Gray went through his log of the previous months with Vancouver and stated that he had seen what was likely to have been a powerful river at 46°10' north latitude. He described how he had tried to enter it, but was foiled by the strength of the current; he told Vancouver that he intended to return to the area and renew his efforts to get into the river. Vancouver was dismissive and is said to have been rather patronizing to Gray, stating that he saw no point in returning to investigate the matter further.

Gray sailed south, and on 9 May 1792 he reached the strait he had failed to enter on his northbound voyage, though he had made numerous attempts to do so. The eleventh of May was a mild day with light winds and calm seas, and Gray assumed, correctly as it transpired, that there would be sufficient depth if he stayed close to the shore. He sailed *Columbia Rediviva* eastwards, with all sail set. Gray described the momentous discovery in his log book:

> . . . at ten o'clock found myself in a large river of fresh water, at a point almost twenty miles from the ocean. *Columbia* moved another fifteen miles up the channel the next day.

Gray had discovered a hitherto unknown great river. He named it 'Columbia' after his ship, and laid claim to the Columbia River on behalf of the United States. His overnight anchorage was a cove with deep water on the north side, where the river is nine miles wide; later it became known as Gray's Bay. Gray bestowed the name Adams on the southern cape, and the northern one he named Hancock. The presence of a big river somewhere on the west coast of America was suspected, but its discovery by a United States sailing ship and her captain was to have significant consequences for the balance of power in the world during the centuries that followed.

Shortly afterwards, Gray encountered the Spanish captain Bodeg Quadra for the second time, and gave him a chart he had drawn. Quadra later met Vancouver and told him of the discovery and gave him Gray's chart. Vancouver directed Lieutenant Broughton to return to the Strait of Fuca and proceed upriver as far as possible. On 21 October, Broughton crossed the bar of the Columbia River, a particularly demanding task as the soundings were variable and the channel difficult to locate.

Twenty miles from the open sea, he left *Chatham* and proceeded upriver by cutter for a hundred miles to a place he named Fort Vancouver, located on the north bank of the Columbia River not far from Portland. The fort subsequently became the town of Vancouver. Broughton was impressed by the size and extent of this great river that was teeming with salmon and had trees reaching hundreds of feet high on each bank. The place where the Willamette River joined the Columbia River was considered by Broughton to be exceptionally beautiful and he gave it the name 'Belle View Point.' The river bank was populated by people who got around in dugout cedar-log canoes; at one place, fifty canoes that had occupants who were armed with bows and arrows, put out to intercept Broughton; they put their weapons down when one of Broughton's crew demonstrated a musket!

Chinook Indians were the indigenous inhabitants of the banks of the Columbia River. They were a peaceful people who depended on fishing and trading, and lived in villages on the banks of the river from its source in British Columbia and Washington State to the sea. What is now called Sauvie Island, the largest island on the river and located just north of where Portland stands today, was the power base of the Multnomah tribe. The Multnomah held an annual fair, where tribes from upriver and downriver joined those from the valleys, mountains, and beaches. They would exchange goods, race horses, gamble, and generally have a good time. The island was then named Wapato, after the palatable and

nutritious onion-like root plant that grew
along the banks of the Columbia. The
wapato bulb, about the size of an egg and
resembling a potato, was harvested by
people in canoes who would get into the
shallow water by the river bank and
loosen the bulbs with their feet. It was a
nutritious and fairly plentiful food, and
an important item of trade. In addition to
the wapato bulb, fish, particularly salmon,
provided the staple diet for those living
along the river.

Broughton charted the Columbia River
from Fort Vancouver to the sea and
claimed the land for Britain. The first trading vessel to arrive on the Columbia was

Captain Robert Gray

encountered by Broughton on his return journey to the sea. The schooner *Jenny*
had presumably been told about the opportunities for trade by Gray. Thirteen
years later, Meriwether Lewis and William Clark would lead the first white men
down the Columbia River to the Pacific Ocean, using Lieutenant Broughton's
detailed map of the river's lower reaches.

Gray returned to Boston where he announced his discovery; later he described
how the news was received with indifference. Captain Robert Gray continued his
career as a seafarer, although he never returned to the Pacific Northwest. In 1806,
while on a voyage to South Carolina, he died of yellow fever. Afterwards Gray's
widow applied to the United States Congress for an allowance on account of her
husband's discovery, but her claim was rejected.

In 1819 the United States claimed Oregon, the area around the Columbia River,
as its territory. The US did not want Britain or Spain, either of which could have
had a claim on it, or Russia, to establish colonies there. Britain and Spain relinquished their claims in favor of the United States. In 1825 Britain and the United
States agreed a joint occupation treaty of 'Oregon Country,' and until 1839 the
only law in the state was the rules of the Hudson's Bay Company. The Hudson's
Bay Company, with its headquarters in Canada, is the oldest commercial corporation in the world. The company was incorporated by royal charter in 1670 as: 'The
Governor and Company of Adventurers of England trading into Hudson's Bay.'

* * *

Sunset and Evening Star,
And one clear call for me!
And may there be no moaning of the bar,
When I put out to sea,

But such a tide as moving seems asleep,
Too full for sound and foam,
When that which drew from out the boundless deep
Turns again home.

Twilight and evening bell,
And after that the dark!
And may there be no sadness of farewell,
When I embark;

For tho' from out our borne of Time and Place
The flood may bear me far,
I hope to see my Pilot face to face
When I have crost the bar.

Alfred Lord Tennyson, *Crossing the Bar*

The notorious bar at the entrance to the river was the reason for the lack of urgency in colonizing the Columbia basin: powerful opposing forces of water created inhospitable, confused, unpredictable, and dangerous waters; the huge volume of river water flowing into the sea, meeting the incoming Pacific swell over a shallow sand bar, was compounded by constantly changing tidal streams. Fresh water is present up to ten miles out from the river mouth, so powerful is the flow of the river. When whipped into frenzy by a storm, the Columbia River entrance is the worst in the world.

> The sea at all times breaks furiously, the surges dashing to the height of the mast head of a ship, and with the most terrific roaring. Vessels have not infrequently to stand off shore until the crews have suffered extremely for food and water. This circumstance

must ever form a barrier to permanent settlement there.
John Townsend, American Anthropologist (quoted by Dietrich)

Crews of Hudson Bay Company ships dreaded having to enter or leave the Columbia River. They often had to stand off for days or weeks on end, waiting for suitable conditions to cross the bar and enter the river; the company's barque *Cowlitz* had to wait 80 days off the bar for calm weather before she could enter the river. Two of 35 ships the Hudson Bay Company brought there were wrecked, with the loss of 28 sailors and traders. In 1810, John Jacob Astor chartered the ship *Tonquin*, commanded by Captain Jonathon Thorn, to carry his fur traders from New York to the Columbia River. Astor started out in the fur trade and afterwards became a financier and one of the first American business tycoons. During the voyage, friction developed between Thorn and the fur traders. Severe squalls and high seas were churning up the waters of the bar when *Tonquin* arrived off the Columbia River entrance on 22 March 1811. But Thorn insisted on sending an experienced young sailor named Fox, with four inexperienced traders, to sound the foaming channel ahead of *Tonquin*. Fox and the boat crew initially resisted, but Thorn ordered them into the boat, and the five were never seen again; as they were leaving the ship one of the four traders, Alexander Ross, stated that his uncle had drowned there a few years earlier and now he was going to join him.

The following day the wind died and Thorn decided to take *Tonquin* across the bar into the river. A pinnace, with five crew under the command of a sailor named Aiken, was sent ahead to make soundings of the channel. On reaching an area of raging surf, where the outflowing river and incoming tide clashed, *Tonquin* overtook the pinnace which had got caught in the foaming water and overturned with the loss of three more crew, two from drowning, and one who made it ashore but died from hypothermia. *Tonquin* received a severe buffeting and narrowly escaped being driven aground and wrecked on the bar, before she made her way into the river estuary. The ship was in no danger when she was off the bar; it was Thorn's overbearing attitude and impatience that cost the lives of eight men.

The United States Navy lost two ships on the bar: *Peacock* in 1841, and *Shark* in 1846. In 1853 the barque *Oracle*, inward bound with building material and construction workers for the new Cape Lighthouse, went aground on the bar and was pounded to pieces by the breaking seas.

During an expedition in 1839, led by Lieutenant George Wilkes on behalf of the United States Government, the sloop-of-war *Peacock* strayed out of the channel and foundered on the spit, subsequently named 'Peacock's Spit.' The purpose of Wilkes's squadron was to survey the Columbia and others rivers in Oregon. Before the loss of *Peacock*, the squadron consisted of six ships: two ships-of-war, a brigantine, a supply ship, and two schooners. After the loss of *Peacock*, Wilkes considered the entrance of the Columbia River so dangerous that he would in future sail north to Puget Sound and return overland from there to reach the river.

Wilkes and his crew carried out a detailed survey of the Columbia River from Walla Walla, about 300 miles inland, to Astoria. Wilkes's survey had far-reaching consequences for the subsequent borders of the Unites States. On his return to Washington, Wilkes reported that the Columbia River was impossible to enter for two-thirds of the year, difficult at other times, and he advised against locating a naval base on the river because of the danger and difficulties crossing the bar. In subsequent negotiations with the British, the Americans insisted on having access to Puget Sound so that their naval ships would have safe anchorages and harbors in the American Northwest; and in the Oregon Treaty of 1846, both nations agreed on the 49th parallel as the boundary between the United States and Canada.

Mexico ceded California in 1848; this and the Oregon Treaty established the western seaboard of the United States, consolidating Gray's original discovery and claim on the Columbia River on behalf of the United States. The river itself would form the boundary between the State of Oregon in the south, and Washington State in the north, the latter extending to the Canadian border.

Writing at the turn of the twentieth century, Lyman stated that without Oregon the United States would probably not have acquired California, and without a Pacific coast the United States would have inevitably been a second class world power, and prey to European intrigue.

Despite its high latitude, the American Northwest is relatively warm in midwinter due to the effect of the warm Japan Current on the Pacific coast, similar to that of the Gulf Stream on Northwest Europe. The Cascade Mountains divide the area into a humid western part with an annual rainfall of 40–50 inches, and a dry eastern part. In the 1840s much of the western part was clothed in dense forests that extended to the banks of the Columbia, including the area where Portland now stands. The Columbia River rises in Lake Bright in British Columbia and flows 1,400 miles to enter the ocean between the long spit of Point

Adams to the south and the rocky headland of Cape Hancock seven miles to the north. By 1900, Point Adams and Cape Hancock were both surmounted by a lighthouse marking the northern and southern limits of the river entrance.

> All other waters have their time of peace,
> Calm, or the turn of the tide or summer drought;
> But on these bars the tumults never cease,
> In violent death this river passes out.
>
> John Masefield, The River

It is not surprising that the bar across the mouth of the Columbia River, with huge seas breaking over its extremities, earned an appalling reputation. But a channel that extended across the bar was discovered; this was about two-and-a-half miles wide and had a depth of 21 feet at lowest tides. It would allow the largest ships of the time to gain access to the river and to Portland, provided there were skilled and reliable pilots available to navigate through it. Later, the shallower parts of the channel over the bar and between Portland and Astoria were deepened, enabling ships of up to 26-foot draft to travel freely between the ocean and Portland.

The earliest known pilot was a local Indian named Comcomly. He, in a ceder dugout canoe, guided ships engaged in the fur trade. Captain George Flavel began piloting ships across the bar in 1846, and was granted a licence in December 1851. For the following 25 years Flavel was in charge of pilotage. He would only recruit experienced master mariners to act as Columbia Bar pilots, a practice that continues to this day.

Portland was then located on the west bank of the Willamette River just south of where the Willamette flows into the Columbia River. With its deep water anchorages and accessibility to the Pacific Ocean, Portland is ideally located for the export of agricultural goods from the Northwest region of the United States. The city itself is set in a pleasant background, with hills rising to the west, and a large expanse of level countryside extending eastwards against a backdrop of mountain tops in the distance.

In 1844 two New Englanders, one from Boston and one from Portland, Maine, opened a store on the west bank of the Willamette River and filed a claim for 640 acres of surrounding land. To name the area, they tossed a coin: Portland was chosen rather than Boston.

The arrival of the Northern Pacific Railroad in 1883, linking the Pacific Northwest to the eastern United States, was a milestone in Portland's development: wheat began to arrive in Portland by rail from the prairies of Oregon and south Washington, and from as far away as Idaho and Montana.

By the beginning of the 20th century, Portland had straddled the Willamette River and was booming. A place that fifty years earlier was a clearing used by Chinook Indians as a staging post for their travels along the Columbia and Willamette rivers, had grown to a city of about 200,000 people. At the time, the average wealth in Portland ranked it the third wealthiest city in the United States.

By then the region had one of the most extensive and well-equipped railroad networks in the world. Portland itself was served by a network of local lines, many of them electric, serving the urban areas, nearby towns, and the wheat-producing prairies. Four transcontinental railroads, Union Pacific, Northern Pacific, Great Northern, and Southern Pacific served the city. By 1907, a new railroad along the north bank of the Columbia River was nearing completion, and Portland was shipping more grain than anywhere else in the world. Big wind-driven square-rigged clipper carriers were transporting grain from Portland to the outside world. South Australia and the Pacific Northwest of the United States provided wheat for Western Europe. In 1907 a total of 1,220 ocean-going ships, registering a total tonnage of 1.7 million, loaded about 3.5 million tons of cargo, mostly lumbar, wheat, and flour. Foodstuffs, including 18 million bushels of wheat, valued at over $10 million, were exported from Portland that year. Grain was measured in bulk, with a bushel representing approximately 36 litres.

Cultivation of wheat in the United States became highly mechanized in the second half of the 19th century. The extensive prairie wheatlands were harvested by convoys of combine harvesters; each machine was pulled by a large team of horses. When the time came to prepare the land for sowing, at least five teams of four horses, each team pulling a large plough, would turn the prairie sod. At the beginning of the 20th century, steam traction engines began to replace horses for drawing harvesters, and gasoline powered tractors were also making an appearance, although they were expensive to maintain and unreliable.

Astoria was also booming. The town had about 15,000 permanent inhabitants and an extra 5,000-6,000 people during the fishing season. Up to 10,000 of mostly Italian, Sicilian, Scandinavian, Russian, and Greek migrants were engaged in fishing at the mouth of the river, where 30–40 million salmon were caught annually on the Oregon side alone, and large Chinook salmon taken from the

Columbia River would average 50–60 pounds in weight. Canning and drying salmon was the big local industry. Canneries located in Astoria and the surrounding area produced between a quarter and a half million cases of tinned salmon each year; each case would contain 24 tins.

The mouth of the Columbia River and the bar was dangerous and there were many tragedies among those who fished there. The salmon catch was greatest as they came to the surface over the bar at night in the dark, and the best time to draw the nets was at the turn of the tide; timing was critical.

> In a fishing boat in the chill of the early morning the fishermen will frequently become bemused and drowsy and neglect the critical moment. When the tide fairly turns on the bar it runs like a mill race, and woe betide the boat that waits too long. It goes out to sea, reappearing perhaps, bottom up, in the course of the day with owners and cargo gone. Some experienced fishermen have asserted that not less than a hundred fishermen are lost each summer.
>
> William Denison Lyman, The Columbia River

Logging was another major industry along the Columbia River. Lyman describes the curious sight of a log boom at the river mouth; millions of feet of logs strongly chained together had arrived from upriver and, as he watched, the boom was being floated across the bar on its way to San Francisco.

* * *

By the 1890s places along Puget Sound, namely Port Townsend, Tacoma, and Seattle, were, in addition to Astoria and Portland on the Columbia River, thriving grain and timber exporting ports. The practice of shanghaiing was widespread and gave these ports a bad reputation. The practice continued until 1910. Port Townsend even had tunnels to support the practice; they extended from the entertainment district to the dockside. Doped men were carried down to the ships through the tunnels, and opium was smuggled in the opposite direction.

The most infamous crimp in Port Townsend was Max Levi; his runners were tough ex-boxers; and his boarding house was built on stilts over the water's edge, so that his boat could be hoisted or lowered into the house by davits. Levi would have two armed runners on each ship in order to prevent any shanghaied sailors from escaping; the runners remained there until it was time for the ship to sail.

In 1899 the German barque *Plus* arrived in Port Townsend. Her crew included two deserters from the Russian navy who were 'run off' by Norwegian Charlie and other Levi runners, with the promise of well-paid work on a local coaster. The following day the hijacked sailors found themselves outward bound on a British four-master. The accumulated pay due to them from *Plus* was forfeited, as seamen were not entitled to wages due to them if they deserted. And they would also lose two or three months pay on the ship onto which they were shanghaied because the captain would have paid 'blood money' to the crimps for his new recruits.

There was an apprentice on *Plus* named Schroder, who later became a ship's captain. He befriended an out-of-work German sailor ashore and had him signed on aboard *Plus*, where he was hidden away by the mate. Next time Schroder was ashore he was made aware that Levi's gang was out to get even with him because he had assisted his young fellow countryman to obtain a berth. As Schroder and another apprentice rowed back to *Plus*, they were intercepted by Norwegian Charlie and another Max Levi runner named Ed Sims. Schroder and his shipmate were wounded in a boathook skirmish, but Levi's men were driven off by the mate of *Plus* and his men. *Plus's* captain ended up, nevertheless, having to pay blood money to Max Levi's outfit for a crew, made up of miners, lumberjacks, and farmers, in addition to the German who had been signed on. And Schroder was warned by the local police not to set foot in Port Townsend again.

Around the same time, the captain of the Yankee ship *America*, loading at Port Townsend, was determined to bypass the crimps; he arranged for a crew to come from San Francisco. The new crew was intercepted by Levi's runners as they disembarked from a steamer in Vancouver, and brought to Port Townsend in a hired tug. There, the hijacked men were offered at the usual fee to the Yankee captain. He refused to pay and instead arranged for another crew to come from San Francisco. This time he went to Vancouver himself to collect them. When he got them back to Port Townsend, Levi's crimps, armed with rifles and revolvers, raided the ship while Norwegian Charlie and Sims threatened the officers with instant death if they interfered. Levi's other runners under Tom Newman then led the bewildered sailors at gunpoint into their boats, and took them ashore. The following day they were offered back to the Yankee skipper at $100 each. *America's* captain realized he was powerless against Levi and his gang, and paid up so that he could get to sea.

The story goes that Max Levi later became religious, but a group of seamen whom he had previously shanghaied, and who recognized the former crimp, roughed him up.

Astoria and Portland were notorious for shanghaiing. In Astoria, drinking saloons, dance-halls, and brothels were everywhere and crimping was rife. Kidnapping of sailors and lumberjacks took place all the time, particularly in the saloons, often by gangs who worked both ports. Armed guards would be placed on ships that had been supplied with crew by the crimp gang, to prevent them being shanghaied by another gang. Astoria's Police Chief in the 1890s was reputed to have been in league with the crimps. The Portland crimp, Jim Turk, shanghaied his own son because of the son's liking for drink, gambling, and women; and a crimp in Astoria is reputed to have shanghaied her own husband.

Crimping in Portland was centered in the area of Lower Burnside, between 2nd and 3rd streets, where the police were tolerant of vice, and where there was lively nightlife until dawn. The area was the location of a number of saloons: Erickson's, Fritz's, Blazer's, and House of All Nations. Nearby were boarding houses for sailors and Willamette Whiskey saloons. These were run by Irish women such as Nancy Boggs, Bridget Gallagher, and Liverpool Lizzie; the latter owned the Senate Saloon in 2nd Street. Ericksons Saloon, on the north-east corner of 2nd Street and Burnside, boasted the longest bar in the world; travellers from near and far are said to have known it as 'The Five Bars under One Roof.'

The blood money extracted from ships' captains for crew was about $60 a head in Portland. It was against the law to take sailors from one ship in port and put them on another. But this was of little concern to the crimps in Portland, as the police were normally in league with them. As soon as a ship arrived in port, crimps and their 'runners-offers' would induce or force the crew to jump ship. The ship's captain had little choice but to let his men go, though he knew he would later have to pay the usual blood money for a new crew. The inducements offered to the gullible sailors were considerable, and they fell for the bait repeatedly. After being 'run off' the sailors would be shanghaied onto another ship. Apprentices were of little value to the crimps and were left alone because they received no pay.

Some captains were strongly opposed to the corrupt and despicable system of crimping, and tried to resist it, putting themselves in great danger by doing so. Captain R F Batchelor of the British four-master *Cedarbank* was vigorously opposed to the practice. *Cedarbank* arrived in Portland with only half her complement of seamen, Batchelor having refused to buy men from crimps before he departed from Hong Kong. As soon as he had cast anchor in the Willamette River, he received a note from the crimps to send his crew ashore. He refused. When the crimps and their runners arrived alongside, he had an anchor dropped into one of their boats, holing it; its occupants had to be picked up by other crimps. Two of the crew of *Cedarbank* were arrested for having broken the law on a previous visit, even though they had never been in Portland before. Shortly afterwards Batchelor took on the crimps, but he was promptly arrested and charged with assault, battery, and attempted murder. The charge of attempted murder was dismissed, but he was convicted of assault and had to serve a month in jail. In court, it transpired that the crimp he was convicted of assaulting was a brother of the Sheriff. Batchelor had armed each of his officers with a revolver to protect the crew before he left; when he returned to his ship only one of his seamen had absconded, and a replacement had been signed on in the proper manner.

As *Cedarbank* was leaving Portland, she was followed by the sheriff and his crimping brother in a boat, demanding that Batchelor turn his ship around and return to the wharf, as they had warrants for the arrest of two of his seamen for stealing overcoats; the two in question hadn't left the ship during *Cederbank's* time in Portland. Batchelor continued down the Columbia River, shouting at his pursuers from the poop that he would look into the matter when he had crossed the bar, and they were forced to give up. Despite being manned with only five seamen and eight boys, *Cedarbank* rounded Cape Horn and arrived at Queenstown in the very good time of 99 days.

Three years later *Cedarbank* arrived in Vancouver. The local crimps received a telegram from their friends in Portland urging them to get the sailors off, and make it as difficult as possible for Batchelor to get replacement crew. Immediately that *Cedarbank* was loaded, Batchelor cast off and set sail. He lost no crew, and became one of only a small number of captains to leave Vancouver without having to pay blood money.

Larry Sullivan, an ex-boxer and gambler, was one of the more notorious of the Columbia River crimps. He opened his first boarding house at the corner of 2nd and Glisan Streets in Portland: women and alcohol were banned, reputedly on the instructions of his wife, Lucille Ayers. In October 1891, he chartered a river boat and arranged to have an orchestra, saloon-girls, plenty of free food, and liquor. He inveigled a group of waterfront down-and-outs and a 21-year-old farm boy from Aquilla, named Ernest Cook, to take a free cruise down the river. At Astoria they were put aboard *T F Oakes*, commanded by Captain Reed, a

Yankee Cape Horner that was finding it impossible to get a crew because of her reputation as a hell-ship. Once on board, the captives were driven into the hold at gunpoint and shackled, until sail was set for Le Havre. Ernest Cook finally arrived back in Portland seven years later. In 1897 Sullivan supplied a full crew, at gunpoint, to the ship *Alexander Black*. He is reputed to have extorted $117 for each man supplied, to penalize the ship's master who had complained about Sullivan's methods to the police.

Ships' masters received little support from the police; on the rare occasions that the police tried to arrest deserters in Portland or Astoria, the crimps would simply transfer them north across the river to the State of Washington, where it was not against the law to desert. Another of the crimps' tricks was to have deserters jailed for minor offences, so that when their ship had sailed they could be shanghaied onto another ship. It was also crimping practice to shanghai men directly from jail, a practice that cost Portland's Police Chief his job in 1890. He had shanghaied a man from jail onto *Sierra Blanca*, and was paid $90 by Captain Craigie. The man, a respectable citizen, was in jail on an unproved charge and later, when he returned to Portland, he was successful in having the Police Chief dismissed for shanghaiing him.

But it was Sullivan's encounter with Captain Llewelyn Rees of the four-masted barque *Morven* in 1905 that had far-reaching consequences for the practice of crimping in Portland and ports of the American Northwest. Sullivan failed to persuade Rees to run off his sailors. The story goes that a battle ensued between the third mate, boatswain, and apprentices as they tried to retrieve a couple of deckhands who were run-off into one of Sullivan's boats that had sneaked under the bow of *Morven*. The crimps and runners were pursued by Rees's men and boys in the ship's longboat. In the ensuing fight the third mate was attacked and injured by a boathook, wielded by one of the crimps. In response, the boatswain picked up his revolver hidden in the bottom of the boat and shot the two crimps dead. A writ was placed on *Morven*, and the boatswain was charged with the deaths of the crimps. Rees sued Sullivan for boarding his ship and causing a riot. It is not clear whether the boatswain was convicted: according to sailor's lore he was acquitted, although the records suggest that he was not; Rees lost the case against Sullivan. When news of the *Morven* episode reached London there was indignation, and strong protests were made to the Federal Government in Washington. Pressure was put on the authorities in Portland; and shanghaiing of seamen in Portland ceased shortly afterwards.

* * *

Chile and Peru supplied almost all of Europe's requirements for nitrate. Nitrate was first exported from Callao, near Lima in Peru, in the early 19th century; the trade started in earnest in the 1870s and 1880s, reaching a peak in the years after 1890; by then a large numbers of ships were involved in transporting nitrate to Europe. South America's west coast had been a source of copper ore for years before the nitrate boom. Copper ore was carried from the interior to the coast by pack animals known as llamas.

Sailing ships loaded cargoes of copper ore, nitrate, and guano at anchorages scattered along the 2,000 mile coast from Payta in the north of Peru to Valdiva 400 miles south of Valparaiso. The busiest nitrate ports were Callao, from where nitrate was first exported, and Iquique in the north of Chile. Callao is located about 12° south of the equator and Iquique is 13° further south. Cargoes were loaded by the ship's crews, bag by bag, a laborious, time-consuming, and costly exercise. Nitrate and guano were transported to Europe in great iron and steel ocean carriers, referred to as nitrate clippers.

The nitrate clippers sailed the toughest sea route in the world, to places that were unsuitable for steamships. South American nitrate ports were dry arid places where water and coal were expensive and in short supply; and further-more, if the weather deteriorated, steamers could not make a hasty exit because they first had to raise steam.

Outward bound carriers had to battle round Cape Horn in the face of the prevailing westerlies, often into the teeth of raging storms that made the voyages difficult and hazardous. Returning east round the Horn could be equally chal-lenging because of unpredictable storms, icebergs, and following seas, capable of overwhelming even the sturdiest sailing vessel.

On the west coast of South America, the prevailing winds and currents were difficult for the nitrate carriers. These forces favored ships sailing north from Cape Horn. The exception was the north-flowing Peru Current, which could whip them past their destination; and then it might take days, or weeks, for them to claw their way south to their intended anchorage. Sometimes captains gave up and altered course for Australia or the Pacific coast of North America in the hope of getting an easier cargo. Most nitrate clippers arrived with coal, iron rails, cement, and machinery from Britain, while others having crossed the Pacific Ocean had coal from Newcastle, NSW.

The South American nitrate ports were open anchorages off an arid and desolate coast, that would have been totally deserted were it not for the nitrate trade. Shanty towns, with narrow disorganized streets of bars, boarding houses, and fandango halls, had grown up around loading terminals and customs posts to cater for the crews of the nitrate clippers. Many of these premises were owned by seamen who had deserted ship, attracted by the cheap alcohol, or by one of the dark-eyed senoritas who had arrived from the interior to work in one of the boarding houses or bars. The other inhabitants consisted mostly of homeless deserters, pimps, and prostitutes.

Sailors would spend shore leave in the local shanty town, while the captain and apprentices went on short expeditions of two or three days at a time, exploring the wildlife along the shore and in the lagoons. The waters of this otherwise deserted coast teemed with fish of many different kinds.

Loading nitrate was a dreary task. Having arrived by rail from the desert, or been hauled down in cable cars from the hills to the shore, the nitrate, packed in 180-kilogram sacks, was taken out in lighters to anchored ships. It was stowed dry in the hold of the ship, as otherwise it would become liquid from contact with moisture, a chemical reaction referred to as deliquescence. Because nitrate was liable to shrinkage, it had to be packed carefully between layers of wood to prevent it from shifting during transportation. This packing technique was known as dunnage. There were other hazards associated with nitrate cargoes. It was potentially inflammable, and liable to catch fire during loading. A number of ships carrying nitrate cargo did catch fire and were lost for that reason. Water was the only way of quenching a nitrate fire; barrels of water were placed alongside each hold during loading. The fumes given off by nitrate were lethal to the animals and insects that inhabited the ships' holds. Because of nitrate's inflammable and explosive qualities it later became an important raw material in the manufacture of munitions.

Guano is bird excrement and gets its name from the South American Spanish word for dung. It coated many of the volcanic islands off Chile and Peru to depths of up to 200 feet. As it was an excellent fertilizer, huge demand developed for guano in Europe. The foul-smelling guano being loaded onboard in the heat of a South American day produced a yellow dust that coated the decks, yards, stowed sails, and all exposed parts of the ship; the fumes given off by the guano cargo drove the rats from the hold, and into the crew's living quarters. The yellow deposits of guano in the rigging and on deck would be washed away by the first squall encountered on the homeward voyage and the nitrate clipper would look good again.

*

The nitrate clippers used open anchorages off the coast and were in danger of being driven ashore and wrecked during sudden storms. On 22 July 1913, the 1,702-ton French barque *Ville de Dijon,* was driven ashore and wrecked with the loss of nineteen crew at Papudo, about 55 miles north of Valparaiso. The barque had arrived a week earlier with coal from Newcastle, NSW. The coastal region of Peru and Chile was subject to earthquakes, and ships were at risk of being suddenly overwhelmed by tidal waves (tsunami).

Ships that were provided with ballast sometimes had to contend with unscrupulous operators who sold and loaded it, but did not stow the necessary amount required to keep the ship upright in high winds or rough seas. Even sailing vessels with a normal amount of ballast were in danger if the ballast shifted, and this could be a problem in really bad weather. The ballast itself was not ideal; it was shingle dredged from a harbor bed and slimed over with mud, and therefore difficult to secure. The nitrate carriers would only travel short distances along the coast in ballast, and, as the weather was usually fine, poor or inadequate ballasting was not normally a problem.

A vessel that may well have been lost as a result of a ballast scam was the 2,025-ton Nantes barque, *Maréchal de Gontaut,* owned by Société Générale d'Armement L'Océan. On 26 November 1913 *Maréchal de Gontaut* left Callao in ballast, bound for Sydney under the command of Captain Huchon, and was never heard of again. It is likely that the barque was overwhelmed after her shale ballast shifted in adverse weather.

Two months before *Maréchal de Gontaut* set out for Australia, the fine 2,665-ton steel full-rigged ship *Dalgonar,* from the Southhampton yard of T B Oswald and belonging to Gracie, Beazley & Co of Liverpool, left Callao in ballast for Taltal in Chile, on what should have been a relatively straightforward offshore voyage. But *Dalgonar* encountered stormy weather and, because she was much lighter than she should have been, began to heel excessively; as a result the shingle shifted and she developed a pronounced list. Despite the best efforts of the crew who shoveled the ballast across to the weather side, it slid back each time, and soon *Dalgonar* was lying on her side. The storm continued for days as the big clipper ship lay helpless on her beam ends. Fortunately for the crew their ship did not capsize. When all attempts to reduce the list failed, it was decided to abandon ship. In the first attempts to launch a boat from the severely listing ship, Captain Isbister and three of the crew were thrown into the turbulent water and drowned.

The mate then cut the masts away and this reduced the list slightly. But the storm continued, and the slight improvement in *Dalgonar's* list was not enough to enable the crew to get clear. On the night of 10 October, the 2,685-ton four-masted barque *Loire* of Nantes, out of Iquique with nitrate for Dover, saw *Dalgonar's* distress signals and altered course to render assistance. The weather was so bad that all *Loire's* Breton crew could do was to stand by in severely stormy weather and remain in sight of the stricken *Dalgonar*, as she lay on her side threatening to capsize at any moment.

There was no improvement in the situation and *Loire's* crew waited night and day for a window in the weather that would allow them to rescue their stranded comrades. For four days, *Loire* flew the flag of the International Code of Signals that read 'I Will Not Abandon You.' Although the weather improvement, when it came, was marginal, it provided the long-awaited opportunity: *Loire's* mate, the elderly Yves Cadic, and his men maneuvered their lifeboat with great skill along-side the stricken *Dalgonar*, and took her crew off. They had to do so from the deck side, while taking care to avoid stumps of the broken steel masts, wire stays, and other debris thrashing around in the water. Then *Loire's* captain, Michel Joffré, maneuvered his big four-master with precision and picked up the rescuers and the rescued. The gallant rescue was carried out about 800 miles west of Coquimbo, Chile, at approximately 29°S 87°W.

Shortly afterwards, as *Loire* rounded Cape Horn, Yves Cadic died. He had com-manded the lifeboat that rescued the crew of the stricken *Dalgonar*, and had not recovered from that demanding ordeal. The rescue, carried out in such appalling circumstances, was long remembered as a great feat of seamanship by the captain and crew of *Loire*. Other large ships that left Callao in ballast at about the same time as *Dalgonar* disappeared without trace.

The crippled *Dalgonar* didn't sink; instead she drifted across the Pacific Ocean for months, until she went aground on Maupiti in the Society Islands. Her rusted steel hulk was still there more than fifty years later. Ten years after the rescue, *Loire* went to the breaker's yard.

* * *

Sail continued to dominate the trade in grain, nitrate, and nickel at the beginning of the 20th century. Coal for use in steamers was frequently carried on the outward voyage from Europe. The carrying of wheat, South American nitrate, and New Caledonian nickel ore to Europe was generating considerable profit and a number of very large sailing ships were launched. These windjammers, as the last of the great clipper carriers were known, were equipped with powerful winches to make sail handling relatively easy. Small steam engines, referred to as donkey engines, provided the power for the anchor chain, cargo winches, and pumps.

Some of the largest and most famous windjammers of the Horn were five-masted bulk carriers built for the nitrate and nickel trade between 1890 and 1911. *France I*, launched in 1890 and lost in 1901, was later replaced by *France II*. Four were German built: *Maria Rickmers* (1890), *Potosi* (1895), *Preussen* (1902), and *R C Rickmers* (1906). *Maria Rickmers* and *R C Rickmers* were not strictly clipper carriers, as their sails were supplemented by auxiliary steam engines. Likewise, the Danish *Kjøbenhavn,* launched from the Leith (Edinburgh) yard of Ramage & Ferguson in 1921, was not considered a true windjammer as she was also fitted with an auxiliary engine.

France I was built in 1890 by D & W Henderson & Son in Glasgow for A D Bordes of Dunkirk. She had a double-bottomed hull that enabled her to take on water ballast. On 14 March 1901 *France I*, under the command of Captain Forgeard, left North Shields on the River Tyne with a cargo of coal for Valparaiso. On 10 May, the 3,624-tonner was struck by a particularly violent pampero off the coast of South America. She was thrown on her side and listed to about 45°. In addition she sprang a leak. On 13 May *France I's* crew abandoned ship, and were picked up by the German four-masted barque *Hebe.*

In 1911, *France II* was launched by Chantiers de la Gironde of Bordeaux for the Rouen company Société des Naires Mixtes. Like *France I,* her namesake, *France II* was a five-masted steel barque with square sails on the forward four masts and fore and aft sails on the mizzen. *France II* was larger and at 5,010 tons the largest of the French sailing juggernauts, and the largest sailing ship in the world when she was launched on 9 November 1911. *France II* and the German *Preussen* were the largest merchant sailing ships ever built. *France II's* cellular double bottom was divided into sections that enabled her to take on 2,685 tons of water ballast. She originally had the benefit of a pair of auxiliary engines, but they were removed at a later date because they were unsatisfactory. *France II's* crew, numbering 45, was provided with good accommodation, state-of-the-art labor-saving devices to work her 32 sails, and an electric lighting plant; she was also equipped with wireless telegraphy. On her outbound voyages, she mostly carried coal from the Clyde to New Caledonia and returned with a cargo of nickel ore. Like the other big ocean carriers of her time, she worked many of the bulk cargo routes of the world.

France II was fitted with two 90-millimetre guns during the Great War. But on the night of 28 February 1917 it was her speed under sail and auxiliary power, aided by the darkness of the night, that saved her when she was attacked by a u-Boat off Cape Finisterre.

In April 1919 her auxiliary engines were removed and she became a true Cape Horner. On the night of 11–12 July 1922, *France II* drifted onto a coral reef off New Caledonia; her hull took a pounding and she grounded on a falling tide. The crew escaped. *France II* was abandoned by her owners. Salvaging her would not have been worthwhile because of the worldwide slump in shipping; in December 1922 her hull was sold for its scrap value of £2,000.

> They saw that the ship to windward was a five-masted, full-rigged ship. She was lying over a little, with her lee scuppers awash, and the sea was gushing from her wash-ports. She was a lofty vessel with masts 200 feet high, towering above the sea, dwarfing the 1,500 ton barque whose astonished apprentices counted forty-three sails, all set magnificently and pulling like horses. The flag at the short gaff on the aftermast was German. The name on the high flared bows was *Preussen*. As she passed and drew steadily ahead, they could read her name again on the shapely counter, and her port of registry. 'Preussen, Hamburg' they read.
>
> Alan Villiers, *The Way of a Ship*

The mighty *Preussen*, the greatest German sailing ship of all time, registered 5,081 tons and was capable of carrying 8,000 tons of cargo. *Preussen* was 490 feet long from bowsprit to taffrail; her main-yard was over 100 feet long. She carried square sails on each of her five masts, making her the only five-masted full-rigged ship ever built. Her main masts rose over 200 feet into the air, and the largest of her sails spread 3,500 square feet and weighed half a ton. Powered by 60,000 square feet of canvas, comprising 30 square sails, six on each mast, and between fifteen and eighteen fore-and-aft, *Pruessen* could reach a speed of 18 knots. Experiments on a model, carried out much later, showed that her sails had to generate over 6,000 horsepower to drive her fully laden hull through the water

Preussen

at 18 knots. The great five-master was manned by a crew of 47 officers and men.

Preussen, built for the Hamburg Flying P Line of Carl Laeisz, was launched from the yard of Johann C Tecklenborg at Geestemünde in 1902; the Laeisz Company was referred to as the 'Flying P Line' because their ships were given names with the initial 'P.' *Pruessen* was the 62nd ship built for the company. It was an exceptionally fast ship, averaging seven knots throughout her career. Captain Boye Petersen, one of Laeisz's most valued captains, was put in charge of her for her maiden voyage to Chile. The great five-master made ten consecutive trips to Chile for nitrate, making good time on both the outward and homeward voyages. *Preussen* made a profitable round-the-world trip that included calling at New York to take on a cargo of case-oil for Yokohama, and later collecting nitrate from Chile before completing the voyage. Petersen decided to relinquish command and went into retirement. He was replaced by Captain Heinrich Nissen who took *Preussen* on a single voyage to Chile with a mixed cargo and returned with nitrate. It was the great five-master's last voyage round Cape Horn.

Preussen, then the 'Pride of Prussia,' left Hamburg at the end of October 1910 with a mixed cargo including coal. The weather was bad with long dark winter nights, rain, fog, and little wind. The tug *President Lion,* towed the great windjammer down the Elbe and through the North Sea to the English Channel, passing through the Dover Strait on the fifth day out. Then the wind began to freshen, and although patches of mist persisted, Nissen decided to cast off from the tug.

It was a strange decision for the esteemed captain to make. Nissen had an impeccable record with a company that demanded the very highest standards from its captains and crews and rewarded them accordingly. Captains Petersen and Nissen were considered by the House of Laeisz to be successors of Robert Hilgendorf, the man considered by many to have been the greatest Cape Horn sailing captain of all time. Hilgendorf though he had retired by then was offered command of *Preussen,* but turned it down, as he was of the opinion that the great Windjammer of the Horn would be better under the command of a younger man. Heinrich Nissen had established his reputation commanding the 1,700-ton ship *Parchim* and the 3,784-ton five-masted barque *Potosi*; on one occasion he sailed *Parchim* 4,871 nautical miles in nineteen days, a tremendous average of just under 11 knots, and he had driven *Potosi* from Iquique at an average speed of 8.6 knots.

The busy English Channel was notorious for collisions between sailing ships and steamers, during the hours of darkness and at times of poor visibility. The Flying P Line had sanctioned the use of the tug, and the commanders of large sailing vessels would normally have availed of their tug's services to extend the tow to the wider western part of the Channel, before casting off. The sea area between Start Point in Devon and the French coast is about 100 miles wide, compared to the 20 miles between South Foreland, just north of Dover, and the French coast at Calais. Extending the tow for another 24 hours would have taken *Preussen* as far as Start Point.

As most of *Preussen's* crew were loosing and setting sail, others were setting off fog-rockets to warn other ships of her position. But before the five-master was fully under way, the forward lookout reported a steamer approaching fast off the starboard bow. It was the cross-channel ferry *Brighton,* en route from Newhaven to Dieppe. Even when the vessels were in sight of each other, *Brighton* failed to slow down, or alter course to pass astern of the sailing vessel as required by the regulations. *Brighton's* captain miscalculated *Prussen's* speed, and tried to cross her bow instead of going under her stern. The steamer, travelling fast, ploughed into the mighty windjammer, holing her badly.

The badly wounded *Preussen* managed to stay afloat because the steam pumps kept the water levels down in her flooded forward holds. She limped into

Newhaven, and having been temporarily repaired there, she set sail for Plymouth. But the winds were variable and she was forced to anchor. It was November, and a winter storm swept through the Dover Strait from the west. Nissen managed to engage tugs, but repeated efforts to tow the 11,000-ton vessel into Dover failed; one tow-rope after another parted, and the stricken *Preussen* was driven onto the rocks under the Cliffs at Dover. For three days, Nissen and his crew refused to leave the ship. The weather did not improve and *Pruessen's* crew had no choice but to abandon ship. Before doing so, a telegram was received by Captain Nissen from Kaiser Wilhelm II. It was read out to the wet, cold, and bedraggled crew who received it with three cheers:

> Deeply moved by the news of the disaster of the proud five-master *Preussen*. I desire to express to the owners my warmest sympathy. I should like a direct report regarding the result of the catastrophe and especially about the fate of the brave crew, which causes me much anxiety.

When the wind dropped, Nissen had part of her cargo discharged into lighters, but a consignment of valuable German-made pianos, destined for Chile, was lost. Later it was discovered that the mighty *Preussen* had broken her back and was beyond salvage. At the subsequent enquiry, Nissen was completely exonerated, but this must have been cold comfort to him and the House of Laeisz for the loss of their valued *Preussen*. The litigation that followed dragged on and remained unsettled at the outbreak of the Great War nearly four years later.

Although it may have been imprudent of Nissen to set sail at the eastern end of the English Channel, he was in no way to blame for the collision that ensued when the steamer *Brighton* attempted to cut across *Preussen's* bows. Captain Heinrich Nissen continued to command Flying P Line ocean carriers, including the famous four-masters *Pitlochry* and *Peking*. When he retired in 1925 he had commanded eight of Laeisz's Cape Horners during the previous 27 years.

Laeisz's Flying P Line operated sailing ships for a century starting in 1839, when its founder, Ferdinand Laeisz, acquired his first ship, the 220-ton wooden brig *Carl*. The company's involvement in the nitrate trade began in 1867 when Ferdinand and his son, Carl Heinrich, bought six wooden barques of between 450 and 500 tons: *Rosa y Isabel*, *Henrique Teodoro*, *Mercedes*, *Ricardo*, *Carolina*, and *Don Julio*, all originally built in Hamburg by the firm of Stülcken for a German company in Valparaiso. In the 1880s, the Laeiszs built a fleet of 1,000-ton, 1,500-ton and 1,700- ton full-rigged steel clipper carriers. Before long, they were operating the largest fleet of the finest sailing ships in the world, and turning in a considerable profit in the Chilean and Peruvian nitrate trade. The ships of the Flying P Line of Laeisz developed a reputation for speed, a reputation that their expanding fleet of four and five-masters would build on.

The advent of the large four-masted barque, with three masts square-rigged and fore-and-aft sails on the after mast, enabled the Flying P line to consolidate its place as the leading shipper in the nitrate trade. The first four-masted clipper barques, registering almost 3,000 tons each, were *Pisagua* and *Placilla,* both launched from Tecklenborg's Geestemünde yard in 1892. On her first voyage to Chile, *Pisagua* arrived in Valparaiso 70 days out from the Channel, and during the following eighteen years she continued to make good passages.

In the early hours of 16 March 1912, *Pisagua,* under the command of Captain R Bahm and fully laden with nitrate, was beating up the English Channel under full sail against an easterly wind; when level with Beachy Head she ran into the outward bound P&O liner *Oceana.* The liner was badly damaged, and it was decided to abandon ship. Seven passengers and a crew member were drowned because the first lifeboat to be launched capsized. The badly damaged *Oceana* was towed into shallow water, but sank shortly afterwards. It was the first time that a P&O passenger was lost in an accident at sea. *Pisagua's* bow was stove in. It was repaired, and shortly afterwards she was sold to Norwegian owners. In February of the following year, she went aground on the South Shetland Islands, Antarctica, south of Cape Horn, and became a total loss.

Captain Robert Hilgendorf assumed command of *Placilla*; he took her to Chile, arriving at her allocated nitrate anchorage 58 days out from the Channel, a time only subsequently improved on by a day, by the mighty *Preussen.*

The success of *Pisagua* and *Placilla* demonstrated the superiority of the large 3,000-ton four-masted barques in the nitrate trade, and Carl Laeisz replaced his smaller ships with similar four-masters, most of them were built by Tecklenborg, and by Blohm & Voss of Hamburg; a couple were also built in Scotland: the fast and powerful *Pitlochry* was built by Stephen & Sons of Dundee and *Persimmon*, originally named *Drumrock,* by Ramage & Ferguson of Leith. At the turn of the 20th century, the Flying P Line was one of the most successful businesses in Hamburg. The Laeisz Concert Hall, built by the family, still stands in the city.

The sailmaker was with us. 'That's just like him' he said. 'This wouldn't have happened with Captain Hilgendorf. You should have seen how he rounded the Horn in a storm; he didn't strike a single spread of Canvas.'

Günther Prien, *I Sank the Royal Oak*

Robert Hilgendorf was born in the small town of Schievelhorst on the Baltic coast in 1852, and started sailing with his father during the summer months; his father was a captain of coastal brigantines and barques sailing out of Stettin. At the age of fifteen, Robert went to sea and spent two years sailing in the Baltic and North Seas before becoming an able seaman. He was conscripted into the Imperial Navy, where he was promoted to boatswain's mate. After completing his service in the navy, he obtained his mate's certificate and returned to the

Captain Robert Hilgendorf

Baltic trade, becoming mate on the barque *Nautik*. He spent two years in the post, often in charge of *Nautik*, whose captain was very old. He then took his master's certificate. Shortly afterwards he went to Hamburg and presented himself to Carl Laeisz, who appointed him mate of the barque *Parnass*. The young Hilgendorf proved to be an outstanding officer, and in 1876 he graduated from the Officer's School of Altona. In 1881 he was given command of *Parnass*.

During the following twenty years, Robert Hilgendorf commanded Flying P Line nitrate clippers. His record as a Cape Horner was magnificent: he rounded Cape Horn 66 times; on eighteen round trips his average outward time to the Chilean ports from the English Channel was 64 days, beating westward round Cape Horn in an astonishingly consistent 7–10 days, and returning with nitrate in an average 74 days. During those twenty years, Hilgendorf sailed nine square-riggers at an average speed of 7.5 knots.

He lost one ship: *Parsifal*. Her cargo of nitrate shifted and she foundered. Hilgendorf managed to get his crew and himself safely into the boats and clear before his ship went down. He retired from the sea at the age of 50 after ten voyages as captain of the big five-master *Potosi*. He handed over command of the nitrate carrier to Captain Heinrich Nissen. After his retirement from seafaring, Hilgendorf acted as a marine surveyor and marine insurance assessor in Hamburg for 30 years. He died in February 1937; then in his eighties, he was pitched from his bicycle following a collision in a Hamburg street. When Erich Laeisz was in charge of the Flying P Line, there was one photograph on the wall of his office where pictures of company ships would normally be on display and that was of Robert Hilgendorf.

> No creation man ever achieved was more in the hands of its master than the ocean-going sailing ship. He was more than her brains, he was her *character*, her resolution, her hope of integrity.
>
> Alan Villiers, *The Way of a Ship*

After the Great War of 1914–1918, the Flying P Line of Laeisz lost their remaining ships, mostly to France, as reparation payments that Germany was required to pay by the terms of the Treaty of Versailles (1919). Erich Ferdinand Laeisz took control of the company after his brother Herbert was killed in the war, and he bought back, at knockdown prices, the ships that he had forfeited. Erich Laeisz had two new four-masted barques built: *Priwall* in 1921 and *Padua* in 1926. *Padua* was the last Cape Horner to be launched. *Priwall* and *Padua* were fast clipper carriers: in 1933 *Priwall* reached Australia 65 days out from Germany under Captain Robert Clauss; *Padua* took only one day longer when it did the trip.

There was a slump in shipping after the Great War, and most Cape Horners were laid up. The European market for South American nitrate had diminished considerably by the 1930s. By 1936, the fleet of the Flying P Line's Cape Horners was reduced to *Priwall* and *Padua*. World War II brought an end to the career of the last two clipper carriers belonging to the House of Laeisz.

The Flying P Line's highly esteemed 3,185-ton four-master *Priwall*, under the command of Captain Adolf Hauth, ended her career in a blaze of glory when she set an all-time record for a westward rounding of the Horn by a sailing ship. At the beginning of November 1938, Hauth guided *Priwall* from 50°S in the Atlantic round Cape Horn to 50°S in the Pacific in a record 5 days 14 hours, beating *Young America's* 1876 record by ten hours: *Priwall* was driven through Le Maire Strait and Drake Passage by a strong north-westerly on the beam, a favorable wind that continued until the great four-master was almost directly south of Cape Horn;

then, following a day of light easterlies, the wind veered to the south and strengthened; the last great nitrate clipper, under full sail, passed south of the Diego Ramirez Islands to reach 78°25'W, before Hauth altered course and took his ship north, driven by a southwesterly.

Priwall was in Valparaiso at the outbreak of World War II, and was presented to the Chilean Navy. She was fitted with an engine and renamed *Lautaro*. Not long afterwards she caught fire when carrying nitrate off the Peruvian coast, and was lost.

Padua spent the war in the Baltic Sea where she was used as a training ship for merchant seamen. In 1946 *Padua* was handed over to the Soviet Union and became the sail training ship *Kruzenshtern*.

Later Alan Villiers met with Captain Hauth in the town of Rendsburg, near the Kiel Canal.

> There I found him, waiting for me at the crowded railway station
> one summer day in 1968. I had not seen him before, but I knew the
> sailing-ship master at once in all the crowd. Such a man stands out,
> the strong character in his face developed through much testing of
> a sort the more ordinary citizens will never know. So I looked at
> the crowd as I walked along the platform and I saw the Priwall's
> master at a glance.
>
> Alan Villiers, *The War with Cape Horn*

The most beautiful and, according to many experts, the finest of the nitrate clippers was another German built and owned barque, *Herzogin Cecilie,* named after the Duchesse Cecilie of Mecklenburgh. The 3,242-ton four-master was launched from the Bremerhaven yard of R C Rickmers, at the mouth of the River Weser, on 22 April 1902 for Norddeutscher Lloyd; the word Lloyd was included in the company name to denote that their ships were built to Lloyds specifications. *Herzogin Cecilie's* elegant lines were matched by her capacity to carry a large cargo and first class accommodation, all on a draught of 23 feet. The hold could carry 4,000 tons. Officers, crew, and up to 60 cadets were accommodated in a deck-house that extended forwards from the poop along two-thirds the length of the deck. The floors of the two decks were hardwood laid on steel. Like other large 20th century windjammers, her steel hull was double-bottomed to take in water ballast. Her tallest masts were 200 feet high, and she was rigged with double topsails and double topgallants; none of her sails had reefs.

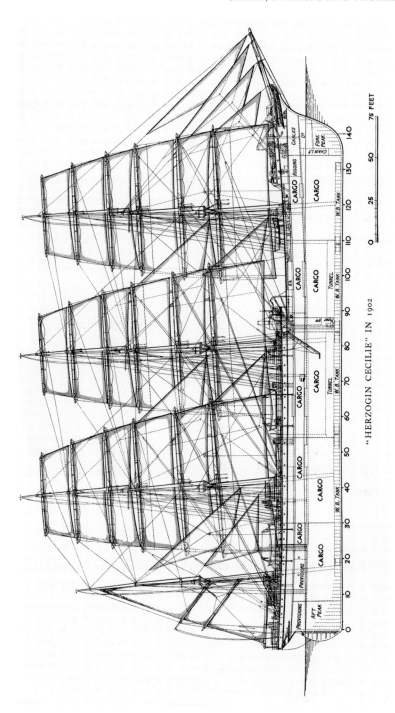

Herzogin Cecilie: Profile of the hull and the plan of the rigging

Captain Max Dietrich commanded *Herzogin Cecilie* on her maiden voyage to Astoria at the mouth of the Columbia River on a voyage that nearly ended in disaster. A pampero struck *Herzogin Cecilie* when she was off the River Plate, and within minutes her spars were carried away, her masts damaged, and her sails were in shreds. Repairs were carried out over six weeks in Montevideo, and the voyage was resumed. During the following twelve years, *Herzogin Cecilie* performed well, mostly in the South American nitrate trade, averaging about seven knots, and achieving 24-hour runs of 300 miles.

At the outbreak of the Great War, *Herzogin Cecilie* arrived at Herradura Bay, Chile, with a cargo of coal and a large number of cadets on board. The captain, Dietrich Bellehr, immediately immobilized his ship in the deepest part of the bay; he placed many essential parts of her steering gear, including the three-ton rudder, on the deck ready to be jettisoned, should an attempt be made by any of Germany's enemies to seize his ship.

As the war progressed, most of the crew left the ship and settled in Chile. In 1920, Bellehr was instructed to make *Herzogin Cecilie* ready for sea. After six years of idleness, it took time and effort to get her ready for sailing again. With no dry dock available, Bellehr managed to heel the giant barque over on one side, and then the other, by filling the ballast tanks on each side in turn. In this way, and with the help of local labor, he managed to clean most of *Herzogin Cecilie's* badly encrusted bottom. Then, with a cargo of nitrate, and a more international crew than he was used to, Bellehr set sail for Europe.

Following her arrival in Germany, *Herzogin Cecilie* was awarded to France as part of the reparation payments. Many of France's own grain and nitrate clippers were lying idle at the time and there was no use for yet another windjammer of the Horn. She was put up for sale. There was little interest in big cargo-carrying sailing ships at the time, and it began to look as though *Herzogin Cecilie* would go to the breaker's yard. Then, in December 1921, a Belgian sailing ship captain, Rubens de Cloux, bought her on behalf of Captain Gustav Erikson of Mariehamn in the Finnish Åland Islands for £4,250, about one-tenth of what she cost when new.

In 1921, about 140 square-riggers carried grain from Australia to Europe; but a decade later the number was considerably fewer. At the beginning of the Great Depression, only half the available ships were chartered. But the demand in Europe for Australian wheat soon increased. In 1931 and 1932, twenty ships obtained cargoes. By then, Australian grain was virtually the only cargo available to the last of the Cape Horn sailing ships. Seventeen of the twenty were registered in Finland; Gustav Erikson owned fourteen of them.

Erikson's venture into grain carrying was the end of an era for the clipper carrier. Without the Australian grain crop, their days as bulk carriers would have been at an end, and Erikson's sailing ships redundant. With their lower overheads when compared to steamers, sailing ships could wait for weeks off jetties adjacent to farmers' land in the Spencer Gulf for sacks of grain to arrive in small quantities.

Erikson operated his ships on low overheads: his office was a shed in the garden; the ships were uninsured; and there was no depreciation because he had bought them at scrap value. He was virtually running them for nothing on the Australian grain run. A number were four-masted barques that had previously belonged to Laeisz's Flying P Line.

He had no trouble finding suitable crew: the captains, officers and most of the boatswains, cooks, carpenters, and sailmakers were Swedish-speaking Åland Islanders. The Ålanders were gifted linguists, and Erikson's captains and officers were usually fluent in English, a requirement for the job; in addition many of the crew had a good command of English. Some of the captains were related; the two Gustafsson brothers had, between them, commanded Cape Horn sailing ships for many years. The crew was kept to the very minimum required to sail the vessel, mainly youngsters and premium-paying cadets. For farm boys on the islands, the low pay and the working conditions were better than the drudgery on the family farm for which they received no remuneration.

Filling the rest of the deck berths was easy because young people of all nationalities were willing to buy a two-year apprenticeship on a Finnish sailing ship. At the time, many European nations required their ships' officer cadets to have served in deep-sea sailing ships. It was not compulsory to serve two years; many young sailors including some girls completed one round trip and then returned to education or civilian employment. They saw it as an opportunity for a challenging adventure.

Erikson was pleased to acquire the large and beautiful four-master *Herzogin Cecilie,* and she became his pride and joy. He lavished more money and care on her than on any of his 22 other ships. His ships were colored black, as that was the cheapest paint to use, but *Herzogin Cecilie* was painted brilliant white.

After a break of almost seven years, *Herzogin Cecilie* resumed sailing the great trade routes of the high seas, and became the flagship of Erikson's fleet. Crewed by Captain Ruben de Cloux and the Åland islanders, *Herzogin Cecilie* gave of her best: her fastest 24-hour run, fully laden with cargo, was a remarkable 336 miles; she frequently reached speeds of over 18 knots. In 1928, Alan Villiers was serving aboard *Herzogin Cecilie* as a seaman when she reached Falmouth, 96 days out from Port Lincoln with 4,500 tons of grain. She was the first ship home that year and well ahead of her rivals.

In 1929 de Cloux retired and the mate took command: *Herzogin Cecilie's* new commander was Mathias Sven Eriksson, a 25-year-old Åland islander. Eriksson knew the ship well and had no intention of working her under easy sail. When outward bound to Australia in the South Atlantic in October 1934, the captain of a passenger liner, sailing in the same direction, ordered full steam ahead to bring his ship alongside so that the passengers would get a close-up view of a great clipper under sail. A gale was blowing. Eriksson set all sail and *Herzogin Cecilie* pulled ahead and reached a speed of 19 knots, a feat acknowledged by the steamer's captain who dipped his ensign and sounded his siren in tribute.

Nineteen knots was not the fastest speed recorded under Eriksson: three years earlier, while on a voyage from Wales to Finland, *Herzogin Cecilie* reached a phenomenal 20.45 knots. During an overnight sprint through the Øresund, Eriksson kept firing rockets to make steamers aware that he was about to overtake them in the dark. His crew remained on deck that night, enjoying an exhilarating experience, and anxiously watching the rigging as it stretched to breaking point. The sea opened up a path for this sailing marvel of the 20th century driven by the energy of wind on canvas, to what may have been as much as 5,000 horsepower.

On 24 April 1936 *Herzogin Cecilie* left Falmouth for Ipswich; there was dense fog off Cornwall and Devon. At about 4am, in very limited visibility due to fog and the darkness of night, this giant sailing ship struck Ham Stone Rock, was pitched into Sewer Mill Cove, and went aground at the foot of the cliffs. There was no loss of life.

The plight of *Herzogin Cecilie* caught the public imagination, and over £1,000 was collected in small donations from a sympathetic English public, as a contribution to the cost of saving the great ship; and the owner Gustav Erikson was willing to spend much more. *Herzogin Cecilie* was pulled onto the shallows of Starehole Bay in order to carry out temporary repairs, as it was thought she would be safe there. But on 17 July a heavy swell was running into the bay, and it lifted her up and bounced her down on the shingle repeatedly. In a relatively short time the four-master's hull was damaged beyond repair.

The passing of *Herzogin Cecilie* signalled the end of the Great Clipper Era. Another war was approaching, and it was only a matter of time before the few remaining wind-propelled juggernauts would vanish from the oceans of the world.

When Alan Villiers joined the former Laeisz nitrate clipper *Parma* in 1933 at Port Victoria on the Spencer Gulf, she was the only four-masted barque owned independently in Mariehamn; the other ten were Erikson's. Shortly afterwards the Scottish-built *Parma*, capable of carrying the largest cargo of any sailing vessel at that time, set sail for Falmouth with 68,000 bags (5,200 tons) of Australian wheat. The crew of 32 included two girls who had signed on as apprentices. Ruby de Cloux was the Captain's daughter, and Betty Jacobson, a Scandinavian, was also a sea captain's daughter. The average age of the deck hands was seventeen. Hilgard, an American who planned to be a naval architect, was the youngest deck hand; when he returned to school at Long Island after the voyage he was still only fifteen.

Parma had a brisk run before the prevailing westerlies of the Southern Ocean, and rounded Cape Horn without mishap, having logged 6,306 miles in 30 days. In the Atlantic, no calms were encountered and *Parma* reached Falmouth after an 83-day passage from Port Victoria, about 600 miles longer than the distance from Melbourne, and 1,000 miles further than the wool clippers had to sail from Sydney. *Parma's* 83 days was the fastest passage of an Australian grain ship in the 20th century, and a great achievement for a four-masted barque that was considered by some to be no match for a true clipper ship.

Villiers described going ashore from *Parma* at Mariehamn:

> Her tall masts disappeared, and the little steamer, bucking in a strong head sea, made me seasick. I had never been seasick under sail.
>
> Alan Villiers *Last of the Wind Ships*

The last year that a fleet of wind-driven ships carried cargoes of grain from South Australia was 1939. That year, twelve Cape Horners brought Australian grain to Europe: *Abraham Rydberg, Archibald Russell, Killoran, Lawhill, Moshulu, Olivebank, Padua, Pamir, Passat, Pommern, Viking* and *Winterhude*. Laeisz's *Priwall* was carrying nitrate from Iquique for the last time. Another sailing vessel that carried grain that year, *Kommodore Johnsen,* was not entirely wind-driven, as she was fitted with an auxiliary engine.

War was declared on 3 September 1939, and an early casualty was Erikson's four-masted barque *Olivebank*. In July she discharged her cargo of wheat at Barry in South Wales and sailed for the Baltic. On 12 September, *Olivebank* struck a mine in a German minefield off Jutland, and sank with the loss of thirteen of her crew including Captain Carl Granith.

Erikson's *Killoran* was also lost in the early part of World War II. *Killoran,* a 1,569-ton barque built in Scotland at Troon in 1905, was captured and sunk by the German surface raider *Widder*, Kapitän zur See Helmuth von Ruckteschell, on 10 August 1940 when on a voyage from Buenos Aires to Las Palmas with a cargo of corn and sugar. *Killoran's* crew was taken on board *Widder*.

The former Laeisz 1,997-ton barque *Penang* went missing in 1941 and was assumed to have foundered off Cape Horn. In 1971 the true fate of *Penang* came to light: on 8 December 1940 she was sunk without warning by *U-140*, commanded by Oberleütnant Hans-Peter Hinsch, and lost with all hands.

Cape Horn

John Kretschmer

CHAPTER 9

The Explorers

*The Horn was a sight I'll never forget. Cape Horn is not beautiful –
it's humbling. It's a brazen, rocky headland that has somehow
defied the ravages of erosion. It jauntily juts its craggy chin into the
cold blue sea, dividing the two great oceans of our planet.*

John Kretschmer, *Cape Horn to Starboard*

Before the Californian Gold Rush there were relatively few voyages round
Cape Horn: traffic was mostly limited to the occasional whaler, ships trading with
Spanish California, and ships engaged in the developing copper ore trade
between Chile and Swansea, South Wales. Ships sailing between the Atlantic and
Pacific oceans had to pass below the islands that comprise the southern tip of
South America; Cape Horn, 55°58'S, is the most southerly of the Horn islands.
Another outcrop of rocks, the Diego Ramirez Islands, lies 50 miles further south.

During the early part of the 19th century, Swansea was the foremost center for
copper smelting and non-ferrous metallurgy in the world. Copper had previously
been imported to Swansea from Cornwall, North Wales, Ireland, Spain, and
Cuba. In the 18th and 19th centuries Cornwall was the largest producer of copper
ore in the world, with production reaching a peak of 180,000 tons in 1860. Chile
also became an important supplier following the discovery of large deposits
there. In 1853, 13,000 tons of Chilean copper ore was imported into Swansea and
this increased to 30,000 tons in 1860.

Copper smelting depended on a readily available supply of fuel, and this
was provided by the nearby coalfields of South Wales. Swansea was a great coal-
exporting port, and the expression 'coal out and copper in' described the main
business of the port. Many of the Swansea copper barques were built at Prince
Edward Island, Canada.

The Vivian family, originally from Cornwall, were the best known copper
smelting entrepreneurs in Swansea; a Vivian father and son studied metallurgy

in France and Germany. The scientific society formed at Swansea in 1835, and known as the Royal Institution of South Wales, included a group of local metallurgists. During the latter part of the century, Swansea's leading role in copper smelting was in decline, as by then it had become more efficient and profitable to smelt copper ore at source and transport it as ingots.

The Dutch explorer, William Schouten, gave Cape Horn its name on 29 January 1616 when he sailed round the most southern point of South America. He was the first European to round the Horn; he named the isolated rock after his home town of Hoorn in Friesland, in the northern part of The Netherlands. Captain Schouten was a skilled navigator and he commanded a ship that set sail in June 1615 as part of an expedition led by the Dutch merchant, Isaac Le Maire. On 24 January, they found and sailed through a channel running in a southwesterly direction between Tierra del Fuego and an island they named Staten Island; the channel itself became known as Le Maire Strait. On leaving the channel, Schouten realized that he was in open sea, in water that was too deep to obtain soundings, and with no land to the south or west. As he sailed further south, he realized that he had reached another ocean when he encountered big waves: he had reached the Pacific Ocean.

Schouten continued sailing in a westerly direction through the Pacific and Indian Oceans until he made landfall in one of the Dutch colonies. There he was promptly arrested by the Dutch East India Company who confiscated his ship, its cargo, and his papers. This powerful commercial organization did not take lightly to the idea of competition in the East India trade from the much smaller enterprise of Isaac Le Maire. The local representatives of the Dutch East India Company refused to believe that Schouten had sailed past the southern tip of America.

After returning to the Netherlands Le Maire's son Jacob, who had accompanied the expedition, published a book describing the voyage and confirming the presence of a stretch of open water south of South America, connecting the Atlantic and Pacific oceans. Jacob Le Maire's book was translated into a number of languages, including English, and was widely read. His description of the voyage gave credibility to Schouten's discovery of a southern sea route to the Far East, and the Dutch East India Company was ordered by the courts in the Netherlands to compensate Schouten.

The Dutch were not the first to discover a route through to the Pacific Ocean from the South Atlantic. In September 1519, the Portuguese navigator Ferdinand Magellan set sail from the small harbor of San Lúcar, the port for Seville on the Gulf of Cadiz, in his quest for a southern channel to the Great South Seas, as the South Pacific Ocean was then known. Magellan, while in the service of the King of Portugal, had seen a chart fairly accurately depicting what would become known as 'Magellan Strait.' During 1421–1423, a Chinese fleet under Admiral Hong Bao sailed from the Atlantic through the strait on its way to Antarctica, and charted its latitude fairly accurately. A copy of Bao's chart is likely to have been the one seen by Magellan.

Magellan, sailing under the flag of Spain, led a fleet of five ships and 265 men. He first sailed to the River Plate and there he wasted time trying to find a passage, though there was no evidence of salt water to confirm a connection with the ocean. By the time Magellan's ships reached *Puerto San Julián* (San Julian) on the south coast of Patagonia at latitude 49°S, rations were low, and there was an attempted mutiny by a number of his most senior officers. Magellan dealt with the revolt by executing two of the leaders and marooning another two, one of them a priest, on the coast; the other mutineers were pardoned.

After sheltering at San Julian over the southern winter, the remaining four ships of the fleet resumed their voyage south; the fifth had been wrecked on the coast during a pampero without any loss of life. On 27 August 1520, after a three-day sail, the fleet rounded a prominent headland and entered a large inlet. It was the feast of the English martyr, Saint Ursula, and they named the headland *Cape Virgenos* after the eleven virgins who were martyred with Ursula in the fifth century; they were on a pilgrimage near present day Cologne; the number of martyrs is often quoted as 11,000. Magellan turned west into the inlet and discovered salt water and a high tidal range, indicating that he was in a channel.

For three months, Magellan sailed cautiously through the channel with the South American mainland to starboard, and an island to the south where many fires were burning. He named the island 'Tierra del Fuego.' Magellan Strait was particularly treacherous with williwaws, blizzards, rain, and poor visibility; and in addition there were two narrows, subject to dangerously unpredictable strong tidal streams. By the end of November, Magellan had negotiated the full length of the channel and passed through the islands to the west to behold a vista of open water. He named the ocean, the largest of the world's oceans, the 'Pacific Sea.'

Williwaws are sudden violent whirlwind squalls. They are the most adverse meteorological phenomenon likely to be encountered in Magellan Strait with winds reaching a speed of 100 knots. They develop from extremely cold south-westerly winds blowing from the Antarctic that become more turbulent as they encounter the elevated southern tip of America. Having crossed Tierra del Fuego and the adjacent archipelago, these unwelcome airstreams plunge down into the void created by Magellan Strait. The sudden, unexpected, and intermittent nature of this meteorological phenomenon would be the cause of much havoc on board vessels sailing in the strait: a ship could be hit by a bolt of wind from above and sent over on her side; and as soon as she came upright she would be knocked over again by the williwaw striking her on the opposite side.

The Spaniards were pleased to have a route between the Atlantic and Pacific Oceans, and afterwards carried out a detailed survey of Magellan Strait. But it proved a time-consuming and dangerous route for ships to use. Many were lost in the strait, and Spain soon decided that the overland route across the Isthmus of Panama was an easier way of transporting people, cargo, and valuables from the Pacific coast.

* * *

Tremendous rivalry existed between the seafaring nations. Spain and Portugal were eager to benefit from the spoils of the lands they had discovered in the New World and the East Indies, and determined to protect their overseas interests against any newcomer intent on expanding its own trading horizons.

At the time, England had no overseas possessions and was not a serious threat to Spain and Portugal in the Americas. But that was about to change in the person of Sir Francis Drake, sailor, adventurer, explorer, slave-trader, and pirate, who became an English national hero for his role in the defeat of the Spanish Armada. Drake was born near Tavistock, on the edge of Dartmoor north of Plymouth, twenty years after Magellan sailed into the Pacific. Drake, whose father is said to have doubled as a sheep shearer and clergyman, became a coastal sailor at a young age, later joining his cousins John and William Hawkins in the iniquitous slave-trading adventures of the early 1560s.

The Hawkins family maintained a fleet of ships that operated from Plymouth. Their main enterprise was the African slave trade; they acquired human cargos by raiding the West African coast of Guinea and then transported their captives across the Atlantic to Central America and the Caribbean. There they where sold as slaves to the Spaniards. African slaves were required as workers in Spanish America to replace the enslaved and dwindling Native American population.

Malnutrition, disease, oppressive working conditions, and the forced separation of men from women had caused the decline of the indigenous population. English involvement in slavery began in 1562 when Sir John Hawkins started trading slaves; Portugal had started the international slave trade in 1530.

Soon the trade between the Hawkins' and the Spanish ceased, and a private war started. Each side attacked the other whenever the opportunity arose, with the aim of acquiring treasure. At the time, Spain and Portugal were shipping immense wealth, mostly in the form of gold and silver, from their conquered lands in the New World back to the home country. Although the English were operating far from home, the Spaniards were more vulnerable because of the valuable treasure on board. Hawkins' ships had some initial success, particularly when they captured a number of Portuguese ships and sent the spoils back to England. But Spain made it increasingly difficult for anyone to attack their treasure ships, and any attempt at robbing their transports of gold and silver would require an element of surprise. Drake excelled at surprise attacks and thus acquired the wealth he desired.

Unlikely alliances developed in order to obtain valuable treasure. In 1572 Drake, a short heavily built man with a neat reddish-blonde beard, led his men ashore in Panama. He was planning to ambush a mule train carrying treasure. He travelled inland to a village located on high ground, inhabited by African slaves who had escaped; free African slaves in Central America were known as *Cimarrones*. In the village, Drake befriended Pedro, the leader of the *Cimarrones*. They shared a common a hatred of the Spaniards: Drake harbored resentment following a previous encounter in which he believed that the Spaniards had behaved treacherously towards him; and the former slaves deeply resented the brutal treatment meted out to them by their Spanish slave masters. Pedro took Drake up a tree to a platform constructed near the top, from where Drake could see both the Pacific Ocean and the Atlantic Ocean. Drake is the first recorded English person to get sight of the Pacific, and he decided there and then that one day he would sail on that great ocean. The first Europeans to view the Pacific were Vasco Núñez de Balboa and his followers when they crossed the Isthmus of Panama in 1513. Balboa waded into the water carrying the flag of Spain and named the ocean the Great South Sea, and claimed it and the coastlines bordering it for Spain.

Drake formed an alliance with French pirates led by Guillaume Le Têtu, with the aim of attacking a train of pack mules transporting a valuable consignment of gold and silver. The attack on the mule train was a success, yielding treasure valued at about £20,000 that was divided equally between Drake and Le Têtu. Drake returned to England a rich man.

Having viewed the Pacific Ocean, Drake drew up plans to extend his policy of piracy and plunder to Spanish and Portuguese ships and settlements on the west coast of America. And he persuaded a number of important people, including Queen Elizabeth, to invest in his venture.

> Then Globe-engirdling Drake, the Naval Palme that wonne,
> Who strove in his long Course to emulate the Sunne.
>
> Michael Drayton, *Polyolbion*

Drake left Plymouth in December 1577 in command of five ships: *Pelican*, 150 tons and carrying 18 guns; the 80-ton *Elizabeth* with 11 guns; and the smaller *Marigold*, *Swan*, and *Benedict* with 12 guns between them. Among the other leaders of the expedition was John Wynter who commanded *Elizabeth*, and Thomas Doughty. Doughty had connections at Court, and was in command of *Swan*. *Pelican*, commanded by Drake, was the flagship of the fleet.

A feature of Drake's expedition was the ethnic diversity of the sailors: Danes, Dutchmen, Greeks, and Africans, including an African who accompanied Drake back from Panama; and a number of Portuguese and Spaniards joined the fleet at a later stage. Mixed nationality crews were to become a feature of British ships for hundreds of years. The true destination of Drake's fleet was a closely guarded secret, so that the Spanish and Portuguese authorities would not become suspicious.

Drake's ships carried a number of partly built pinnaces that could be assembled by the ships' carpenters for use in shallow water; their function was to ferry Drake and his men ashore during raids on towns and settlements. Near the Cape Verde Islands, Drake captured six Spanish and Portuguese vessels. He also captured a 40-ton Spanish fishing vessel named *Christopher* and used it as a replacement for the smallest vessel in his fleet, the 15-ton *Benedict*.

Shortly afterwards he captured a Portuguese vessel, *Santa Maria*, loaded with wine and other merchandise, and took the commander, Nuão de Silva, prisoner. Drake commandeered *Santa Maria*, renaming her 'Mary,' and put Doughty in charge of the captured vessel. De Silva kept a detailed journal of his voyage with Drake; he was well acquainted with the coast of South America and proved to be a valuable pilot to Drake's fleet. A friendly relationship developed between Drake and de Silva, in sharp contrast to the discord and acrimony that was developing between Drake and Doughty.

By the end of June 1578, with the fleet nearing latitude 50°S, Drake put into San Julian, where Magellan had wintered 58 years earlier. The fleet was now reduced to four vessels; *Swan* and *Christopher* were earlier set on fire on Drake's orders after he stripped Doughty of his command, and made him a virtual prisoner. Trouble started as soon as Doughty was put in command of *Mary*. Initially there was a confrontation between Doughty and Drake's brother, Thomas. Drake is said to have been affronted by Doughty's assertion that Thomas Drake was involved in disorder that broke out on board *Mary* when members of the crew raided the wine cargo on board and started drinking. Two camps developed: one that supported Doughty and the other led by Thomas Drake that vilified Doughty. Francis Drake began to see Doughty as a danger to the success of the expedition, and Doughty and his supporters voiced concerns about Drake.

Setting out from Plymouth, Francis Drake, Wynter, and Doughty were listed as equals in the enterprise, although Drake was considered to be the commander of the fleet. When they reached San Julian, Drake put Doughty on trial before a jury for attempting to cause a mutiny. The jury of seamen was pressured by Drake to find Doughty guilty, which they did, and Doughty was beheaded at the site of the earlier Magellan executions. This course of action was unlikely to have had the support of many in the fleet.

Drake's fleet spent a couple of months at San Julian sheltering from the worst of the austral winter, before they set sail for Magellan Strait, three to four sailing days away. *Mary* was abandoned in San Julian. *Pelican, Elizabeth,* and *Marigold* passed through Magellan Strait to reach the Pacific in September. They then sailed south, expecting to discover a further expanse of territory; geographers of the time believed there was another great land mass below South America, what is now known as Antarctica. The fleet was driven further south by adverse winds to approximately 57° latitude. There, Drake realized that the Atlantic Ocean and the Pacific Ocean met as a wide expanse of water which would afterwards be known as 'Drake Passage.'

Drake's voyage through Magellan Strait and in the Pacific Ocean had taken its toll on the crews: it is estimated that 80 or more men perished from cold, hunger, disease and shipwreck. Eight sailors set out in a poorly equipped pinnace, without food or a compass, and went missing. However, they survived the rigors of the elements in an open boat, and made their way through Magellan Strait to the Atlantic Ocean. There they headed north and, after an incredible 1,200-mile journey along the coast of Patagonia, arrived in the River Plate.

The fleet managed to stay together until the night of 30 September when *Marigold*, commanded by Doughty's friend John Thomas, went missing. *Marigold* and her crew of twenty were never heard of again. The two remaining ships sailed north and after a week arrived near the western entrance to Magellan Strait; there they became separated and Drake lost contact with *Elizabeth*. Wynter was in command of *Elizabeth*; he sailed her into the strait and remained there. The crew, many of them friends of Doughty, were demoralized from hunger and cold. In November, Wynter sailed *Elizabeth* back through Magellan Strait and returned to England where he reported the execution of Doughty and the disappearance of Drake and his ship.

Drake's ship, *Pelican*, by then renamed *Golden Hind*, was driven in a south-westerly direction by storms to 55°S, before Drake could set a course in a north-westerly direction. *Golden Hind* sailed north in the Pacific Ocean. Drake had his first success at Valparaiso: he captured a treasure ship, raided a church, and pillaged warehouses; he also managed to acquire charts of the coast. Unarmed Spanish and Portuguese ships expected to be able to sail the Pacific Ocean unmolested, and were no match for the heavily armed *Golden Hind*. The element of surprise was in Drake's favor, and he captured a number of ships, including at least one galleon loaded with quantities of gold, silver, and other valuables. He raided coastal settlements as far north as present day California. His success enabled him to replenish his supplies so that his sailors were spared the deprivation and hunger suffered by Magellan's sailors 60 years earlier, when they had to exist on powdered sea biscuits crawling with worms and wet with rats urine.

Drake put Nuão de Silva ashore, and set out for home going west across the Pacific with a crew further depleted by death from skirmishes and disease. Apart from going aground for a short period on a reef in the China Sea, his voyage home around the Cape of Good Hope was uneventful. *Golden Hind* arrived back at Plymouth on 28 September 1580 carrying incredible wealth. Earlier, when Wynter had arrived home he was hailed for his epic voyage, having proudly claimed that he had returned without retracing his westerly voyage through Magellan Strait.

Drake, returning after three years and having been presumed lost, received a hero's welcome and was hailed as the first Englishman to have sailed around the world. About six years after Drake's return, a crew member of the pinnace that had earlier made it to the River Plate, Peter Carder from Veryan in Cornwall, arrived back in England to an enthusiastic reception. Drake's valuable cargo yielded great profit for himself and his investors. In 1581, Queen Elizabeth knighted Drake and had his ship brought ashore at Deptford as a permanent monument to his remarkable voyage.

* * *

Drake Passage extends southwards from Cape Horn to the edge of ice-covered Antarctica; the channel is about 200 to 400 miles wide, depending on how much of the ice plate is extending into the Southern Ocean from Antarctica. Few sailors ever had a close-up view of Cape Horn, as ships sailing from one ocean to the other normally gave the well-known navigation hazard a wide berth.

The unique Southern hemisphere meteorology, interfaced with the land-masses of the southern tip of America and the Antarctic Peninsula, made for exceedingly hostile weather conditions encountered by clipper ship sailors. A band of low pressure, the circumpolar low-pressure trough, lies over the Southern Ocean between the high pressure zones of the oceans to the north and Antarctica to the south. The westerly Southern Ocean winds, generated by very deep depressions, flow in an almost uninterrupted pattern around the southern hemisphere. Marked differences in temperature between the equator and the South Pole, greater than the differences in the northern hemisphere, contribute to the depth of these depressions, and result in almost constant gales, rain, storms, poor visibility, and blizzards. Troughs of low pressure are at their deepest at the time of the equinoxes, giving rise to the much feared 'equinoctial storms.'

An east-flowing current, the Antarctic Circumpolar Current flows freely round Antarctica between the southern latitudes of 40° and 65°; it is driven by the prevailing westerlies and transports the largest volume of water of any of the ocean currents. The main obstacles to the Circumpolar Current are the southern tip of South America and the Antarctic Peninsula. Almost all the continent of Antarctica lies within the Antarctic Circle; the exception is the Antarctic Peninsula, the northern end of which extends into the Southern Ocean to about 66°S opposite Cape Horn, to form the southern limit of Drake Passage. The waters of the Circumpolar Current converge as they pass through Drake Passage, resulting in the greatest movement of water between two land masses anywhere in the world; their convergence increases the speed of the current to almost two knots, and the water becomes even more turbulent as a consequence. Between

65°S and the Antarctic coastline, there is a west-flowing current driven by the easterly coastal winds.

During the clipper era, Drake Passage became one of the busiest shipping lanes on the high seas, and remained so until the early part of the 20th century. Few steamers ventured near Cape Horn as there was inadequate refuelling facilities for vessels embarking on such a long voyage; the square-rigged clippers were capable of sailing half way round the world non-stop. Steamers encountering adverse weather off the Horn would have been tossed around like corks, whereas clippers' sails provided some stabilizing effect.

> In the great days of sailing in the 80s and 90s many had rounded it twenty or even thirty times – recognized by every shellback as the fiercest enemy of the race.
>
> Basil Lubbock, *The Last of the Windjammers*

Clipper ships encountered extremely severe weather when sailing off Cape Horn; much worse than they were likely to encounter elsewhere. The ocean between Cape Horn and Antarctica was the most inhospitable, unpredictable, and dangerous channel in the world; an area with a reputation for extremely adverse weather, and the steepest seas anywhere on the oceans. The great waves of the Southern Ocean became bigger, steeper, more unpredictable, and more threatening as they were channeled between the southern tip of America and Antarctica.

On the approaches to Cape Horn, clipper crews prepared for extreme weather conditions: they bent on the strongest canvas; ropes and wire stays that showed any signs of wear were replaced; boats and deck equipment were double lashed; battening of the hatches was reinforced; skylights were boarded up; purchases on the rudder tackle were checked, reinforced, and replaced where necessary; and lifelines were stretched along the main deck. When off the coast of Argentina, ships heading west took the added precaution of removing the hatch tarpaulins, so the hatch covers could be caulked with oakum in anticipation of sailing into the teeth of relentless Cape Horn storms.

Sailors rounding Cape Horn lived in oilskins and rubber boots, only taking them off to get into their bunks. Big seas breaking on deck frequently engulfed them in water; those rounding the Horn for the first time quickly learned to grab hold of something secure and hold on for dear life, as running away from an approaching sea considerably increased the risk of being washed overboard.

When caught in a particularly big sea it was often impossible to hold on indefinitely, because of the great weight of water; the immersed sailor would be taken by the receding water across the deck and deposited in the lee scuppers, bruised, cut, and nearly drowned. Those in greatest danger were the crew on deck hauling the braces: whole watches were washed away when wearing ship in bad weather in the seas off Cape Horn.

Iron and steel hulls increased the strength of the clippers, but were of negligible reassurance to those coping with the rigors of the Horn. Few ships escaped the battle with Cape Horn without scars. The greatest difficulties were encountered by vessels trying to force a passage in a westerly direction because the prevailing westerly winds and currents almost constantly forced them back. Doubling the Horn involved passing from 50°S in the Atlantic, and continuing quite a distance west past Cape Horn (67°17'W), by sailing as far as longitude 80°W, before altering course north in the Pacific to latitude 50°S. Sailing the extra distance west was necessary to avoid being set to leeward by the westerlies onto the islands and reefs off the western end of Magellan Strait, where numerous sailing ships were lost.

Westerly gales sweep through the Southern Ocean almost continuously; they are strongest and most persistent in the seas off Cape Horn itself. Westbound sailing ships were frequently driven even further into the freezing south as they struggled to find a way through. The landmasses of South America and Antarctica bordering Drake Passage increase the speed, turbulence, and unpredictability of the westerlies by interrupting and deflecting their flow over the Southern Ocean. The winds from the west vary in direction from north-north-west to south-south-west; they are bitterly cold as they come off the Antarctic ice, particularly when accompanied by hail, sleet, and snow. At times the difference between night and day is a matter of degree: total blackness at night compared to the dismal grey darkness of the day. It was unusual for ships sailing eastwards round Cape Horn to be headed by strong winds.

* * *

Sailing in the Southern Ocean and rounding Cape Horn gave clipper ship sailors an opportunity to visualize the unique wildlife that inhabits the waters at the edge of the Antarctica. One of the most abundant seabird populations anywhere in the world is in Antarctica and the Southern Ocean; birds are an important part of the Antarctic ecosystem, with most species nesting all along the coast.

> . . . the great albatross, the squawking mollymawk, the fluttering
> Cape pigeon, black hen and the penguin navigate to the southward
> of Cape Stiff.
>
> Basil Lubbock *The Last of the Windjammers*

Foremost among the bird population is the albatross, the great majestic bird that has captured the imagination of travellers to the Southern Ocean from earliest times. The Antarctic and bordering waters is the home of the albatross, with only a few of the species encountered elsewhere in the world. With its long narrow aerodynamic wings, the albatross is the largest flying seabird. Mollymawks are a smaller version of albatross.

The largest of the species is the mighty wandering albatross, with a wingspan of approximately twelve feet; and there is also a slightly smaller royal albatross. The wandering albatross is predominantly white in color with black areas over much of the wings; the bird's bill is a pinkish white with a yellow hooked tip. At sea, the adult wandering albatross may be difficult to distinguish from the royal albatross; the latter is almost as large, but is almost entirely white in color. Albatrosses breed on remote Antarctic islands. The bird is a great traveller and a master of the elements, circumnavigating the globe in the southern latitudes many times in a lifetime. Borne by the strong winds of the Roaring Forties, the albatross glides effortlessly around the world and can live a long life that stretches into decades.

Cape Horn sailors marveled at the ease with which the albatross glided low over the waves without flapping its long, relatively narrow, picturesque wings. These magnificent birds stay airborne most of the time, using minimal energy as they travel vast distances, flying just above the surface of the sea in search of food such as fish and plankton. Albatrosses are hunters, acquiring their favorite food, squid, by swooping after dark to snatch them from their nocturnal location below the surface of the sea.

Wind deflected from the windward surface of the waves provides the upward flowing air that gives the big wandering albatross lift and flying power. Albatrosses rely on the strong winds of the turbulent Southern Ocean for their graceful and effortless gliding flight: they gather speed downwind, and lose speed as they gain height flying into the wind; they follow a regular pattern of long sweeping glides on outstretched wings, flying into strong winds to gain height, coasting across the face of the wind and turning downwind to glide, gain speed, and lose altitude before they dip one wing to leeward and bank as they turn to rise into the wind again. Albatrosses have been known to follow a ship for days without flapping their wings, apart from making slight adjustments to their effective wing area. During calm weather, these great birds spend their time resting on the water. They require wind to start flying again: they take off from water by heading into the wind, furiously flapping their wings and thrashing the surface with their webbed feet until they become airborne.

Writers and sailors have given the albatross a certain mystique. Coleridge immortalized the albatross by alluding to the superstition attached to the deliberate killing of these unique birds:

> At length did come an Albatross,
> Through the Fog it came;
> And an it were a Christian soul,
> We hail'd it in God's name.
>
> The Marineres gave it biscuit-worms,
> And round and round it flew:
> The Ice did split, with a Thunder-fit;
> The Helmsman steer'd us thro'.
>
> And a good south wind came up behind,
> The albatross did follow;
> And every day for food or play
> Came to the Marinere's hollo!
>
> Samuel Taylor Coleridge, *The Rime of the Ancyent Marinere*

Many Cape Horn sailors had little hesitation in trapping and killing the albatross for its meat, creating instruments such as needles from the bones, and using the feathers to supplement their clothing. Superstition was related to the sooty albatross, a smaller bird than the wandering albatross, and colored a pale sooty shade of grey with a black beak that has a line of light blue running along the underside. The sooty's wings are proportionally longer, narrower, and more elegantly pointed than any other bird; long pointed feathers form its slender wedge-shaped tail. The sooty has staring eyes surrounded by white eyelids. It was the inquisitive eyes, always looking and appearing to inspect every spar on the ship, as though searching for something, that fascinated sailors and led to the superstition that individual sooty albatrosses were reincarnated sailors who had fallen overboard and drowned in the Southern Ocean.

Sailors were enthralled by the apparent inquisitiveness of the sooty albatross: following ships closely, flying ahead before dropping back to keep station with one wing tip almost touching the yardarm, and holding that position with scarcely any wing movement; from time to time the sooty would change position by flying forward or dropping back to keep station alongside one of the other yardarms at the same level. L Harrison Matthews alluded to the sailors' superstition of the sooty in his *Wandering Albatross:*

> Hermann watched him glide alongside the weather leach of the main lower topsail just above the main yard-arm, and looking down on the bulging belly of the course. 'See what he's doing?' he said. 'He's having a look at the bunt-line and clew-line lizards to see they're all clear for running and won't foul if we have to clew up in a hurry for the next squall; they always do that. I wonder how long ago he went overboard.'

Various species of petrel, varying in size from small to quite large, inhabit Antarctica and the Southern Ocean. Best known to Cape Horners was the Cape Petrel, known as Cape Pigeons, a species of Southern Ocean diving petrel that is present in large numbers off Cape Horn. They followed sailing ships, attracted by discarded scraps of food and offal that were thrown overboard.

Cape Petrels have a colorful black and white plumage: black legs and head, including beak; their back is speckled black on white, the tip of their tail is black, as are the edges of the wings; when in flight, characteristic, fairly large, white patches are present on the otherwise black outer parts of their wings. Cape petrels are skilled at collecting food on the wing: they fly with their heads submerged below the surface of the water, collecting and trapping food in their mouths by means of a series of serrations on each side of their partially closed bills that permits excess water to drain away. Other species of petrel encountered by the sailors were Wilson's storm petrel, the southern giant petrel, the Antarctic petrel, and the blue petrel.

Cape Horn sailors would have regularly sighted the great blue whale, not only the largest of the whale species, but also the largest existing mammal on earth. Blues weigh about 150 tons on average, and are about 100 feet in length; their skeleton alone can weigh over 22 tons; their streamlined torpedo shape and muscular tail-stock allows them to move through the water at speeds in excess of 20 knots. Called blue because of their blue-grey color, the Antarctic species is larger than northern hemisphere Blues. They have a lifespan of up to 70 years or more, and travel widely, feeding in the seas around Antarctica and travelling to warmer climates to calve. Blues send plumes of spray nine feet into the air; and they emit low-frequency sounds and moans that are said to travel through water for thousands of miles.

Blues breathe air in through two blowholes located on the top of the head, and blow air from their lungs out through the blowholes, so-called because stale air is expelled as spray, referred to as a blow. As the Blue dives, it raises its big tail-fluke into the air before disappearing below the surface. Their favorite food is krill, small organisms a couple of inches in length that are present in large numbers at the surface of the ocean; its 70-foot-long mouth takes in 60 tons of water and food in one gulp, before squeezing the water out of its mouth to retain the food. Each Blue requires about 3.5 tons of krill each day. They increase their weight by up to 40 per cent when they are in the rich Antarctic feeding grounds, enabling them to travel north and stay in warmer waters for a number of months before giving birth to their offspring.

Blues are often first sighted when they come to the surface to blow, or when they raise their tail-fluke into the air to dive below the surface. During the sailing ship era, Southern Ocean sailors were among the few people who had the privilege of viewing the Great Blue. A plume of spray, followed by its large tail-fluke rising into the air as it dived, would be the signal that alerted most sailors to their presence. On the rare occasions when the sea was relatively calm, one of these magnificent streamlined creatures might be seen below the surface making its way past the ship; sailors in the rigging would have had a grandstand view of this underwater giant mammal as it swept past below the surface. As the largest creatures in the ocean, Blues are safe from other predators, with the exception of killer whales hunting in packs and human hunters using exploding harpoons.

CHAPTER 10

Rounding the Horn

Rounding the Horn, such seas!
and at the edge of sight
always an iceberg crest.
Strapped in my bunk at night
feeling the ship drop
too far and fast to stop,

I waited for the blow,
the torn plates spouting, time
after time. But then
shuddering she would climb
out from under the wave
pouring into her grave.

If she was his patient,
my dear ship's doctor said,
he would a hundred times
have given her up for dead,
but still her pulses beat
strongly under our feet.

Jon Stallworthy, *Rounding the Horn: The Return*

At the dawn of the 20th century, up to forty clipper carriers were likely to be in sight of Cape Horn, the worst corner in the world, at any particular time. The relentless gales sweeping around the globe, just north of the Antarctic continent and ice shelf, engulfed sailing ships in squalls of dense hail, sleet, and snow, and sometimes left a thick layer of slush on the sea; Cape Horn blizzards could whip up snowdrifts on the surface of the ocean. In storm force winds that blew from the west for weeks at a time, angry seas could build to 120 feet. From time to time, a massive rolling wave would advance and make even a large clipper look small. Occasionally, the front of one of these advancing high rollers, travelling at 22–27 miles per hour, would grow into a steep wall of green water to become perpendicular, before the crest overtook the trough to break into a 20–30 foot high wall of boiling white surf, capable of engulfing and destroying everything in its path. These huge waves, with their breaking crests, were known as greybeards by the seasoned Cape Horner. Rogue waves are capable of developing anywhere during stormy weather, but those encountered by the Cape Horners were capable of engulfing and destroying even the strongest and biggest ship. Rogue greybeards accounted for a number of clipper ships and their crews that disappeared without trace.

One of the best descriptions of what it was like for clipper ship sailors rounding Cape Horn was given by Basil Lubbock shortly after his first ocean voyage, when he sailed as a crew member of the clipper carrier *Royalshire* from San Francisco to Queenstown at the turn of the twentieth century.

> Great Cape Horn greybeards, with crests a mile and a half long, roar up behind us, and at one moment you see a green sea with a boiling whirlpool of foam on its top, which looks as if it must poop you, and wash you away from the helm; the next moment the gallant vessel has lifted to it, and it roars past on either hand, breaking on to the main-deck with a heavy crash and clanging of ports, then sweeping forward in a mighty flood of raging, hissing, seething, icy-cold water ... It is glorious to watch a great sea break: as it curls over, there is a most beautiful deep-green colour in the very heart of the breaker ...
>
> It really is a magnificent sight: huge mountains of water with 10 feet of foam on their crests rush after us as if they would devour us; like great beasts of prey they rage around us, then fling themselves upon the straining, groaning *Royalshire*, they swarm all over her, and seem as though they would rend her limb from limb.
>
> A Basil Lubbock, *Round the Horn before the Mast*

Alfred Basil Lubbock, a 22-year-old Eton-educated adventurer, joined *Royalshire* in July 1899 at San Francisco where she was loading a cargo of wheat before setting out for Europe by way of Cape Horn. *Royalshire* had arrived in San Francisco with a cargo, the first coal to be exported from Japan to the United States. Lubbock was returning to England, and signed on as an ordinary seaman. He had arrived from the Yukon Territory in Northwest Canada where he had taken part in the great Klondike Gold Rush of 1897–1898. Lubbock had no previous experience as a sailor, but he persuaded the captain that climbing and working the rigging would pose no significant challenge to him, as he was used to hair-raising experiences scaling steep cliffs when prospecting in the Yukon. The young prospector turned sailor became a great admirer of sailing ships, and shortly afterwards published *Round the Horn before the Mast* based on his experiences aboard *Royalshire*. Lubbock continued to write, publishing a total of about twenty informative books on clippers, other great sailing ships, and those who sailed them.

Royalshire, actual name *Ross-Shire*, was a magnificent 2,257-ton four-masted barque launched from the Scott yard at Greenock in 1891, owned by Thomas Law's Shire Line of Glasgow, and commanded by Scotsman Captain Andrew Baxter; her other officers were also Scots. Baxter, one of the most renowned sailing ship captains of his era, was on his 30th passage round Cape Horn and would afterwards describe the mountainous seas encountered on the voyage as the biggest he had ever seen. He retired from seafaring after the voyage and later became a master stevedore in New York. On 23 December 1900, *Ross-Shire* caught fire following an explosion in the hold while loading nitrate at Pisagua, and burned to the waterline; 500 tons of coal was still to be unloaded when the explosion occurred. The crew escaped.

Baxter described a narrow escape on a previous westbound voyage when *Royalshire* was beating against a particularly strong Southern Ocean gale in such reduced visibility that it was impossible to see more than a ship's length ahead. The lookout had shouted with great urgency 'breakers ahead' as out of the mist appeared a great towering island of rock: they were heading straight for the Cape Horn itself; Baxter put the barque about immediately and, as *Royalshire* came into the wind, the huge seas rolling in to break on the rocks swept across the deck, tearing away the boats and the standard compass. A few minutes delay and the great barque would have struck the rocks and gone down with all hands.

On Lubbock's eastbound voyage, *Royalshire* passed well to the south of Cape Horn. The weather was at its worst, requiring sail to be reduced to storm jib, three lower topsails, main upper topsail, and main lower topgallant. *Royalshire* was engulfed in squalls of hail as she was chased by mile-long greybeards, their crests white with foam and spray; mountain-like seas overtook her with at least a mile from crest to crest and deep valleys in between. There was not an albatross to be seen, although the foul weather had not deterred a number of Cape pigeons and mollymawks.

One immense sea broke on deck and passed over Lubbock, who estimated that the surface was well above his head. Enveloped by this great mass of water, he held his breath and grabbed the end of a clewline as he was swept overboard; as the water cleared over the lee rail Lubbock floated back to safety. The main upper topsail split, and the main lower topgallant was quickly taken in, leaving *Royalshire* to run before storm force winds under a single jib and three lower topsails.

Going aloft in such appalling conditions was particularly unpleasant, as well as exceedingly dangerous. The ice-cold southern wind from Antarctica soon numbed fingers, adding to the difficulty of handling sail. Unfurling canvas that was frozen stiff required tremendous effort on the part of sailors whose hands were already numbed by the cold; numb fingers soon became painful and started to bleed. Taking in sail was no easier: in the bitterly cold weather, with the rigging covered in ice, the solidly frozen sail had to be punched soft before being furled with one hand as the other clung on, and the sailor's feet balanced on the foot-rope of a perilously swaying yard, with the lower yardarms dipping intermittently into the whirling crests of spray-covered waves. Before going aloft, the watch would have worked on deck, hauling the sail up, using the clewlines, buntlines, and leechlines to spill the wind.

While working aloft was demanding, and a far from pleasant task, it did have the compensation of providing an unrivaled view of the ship and the turbulent seas. Lubbock describes working on the foreyard on a dark southern night, with occasional breaks in the darkness when the moon peeped out from behind the scudding clouds to illuminate the frothing white tops of giant waves, rolling by as great ink-black mountains alongside and level with him. On the peak of one of the mountainous seas, the view was like looking from the top of a mountain to smaller mountains and hills, with a valley one to two miles away.

On a number of occasions, huge seas broke over the decks pooping *Royalshire*. Sailors did not like to be pooped, and many of the crew were anxious and uneasy as large waves breaking over the stern threatened to send *Royalshire* to Davy Jones's locker. Every so often a terrific crash would be heard as a huge sea fell on the poop deck, before it swept forward to cascade onto the main deck. On one occasion, the mate attempted to get a sun sight: as he sheltered in the lee of the chart house the ship was pooped by an immense sea; he was swept off his feet and washed forward, valiantly clinging on to his precious sextant, and only saved from being thrown down onto the main deck by the poop-rail.

As a particularly big sea broke aboard, some of the crew feared that it would drive *Royalshire* under, and she would not recover. The mate expressed his concern about the constant pooping, relating the number of ships that had been lost with all hands from running for too long before a storm. He, like the captain and the second mate, had nerves of steel, and appeared to be the least anxious of those on board; Baxter and his officers did not expect any of the crew to go anywhere on deck or aloft where they would not have been prepared to venture themselves.

> I gave one look astern, and there, towering high above us, was a huge monster, roaring and hissing as it curled its top; it looked as if it must break full on to the poop, and was a sight to strike terror into the stoutest heart.
>
> Would she rise to it or, or was it our last moment on earth? Up, up, up went the *Royalshire,* good old ship, she was going to top it after all; but though she did her best, the heavy weight aft held her down, and she did not quite get there.
>
> With a deafening thud, the top of the monster curled into boiling surf and fell upon us, overwhelming the helmsmen, who clung desperately to the wheel, and dipping us to the waist as we hung in the weather jigger rigging.
>
> In a roaring torrent it poured across the poop, and then, like an earthquake, the wave fell aboard the whole length of the port-rail. Such a height was it, that it toppled over in a terrific breaker upon the top of the midship house; the gig's side and bottom fell out; as if hit by a thunderbolt, the lamp-locker door was smashed down and all the lamps washed out (luckily Don was not inside this time, or he would have certainly been drowned) and it filled the main-deck above the hatches until the water was on a level with the poop.
>
> The poor old ship gave a sickly roll under the terrible weight of water, and dipped Loring and myself up to our necks in the next sea

as we clung on to the port jigger-backstays.

All the life seemed struck out of her; she swung nearly five points off her course, and old Foghorn Jennings and the second mate were working like demons as they hove the wheel up.

'If she gets another on top of this, she'll go down like a stone!' yelled Mac in my ear.

A Basil Lubbock, *Round the Horn before the Mast*

Working on deck was hazardous for the crew. Huge breaking waves were likely to sweep across the deck, taking everything in their path. Hauling on the braces, which required the crew to be on deck, was particularly hazardous in foul weather. Sailors on *Royalshire* were frequently washed along the deck into the lee scuppers and only saved from going overboard by grabbing and holding on to one of the lifelines, ending up cold, bruised, and cut, narrowly escaping death by drowning each time they were swept off their feet. Oilskins and rubber boots were of little use to those who repeatedly got immersed in freezing water during their watch. A golden rule for those on deck was not to run from the sea but to grab hold of the nearest thing, and hold on for dear life; without a firm hold on something fixed to the deck there was a great risk of being washed overboard.

Notwithstanding the cold, the discomfort, the wet, the man-killing work in the pitch darkness, and the washing about the decks, I thoroughly enjoy it all. One is stirred up by the danger; one works like fury, whether up aloft getting in sail or on deck up to your middle in water, occasionally hanging on for dear life until you think your lungs will burst, so long is the water in clearing off.

It is wonderful too, how one gets used to being knocked down and floated about the deck in a half drowned, half-stunned condition.

A Basil Lubbock *Round the Horn before the Mast*

On a previous *Royalshire* voyage one wave surged across the decks, flooding the crew accommodation on the half deck, despite the tightly shut doors; one of the crew was nearly drowned when he was unable to get his head above water as he floated off the bunk. Water also invaded the galley and quenched the fire, with the result that there was no hot food or drinks for the crew. Even the forecastle was inches deep in water.

A landsman has no idea of the various noises on board a wind-jammer in a storm. Every part of the ship groans; up above the gale roars, sings, and whistles through the rigging; one backstay produces a deep note, and one could fancy an organ was being played aloft; others shriek shrilly like telegraph wires; some hum, some ring, others twang like banjo strings; and above all is the crash of the seas falling on the main-deck, and the clang of hardly-used ports as they are banged first open and then shut by each succeeding wave.

A Basil Lubbock *Round the Horn before the Mast*

* * *

Other ocean carriers fared less well off the Horn. In 1878 the homeward-bound Scottish ship *Ben Voirlich* broached when running before strong gales to the west of Cape Horn. A huge sea was running and the helmsman, unaware or ignoring the rule not to look behind at the following sea, saw a huge Cape Horn grey-beard approaching the stern and let go the wheel from sheer fright. As *Ben Voirlich* broached, she was hit by another huge sea that broke over her quarter, swept over the poop, destroyed the cabin, put her over on her beam ends, and completely disabled her; nine of the crew were washed overboard and lost. The survivors fought to get her back on an even keel, but it was an hour before *Ben Voirlich* responded to the wheel, slowly righting herself and bringing the wind astern.

Another ship that had a narrow escape off Cape Horn was the Robert Duncan built *Invercargill*, commanded by Captain Tom Bowling from Kingstown. A trusted captain with the Shaw Savill Line, he had commanded the greatly admired clipper ship for thirteen years. Bowling, who had spent a remarkable fifty years at sea, thirty in command of sailing ships, was well known for the expertise with which he handled the beautiful *Invercargill*. At the end of September 1904, he encountered the worst storm of his career: *Invercargill* left Sydney for Queenstown on 27 August with a cargo of wheat, and was thrown on her beam ends by a huge breaking greybeard off Cape Horn; the cargo shifted to port, and the port bulwarks were carried away. The crew set to work at the Herculean task of shifting cargo by hand to the windward side of the ship, and eventually succeeded in righting her. *Invercargill* continued her passage only to be sent on her beam ends again in the North Atlantic at 45°N, 20°W during a December storm. Only by jettisoning part of her cargo could Bowling get his ship back on an even keel, and take her limping into port.

Ships rounding Cape Horn steered clear of the South American coast to avoid being struck by a pampero; the sudden offshore white squall that was occasionally encountered by ships sailing near the coast of southern Patagonia. In 1894, *Auckland*, while voyaging before light winds under a clear cloudless sky, was rounding the Horn on a voyage from New Zealand when she was enveloped in an extensive white haze. The captain, aware that this was an omen for a change in the weather, mustered all hands to reduce sail. As the crew were starting to take in the fore and main upper topsails, a squall suddenly hit the ship. *Auckland* was hit on the beam by the wind, sending her over on her side; she was starting to come up and right herself when a second blast of wind sent her on her beam ends again; as the crew began crawling towards the weather side, there was a tremendous bang as the foresail was carried away, probably saving *Auckland* from going under; one of the crew who was nearby had instinctively cut through the six-inch thick manila hemp foresheet with his knife and, only then, did *Auckland* begin to right herself.

Even if there was a lull in the Cape Horn gales and the wind died, there was unlikely to be respite from the Southern Ocean swell that heaved a ship up before depositing her down in a gradual long slow motion while the sails flapped from lack of wind. The absence of wind, an occasional occurrence off Cape Horn, could be frustrating for the sailors, anxious to maintain speed and get well clear of this isolated, unpredictable, and desolate outpost. The unpleasantness caused by the erratic motion of a stationary ship during an interlude of calm is vividly expressed in rhyme:

> The wind shrieked through the rigging
> Like a fiend on that wintry night,
> As we drove under reefed topsails
> Through the storm-torn billows white.
> For days we had run before it,
> Now its strength was spent, and the balm
> Of rest to be sank o'er the sea,
> What is known as a Cape Horn Calm.
> But the great grey swell was heavy,
> How she rolled and her deck was wet;

All day long we were loosing sail
And her every stitch had been set,
But she lolled like a lazy monarch
And never the dog-vane stirred,
Swinging to the roll from the South Pole,
And hardly a sound was heard.

Save the patter of many reef-points
And the wheeze of the blocks aloft,
And the groans of the frozen deck-planks
That were buried in snowflakes soft
And the wail of some lonely seagull
Resting still on the ocean's face,
That seemed to cry to the passer-by,
"Here is limitless time and space".

R B, *A Cape Horn Calm*

And few Cape Horners would have recognized the idealistic picture of Cape Horn penned by a ship's doctor rounding the Horn aboard a steamer during calm weather in the early part of the 20th century:

As the sun sank into the water the whole western sky was a mass of tawny gold. Away to the east stretched an opaque rich purple mist for miles along the horizon and above it a gauzy layer of beautiful pink-shaded sky. As the sun sank lower the sky in the north assumed a deep salmon colour, all the other tints remaining. Gradually the surface, which at this time was as placid as a sleeping child, became terraced over with patches of pink sea almost too beautiful and unearthly to believe. Side by side the other half of the sea to the horizon was changed into a mass of molten gold with a purple streak of sea where the purple mists refracted from the surface. Just as the whole gorgeous display was at its height the half-moon glittered on the water with rays of pure silver colours and into the path of the rays came a herd of beautiful dolphins, some strung out in a 'follow-the-leader' fashion and looking for all the world like one gigantic monster about fifty feet long. Indeed, at first I thought it was a whale or a sea-serpent (a serpent in the

Garden of Eden) until they finally broke formation and darted past with incredible speed, showing their pure white underparts.

M F McElligott, *Cape Horn Sunsets*

Few ships were unlucky enough to get into trouble during a Cape Horn calm. The medium clipper *Dreadnought* was one that did come to grief because of lack of wind off the Horn. Having established her reputation as a fast and commercially successful transatlantic packet during her ten years as an Atlantic Ferry between New York and Liverpool, *Dreadnought* was put on the San Francisco run.

On 4 July 1869, when under the command of Captain P N Mayhew, and 67 days out from Liverpool, *Dreadnought* was becalmed on the approach to Cape Horn, and carried by the strong current towards the rocky shore of Cape Penas, on the north-east coast of Tierra del Fuego. The coast was steep, with no opportunity to anchor because of the depth of the water. As she approached the shore, *Dreadnought's* crew took to the boats and attempted to tow the 1,400-ton heavily laden ship through the Cape Horn swell against the current. But their efforts were in vain. A Cape Horn calm would be the nemesis of one of the most famous of the transatlantic packets; a ship that had earned the accolade 'Wild Boar of the Atlantic' was carried by the breaking swell onto the rocks, and quickly wrecked. Mayhew and the crew got safely ashore.

Seventeen days of hardship followed for Mayhew and his group. They were subjected to hunger and exposure as they made their way to Cape San Diego bordering Le Maire Strait, where they arrived on 20 July. At daylight on the following day, sail was sighted, and contact was made with the Norwegian barque *General Birch,* commanded by Captain Amuseden, out from Hamburg and bound for San Francisco. *Dreadnought's* full complement of 34, including the stewardess and a 12-year-old boy, were taken aboard the barque. On 17 August they were landed at Talcahuano, Chile, where a number of crew were hospitalized with frostbite, while the rest travelled on to Valparaiso aboard the steamer *Bio Bio.* American underwriters paid out $83,000 insurance for the vessel and cargo to the owner, John Parrott of San Francisco, who had purchased *Dreadnought* a year earlier.

A ship that went aground at Cape Horn but had the distinction of surviving was the 1,765-ton French barque *Vendée,* built by Dubigeon for Raoul Guillon. Having left Portland in late June 1908 with a cargo of wheat for Europe under the command of Captain Rigault, *Vendée* became embayed in Kendell Cove on the south-west of Wollaston Island on 1 September when rounding Cape Horn at night during a snowstorm. It was fortunate that she grounded on a sandbank, as it proved possible for a small steamer to pull her free, refloat her and tow her to Montevideo for repairs. *Vendée* continued to sail the world until she was laid up in 1921. Five years later she went to the breaker's yard.

* * *

Ice was an additional hazard for ships rounding the Horn, particularly during the austral summer when the Antarctic ice shelves were calving. Antarctic ice freezes solid to the land in winter. Ice breaks off from glaciers or ice shelves as icebergs, frozen masses of fresh water. There are three general categories of ice encountered at sea: icebergs, growlers, and bergy bits. For every ton of iceberg above water there is 8-9 tons below sea level. Icebergs are particularly hazardous during the hours of darkness because their presence results in a drop in temperature that can cause reduced visibility, often accompanied by a persistent snowfall. Growlers are large, more or less flat pieces of ice, quite extensive and often green in color; they barely show above the water, and are frequently not noticed until it is too late. Bergy bits are small but in Antarctica can be the size of a small house.

Icebergs are more numerous and larger than those in the Arctic because of the extensive ice shelves in Antarctica; Arctic icebergs mainly originate from calving glaciers. A glacier is a mass of ice on the earth's surface. Strictly defined, it is a valley glacier although the term glacier is often used when referring to an ice shelf or the ice cap.

The ice covering the Antarctic Continent is built up over thousands of years from layers of snow and ice that form ice sheets and gradually flow to the edge of the continent as ice streams. From there they float onto the water as ice shelves. Ice sheets are maintained by a balance between snowfalls on the continent, and the flow of ice crossing the coast. Moist air going south to Antarctica from the mid latitudes precipitates to fall as snow.

Antarctic ice shelves are floating flat layers of ice up to thousands of feet thick. They extend out into the sea from the land to form part of the coastline; and, when they fracture, they break off into large Southern Ocean icebergs. Ice shelves account for nearly half the coastline of Antarctica. The remainder consists of grounded ice walls, glaciers, and rock. One of the region's more rapidly flowing ice streams feeds the Ross Ice Shelf in the large inlet of the Ross Sea, almost directly south of the North Island of New Zealand, well to the west of Cape Horn.

Icebergs from the calving Ross Ice Shelf are particularly large, and are carried eastwards by the Antarctic Circumpolar Current, through Drake Passage and the waters off Cape Horn, into the Atlantic Ocean.

> Listen, Stranger! Mist and Snow,
> And it grew wond'rous cauld:
> And Ice, mast-high came floating by
> As green as Emerald.
>
> And thro' the drifts the snowy cliffs
> Did send a dismal sheen;
> Ne shapes of men ne beasts we ken –
> The Ice was all between!
>
> The Ice was here, the Ice was there,
> The Ice was all around:
> It crack'd and growl'd and roar'd and howl'd –
> Like noises of a swound.
>
> Samuel Taylor Coleridge, *The Rime of the Ancient Marinere*

Icebergs drifting past Cape Horn were directly in the path of sailing ships, and posed a hazard in the South Atlantic as far north as latitude 40°S. Viewing icebergs from a safe distance on a Cape Horner provided a magnificent spectrum of color: white, blue, green, brown, and even black; some composed of dense ice radiated an azure blue; those colored white contained a large number of trapped air bubbles; dark greenish icebergs were from the bottom of the glacier; rocks and sediment from glaciers colored icebergs brown and black.

About ten per cent of the volume of an iceberg is above the surface of the water. Large Southern Ocean icebergs acquire a variety of shapes and sizes that vary with the depth and contour of the ice shelves from which they originate. Among the most awesome sights for the Cape Horn sailor would have been large flat icebergs: sheets of ice stretching for miles, with cliff-like sides rising hundreds of feet into the air. Some icebergs towered 1,000 feet in height and had local cliffs rising to as high as 1,500 feet. One iceberg was estimated to be about 50 miles long and 40 miles wide, significantly larger than the Isle of Wight. In 1884, the German barque *Emil Julius* reported an iceberg 1,700 feet high; in 1893 the crew of *Loch Torridon* and other ships reported icebergs as high as 1,500 feet, and one that was 50 miles in length.

Richard J Woodget

Southern Ocean Iceberg

Fewer forces of nature were more hazardous to sailing ships than floating islands of ice. One gigantic iceberg is reported to have had a bay opening 40 miles wide: a vessel being steered into it, thinking it was the open sea, would have had little chance of getting out again. Smaller icebergs, including those that calve from glaciers, take a variety of changing shapes as they begin to melt under the influence of warmer weather. One Southern Ocean iceberg is said to have drifted for two years until it finally wasted away.

There is a characteristic loud cracking sound that emanates from icebergs during calving. Sailing ships were advised to pass to windward of calving icebergs in order to avoid floating ice that had become detached and collected in the lee of the iceberg.

> The most phlegmatic ocean traveller would be jerked out of himself by the announcement that his ship was now heading for a region of uncharted reefs and shoals, even if it were clear weather and daylight. But in dirty weather and night time it would appear little short of madness. Yet that is to all intents and purposes, what sailing through berg infested waters amounts to.
>
> W M Hutton, *Cape Horn Passage*

*

John Gilpin, the ship that won the celebrated 1852–1853 California Clipper Race on her maiden voyage, set sail from Honolulu on 30 November 1857 with 7,500

Sailing through the Ice Field (*ILN*)

barrels of whale oil and fifteen passengers. She had rounded Cape Horn and was running before heavy seas when, at 2.30am on the morning of 29 January, she was struck by what felt like a large breaking wave. The ship had hit the submerged part of an iceberg, was holed, and began to take water. The following day, with fifteen feet of water in the hold, Captain John F Ropes decided to abandon ship. As the crew were preparing to leave, the ship went on fire, probably from an over-turned oil lamp, but everyone got away safely. The crew were picked up by the British ship *Hertfordshire,* bound for Cork, and landed at Bahia Blanca.

Indian Queen, advertised by the Black Ball Line as a sister ship of *Marco Polo,* left Melbourne on 13 March 1859 carrying 40 passengers and a cargo of wool and gold dust. On 31 March she had reached 58°S and was more than half way to Cape Horn when, in a heavy swell, she sailed along at a steady 12 knots ahead of a brisk north-westerly wind in wet, foggy, and very cold conditions. Suddenly, at two the following morning, there was a tremendous crash followed by a grinding noise along the port side; *Indian Queen* came to an abrupt halt. The watch below and terrified passengers rushed on deck. They found the ship lying broadside to a huge iceberg, with masses of ice covering the deck. The spars and rigging were in ruins: the foremast was broken off close to the deck, and was held at an angle by

277

Indian Queen strikes iceberg *(ILN)*

the rigging; all spars and sails above lower mast level were hanging over the starboard side; the main yard was broken in two; although the mizzen topmast remained intact, its topsail yard was broken and useless; and the bowsprit was suspended in the water underneath the bow.

No one was present on deck, the wheel was unattended, and the port lifeboat was missing. The perplexed gathering was somewhat reassured when the carpenter, Thomas Howard, appeared and announced that the ship was not taking water. Shortly afterwards the second mate, a man named Leyvret, also appeared. Leyvret related how panic had ensued when *Indian Queen* crashed into the iceberg, and how most of those on watch, including the captain and mate, seventeen in all, had gone off in the lifeboat. Among those still on board was an apprentice who was the captain's son.

The passengers, cooks, stewards, and remaining crew were divided into two watches. They immediately set about shoveling the ice overboard, and clearing up the tangled rigging. The captain's son was put on the wheel. Cries for help could be heard from the missing boat; it was seen being tossed about in the swell as it tried to make it back to the ship. The boat seemed to be without oars and, before anyone had time to realize what was happening, it swept past the ship, propelled by the backwash of water off the face of the iceberg, and was never seen again.

The crossjack was backed with difficulty, and the head of the spanker taken in. The crippled *Indian Queen* began to move slowly astern along the side of the iceberg, and soon reached smooth water to leeward. As dawn broke, crew and volunteers started to cut away the wreckage, starting with the tangle of broken spars and stays attached to the broken main yard. Then there was a cry: "Ice to Leeward," and a huge iceberg loomed out of the fog. The crossjack, the only serviceable yard and sail, was braced up; the spanker was set; and a foresail rigged after a fashion. A tense crowd on deck watched and waited as *Indian Queen* limped slowly ahead, dragging the wreckage of tangled masts, spars, and torn sails alongside. To everyone's relief the menacing iceberg was passed with barely 300 feet to spare.

That hurdle had barely been overcome when the damaged foremast came crashing down onto the longboat; the added strain of the jury-rigged foresail was too much for the damaged mast; no boats were left as the ones on board had been smashed by the falling spars.

A roll call accounted for the remaining crew and passengers: in addition to the carpenter and second mate, the boatswain, cooks, stewards, doctor, purser, thirty male passengers, three women and seven children were on board. A course north was set, and before long the almost mastless clipper was moving at 3–4 knots before a cold south wind, drawn by a jury rig composed of a lower studding-sail and a staysail set on the main. Shortly afterwards, a mountainous square-shaped iceberg loomed into view. *Indian Queen* cleared the iceberg just before it dramatically broke in two; the smaller part of the berg slid into the sea, creating a great wave in front of it, and continued to travel until it was between two and three miles distant from its parent.

It was reckoned afterwards that the collision had occurred at about 60°S. Seven days later latitude 54°S was crossed and *Indian Queen* finally cleared the ice field. After crossing 49°S a course was set for Valparaiso, about 3,800 miles away. The ship's speed improved by a knot after rigging sheers were added and a topmast secured to the stump of the foremast. Under her improvised rig, *Indian Queen* gradually moved north.

Sail was sighted on 7 May. It was the New Bedford whaler *La Fayette*, whose captain came aboard, gave the crew what assistance he could, and corrected their longitude which was in error by three degrees. The following day, *Indian Queen* fell in with the French man-of-war *Constantine*, and the captain promised to guide *Indian Queen* into port. Two days later, as they approached Valparaiso, boats from *HMS Ganges* came out to meet the disabled *Indian Queen* and towed her into the roads where she anchored, 40 days after her collision with the iceberg.

On 3 May 1859 the five-year-old medium clipper *Fleetwood,* built at Portsmouth, New Hampshire, struck an iceberg off Cape Horn when running under single-reefed courses and a close-reefed topsail, and sank. The crew got away in two boats. Five days later the mate and four seamen were picked up from one boat by the British barque *Imogene*. The seventeen occupants of the other boat, including Captain Frank Dale, his wife, son, and one passenger, were never heard of again.

Certain years are remembered for the great mass of ice released into the Southern Ocean as the result of a particularly large ice shelf breaking free. In 1860, when near Cape Horn on a voyage from Baltimore to San Francisco, Donald McKay's medium clipper, *Chariot of Fame,* commanded by Captain Alan H Knowles, encountered three huge icebergs in a field of ice that stretched as far as the eye could see. In 1868 Captain Johnson and the crew of *Panther,* a medium clipper built by Paul Curtis of Medford, had an anxious week off Cape Horn surrounded by huge icebergs.

Icebergs and ice reacting with warmer water caused fog, adding to the hazards faced by ships sailing through ice fields. In 1877, ships sailing from Australia and New Zealand encountered a significant amount of ice and fog. Two clippers on a heading for Cape Horn, one loaded with Australian wheat and the other with a cargo from Timaru in New Zealand, were never heard of again and were assumed to have collided with icebergs and foundered.

A ship under the command of Captain J T Rolls, recognized as one of the finest clipper commanders of the time, had a narrow escape on a voyage to London. Rolls's ship left Auckland with a cargo of wool, kauri, and gum in February 1877 and ran into fairly thick fog about 1,000 miles west of Cape Horn. In the early hours of the morning, the lookout reported a small 60-foot-high iceberg directly ahead: the helmsman was immediately instructed by Rolls to luff; the ship came into the wind and just cleared the weather side of the berg, hitting small pieces of ice that covered the sea. The watch then took out a number of sails and trimmed the yards to reduce speed. All hands were now on deck, stationed at the masts. Shortly afterwards a mountain-like iceberg loomed out of the fog on the lee bow. Rolls was standing by the man at the wheel and immediately ordered the wheel hard down to take the ship round on the other tack, while the crew worked frantically on the braces to bring the ship round. Having cleared that hazard, ice was reported on the weather bow; this time the helm was brought hard up and the yards squared to take the ship away from a small 60-foot high iceberg with ice all round it. Not long afterwards, icebergs were seen on the port and starboard bows, but fortunately there was enough room to pass between them and get through. Within three hours of encountering the first iceberg, the ship emerged from fog and ice to sail under a clear sky. The crew, with the exception of the officer of the watch, two lookouts and the seaman on the wheel, were all issued with half a tumbler of Jamaican rum.

In 1892–1893, a huge ice field was reported east of the Falkland Islands, stretching for almost 300 miles from east to west and 100 miles from north to south. It was one of a number of vast stretches of ice that resulted from a particularly massive sheet of ice that broke away from the ice shelf, and drifted eastwards past Cape Horn. In May 1892, *Kinfauns* sailed through a 400-mile field of ice, encountering at least 100 icebergs on one morning alone. Less than two years later in February 1894 Captain Woodget, driving *Cutty Sark* in his usual relentless manner, cut through an ice field along a narrow corridor between great cliffs of ice, and got clear.

In 1906 the Irish four-master *Fingal*, outward bound to British Columbia, reported large amounts of ice off Cape Horn; the ice was accompanied by extremely low temperatures that froze the deck gear solid.

The French 2,020-ton steel barque *Hautot* may have been a casualty of the ice that covered a large part of the South Atlantic from Cape Horn to the Falklands in 1906. *Hautot* left New Caledonia on 4 July with a cargo of nickel ore for Glasgow, and was never heard from again. It was subsequently reported that her wreck was seen in the middle of a huge ice field, too dangerous to approach.

The Long-Courier, *Daniel,* and the British *Netherby*, also went missing during the latter part of 1906, and were thought likely to have collided with icebergs. On 3 July 1906, the 1,819-ton ship *Daniel* left Bellingham, Washington State, under the command of Captain David with a cargo of timber and was never heard of again. Timber was seen floating between the Diego Ramirez Islands and Staten Island around the same time; and it is likely that *Daniel* foundered there following a collision with an iceberg.

Other vessels passing through the ice field reported seeing three abandoned ships: in September a capsized derelict ship was seen floating among the icebergs, with no trace of her crew; shortly afterwards the French ship *d'If* came across a large three-master held fast in the ice with no trace of life. Subsequently *Emilie Galline* collided with an iceberg in which a large square-rigged ship was embedded. The unidentified wreckage, seen on an iceberg by a number of ships, was thought to be the remains of *Osmsary*, also reported missing without trace in 1906. A number of outward bound vessels were unaccounted for in that year and assumed to have foundered after colliding with icebergs off Cape Horn.

The years 1907–1910 were remembered for the great number of immense icebergs that broke off the Ross Ice Shelf and drifted into the path of Cape Horners. In 1908, icebergs were reported as far as 49°S and 50°W. In June of that year *Largo Bay*, on her arrival at Queenstown, reported having seen 41 icebergs in one day off the Falkland Islands. During the Antarctic summer of 1908, the Glasgow barque *Dee* sailed through a sea of ice, passing 150 icebergs of between one and five miles in length; one iceberg was 50 miles long. It took *Dee* 16 hours to pass through the ice, during which time she came across a partially dismasted barque. *Dee* moved closer to offer assistance, and identified the barque as the Norwegian vessel *Trafalgar*; several spars were missing and her bulwarks were stove in following a collision with an iceberg. *Trafalgar's* captain wanted to try and reach Buenos Aires; he succeeded, arriving there on 28 September.

In September 1908, *East Indian* of Greenock, under the command of Captain M'Kinley, was sailing in fog when she struck a huge iceberg that towered above her masts. M'Kinley and his crew were fortunate that the ship's hull did not come in contact with the berg; some of her yards, including the foreyard, came crashing down, as overhanging pieces of ice broke loose and crashed onto the deck. As *East Indian* negotiated a way clear of the iceberg, her mizzen mast made contact and buckled in two. She then found herself surrounded by icebergs. The following morning she hit another iceberg, but was undamaged. Her hull, however, received some damage when she struck a third iceberg a week later.

Another near disaster in 1908 is described by P A Eddy, who was a crew member on board the three-masted full-rigger *Cambrian Lass,* then carrying wheat from Portland to Queenstown. Having cleared Cape Horn, *Cambrian Lass,* sailing before a moderate wind, encountered a particularly dense bank of fog accompanied by bitterly cold air, indicating the proximity of ice. The captain posted two lookouts on the forecastle and two boys on the poop, one boy to keep a lookout on each quarter; in addition three long blasts were sounded on the foghorn every few minutes so that any echoes emanating from an iceberg would warn of a hazard ahead. At six in the morning, the lookout on the port bow cried out: "Ice! ice right ahead!" as a massive white-grey iceberg appeared out of the dense fog. The great ship immediately turned to port, but it was too late: *Cambrian Lass* crashed into the iceberg, with the jib boom and the weather foreyard yardarm taking the full impact of the collision; the 100-foot foreyard came crashing down taking with it sails and rigging gear; the jib boom buckled and the figurehead disintegrated; huge lumps of ice, weighing up to half a ton, fell from the iceberg, some crashing through the deck and coming to rest on the wheat in the hold, while others holed a large lifeboat and smashed one of the other boats. *Cambrian Lass* came to a halt in the lee of the iceberg, calculated to be 150 feet high and three miles long. Fortunately no one was injured and the ship was not taking water. The foreyard and other gear were cut away, the decks cleared of ice, and patches of canvas and timber were nailed down to cover the holes in the deck caused by the ice crashing through. Later in the day, the fog cleared to reveal icebergs of all shapes and sizes in every direction. During the following days, temporary repairs were carried out and a mooring chain was passed around the ship onto which a temporary bobstay was shackled to support the bowsprit. The captain assembled the crew and put it to them that they could put into Port Stanley for repairs, or continue under jury rig on the long haul to Cork. By a large majority it was decided to take the latter course of action, and the wounded *Cambrian Lass* set out for Queenstown minus her foresail and fore lower topsail, and made it.

CHAPTER 11

At War with Cape Horn

The wives and the girls watch in the rain
For a ship that won't come home again.
John Masefield, *The Yarn of Loch Achray*

Some years are memorable for the ferociousness of the weather off Cape Horn, particularly for ships battling into the teeth of relentless storms and adverse currents as they valiantly fought against the great west wind that was king in the Southern Ocean. The short days and almost endless nights of May, June, and July were dispiriting for clipper crews. In July 1895, a hurricane of such strength was blowing off Cape Horn that fourteen ships had to put back to Port Stanley and Montevideo for repairs.

The Cape Horn winter season of 1907 was a ferocious one. The big and famous four-master *Shenandoah,* outward bound to San Francisco from Baltimore, was damaged in a storm and began leaking badly off Cape Horn. *Shenandoah* turned around and headed for Australia where she put into Melbourne for repairs.

In October of the previous year, the 1,941-ton *Duchesse de Berry* belonging to Société Générale d'Armement l'Océan of Nantes was wrecked on the east coast of Staten Island, after she struck the Penguin Rocks near St John Bay. Captain Gautier de Kermoal and his crew were saved and taken to Punta Arenas. It was the ship's third failure to round the Horn on an outward voyage and earned her the title: 'the ship that could not pass Cape Horn.' In 1902 she had set out on her maiden voyage with a cargo of coal from Penarth for San Francisco, but the newly-built Long Courier received such a battering off Cape Horn that her cargo shifted, she developed a leak, her bulwarks were carried away, and she lost three of her four boats. Badly damaged, *Duchesse de Berry* retreated to Cape Town where she spent months undergoing repairs before completing the voyage to San Francisco, by sailing east. Her second attempt to round the Horn with a cargo of coal from Swansea for San Francisco in 1905 also ended in failure; she was once again forced to turn around and head east for the Pacific by way of the Cape of Good Hope. And the following year, *Duchesse de Berry* became enveloped in fog as she approached Le Maire Strait, struck the Penguin Rocks, and sank.

But it is the austral winter of 1905 that is best remembered for its fierce relentless storms, the worst ever recorded in the long history of seafaring; the weather encountered in the waters bordering Cape Horn by ships and their sailors was appalling, and accounted for considerable loss of life.

> . . . there emerges a picture of several hundred rather wonderful creations slogging it out against the gales of the Horn, taking on the ice, the lee shore, the merciless thrashing of the overwhelming sea and the remorseless howl of the hurricane wind, quietly rescuing one another in their open boats if necessary, smashed on a thousand rocks and inlets, with incredible casualties accepted as part of the risk of their workday world – commanded and manned by men many of them outcasts, some with grievous inadequacies. They died on the job, neglected and forgotten. Many of their ships were driven away, sometimes engulfed in the seas they fought.
>
> Alan Villiers, *The War With Cape Horn*

In 1905 the crew of the relatively small ship *Pengwern* risked being charged with mutiny off Cape Horn when they requested the captain to turn around because of the atrocious conditions. The ship's mixed cargo, including railway iron and barrels of cement, had been badly stowed and was constantly shifting. *Pengwern* had sustained damage to her deck and rigging, and was hammered by the unrelenting Cape Horn storms, before she retreated to Montevideo for repairs and to have her cargo re-stowed. She then made a satisfactory voyage round the Horn to Antofagasta.

About 400 square-riggers were estimated to be passaging round Cape Horn that year; the sailors and ships attempting to round the Horn from east to west during the endless nights of that particularly bad winter suffered most. A couple of dozen first class sailing ships retreated in a damaged state from the pitch of the Horn.

Villiers described the extreme hardships endured by Captain John Jones, of Caernarvonshire, and his crew aboard *Deudraeth Castle*:

But the gales shrieked in his (Jones) face endlessly. Try as he might, he could not make westing. He could make something but then he could not get north again. He held a press of sail; the wretched wind screamed at him; cold sea filled the decks; the crew suffered from frostbite, lack of warm food (galley washed out), cut hands, cracked fingers, festering torn-out nails – all those common ills of the winter west-bound Cape Horn ship, bearable unless too long continued. Then a violent shift of wind caused rigging damage too great to repair aboard.

Alan Villiers, *The War With Cape Horn*

Deudraeth Castle set sail in early April from Britain with a load of cement and coal for Valparaiso, and arrived off the Horn at the very worst time. She was one of at least 50 clipper carriers that were mauled by extremely turbulent hurricane force winds and tremendous seas sweeping through Drake Passage that winter. After weeks of failing to make progress against the adverse forces of nature, and with her cargo of coal heating up and creating the risk of a sudden fire, Jones had to turn round and head for Montevideo. There, the hot coal was unloaded and allowed to cool down before it was returned to the hold. Because the coal was wet when it was originally loaded, it had gained heat during the long voyage. The westerly gales continued unrelentingly and it was not long before *Deudraeth Castle* was again being buffeted by blizzard, wind, and wave off Cape Horn.

The clipper had to turn round again and head for shelter and repairs. She put into the Falklands, to the great advantage of the locals. Having repairs carried out at Port Stanley was expensive, as damaged Cape Horners forced to go there had little choice. Following essential repairs, Captain Jones was off again to round Cape Horn. With the worst of the winter over, Jones was optimistic that he would make it round Cape Horn on the third attempt. But the westerly gales continued as *Deudraeth Castle* sailed south under short canvas on a starboard tack, trying to find the slot she needed below the persisting westerlies. The furious gale force winds then backed to the southwest, forcing Jones to wear ship and head north again. In the perverse attitude of the westerlies, the wind then veered to the west and the north-west making any headway impossible. By then, *Deudraeth Castle's* rigging was showing signs of considerable strain, the coal was heating up again, there was limited visibility, and although Jones knew what direction he wanted his ship to take, he was unsure of even his approximate position, as he had not been able to get a sun sight because of the persistently overcast sky.

Deudraeth Castle's cargo was destined for Coquimbo, an open anchorage on the Chilean coast about 800 miles north of Valparaiso. It was by now a loss-making voyage, even if Jones managed to deliver the cargo of coal and receive the full freight. Thirty-five days out from the Falklands, disaster struck when the foremast began to come apart: first the topgallant yards were damaged and immobilized, making them useless; almost immediately afterwards the foreyard, a 90-foot bar of heavy iron, became loose, slipped, and came crashing down, end first like a giant spear, puncturing a hole in the wooden deck.

To Jones and his crew this was the last straw: they were already cold, hungry, exhausted, and demoralized in the inhospitable stormy seas off Cape Horn; and *Deudraeth Castle* had a hole in her deck and spars were thrashing around out of control. The great barque was by now unmanageable, and it was only a matter of time before she would sink, as the breach in her deck would enable the raging seas to swamp and overwhelm her. There was nowhere to go for refuge or escape, there were no other vessels in sight, and the one remaining lifeboat, the crew's only chance, would be smashed to bits if any attempt was made to launch it. The intact boat was prepared by the crew so that it would float away if the ship sank beneath them.

Taffy, the youngest apprentice, was sent aloft to the top of the swaying mainmast to see if land was in sight. After reaching the top and looking around, he came sliding down the lee backstay to the deck, excitedly announcing that sails were heading towards them. Jones immediately set his red ensign upside down to indicate that his ship was in distress. The other ship, *Pass of Killiecrankie*, on seeing *Deudraeth Castle's* distress signal, hove-to a short distance off. Fortunately there was a respite in the weather, and having poured what oil they had on rough waters the remaining lifeboat containing Jones and his crew was launched successfully, and they were rescued by *Pass of Killiecrankie*.

Jones and his crew had expected *Deudraeth Castle* to sink immediately, but she was later seen south of the Falklands by a German ship and boarded by the mate. He reported that the hatch covers had gone, and the coal-filled holds were waterlogged; the hatch covers had been removed by Jones to ensure that the barque would sink after she was abandoned.

About a dozen ships went missing without trace in the region of Cape Horn in 1905 including four British and one Danish vessel.

Sudden dismasting was another Cape Horn hazard that terrible winter.

Garsdale, a ship of 1,755 tons commanded by Captain W J King, sailed from the River Tyne in June and ran into trouble trying to round Cape Horn. While battling to make headway against the horrors of Drake Passage, an 18-year-old seaman was washed to his death from the jib boom. Shortly afterwards, when beating against a strong westerly gale and huge seas under considerably reduced canvas, *Garsdale's* main backstays gave way, bringing down the mainmast, followed by the foremast and part of the mizzenmast; the falling foremast and yards smashed the foredeck boats to pieces. Within minutes *Garsdale* was immobilized, and wreckage from the masts and yards thrashed about threatening to hole the ship; the broken mast was pounding the hull like a battering ram. The crew worked to cut away the wreckage, a task that took three days to accomplish. Meanwhile, *Garsdale* continued to be thrown around by wind and wave as she lay helpless at the mercy of a storm, unrelenting in its ferocity; one of the two remaining lifeboats was smashed by heavy seas breaking over the stern.

Three days after the dismasting, the Italian ship *Ascensione* came on the scene and stood by all day, but during the night contact between the two ships was lost. The weather eased a little and two days later, on 12 September, the 2,851-ton Long Courier *Bérangère* arrived on the scene.

With *Bérangère* commanded by Captain Baudouard standing by, *Garsdale's* beleaguered crew had no option but to launch their remaining boat, a daunting and terrifying task, as there was no other way of getting off the stricken ship apart from jumping into the confused water in the hope of being picked up by *Bérangère*. Most of *Garsdale's* crew boarded the boat but it got damaged when it smashed against the side of the ship as it was lowered into the sea. Magnificent seamanship by Baudouard and his crew, particularly those who manned *Bérangère's* boat, saved the nineteen occupants of the damaged boat. Captain King and four of his crew remained on board *Garsdale*. They jumped into the raging sea, one at a time, and were rescued with considerable skill by the crew of the French four-master. Twelve years later *Bérangère* was sunk by *U-62*.

* * *

An eyewitness account of what it was like beating against the westerly Cape Horn hurricanes that particular winter was related some years later by Captain William H S Jones. Jones was a 15-year-old from Southend-on-Sea, a town on the northern fringe of the Thames Estuary, when he joined *British Isles* as an apprentice in 1905 for what became an epic voyage. He later would become a master mariner and described his first seagoing experience in *The Cape Horn Breed.*

> I am not likely to forget my first passage in the *British Isles* nor is anyone else who took part in it; for it so happened that this voyage has passed into sea history as one of the most eventful, and in some ways, most disastrous of sailing-ship voyages in the last days of sail.
>
> William H S Jones, *The Cape Horn Breed*

William Jones joined *British Isles* at the East India Docks in London where she had arrived from San Francisco with a cargo of tinned salmon. *British Isles,* with Britannia as her figurehead, was one of the largest and finest of the ships sailing under the red ensign at the time. Built at the Clyde yard of John Reid in 1884 at a cost of £48,000, she was a steel three-masted clipper ship of 2,287 tons register, with a cargo capacity of 4,000 tons. The full-rigger crossed royal yards on her foremast and mainmast, and she carried double topsails and double topgallants. Her generous spread of canvas, fine lines, and competent crew enabled her to gain a reputation for speed, particularly when the wind was abaft the beam; in one 24-hour period she covered 383 miles, an excellent achievement for a ship of her type. When under the command of Captain J M Stott in 1898, she recorded the fastest time from London to Sydney, sailing from port to port in 80 days, covering 4,410 miles in eighteen consecutive days, at an average speed of 10 knots. Another particularly memorable performance was when she overtook the famous German five-master *Preussen.*

The commander of *British Isles* was 31-year-old Captain James Platt Barker from Cheshire who had gone to sea as an apprentice at the age of 15, after preliminary training at the Trinity House Navigation School in Hull. Barker was clean-shaven, strongly built, and recognized as a master mariner of outstanding ability who exercised authority by his mere presence. When he took command of the ship *Dovenby Hall* in 1900, he became one of the youngest ships' masters sailing under the British flag.

British Isles was towed from the Thames in ballast to Port Talbot in South Wales by the tug *Sarah Jolliffe.* Her deckhands were recruited there, personally chosen by Captain Barker from the crowd of men available in Cardiff. The captain's wife and two children were surprise passengers; they would travel in the relative luxury of a cabin under the poop. *British Isles* was worked by a crew of mixed nationalities: six British, one Irish, one Greek, with a number of Danes, Swedes,

Norwegians, and Germans. This was in no way accidental; many ships' masters thought a mixed crew was a good way of avoiding troublemakers, as men of various nationalities were less likely to band together and ferment discontent. The Scandinavians and Germans serving on British ships were first-class sailors, who could be relied upon to take meticulous care when working aloft. They were also highly skilled at splicing, seizing, and securing gear.

At Port Talbot, *British Isles* took on a cargo of 3,600 tons of coal (black diamonds). The ship was then towed by *Sarah Jolliffe* into the open water of the Western Approaches where sail took over from steam. Shortly afterwards *British Isles* was moving under full sail to royals at 11 knots on course to Cape Horn, bound for Pisagua on the north coast of Chile 10,000 miles away.

> A large vessel driving through the water under full sail is a never-to-be-forgotten wonder, to those who have experienced it; and the throbbing of a steamship can offer nothing to compare with it; for, under sail, man is in harmony with nature. On deck, with the ship running free, is a silence which can almost be felt; and from aloft comes a comforting sound as the wind hums and sighs through the riggings, or the parrals of the yard creak and occasionally groan as the vessel rolls. At night, the vast expanse of tumbling water all around can be dimly discerned by starlight, and the stars themselves, in that far greater expanse overhead, glimmer above the mastheads, to be momentarily obscured by the curves of the bellying canvas. Now we are free of land and its dangers, and the chart shows open ocean for thousands of miles ahead.
>
> William H S Jones, *The Cape Horn Breed*

There were other ships loading coal at Port Talbot alongside *British Isles*, the most notable was beautiful *Susannah*, a German ship with a reputation for speed. *Susannah*, bound for Iquique, sailed a few hours before *British Isles*. The crews wagered with each other as to which of the two reputedly fast ships would reach their destination first. *Susannah* had the advantage of a full crew; *British Isles* was undermanned, with a crew of only 33, half her full complement. Ships were often undermanned to save money.

The trader, in many cases also the ship's owner, would purchase coal at the coalfields, and sell it at the ship's destination at a considerable profit. *British Isles's* 3,600-ton cargo of coal was expected to fetch £4/10s a ton; it had been purchased at the pit head for 10s a ton, to yield a profit of about £14,400. The cost of crewing the ship was negligible: seamen were paid £3 per month and given meager rations; the apprentices were paid £4 per year, plus their food. Both groups had to provide their own clothing, including foul weather gear, which could be purchased at inflated prices from the Captain's slop chest.

On her first night under plain sail, a moderate north-westerly gale drove *British Isles* through the water at a steady 12-13 knots. At dawn, sails of another ship were seen on the southern horizon. During the morning, *British Isles* gained on the other ship, and within hours got close enough to identify her rival *Susannah*. Later in the day the gap between the two ships narrowed as the gale freshened and both reduced sail. During the next night a full gale was blowing, and the deck was covered in surging water as *British Isles* charged ahead, logging 14 knots. Next morning *Susannah* was nowhere to be seen.

Barker ordered a complete change of sail, and fair weather canvas replaced heavier fabric sails as they picked up the westerlies of the southern hemisphere. A full 12-hour day of strenuous labor was put in by every member of crew: as soon as the old sail was taken off and lowered a new sail was sent aloft, stretched out above the yard, and instantly bent; every piece of canvas, every rope wire and other sail tackle had to be manipulated by hand. It was dangerous, backbreaking, and demanding work.

> All day long we were hounded up and down the rigging, at work at heights of 40, 70, 90 and 150 feet, on each successive yard, balancing against the steel spar while standing on a swaying foot-rope, so as to be able to haul with both hands to stretch the heavy sail along the yard. To hold on with one hand, and pull with the other, would have brought a tirade of sarcasm, not only from the Old Man on the poop, but also from the seasoned shellbacks working alongside us, who despised such excessive caution. Yet, as we balanced, and held on with our belly-muscles, while grasping at the folds of stiff canvas, which gave but a precarious handhold, or crouched on the foot-rope under the yard, the green water swirling below, at varying distances beneath us as the ship rolled, was a constant reminder of the penalty for carelessness or incompetence when

working aloft.

William H S Jones, The Cape Horn Breed

A few days later smoke was seen coming from the hold, indicating that the cargo of coal was on fire, a serious situation that would threaten the ship and the crew if it spread. The hold was opened, a procedure which could have converted smoldering coal into a blazing inferno because of the inrush of air. Steam was coming off the hot coal, but to everyone's relief the cargo was not on fire, although the situation remained serious. The cargo of coal had been loaded in Port Talbot when it was damp from rain. Thermometer readings during the previous two weeks had indicated a rising temperature in the hold, but Barker had resisted the mate's urging to put into port and investigate; the mate had also voiced his concerns to forecastle hands, an act that could dent his credibility and would have led to trouble with the captain if he had heard about it.

> To the average sailor, navigation was a mystery. It was always a surprise when land came up over the horizon after the ship had been for weeks or even months in the wide waters of the ocean. The discipline of the ship was maintained partly by the respect felt by the fo'c'sle hands for the navigating abilities of the officers, which enabled them to bring the vessel to her port of destination by invisible routes over the pathless seas. On that knowledge the safety of all depended. The Captain's word was law, and had to be so. When he gave orders for the coal to be dug out, all doubts were at an end. There are no committee meetings at sea to debate what might be best for the safety of the vessel. 'The Old Man knows best' was the argument to settle all arguments. His decisions had to be taken, and obeyed, instantly, on the basis of his superior knowledge of all the circumstances of the case and his ability to weigh the pros and cons, and to anticipate contingencies that could occur.
>
> William H S Jones, The Cape Horn Breed

Eight men at a time dug out the hot coals and shovelled them onto the deck, where they were cooled by washing with seawater. For four days they toiled to get to the seat of the fire; thermometer readings had risen to 200°F as they dug deeper. Shoveling coal was hard, made much worse when the soles of one's feet were getting scorched through boots that shrivelled from standing on hot coal.

Coal that burst into flames as it was lifted out was immediately dumped over-board. After the hot coal was removed and treated on deck, it was shovelled back into the hold. The men, but not the apprentices, were given a liberal tot of rum when the operation was complete.

Then the wind strengthened, accompanied by squalls and rain. One particular squall struck the ship abeam, and sent her heeling over until the lee rail was under water. With a frightening rumble, loose coal in the hold shifted to the lee side, the extra weight leaving *British Isles* listing 45° to port. There was turmoil on deck, but the crew were fortunate that the three-master was under lower topsails, foresail and jib; if she had been carrying more sail the ship would almost certainly have capsized.

In atrocious working conditions the crew managed to stow the foresail, put the helm over, and bring *British Isles* round until she was hove-to. There she remained for four days as the storm raged, buffeted by hurricane force winds and driving rain, while a raging sea tossed this powerful clipper around like a cork. During the storm one of the crew, named Witney, was swept into the scuppers and flung violently against the poop ladder, breaking his leg in three places. All this time *British Isles* was listing markedly to port.

It was necessary to get the ship on an even keel as soon as possible, but even after the gale had abated big waves occasionally broke on board, making it too dangerous to open the hold. Barker sent the seamen and apprentices into the hold through the lazarette door; from there they groped their way forward on the coal, until they were under the main hatch; it was pitch dark as a naked light was likely to ignite coal-gas. Then they shoveled as hard as they could. They received little sympathy for their strenuous efforts in such appalling conditions; instead they were goaded with verbal abuse to spur them on to even greater effort. *British Isles's* list was not eliminated completely, and would continue to hamper her progress for the rest of her voyage.

At the end of the first week in August, 57 days out from Port Talbot, *British Isles* was fortunate to be able to cruise through Le Maire Strait under a clear sky, running before a leading east wind under plain sail. Cape Horn was only 150 miles ahead. The following day, *British Isles*, with all sails set, crossed the 67° 17'W longitude meridian of Cape Horn, well to the south of the famous landmark, a remarkable achievement in the middle of the austral winter.

Within hours of passing Cape Horn, the wind dropped and the ship was becalmed. Then the sky clouded over and a mass of threatening black clouds became visible on the western horizon. Shortly afterwards snow began to fall, and it became so cold that icicles formed on the rigging. At dusk all hands were called on deck to stow the sails, with the exception of the foresail, the lower topsails, and the storm jib. It was extremely uncomfortable for the crew who were aloft for hours on end, working on yards covered in ice, manipulating frozen sails and ropes with hands numbed by temperatures well below freezing. By ten in the evening the sails were snugly stowed, and everything was tied down on deck. The listing *British Isles*, now almost motionless, lay at the mercy of the approaching Southern Ocean storm.

Her crew didn't have to wait long: a white mass advanced relentlessly towards the ship from the total darkness of the west, accompanied by extremely turbulent water, churned up by the advancing storm. Within minutes a squall of hurricane force hit the ship, driving the lee rail under water, and immersing the crew working the braces in ice-cold water; a deluge of hail and sleet followed. One squall followed another as mountainous seas, with white foaming crests, swept relentlessly in from the west. The crew had to work waist high in the swirling ice-cold water, tenaciously holding on to the lifelines or any fixed structure as they carried out orders they knew were essential for the survival of the ship and themselves, too busy and preoccupied to even think about their perilous situation.

No further progress westward was made as *British Isles* was driven south towards frozen Antarctica. It was not long before she was pushed eastwards past the meridian of the Horn, crossed previously with such optimism.

And as though this setback was not enough, on the sixth day of the storm, tragedy struck to further dishearten the already demoralized crew: a sudden hurricane-force squall split the mizzen lower topsail, requiring the deck watch to go aloft and secure the torn sail. A two-hour struggle followed, with the crew spread out on both sides of the yard, battling with the frozen canvas that bellied out with the force of the wind despite being clewed up; during a lull, the canvas was gathered in, laid on the yard, and held down as the gaskets were passed over it. Jones, who was one of those on the yard, describes how suddenly a squall ripped the canvas from the grip of those on the weather side, and bellied out again with a loud bang. Just then an experienced seaman named Davidson was leaning over the yard and holding the sail with one hand, without his feet on the footrope while he reached over to catch the bunt-gasket that was thrown to him: the sail was ripped from his hand by the squall, and before he could get his feet back on the footrope he was catapulted through the air into the icy ocean below. Against all the odds, Davidson managed to grab a rope trailing in the water, but within seconds his numbed fingers let it go, and he was never seen again. Captain Barker asked for volunteers to man the lifeboat, but there were none. He could have ordered a crew to man and launch the boat, but he had no wish to do so, as everyone knew that a small boat would not survive in the raging sea.

There was a further tragedy later the same day: another experienced and respected seaman named West was caught on the main deck by a breaking sea that flung him violently into the scuppers; he sustained a severe head injury that left him unconscious and with an open scalp wound. After the wound was dressed by the captain and the carpenter, West was secured in the other bunk of the spare cabin with Witney, the man with the broken leg.

The loss of three forecastle hands further depleted the already meager crew. As the ship drifted south, the temperature dropped to around 20°F below freezing, and every part of the ship open to the air became enveloped in thick hoar frost. Touching ironwork or wires with bare hands caused an instant cold burn and water freezing inside sea boots was likely to result in frostbite.

Within three weeks, nine of the remaining seventeen seamen were disabled and unable to work because of frostbite to their hands and feet. They were in agony. A number of them recovered, but took several weeks to do so. In other cases, gangrene set in and resulted in the loss of fingers and toes.

Conditions did not improve: westerly storms followed, one after the other, without respite, day after day, and week after week, with the ship under lower topsails and hove-to for much of the time. *British Isles* was driven further south, while edging a bit to the west by wearing ship as the wind changed between north-north-west and south-west.

On numerous occasions, the mate urged Barker to abandon attempts to round the Horn, and instead head for the shelter of Port Stanley; with a following westerly wind the Falkland Islands was about three sailing days away. Barker refused to head for a refuge port unless there was a dire emergency, instead stating his intention of waiting for the break in the westerlies, a break that would come sooner or later, and enable him to set a westward course at the opportune moment.

Twenty-seven days on and there was no respite for the crew of *British Isles*, or any other ships trying to make a westing under sail, as westerly storms swept relentlessly through Drake Passage. The fore and main lower topsails, the only sails set, were rapidly shredded and reduced to rags fluttering from the yards when the ship was pounded by yet another hurricane force squall, leaving *British Isles* helpless under bare poles. Canvas needed to be set, as the only way to get her under way was by replacing the three lower topsails with new ones.

It was necessary to get aloft and bend new sail for the ship and her crew to survive. All hands were summoned on deck. The number of active seamen now numbered twelve, including the four apprentices. The three remaining older seamen were tough sailors whose experience, confidence, and optimism were necessary to encourage the others in their determination to overcome the adversities of that particularly severe Cape Horn winter. They were Hans Hansen from Sweden, Otto Schmidt from Germany, and an Irishman, Paddy Furlong. The three had a lot in common: they were each about fifty years of age, were unable to read or write, and had spent their working lives at sea. Furlong was an outstanding seaman and a natural leader of sailors at their work; he was always organizing the men bracing up or squaring the yards and he provided the words for the 'sea shanty' to which all rope pulling on board a sailing ship was done. He was an excellent teacher, and it was from him that Jones, on this his first and most memorable voyage, learned the essentials of seamanship:

> Paddy Furlong was my instructor, and I could only marvel at his skill and sureness, patience and endless good humor, and the neat finish of his work, however complicated a task might be.

Furlong had served on numerous clippers, including Yankee 'hell ships,' and had a fund of stories to tell about brutal masters and bucko mates.

The disabled ship continued to drift south with her head to wind on a starboard tack, controlled by one jury-rigged sail and the helm lashed hard down, as ferocious winds continued to sweep in from the west. There was still no sign of the easterlies that might be expected in these high southern latitudes. By now *British Isles* had drifted into the ice floe region, where pack-ice added to the risk of her becoming icebound. On the edge of the Antarctic ice shelf, *British Isle's* hull reverberated with the sound of large fragments of ice hitting, scraping, and grinding her steel plates. The pack-ice consisted of flat-topped pieces of sea ice, waisted at the waterline, that could freeze into a solid sheet of ice and completely immobilize the ship.

The first mate was twenty years older than the captain and held a Master's Certificate, but he had failed to get his own command. He caused discontent among the forecastle hands by expressing his doubts about the ship and the likelihood of rounding the Horn. Earlier, he had tried to persuade Barker to give up the struggle and sail for the shelter of the Falklands. As the ship drifted south towards the Antarctic Circle, the mate began to frequent the forecastle to air his views freely with the men. They were bearing the main brunt of the Cape Horn onslaught, and easily persuaded that the best course of action would be to run for shelter.

After one of these discussions with the crew, the mate said that he was feeling unwell and took to his bed. The following day twelve of the crew, including four who were suffering from frostbite, requested to see Barker, who already knew about the discontent; he agreed to meet them.

Captain Barker entered the mess-room, where the men had gathered. He was carrying a revolver and accompanied by the second mate, the carpenter, the sailmaker, and four apprentices. Barker immediately took a seat at the head of the table. The men were at the other end of the table, and Barker asked their spokesman to declare himself, and speak up. Furlong spoke, and asked Barker if he would put the ship around and head for Port Stanley. The grim-faced Barker fumed, telling the men that they had signed articles to obey orders, and that the ship was not heading for Port Stanley. He proceeded to pressure Furlong into admitting that it was the mate who had suggested he might be willing to change course if asked to do so by the crew. Barker then sent his young brother-in-law, the second mate, to get the first mate. He returned with the message that the mate was too sick to get out of his bunk. Barker stood up and left the room taking with him his revolver and ordering everyone to stay where they were while he fetched the mate. A few minutes later the mate, now fully dressed, came through the door ahead of Barker whose revolver was pushing into his ribs. Barker asked the mate if he wished to be charged with inciting mutiny. During a brief exchange the ashen-faced mate claimed to have meant no harm, admitted he was wrong, and pleaded for another chance. After the mate promised that there would be no more trouble-making and that he would obey orders at all times, Barker sent him back to his cabin. He then turned to the men and asked if they had any more complaints, to which there was a prompt reply from Furlong that they had none. He then told the crew to carry on with their duties, informing them in no uncertain terms that he was not running for Port Stanley or anywhere else just because a few sails had blown away, and saying that there was enough canvas to make new sails.

The mate was back on duty the following watch. He never again went to the forecastle to speak to the crew, except on matters related to the working of the ship.

As *British Isles* battled with Cape Horn, Barker's wife and two children stayed in their cabin; from the first day of the storms they had not ventured on deck. Mrs Barker suffered from seasickness, and the voyage had become a prolonged ordeal.

British Isles was strongly built. Her steel hull gallantly climbed the huge waves that frequently broke over her and crashed onto her ice-covered deck. The wind roared relentlessly like a pack of lions, and the growling ice scraped the hull. *British Isles* was now approximately 65°S, about 550 miles south-south-east of Cape Horn, and 300 miles south of latitude 60°, the safe southern limit specified by the Board of Trade.

Thirty-two days passed before the westerly gales moderated. Preparations were then made to bend the repaired fore lower topsail onto the yard. By dawn the following day the seas had moderated, even though gale force winds continued, and Barker announced that he intended to wear ship. This would take *British Isles* away from the ice, but it would mean sailing towards the east, and away from his goal: the Pacific Ocean.

Buoyed up by the prospect of getting a safe distance away from the desolation of Antarctic pack-ice, the crew worked with a will to bend and set the fore lower topsail, in what were appalling and extremely dangerous conditions. Then the fore lower topsail and storm jib were set, and the fore braces manned. Barker, standing on the poop, was ready to give the order to wear ship in gale force winds. All he needed was a 'smooth' wide valley of relatively flat water, with waves of diminished height, the smaller waves that normally follow the occasional towering wave.

As one of these monsters passed underneath, Barker gave the order to hard up on the helm, and haul on the weather fore brace: *British Isles* came round safely without being struck by a big sea forward, which could have prevented her coming round and have laid her in a trough at the mercy of the following waves. After a welcome breakfast the men repaired, bent, and set the main and mizzen lower topsails, enabling the ship to make way in a northerly direction away from the pack-ice amid renewed optimism on board.

The sea can be a tyrant, and nowhere more so than where the Southern Ocean narrows at Drake Passage. A squall of exceptional violence struck at four the following morning. There was a great crash as the main topgallant mast and yards were carried away, falling in a tangle of wreckage, and ending up suspended from the rigging with the ends of the steel spars pounding the bulwarks. The fore and main lower topsails, bent and set with so much human endeavor during the previous 24 hours, were shredded with such force that large pieces of canvas were torn from the yards, flung to leeward, and swallowed by the foaming sea. Surprisingly the mizzen lower topsail survived the onslaught; the crew quickly clewed up one side to take some of the pressure off it. But there was no let-up. Jones described the scene at daybreak:

> At dawn the storm was raging with such ferocity that the only way of moving about on the poop-deck was to crawl on our hands and knees. The seas were again mountainous ridges of terrifying proportions, some towering to 60 feet above us as we wallowed deep in the troughs before them.

And so it continued all day: the crew, lashed to the rail, looked on helplessly as the dangling topgallant mast and yard smashed the bulwarks to bits. Visibility was limited to the ship itself, as needles of ice flying in the spindrift made it impossible to look into the wind. Jones said afterwards that he did not know how a ship could take such a pounding and survive; he never again encountered anything as ferocious during his fifty years as a seafarer.

The climax for the crew came at six in the evening when a mountainous sea crashed onto the deck causing mayhem. The crew lashed to the rail were completely immersed in water, nearly drowned, and left gasping for air. Hieronymos, the Greek seaman, was found lying face down and unconscious in the scuppers, his leg jammed in a washport, and with the heavy iron door pounding it to pulp. He was quickly pulled clear by a number of crew, who were not sure if he was still alive. He was dragged to the starboard forecastle, where he was given first aid by the steward and carpenter.

Meanwhile, Barker and the mates, having hauled themselves by the lifelines in reply to calls for help, found that the port forecastle had been stove in by the crashing sea, leaving the seamen who had been incapacitated by frostbite lying in swirling water calling for help. At the same time, someone was shouting that Nielsen, a Danish sailor who had been on lookout duty standing between the boats on the deckhouse, was missing; he had vanished without trace and was never seen again. The four boats on the deckhouse had been washed clean away, leaving *British Isles* without any lifeboats.

The crashing sea had also smashed the heavy deal timbers that reinforced the hatch and protected the tarpaulin covering the main hatch covers; the bare tarpaulin was no match for the angry wind and sea, and was quickly ripped off. It was not long before water began entering the hold and threatened to sink the ship.

The situation was now critical: the crew was reduced to six totally exhausted seamen and four equally exhausted boys; two seamen had been lost overboard; two were seriously injured; ten more were out of action with frostbite of their fingers and toes; the deck was breached resulting in a serious risk of the hold being flooded and the ship foundering; and there were no boats left, although they would have offered little consolation in the horrendous seas that were running.

It was 13 September and 35 days into the persisting westerly storm when a quick decision was made by Barker to turn the ship and run for shelter. The fore-sail was reefed and set, the helm was put up, and the yards squared; and it was not long before *British Isles,* with the wind on her port quarter, was running in a north-easterly direction.

Tremendous seas rolled in from astern, many of them towering over the poop, lifting the ship's stern before passing underneath, as their foaming crests sent breaking seas over both rails onto the deck. At times, most of the rudder was out of the water, increasing the danger of the ship broaching, if caught by a huge wave breaking over the quarter at the same time; with insufficient crew to let the lines run free, the sails would be taken aback as the ship ran into the wind, her masts would probably disintegrate, the spars would be carried away, and in all likelihood the powerful clipper would have capsized. It required the undivided attention and constant alertness of the experienced seamen at the helm to prevent the ship from broaching.

But there was no break for the exhausted officers, seamen, and apprentices: the crew were put to work covering the hatch with another tarpaulin, securing it, and battening down more deal planks on top of the canvas before securing them with wire lashings. Then the broken and tangled rigging had to be cleared aloft, the loose mast and topgallant yard hauled aboard and secured to the deck and the tangled wire and ropes cut away and thrown overboard. And if that wasn't enough, the pumps, located abaft the mainmast where those working them would be almost constantly immersed in ice-cold water, had to be manned by the same few men and boys working in back-breaking relays in order to pump water from the hold.

It soon became clear that the rogue wave had caused other damage to the vessel. During the cleaning up operation on the rigging, the second mate discovered that the lower mainmast was sprung, and had cracked below the top, requiring all sail to be removed from that mast and securely stowed.

After running before the gale for four days the sea moderated, an indication that British Isles was beginning to come into the lee of Staten Island. As they neared the island, it became obvious to Barker and the crew that they were not alone in seeking shelter: there were about twenty other sailing ships there, driven back by the relentless storm. British Isles, one of the last to seek refuge, was later found to have had the worst mauling of those that survived.

It was never known how many ships were overcome and foundered, but a number of those appearing on Lloyd's list of missing ships at about that time went down with all hands off Cape Horn during that atrocious winter.

A careful inspection of the rigging was made by the captain and mate. They found that the foremast had also sprung near the cap, and the jib boom was cracked. It took two days of hard work, mostly by Barker, the mate, and the carpenter, with assistance from the crew, to carry out temporary repairs.

As they were carrying out the work, the crew enviously eyed one of the famous German four-masted barques of the Flying P Line as she passed Staten Island on her way to Cape Horn. Travelling at about five knots, she was taking the storm in her stride as she sailed close-hauled on a starboard tack, looking splendid under six topsails, reefed courses, and a number of jibs and staysails. These big four-masted sailing ships were built and equipped for Cape Horn, with a crew of about 40 seamen to work the special brace, halyard, and other manual winches.

While the skeleton crew of British Isles was frapping the masts the weather improved. After 40 days, the worst storm ever experienced by hardened Cape Horners appeared to be blowing itself out: the wind moderated and backed to the east, and the seas calmed to a steady heavy swell.

Forty-five days after previously passing Staten Island, Barker took advantage of an easterly breeze. The crew set the six topsails, foresail, mainsail, two staysails and two jibs, and British Isles was under way again. Two of the men who had been disabled with frost-bite returned to work, fit enough to take the wheel and perform lookout duties.

But the following day, the wind backed to the north-west, increasing to gale force during the night. Confused cross seas, built up by the freshening north-westerly wind running into the residual south-westerly swell, carried water over both sides of the ship to break on deck.

Wishing to make as much ground as possible, Barker continued to push his ship under twelve sails, including the large spreads of mainsail and foresail. But at four in the morning all hands were called on deck to haul and stow the mainsail, 3,700 square feet of heavy canvas suspended from a 105-foot-long yard. It was a demanding job that kept the deck crew working in an icy wind, while under attack from ice cold water and spray.

The six seamen and four boys were then sent aloft on the main yard to take in and secure the mainsail. As they were hauling in the weather side of the sail and spilling its wind, the mate was easing off the mainsheet, a heavy wire attached to one lower corner of the sail and the other end round a capstan on the main deck aft. As the mate continued to ease away the sheet, *British Isles* was struck by a violent squall. The force of the wind bellied the mainsail, putting such enormous pressure on the metal sheet and capstan that the pin securing the capstan to the deck sheared. The unsecured capstan went spinning across the deck, trailing the thrashing wire along the deck, narrowly missing the mate who instinctively jumped out of the way in time, saving himself from almost certain death, before crashing into the bulwarks. Above deck the wind shredded the loose mainsail, the remains of which were hauled in and stowed by those on the yard, urged on by the second mate's frantic roaring, and Paddy Furlong's bellowing chant of *Haul we High*.

There was still too much canvas set. No sooner was the tattered mainsail safely clewed up, than Barker, furious at the turn of events, ordered the crew who had just finished stowing the mainsail to take in the upper topsails. They lowered the topsail yards by slowly releasing the halyards. As they were lowering one of the yards, a gust of hurricane strength from the south-west hit the ship, and laid her over with the lee rail under water. It was lucky that *British Isles* did not capsize because of the persistent list to port caused by the uneven trim of the coal in her hold. The ship stabilized at an angle of 40° and the crew, working on the sloping deck under a constant barrage of ice-cold water, managed to tuck the three upper topsails safely under the yards.

But even with the upper topsails stowed, the ship was over-canvassed and the captain ordered the foresail to be taken in. Clewing up the foresail, almost as big as the mainsail, was another laborious task.

After the foresail was hauled up, the ship settled on a more even keel although she continued to roll . Hove-to in mountainous seas, *British Isles's* continued to roll with her masts and yards passing through an arc of up to 60°. But despite this, the five clewed-up sails had to be stowed and secured in their gaskets, an extremely difficult and dangerous task for those going aloft to work on the swaying yards.

> The main yard was rising and falling violently as the ship rolled in the heavy sea. To step out from the rigging, as it seemed into empty space, when one's leg reached out to feel for the foot-rope was, in the weather prevailing, a matter of life and death.
>
> For three hours, the six seamen and four boys lay out on that ice-covered steel yard in the pitch darkness, grunting, cursing and groaning as we labored in the darkness to co-ordinate the efforts of gathering in the frozen and bellied out pieces of canvas. These stood out like boards, and whipped back at the yard, while we clung to the swaying yard with the pressure of our doubled-over bodies.
>
> Bit by bit we got it stowed and secured with the gaskets. Then we clambered down to the main deck, and, without respite, waded through the icy water and climbed the fore-rigging to stow the foresail.
>
> William H S Jones, *The Cape Horn Breed*

The huge foresail, which was not torn, was frozen stiff and extremely heavy. As the depleted crew battled with this monstrous sail, one of the crew, a seaman named Henderson, got his fingers trapped between the footrope stirrup and the yard while throwing up a gasket to men leaning over the fore side of the sail; his half-frozen fingers lost their grip and, as the ship rolled to windward, he fell from the yard with a chilling cry of utter despair and plunged through the darkness into the roaring sea 60 feet below. Nothing could be done for the unfortunate man, and so the others remained aloft, mustering all their remaining physical and mental resources to finish stowing the tattered sail. Henderson was a good shipmate; he was the third man lost overboard on the voyage, and everyone was wondering who would be next.

It was late in the evening, they had been working continuously since noon, and when the men and boys finally reached the deck exhausted, frozen, and dispirited, the captain abandoned plans for stowing the topsails until the following morning.

*

Eight days out from the shelter of Staten Island, at noon on 28 September, the gale abated and the sea became calmer. All sail was set and the yards squared to take advantage of a wind that had veered to the north-east. The following day it veered further, until it was a south-easterly. A new mainsail was dragged from the sail locker, hauled aloft, bent to the 105-foot steel yard and set, a task that took the depleted crew seven hours of labor-intensive effort. A new lower topsail was then bent and set, a much easier task.

Under a clear sky and with all sails set, with the exception of the upper topgallants and the royals, *British Isles* logged 10 knots as she forged ahead with Cape Horn abeam, 52 days after previously leaving it to starboard. During the following ten days, sailing on alternate tacks as required by the varying wind directions, progress was made towards the Pacific Ocean.

Of the twenty seamen who had signed on for the voyage, three had been lost overboard, three were seriously injured; and frostbite had severely incapacitated five and partially disabled two. This left seven able-bodied seamen and four apprentices, far fewer than the optimum forty, *British Isles's* full complement and the number required to sail her with relative ease.

Two of the injured were secured in bunks in the spare cabin aft: Witney, the man with the badly broken leg was improving, although he had lost weight, remained weak, and was unable to walk; West, with a serious head injury, was unconscious much of the time, and seemed near to death. The condition of Hieronymos, who was lashed down in his own bunk in the forecastle where the conditions were terrible, was causing serious concern, because gangrene had developed in his badly damaged leg.

> Since the port forecastle had stove in, fifteen men were bunked in the starboard forecastle, of whom seven, including the Greek were unable to rise from their bunks. The portholes were sealed for weeks, and the only fresh air admitted was when the door was opened for a second or two, as a man made a dash to get in or out. Smoke from the bogie-stove, mingled with tobacco smoke, stale breath, and the stink of unwashed bodies and clothes, made a thick fog, which was also pervaded by something sinister and dreadful–the vile, decayed stench of gangrene, a potent of death.
>
> William H S Jones, *The Cape Horn Breed*

Hieronymos's gangrenous leg was the main source of the awful stench, although the frostbitten gangrenous toes of the sailors also contributed. He frequently became delirious, groaning and sometimes shouting loudly with intense pain. Barker's medical knowledge was limited to first aid and, with no suitable pain-relieving drugs on board, he prescribed the occasional tot of rum.

One day Grönberg, the carpenter, reported to the captain that Hieronymos had lost consciousness and appeared to be approaching death. The captain hurried to the forecastle where he found that the gangrene had spread. Before the captain had time to consider what to do, Grönberg advised him that the only way to save Hieronymos's life was to cut off his leg. Captain Barker was not a man to shirk tough decisions: after a short pause he agreed to amputate the Greek's leg.

It would be an extremely demanding task, one that would have deterred even the stout-hearted, but to Barker there would be no obstacles as he set about his unenviable job. There were no anesthetics in the medicine chest, no instruments on board for performing major surgery, and nowhere to get advice, as the *Ships Medical Guide-Book* contained no information on how to amputate a limb. Grönberg was given the task of sharpening the cook's meat saw and knife before sterilizing them in a bucket of boiling water; an iron poker was to be used for cauterizing the wound, and this was placed in the coals of the forecastle stove.

As the ship continued to pitch and roll in the heavy Southern Ocean swell, the patient, by now deeply unconscious, was lifted from his bunk and strapped down on the forecastle table. Barker then set about his task in the poorly lit forecastle, assisted by the second mate and Paul Nelson, the senior apprentice; Nelson's role was to stand by with a bottle of brandy, ready to sustain the surgeon and his assistant. The grisly procedure took place in full view of the six seamen who were immobilized in their bunks with frostbitten toes.

Afterwards Nelson gave a graphic account of the procedure to the other three apprentices, Ison, Love, and Jones:

> Overcoming nausea at the terrible stench of the gangrene, the Old Man, after binding and tightening ligatures on the thigh, cut through the living flesh, above the knee, and bared the bone. Blood spurted from several arteries. With the red-hot poker the Captain instantly cauterized the cut, and stopped the bleeding, as the stench of burning flesh filled the forecastle. Then, seizing the meat-saw, he quickly cut through the thigh-bone, and applied the red-hot poker again, and again. Grönberg, picking up the putrid

severed leg, rushed out of the door and threw it overboard.

It took half an hour to complete the operation, with Hieronymos unconscious throughout. The cauterized stump was bandaged and the ligatures left in place. The patient was then placed back in his bunk and tightly secured. A couple of hours later Hieronymos regained consciousness, but continued to suffer from intense, and at times intolerable, pain.

In the early hours of 9 October, John West died from his head injuries. Two hours later he was buried at sea, sewn into a canvas shroud weighed with scrap iron at the feet, as the captain read the prayers. Cape Horn had claimed another victim.

Three days later there was a remarkable improvement in the weather and the wind dropped to a light breeze. Grönberg had fashioned a replacement main topgallant mast from one of the spare spars carried on deck, and the calmer conditions were an opportunity to rig it. Although the weather had improved considerably, it was still going to be a demanding and dangerous task to step a topgallant mast on a ship that still had a permanent list to port; every movement of the deck would be exaggerated for the men and boys working 100 feet above the deck.

British Isles was a big ship under sail, with extremely tall masts and long yards; in port she towered above other three-masted ships. Barker's decision to rig the main topgallant mast at sea would not have been taken lightly. They were now in the Pacific, about 2,000 miles from Pisagua, a 10-14 day sail in favorable conditions, and the addition of main lower and upper topgallant and royal sails was unlikely to reduce the voyage time by more than a few hours, or at the very most a day. Intense pride in his ship and his own seamanship, combined with national pride, almost certainly drove this uncompromising tough master mariner to carry out this seemingly non-essential task at sea.

It required the combined expertise of the captain and the mate, who had shown himself to be extremely able and competent since the earlier incident, to get the job done. The new mast, about 70 feet long, was hoisted 100 feet above the deck. It was then raised upwards through the topmast cap until its heel was high enough to be fidded to the head of the topmast, after which the overlapping parts of the two masts were firmly and securely frapped together. The upper topgallant yard was hoisted into place; sail was then hauled aloft, bent, and set. These challenging and demanding tasks were completed by splicing the main brace.

The following day a fresh south-south-west breeze replaced the variable winds, and drove the tough clipper north towards Pisagua with sail set to upper topgallants. After three days comfortable sailing before the wind, *British Isles* crossed the 50°S parallel of latitude in the Pacific; it had taken 71 days to double Cape Horn, the 1,500 miles from 50°S in the Atlantic.

The winds remained favorable and good progress was made on the voyage north, except for one day when a sudden gale arose and blew out two topsails and a staysail. This meant further long hours for the meager crew as they worked on deck and aloft, taking down the torn sails, before hoisting new ones up and bending them.

Three of the men who had suffered from frostbite were able to return to light duties, and subsequently recovered completely. The more seriously incapacitated were carried on deck each day to benefit from the warm weather. Two of those were in a fairly serious condition with swollen feet and legs colored the blue-green of gangrene; they would require major surgical treatment to arrest the progress of the disease. The two with gangrenous toes would have to have them amputated on reaching Pisagua.

Hieronymos was improving slowly; he was still in pain, but it was easing and he was beginning to smile a little. Witney's leg fractures had set, and he was able to hobble along the deck supported by a shipmate. Barker had done a good job setting his fractures, but Witney remained weak and emaciated; the ship's rations were providing inadequate nutrition for the recovering invalid. Food provisions and water were extremely low, and were severely rationed.

*

On 26 October, an apprentice was aloft on the upper fore topgallant yard when he saw land in the distance; his repeated shouts of 'land ho' brought the crew out on deck. There was intense jubilation as the coastline of Chile appeared over the horizon. Soon the coast was clear from the deck, with its rocky capes, bays, beaches, and the red foothills of the lofty Andes Cordillera sweeping down to the sea; about 40 miles inland, the mountains rose to 20,000 feet, their peaks covered with glistening white snow and ice.

As they closed on the shore the town was clearly visible. Pisagua was a disappointing collection of mud huts near the waters edge, in front of steep hills bare of vegetation. It was one of the principal nitrate ports of Chile, and there were about twenty ships of different nationalities anchored in three lines about half a mile from shore, discharging cargoes of coal, or taking on nitrate that had come from the mines in the interior. The area was one of the driest places on earth with a rainfall of less than five inches a year and no vegetation of any sort.

British Isles was maneuvered into the anchorage in light airs under full sail, and brought safely to anchor under canvas, 139 days out from Port Talbot, and nearly two months overdue. Her late arrival was greeted with relief by the crews of the other ships and the British Consul. Several other vessels were overdue, believed to have been overpowered by the seas off Cape Horn. Among them was the German *Susannah*, long overdue at Iquique, 40 miles to the south. *British Isles's* battered state testified to her battle with the old adversary, the Cape Horn grey-beard: her boats were gone, their davits buckled; her sides were red with rust, and her bulwarks shattered; and her royal yards were missing, used to fish (strengthen) two of the masts.

A few hours after anchoring, a Chilean doctor, impeccably dressed in tropical whites, wearing a panama hat, and smoking a cheroot, arrived on board. After briefly examining the injured, he made arrangements for seven of them to be taken to hospital the following day.

A high price in human life and suffering was paid by the crew of *British Isles* for transporting 3,600 tons of coal from Europe to the west coast of Chile. Conditions at the hospital in Pisagua were appalling: two of the seven seamen that were transferred there died; one of those with gangrene died after having his leg amputated, and Witney, the man with multiple fractures of the leg died. The other seaman with severe gangrene from frostbite had his leg amputated success-fully. Hieronymos had more of his leg amputated to arrest further gangrene that had developed. He and the other amputee eventually got back to England, each with a wooden leg. The three with less serious frostbite had amputations of their toes, and recovered.

The apprentices were to become involved in further drama during their stay in Pisagua. One afternoon they were rowing Barker ashore when he noticed a commotion on another boat that had stopped on its way to the anchorage. Barker, fashionably attired in his business clothes consisting of striped trousers, morning coat, and bowler hat for his visit ashore, ordered the apprentices to row as fast as they could, while he steered straight for the other boat. As they drew near, it was obvious that two sailors, who comprised the crew, were attacking their captain, who was in the bottom of the boat. When the gig came alongside, Barker leapt into the other boat and with a swift uppercut lifted one of the sailors clean out of the boat and into the water. The other sailor had armed himself with the tiller and was about to smash it onto Barker's head when Paul Nelson, just in the nick time, jabbed the sailor in the belly with his oar; before he could recover, Barker locked the sailor's head under one arm, and pounded his face until he was unrecognizable.

It then came to their attention that the man in the water was drowning. Without a moment's hesitation Barker, in morning suit, bowler hat, and boots, jumped into the water and dragged the man to the boat; the apprentices helped get the unconscious half-drowned sailor on board. Barker pulled the man's tongue forward to clear his airway, and applied artificial respiration with vigor and violence by pummeling and squeezing his chest, bringing up salt water and returning him to consciousness. The sailors were then tied down in the boat which was towed ashore by the apprentices, where the two were handed over to the authorities and thrown into the filthy calaboose.

The other captain, an elderly man, had been badly beaten and was bleeding from cuts to his face and head. The two sailors had earlier rowed him ashore and used it as an opportunity to consume a large quantity of *pisco*. On the return trip, the captain severely reprimanded them for being drunk in charge of the boat, whereupon they attacked him. Without the timely intervention of Barker, they would probably have killed him. Incidents like this were normally avoided by captains insisting that their apprentices and not sailors rowed them ashore.

Callao, the port for Lima, the capital of Peru, was about 640 miles to the north, and it was to there that *British Isles* sailed to have repairs carried out after her cargo was unloaded and she had taken on 800 tons of ballast. A plentiful supply of wood, water, and provisions, as well as a good anchorage, had made Callao one of the foremost ports on the west coast of South America from the time of the Spanish Conquest.

The cost of repairing the damage sustained by *British Isles* off Cape Horn was going to be high. It would normally be covered by insurance, but the owners had taken the risk themselves, not a good decision in the circumstances, as the premiums paid to the underwriters would have been much less than the subsequent cost of repairs. Cables were exchanged between Barker and the owners. So expensive were the repairs likely to be, particularly the cost of having the foremast and jib boom lifted out and taken ashore to be repaired, that the owners considered selling *British Isles* as she lay, rather than incur the expense. Barker, indomitable as ever, decided that the crew could lift the foremast out under his supervision, and the blacksmiths would repair it on deck, an incredibly demanding task to perform on board ship.

The foremast was 130 feet high, and three feet in diameter at deck level; the lower mast weighed ten tons and had to be lifted 25 feet to bring the heel of the mast to deck level, so that it could be laid along the deck for the blacksmiths to work on. The task was accomplished by using sheer legs, composed of the robust fore and main yards as well as a topsail yard, and the physical strength of the crew, who were using block and tackle. The operation was supervised by Barker. His small team were dedicated and highly motivated; he relied heavily on the experience of older crew members, such as the mate and Paddy Furlong; there was also the second mate, carpenter, five sailors, and four boys. A new set of sails and four boats, to replace those lost, were sent out by steamer from England. After four and a half months *British Isles* was ready to set out for Australia in ballast.

Susannah, the German ship that left Port Talbot on the same tide as *British Isles*, also had a particularly bad time rounding Cape Horn. She took 99 days to double Cape Horn, 28 days longer than *British Isles's* epic slog. Chronometer error was the main contributor to *Susannah's* delay. There was only one marine chronometer on board, and it was set at Greenwich Time on leaving port. Captain Jürgens suspected that the time was wrong when his navigation wasn't accurate, and he had no way of establishing longitude.

Jürgens lacked confidence to alter course in a northerly direction, fearing that he might be driven on to the Chilean coast, and *Susannah* sailed hundreds of unnecessary miles. Having sailed further west than necessary against the prevailing winds, she was swept back with the next westerly storm. Eventually *Susannah* arrived in Iquique after a 207-day voyage from Port Talbot.

British Isles

EPILOGUE

Preceding page: Youth Hostel *Af Chapman* (Poxnar)

CHAPTER 12

The Last Sailing Fleet

I saw the great French square-rigged merchantmen, racing visions
of pale grey loveliness beneath towering, perfect suits of gale-filled
sails heading towards Hobart in Tasmania (for I was raised in those
parts), towards Nouméa in New Caledonia, or perhaps Chile or
California.

Alan Villiers, *The Bounty Ships of France*

France, a country with a long-established merchant sailing tradition, was relatively late in establishing a sizeable deep-water sailing fleet. In the years after 1881,
when France introduced a system of subsidy known as 'bounties' for its merchant
marine, a growing number of French registered clipper ships and clipper barques
took to the seas. Subsidies were paid towards the operating cost, calculated
according to the amount of cargo carried and distance sailed. In 1893 the subsidies were increased, following which increased shipbuilding took place in France
to supplement their existing fleet of mostly Glasgow-built iron and steel Cape
Horners.

Thanks mainly to Henri Picard, Allan Villiers, and Captain Louis Lacroix we
are well informed about France's great fleet of clippers. The majority of *Long-
Courriers Cap-Horniers* (Long Couriers) were built at the turn of the 20th century;
in the years 1897–1903 a total of 212 Long Couriers were launched from French
shipyards, mostly onto the River Loire at Nantes and St Nazaire. These vessels
would extend the great Clipper Ship Era well into the 20th century.

French-built Long Couriers were large steel full-rigged ships and barques, and
included a number of four-masted barques; *France I* and *France II* were the only
five-masted Long Couriers. Thirty-four of the Long Couriers launched in the first
few years of the 20th century were three-masted, full-rigged ships in the classic
clipper design. Like the original clippers they had beautiful lines. The three-
masted barques had similar lines to the full-rigged ships. France's three-masted

ships and barques averaged 2,000 tons net and had a cargo-carrying capacity of about 3,000 tons. It was possible to recognize the great French Long Couriers by their characteristic light grey hulls and well-kept appearance.

French ships were sailed only by French crews and France considered the privately owned and operated ships and their crews a national asset. In return for agreeing to be reservists in the French Navy, sailing crews were reasonably well looked after. The lot of the common sailor was considerably better than on ships of other nations: the food was good, the crew accommodation was dry, relatively comfortable and spacious, with separate quarters for eating meals. This differed from the ships of other nations where seamen were obliged to eat on the floor or bunk of a crowded damp forecastle. Frenchmen who spent their life in the French Merchant Marine were entitled to a state pension from the age of fifty. Deep-water sailing as a profession was first encouraged by Jean-Baptiste Colbert who founded the merchant marine when he was King Louis XIV's minister of finance between 1665 and 1685. Joseph Conrad, because he was of Polish birth, was obliged to quit France and join the British Merchant Navy to further his ambition of becoming a master mariner.

* * *

The famous artist Paul Gauguin spent his formative years as a merchant seaman. Gauguin was born in Peru but was a French national. His mother was half French and half Peruvian Creole with Inca blood, and she claimed that her family also had Spanish royal blood. Two long voyages with his family between Peru and France by way of Cape Horn had created the desire in the young Gauguin to become a sailor. On an outward voyage, his father had collapsed and died at Puntus Areñus, Magellan Strait.

When she realized that Paul wanted to go to sea, his mother urged him to enter the *Ecole Navale* and become a Naval Officer. But he was unwilling to put in the necessary preparation required to pass the difficult entrance examination, though he was an able pupil at school. Instead, the young Gauguin entered the merchant service as a *pilotin*, the term for an apprentice, on the first rung on the ladder to becoming an officer in the French Merchant Marine.

In 1865, when he was seventeen, Gauguin went to sea on the 1,200-ton *Luzitano*, sailing between Le Havre and Rio de Janeiro. After three years, he quit the merchant marine in order to enter the French Navy as a seaman, third-class. He was assigned to *Jérôme Napoléon*, a wooden-hulled schooner-rigged yacht with an

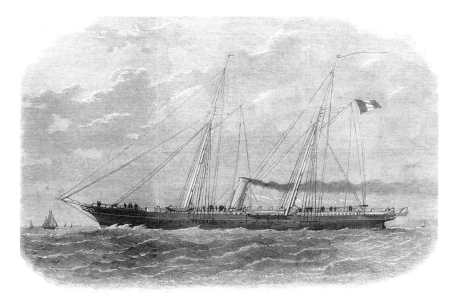

Jérôme Napoléon (ILN)

auxiliary steam engine; the emperor, Napoleon III, who owned the yacht and after whom it was named, had put it at the disposal of his cousin. After spending two years as a stoker, Gauguin was transferred to the bridge and promoted to seaman second class. In 1870, while returning from a cruise to Greenland, the Franco-Prussian War broke out and within two months Napoleon III's Empire collapsed. Gauguin's ship, then in Copenhagen, was renamed *Desaix*. Gauguin continued to serve on board the renamed yacht until the following April when he was given a certificate of good conduct and ten months leave with the right to extended leave.

Gauguin then joined the office of a Parisian stockbroker where he was spectacularly successful at conducting business. On Sundays and holidays he devoted himself to painting and sculpture. He became an early admirer of the Impressionists and acquired a sizeable collection of their paintings, including works by Paul Cézanne, Claud Monet, Edouard Manet, Camille Pissaro, Auguste Renoir, Alfred Sisley, Armand Jonkind, and John Barthold Guillaumin. Gauguin was tutored by Pissaro. His talent as an artist was recognized when he exhibited at the 5th, 6th, and 7th Impressionist Exhibitions during the years 1881 to 1883. Soon afterwards he left stockbroking to devote himself full-time to painting.

Gauguin's early success as an artist was not matched by a great interest from collectors in his work, and he was obliged to sell his treasured collection of other Impressionists' works. He later relinquished Impressionism for what was to become his own personal naive style, based on the primitive art of earlier cultures and possibly influenced by his travels as a sailor.

* * *

France began the twentieth century with a significant fleet of deep-water Cape Horner's, the last great fleet of ships to be propelled solely by the wind. In the South American nitrate trade, the shipping firm founded by Antoine Dominique (A D) Bordes in 1847 at Dunkirk was the only real rival to Laeisz's Flying P Line of Hamburg. French ships were also conveying an increasing amount of wheat from Australia and the American Northwest, as well as nickel ore from New Caledonia. Outward-bound, the Long Couriers carried British coal, cement, railway iron, and machinery.

The steel-hulled Long Couriers were excellent passage makers. On her maiden voyage *Ernest Reyer*, a worthy successor to the great clipper ships of earlier years, reached Hobart 69 days out from the English Channel. *Ernest Reyer*, a 2,257-ton ship, was launched in February 1902 from the Rouen yard of Chantiers de St Nazaire for N & C Guillon of Nantes. The company's two-year-old barque of the same name had been wrecked on the coast of Oregon three months earlier.

In February 1916 *Ernest Reyer* was about to set out from Cape Town for Falmouth with a cargo of maize when her captain, Jules Rioual, had a premonition that he would not arrive at his destination. Rioual gave a letter to Lieutenant-Colonel H L Jones RM with instructions to post it to his wife when he was reported missing. Five months later *Ernest Reyer* was posted as missing. After the war it was discovered that u-Boat *U-69* sank *Ernest Reyer* on 17 April 1916 in the Western Approaches at 49°N 08°10'W.

Crillon, a 1,979-ton ship, built in 1902 at the same Rouen yard, equalled *Ernest Reyer's* 69 days on a voyage from Europe to Australia, the precise details of which are unavailable. *Crillon* was one of the Long Couriers that survived long enough to be laid up in the 1920s and ended up in the breaker's yard.

A fast passage of 66 days to Hobart from Liverpool was notched up by the 1868-ton Nantes barque *Ernest Legouvé* in 1905. Twelve years later on 5 April 1917, *Ernest Legouvé* left Northfleet on the Thames with cement for Buenos Aires. Three days later, while still under tow by the British tug *Joffre* in the English Channel, she was torpedoed and sunk by *U-B-32* with the loss of Captain Le Pannerer and nineteen crew; the second mate and three sailors were rescued by the tug.

One of the finest and fastest of the Long Couriers was the four-masted barque *Valentine*. The 2,756-tonner was launched from the Rouen yard of Chantiers de Normandie on 8 November 1900 for A D Bordes. When under the command of Captain L Gardanne in 1902, *Valentine* had the best run home of the year for a Bordes nitrate clipper, with a time of 73 days from Iquique to Falmouth. And *Valentine* also recorded the fastest time for a westward voyage of any Bordes nitrate clipper when she arrived at Iquique 61 days out from the Isle of Wight. Later on 29 January 1904, *Valentine* reached Dunkirk 70 days out from Iquique. Sadly, on 2 November 1914 *Valentine,* when outward bound from Port Talbot, was captured by the German battle cruiser *Leipzig* off the coast of Chile, where *Leipzig* was cruising in company with the surface raider *Prinz Eitel Friedrich*. A prize crew was placed aboard *Valentine. Prinz Eitel Friedrich* then towed the barque to an anchorage on the coast where *Valentine's* cargo of coal was unloaded and used for bunkering German ships. After most of the coal had been taken off, *Valentine* was towed out to sea and sunk. Captain F Guillou and his crew were taken to Valparaiso on board the steamer *Sacramento.*

The robust Long Couriers, with their predominantly Breton crews, acquitted themselves well when rounding Cape Horn, particularly in the early years of the 20th century when conditions there were among the worst on record. Cape Horn did claim a number of these strong steel-built sailing ships; some are known about; others listed as missing are suspected to have foundered in those stormy waters.

On 1 August 1901, the 1,705-ton Nantes barque *Fervaal* was on her second voyage, outward bound to Portland under Captain Mabon, when she was wrecked on Staten Island near St John's lighthouse. Two of her crew were lost. The others were rescued by the Argentinean naval vessel *Primo de Mayo.*

In 1906, a particularly hostile year off the Horn, three Long Couriers are believed to have come to grief there. *Duchesse de Berry* struck the rocks on the east coast of Staten Island in fog on 19 October 1906 and sank, without loss of life. Two others, the 1,819-ton St Nazaire ship *Daniel,* and the Rouen-owned 2,020-ton barque *Hautot,* went missing and were believed to have foundered off Cape Horn.

France started to operate sailing oil tankers early on. *Ville de Dieppe*, a 1,228-ton iron barque built at Southampton in 1888 by Oswald, Mordaunt & Co for L Robbe & Fils of Dieppe, was the first. *Ville de Dieppe* carried cargoes of bulk petroleum across the Atlantic. In 1900 she was badly damaged by fire in Philadelphia. She was acquired by Norwegian owners in 1903. In April 1917 *Ville de Dieppe* was captured and sunk by *U-C-21* twenty miles west of Ile d'Oléron, having left La Rochelle–La Pallice in ballast bound for New York. There was no loss of life.

Quevilly, a 2,418-ton four-masted barque, was built in 1897 at the Rouen yard of Laporte & Co to carry petroleum from Philadelphia to Rouen. The four-masted tanker performed well under sail, with an eastbound time across the Atlantic of 14 days in 1906. In 1910, *Quevilly* became a twin screw motor vessel after being fitted with MAN oil-powered engines. She continued to carry bulk petroleum until she was purchased by a Norwegian company who used her to carry whale-oil, although afterwards she reverted to carrying petroleum. On 21 October 1939 *Deodata*, as she was then named, struck a mine in the North Sea when she was on a heading for Grangemouth, and sank fairly quickly. The crew, three of whom were seriously injured, were rescued.

The other sailing oil tankers were the 1,673-ton barque *France Marie*, and her sister ship *Jules Henry*, both launched from the yard of Chantiers de la Méditerranée, Le Havre, in 1900. *France Marie* spent eleven years conveying petroleum from Philadelphia to Marseilles. After a brief spell in Belgian hands, she was acquired by a Texan oil company. *Jules Henry* was also a regular petroleum carrier on the Philadelphia to Marseilles run. On 1 August 1909, when moored alongside in Marseilles, she was badly damaged by an explosion in her tanks that killed nine workers. In 1913, *Jules Henry* was reconstructed, enlarged, and had engines fitted in Rotterdam. For the following twenty years, the former four-masted barque no longer resembled a sailing ship as she carried bulk oil cargoes from Constanta in the Black Sea to Marseilles. In 1934 she was broken up and sold for scrap.

Coal was another combustible cargo; when loaded wet it was prone to gain heat during a voyage and catch fire. A fire in her cargo of coal accounted for the loss of *Astrée*, a 1,987-ton steel ship launched onto the River Clyde in 1890 by W Hamilton for A C Le Quellec of Bordeaux. In September 1901, *Astrée* was about to round Cape Horn with a cargo of coal from North Shields for Valparaiso when she caught fire and was abandoned by Captain Jouanjean and his crew. Three of *Astrée's* four boats managed to reach Staten Island, landing near St John's lighthouse, but the fourth boat with six survivors was never seen again.

Turgot, a 1,959-ton barque launched from the yard of Chantiers de la Loire at

Nantes in 1902, and owned by Compagnie Maritime Française of the same city, left Antwerp for Seattle under Captain Roze in May 1909 with a cargo of coke, bricks, and tarred oakum. On 11 June, as she was sailing past the Cape Verde Islands, a fire started on board and spread rapidly. Roze and his crew abandoned the blazing ship and survived.

In 1891, the 1,114-ton barque *Duchesse Anne* was launched from the Nantes yard of Chantiers A Dubigeon for L Bureau & Fils. In 1902, Louis Lacroix was serving as *Duchesse Anne's* first mate when she arrived in Falmouth on 7 June, 89 days out from San Francisco 'land to land.' She was then sold to G C Brövig of Farsund, Norway, and renamed *Andrea*. On 8 October 1913, *Andrea* left the River Tees in Northeast England under the command of Captain Ellertsen with 1,400 tons of coal for Gregory Bay in the Magellan Strait. A fire developed in her cargo and, by the time she arrived at her destination 83 days later, it had taken hold and she burned out.

Another Long Courier that was lost to a coal fire was the 2,100-ton Nantes barque *La Blanche*. After leaving Port Natal on 16 June 1916, a fire developed in her cargo of coal and spread rapidly. Captain Lorant and his crew abandoned ship north-east of the River Plate, and shortly afterwards *La Blanche* sank. *Général de Sonis* was within sight and picked up *La Blanche's* crew.

Firedamp, a mixture of methane, air, and coal dust that explodes on ignition, probably accounted for the loss of the Bordes 3,094-ton *Dunkerque*, built by Russell & Co on the Clyde in 1889. *Dunkerque*, under the command of Captain J Voisin, went missing after leaving Cardiff with coal for Rio de Janeiro on 23 June 1891. Four days later, an empty boat belonging to *Dunkerque* was found in the Western Approaches; it is thought likely that the large steel four-master was destroyed by a firedamp explosion shortly after departure.

A number of France's Long Couriers were lost in the Roaring Forties. Even a strong steel hull could be strained to breaking point when assailed by the relentless onslaught of the stormy Southern Ocean. The 1,949-ton barque *Gaël*, launched on 13 September 1901 from the St Nazaire yard of Chantiers de la Loire for Celtique Maritime of Nantes, was a good passage maker with a 43-day run from San Francisco to Sydney to her credit. On 22 May 1909, *Gaël* left London under the command of Captain D Métayer with a load of cement bound for Portland and called at Cherbourg and Hobart. Métayer had a reputation for pushing his ship to the limit. After rounding the Cape of Good Hope, *Gaël* took quite a punishing from the recurrent gales of the Roaring Forties as she headed for Tasmania. On 17 August, four foot of water was found in the hold, and Métayer gave the order to alter course towards the Australian coast. Despite constant use of the steam pump, it proved impossible to keep ahead of the ingression of water and four days later *Gaël* began to sink. Métayer and his crew abandoned ship about 200 miles off the south-west corner of Australia and got away safely in the boats before *Gaël* sank. Five days later they landed on Australian soil. It is not known why *Gaël* sprung a leak. Cement is a particularly heavy cargo; the weight of the cargo may not have allowed the steel plates any degree of flexibility and put a considerable strain on the riveted seams, so that openings developed between them.

Montebello, built in 1900 by Chantiers de la Loire of Nantes for R Guillon & R Fleury, was another Long Courier lost in Australian waters. In 1906 *Montebello* reached Hobart from Brest in an excellent 74 days under Captain Kervegan. On 6 November, Kervegan received orders to sail from Hobart to Port Pirrie in the Spencer Gulf to collect a cargo of wheat.

Kervégan had an unenviable task: he would have to sail the 1,725-ton barque in ballast into the prevailing winds of the Roaring Forties, with the iron-bound west coast of Tasmania as a lee shore; Kangaroo Island, south-east of the entrance to Spencer Gulf, was in his direct path and he was obliged to set a course to take his ship well clear on the west side of the island. By the time *Montebello* was approaching the entrance to the gulf the weather had deteriorated: it was a dark cloudy night, there was a howling south-westerly gale, Kangaroo Island was a lee shore, Kervégan was unsure of his position as he had been unable to make a reliable celestial observation, and he was also unaware that his ballasted vessel had been set to leeward more than he had estimated. In the early hours of 18 November, breaking waves were heard directly ahead; but it was too late: *Montebello* struck the rocks on the weather side of Kangaroo Island and the force of the collision sent the mainmast over the side; shortly afterwards the forepart of the ship came away. Kervégan and his 23 crew were extremely lucky to escape alive as the storm raged around them. They were picked up by SS *Governor Musgrave* and landed at Port Adelaide two days later.

Anjou, a 1,572-ton barque built by Dubigeon at Nantes in 1899 and owned by Raoul Guillon, left Sydney in January 1905 under Captain Le Tallec with a cargo of wheat, bound for Falmouth for orders. On 4 February, when on a heading for Cape Horn she became enshrouded in fog, and ran into the cliffs on the west side of one of the Auckland Islands, a group located 300 miles south of New Zealand at 51°S. The islands are on the Great Circle route from Australia to Cape Horn, and their shores claimed a number of Cape Horners. *Anjou* struck with considerable force; the impact threw her over on her beam ends and smashed one of the boats. Le Tallec insisted that everyone remain on board the crippled barque until first light. The crew spent a most uncomfortable night as their listing vessel was pounded against the cliff. At daybreak, Le Tallec and his crew managed, with considerable difficulty, to get clear in the three remaining boats. They rowed along the coast for about twelve miles until they found a place to land and, from there, they set out for a safe haven on foot. Twelve days later, they arrived at a location where emergency provisions were stored. Under Le Tallec's direction, they managed to stay alive for three months, before being rescued by the New Zealand steamer *Hinemoa*. Captain Le Tallec was subsequently commended for his actions.

On 18 February 1907, the seven-year-old 1,949-ton barque *Marguerite Mirabaud*, belonging to Société des Voiliers Français, went ashore on the South Island of New Zealand, some 30 miles south of Dunedin when heading for Tahiti with a cargo of coal. The crew was saved, but *Marguerite Mirabaud* became a total loss.

The Antipodes Islands in the Roaring Forties, located south-south-east of New Zealand between 49°S and 50°S, claimed the 2,410-ton four-master *Président Félix Faure* that was built by Chantiers de la Méditerranée. It was a fine and fast barque with crossed skysail yards. *Président Félix Faure* was owned by Compagnie Havraise de Navigation à Voiles and commanded by Captain Noël. While travelling to her home port of Le Havre with a cargo of nickel ore from New Caledonia on 13 March 1908, she ran into one of the Antipodes Islands in thick fog and was wrecked. The crew managed to get ashore safely in the one undamaged boat, and survived on spartan rations until they were rescued by HMS *Pegasus* two months later and taken to Lyttelton, New Zealand.

On 20 May 1906, the 1,719-ton seven-year-old Nantes grain-carrying barque *Cassard,* was on a voyage to Falmouth from Australia when she was wrecked on Bleaker Island in the Falklands, having encountered gale-force head winds accompanied by poor visibility after rounding the Horn. Captain Lemoine and his crew survived.

Another Long Courier that foundered in the Falklands was the *Hélène Blum*, a 1,757-ton full-rigged ship launched from the yard of Chantiers Maritimes du Sud-Ouest onto the River Gironde at Bordeaux on 12 September 1901. *Hélène Blum* was named after the wife of a San Francisco ship's chandler with a significant shareholding in Société des Voiliers de St Nazaire, the company that had the boat built. On 24 May 1908, *Hélène Blum*, when on a voyage from Bristol to the Falkland Islands under Captain F Hervé, struck the Seal Rocks at the entrance to Port Stanley and sank. Her crew was rescued by the tug *Sampson*. *Léon Blum*, named after the ship chandler himself, was a 2,316-ton ship built in 1902 by Chantiers de Normandie, Rouen, for the St Nazaire owners of *Hélène Blum*. In November 1917 *Léon Blum* went aground at night on the approaches to Dakar, Senegal, as she neared the end of a voyage from Adelaide under the command of Captain Grondin; she was abandoned to become a total loss.

The reef-strewn South Pacific, particularly in the area around New Caledonia, was a dangerous place for ships with a deep draft, and became a graveyard for a number of Long Couriers. The exact position of some reefs was uncertain, while others were charted as of 'doubtful existence,' uncertainties that made pilotage and navigation difficult and hazardous.

On 6 February 1900 *Emile Renouf*, a four-masted barque of 2,425 tons, launched onto the River Seine from the yard of Chantiers de la Méditerranée in Le Havre for E Corblet three years earlier, ran onto a reef near Mare Island, Loyalty Islands, shortly after leaving New Caledonia with a load of nickel ore. Captain Boju and his crew managed to get the laden barque off the reef, but she sank almost immediately. The schooner *La Perle* rescued the crew.

Notre Dame de la Garde, a 1,954-ton barque belonging to Société Marseillaise de Voiliers, Marseilles, was nearing the end of a voyage from Le Havre when she ran onto Brany Reef, within eighteen miles of Tchio, New Caledonia, on 7 August 1901 and was lost without loss of life, just fourteen months after she was launched at Nantes.

Another 20th century sailing ship lost in the South Pacific within a couple of years of being built was the 1,731-ton barque *Tourville*, launched in 1902 by Chantiers Nantais de Constructions Maritimes for Bureau Frères & Baillergeau of Nantes. On 18 June 1902, *Tourville* set out on her maiden voyage to New York under the command of Captain Yvon. She was not destined to return home. From New York, *Tourville* made the first of two voyages to Australia with case-oil. Having delivered the second cargo to Hobart and Hakodate in Japan, *Tourville* set sail in ballast for New Caledonia, where on 1 June 1904 she went aground on a coral reef near Mare Island and foundered without loss of life. It subsequently transpired that the position and extent of the reef, as marked on *Tourville's* charts, was incorrect.

On 27 May 1904, the 1,818-ton two-year-old St Nazaire ship *Ville de St Nazaire*, was two days out from Kanala, New Caledonia, under the command of Captain David, with nickel ore for Le Havre, when she hit the Kuakue Rocks and sank without loss of life.

Haudaudine, a 1902-built ship belonging to Société des Armateurs Nantais, was leaving Kataviti, New Caledonia, under tow from the steamer *Saint Pierre* on 26 January 1905 with a cargo of nickel ore when the rope parted before she was clear of the fairway. *Haudaudine* drifted onto a coral reef, was holed, and sank.

On 8 November 1909, the 2,016-ton Nantes-built barque *Armen* belonging to Compagnie Navale de l'Océanie of Paris, having arrived in ballast from Hamburg, was becalmed off Nouméa. The strong current carried the helpless *Armen* onto the rocks, where she was wrecked.

The last large steel barque to be built in Nantes was the 2,311-ton *Rochambeau*, launched in November 1902. As she was nearing the end of a voyage from Glasgow to Tchio, New Caledonia, on 30 August 1911, she struck the Main Reef, became stranded, and subsequently broke up. Captain Créquer and his crew were saved. Earlier the same year, *Rochambeau* ran into and sank the British schooner *Flora Emily* off the south coast of Ireland. The schooner's crew were rescued and landed at Queenstown.

In October 1913 the 1,948-ton Nantes barque *La Tour d'Auvergne* was wrecked on a reef near Palmerston Island in the Cook Islands when heading for New Caledonia from Tahiti. Her crew were rescued by the Sydney barque *Antiope*.

Another casualty in the Pacific was the unlucky 1,732-ton Nantes barque *Connétable de Richemont*. On her maiden voyage from Swansea to San Francisco in 1901, Captain Thoreau and a number of the crew died at sea. Her second voyage under the command of Captain J Rault was to be her last. Having collected a cargo of case-oil, as kerosene packed in containers was called, at New York and delivered it safely to Hong Kong on 17 July 1903, *Connétable de Richemont* set sail for Chile in ballast. But it was a slow voyage. The barque encountered calms and head winds, and at one point was so low on board that Rault had to purchase victuals from the United States steamer *City of Peking*, for $60. Despite the extra victuals Rault was obliged to alter course for Honolulu to re-provision, as he was running low on food and water. On 10 October, *Connétable de Richemont* ran onto and stranded on the French Frigate Shoals, a stranding that was subsequently blamed on chronometer error. The following day, Rault and his crew set off in three boats and a week later arrived at a small island near Niihau in the Hawaiian Islands. Two expensive expeditions to salvage the stranded *Connétable de Richemont* were unsuccessful.

In the Atlantic Ocean, Ascension Island, Cape Verde Islands, Azores and the Caribbean claimed six of France's Long Couriers. The first was the 1,558-ton barque *Normandie*, launched by Dubigeon of Nantes for Raoul Guillon in 1899. *Normandie* was wrecked on Ascension Island on the return leg of her maiden voyage to San Francisco under Captain Le Provost de la Maissonnière, without loss of life.

A vessel lost because there was no wind in her sails was the 1,735-ton full-rigged ship *Vauban*, belonging to Compagnie Maritime Française of Nantes. On 30 June 1906 *Vauban*, while on her way to San Francisco from Cherbourg under the command of Captain Le Dantec, was becalmed and carried by the current onto the Varandino Rocks, south-west of the Cape Verde Islands, to became a total loss. The crew escaped unharmed.

Caroline, a 2,392-ton four-masted barque, was built by Chantiers de la Loire, Nantes in 1895 for Bordes. *Caroline* was returning from Iquique in 1901 when, on 3 September, she became fogbound as she approached the Azores and went aground at Magdalena Point on the west coast of Pico Island and was wrecked. Her crew was rescued.

When the fourteen-year-old 1,917-ton barque *Bidart* reached the North Atlantic in May 1915 with a cargo of New Caledonian nickel ore for Glasgow, half the crew were disabled by scurvy and Captain J Blondel decided to put into the Azores so they could receive medical attention. In addition to his severely reduced crew, Blondel had to contend with overcast skies for three days during his approach to the islands and was unable to get a celestial position fix. On 24 May, in reduced visibility due to fog, *Bidart* was caught in gale-force winds and went aground on Faja Grande, Fayal, where she was pounded by heavy seas and broke up. Three of the crew were drowned.

On 21 January 1907, the first of two Bordes' Long Couriers to be named *Antonin* was lost on a reef off the Florida coast when on a voyage from Pensacola with a cargo of timber for Montevideo. There was no reported loss of life. *Antonin*, a 1,681-ton iron ship from the Glasgow yard of J Reid & Co, was launched in 1875 as *Killean* for Mackinnon, Frew & Co of Liverpool, and in 1893 was acquired by Bordes.

The 2,612-ton four-masted barque *Antoinette* successfully thwarted u-Boat attempts to destroy her in October 1917 when she was under the command of Captain P Lechevanton. Two years later, the four-master came to grief in the Caribbean when heading for New York from the Panama Canal with a cargo of Chilean nitrate: on 21 December 1919, *Antoinette* struck the Serrana Rocks about 200 miles off the coast of Nicaragua and sank, without loss of life.

* * *

> Scurvy amongst them is rare, in 1933: though some still die. The *Olivebank* lost a few boys once, and the little *Flavell* had to land some into hospital after a passage of 210 days from Geelong to Falmouth. Just the other day the barque *Plus,* homeward bound with guano from the Seychelles to London, put into St Helena for food and medical attention for her scurvy-struck crew. But she had been at sea almost four months then, on a passage that should have taken no longer than two.
>
> Alan Villiers, *Last of the Wind Ships*

In the 20th century scurvy, caused by a deficiency of vitamin C, continued to be a problem for some sailing ship crews. On her maiden voyage in 1901 the 1,923-ton barque *Neuilly,* belonging to Société des Long-Courriers Français, Le Havre, arrived at New Caledonia 148 days out, with nearly half the crew afflicted by the disorder. On 1 October 1917 *Neuilly,* loaded with 3,000 tons of Australian wheat, was about 300 miles from Bordeaux when she was intercepted and sunk by *U-90* with no reported loss of life.

On her maiden voyage from Penarth, South Wales to San Francisco in 1901, the 1,974-ton barque *Olivier de Clisson* took 224 days; part of the time was spent on a stopover in French Guiana after she failed to round Cape San Roque. By the time *Olivier de Clisson* arrived in San Francisco, the crew was afflicted by scurvy and three deaths resulted from the disorder. Five years later, *Olivier de Clisson* developed a leak in the Atlantic near the Cape Verde Islands, and soon after the crew abandoned ship she capsized and sank.

Crew members of *Biarritz*, a 2,252-ton St Nazaire-built ship, were found to be suffering from scurvy when she docked at San Francisco after a 170-day voyage from Cardiff in 1906. On 30 September 1917, *Biarritz* caught fire off the Brazilian coast during a voyage from Leith to Montevideo and was abandoned by her crew.

In 1912, many of the crew of the 1,859-ton Chantiers de Normandie of Rouen built barque *Elisabeth*, belonging to Tiberghien & Fils of Dunkirk, developed scurvy when on a voyage from New Caledonia. There were three deaths, and Captain J Blondel put into Recife so that the remainder of the crew could receive medical attention. On 3 June 1917 *Elisabeth*, loaded with nitrate from Pisagua, was captured and sunk by *U-C-29* in the English Channel a few miles south-east of Lizard Point. Four days later *U-C-29* was herself sunk off the south-west coast of Ireland by the Q-ship *Pargust*.

* * *

The notorious Columbia River Bar claimed a couple of Long Couriers. On 4 December 1902, one year after she was launched by Chantiers de la Loire, Nantes, for N & C Guillon, the 1,730-ton barque *Ernest Reyer*, the first of two Long-Couriers to be so named, arrived off the Columbia River entrance during a severe north-westerly gale. Despite the best efforts of the crew, *Ernest Reyer* was unable to cross the bar and was driven ashore. Her crew was rescued with considerable difficulty, and within a few days this fine steel barque was a complete wreck. Seven other vessels were lost in the area during the storm.

In January 1909, the 1,698-ton ship *Alice* belonging to Société des Voiliers de St Nazaire, one of the few French clipper ships to cross skysails on her three masts, was waiting to cross the Columbia River Bar with a cargo of cement for Portland when a storm developed and she was driven ashore seven miles north of the river entrance. Her crew was saved, and soon *Alice* became a complete wreck.

Another Long Courier that came to grief on the coast of the American Northwest was the year-old 1,728-ton Nantes-built barque *François Coppée*, belonging to N & C Guillon. On 20 November 1903, *François Coppée* went ashore about 35 miles north of San Francisco at night in fog, and was quickly overwhelmed by heavy seas. Captain Irruye could not get a celestial position fix during the previous three days because of persistent cloud. Irruye and eleven of his crew were drowned.

The American Northwest was the scene of another tragedy involving a Long Courier. On 2 January 1902, the 1,726-ton Dubigeon-built barque *Max*, belonging to G Ehrenberg of Le Havre, was approaching the Californian coast near Mendocino when she collided with the American steamer *Walla Walla*, out of San Francisco and bound for Puget Sound with 142 passengers and crew. *Walla Walla* sank in less than 15 minutes with the loss of 42 lives. *Max's* bows were badly damaged, and three days later, minus her bowsprit, she limped into San Francisco. A decade later, *Max* went aground at Huily Point on the Chilean coast when on a short passage from Valparaiso to Talcahuano and became a total loss.

A collision in the waters off the United States East Coast resulted in the tragic loss of one of France's largest Long Couriers, the 3,194-ton four-masted barque *Hélène*, purchased by Bordes in 1909 from S Goldberg & Sons of Swansea. *Hélène*, originally named *Andorinha* when she was launched from the yard of W Pickersgill & Sons in Sunderland seventeen years earlier, became the largest vessel in the Bordes fleet. In February 1919, when under the command of Captain Maisonneuve, she left Baltimore for Nantes with a load of steel. Shortly afterwards, on 22 February, *Hélène* collided with the Norwegian steamship *Gansfjord* off the coast of Virginia and sank within minutes. Seventeen of her crew went down with her.

Two Bordes four-masters were in a collision that did more damage to the reputations of their captains than to the ships. *Rhône* was a four-masted barque of 2,610 tons that was launched from the yard of Chantiers de la Méditerranée at La Seyne in 1896. W B Thompson of Glasgow built *Pacifique*, the second Bordes vessel to sail under that name. In 1907 *Rhône* collided with *Pacifique* during daylight hours in excellent visibility near the Falkland Islands. In the collision, *Rhône* and *Pacifique* escaped serious damage, but both captains were found to have been at fault and were dismissed by Bordes.

In 1902 *Pacifique* had received a particularly bad mauling off Cape Horn, when on a passage from the Tyne to Valparaiso with coal. The 2,055-ton four-master was forced to return to Montevideo after huge seas swept her decks, carrying away Captain Leyat, five of the crew, three boats, and the bulwarks; her rigging was also badly damaged. *Pacifique* was lost in 1916 when she went missing after leaving Penarth on 21 October bound for Port Arthur.

Fifty years earlier, Bordes first ship named *Pacifique* was launched as *Berkshire* from Barclay, Curle & Co's yard on the Clyde, and came into Bordes ownership in 1889. The iron four-master was involved in a serious collision in October 1895; the 1,472-ton *Pacifique* was run down in the North Sea off Dudgeon by the German steamer *Emma* and sank within minutes, with the loss of Captain Lebras, a coastal pilot and ten crew; the other eleven were rescued by *Emma*.

Yet another ship named *Pacifique*, an iron four-master, was launched at Whitehaven in 1886 as *Gilcruix*, for North Western Shipping of Liverpool. The Poet Laureate John Masefield served on the 2,108-ton *Gilcruix* during his short career as a sailor. In the 1890s, *Gilcruix* was sold to Knöhr & Burchard of Hamburg, to become *Barmbek*. On 18 August 1914, she was captured in the English Channel south of Lizard Point by a French patrol vessel while on a voyage from Portland to Ipswich, to the surprise of her German crew who were unaware that war had broken out. On 2 March 1921, when owned by Chantiers Navale de l'Océanie of Brest, and en route from Fredrikstad, Norway, to Australia with timber, the now named *Pacifique* collided with the American steamer *Naamhok* in the English Channel south of St Catherine's Point. The disabled *Pacifique* was towed into Le Havre by the Norwegian steamship *Tiro*, and two years later she was broken up at Caen. *Naamhok* was found to have been at fault and was required to pay £44,000 damages.

Following Guglielmo Marconi's first ship to shore radio transmissions in 1898, warships, and most steamers, were equipped with wireless telegraphy. But France's Long Couriers, like their clipper predecessors, were not equipped with radio communications, and had no way of sending distress signals or making contact with other vessels or shore radio stations. It was not surprising, therefore, that a number of Long Couriers were lost without trace. A total of 55 sea-going ships registered in various countries were reported missing in 1905 alone.

> Nobody ever comes back from a 'missing' ship to tell how hard was the death of the craft, and how sudden and overwhelming the last anguish of her men.
>
> Joseph Conrad, *The Mirror of the Sea*

Persévérance, an iron 2,511-ton four-masted barque built for Bordes by Thompson of Glasgow in 1886, left Rio de Janeiro in ballast bound for Antofagasta on 3 July 1891 under the command of Captain J Lequerhic and was never heard of or seen again. *Persévérance* would have been rounding the Horn during the latter part of the austral winter and may have foundered there.

Bordes were unlucky with another Clyde four-master, the 2,017-ton *Amérique*. Launched in 1892 from the yard of Robert Duncan for Lyle Shipping of Greenock and named *Cape Clear*, she was acquired by Bordes in 1899 and renamed *Amérique*. At the beginning of August the same year, Bordes most recent acquisition set out from the Tyne for Valparaiso under the command of Captain Plusquellec. On September 22 *Amérique* was seen, and Plusquellec was spoken to off Cape Horn, after which the four-master disappeared without trace. One explanation for *Amérique's* loss might be that she collided with an iceberg and sank.

Two of the first French-built steel Cape Horner's were launched by Chantiers de la Loire; *Marie Alice* at Nantes in 1889, and *Pierre Corneille* from their St Nazaire yard in 1891. The relatively small 999-ton barque *Marie Alice*, owned by V Vincent of Nantes and commanded by Captain Ancelin, was last seen on 12 February 1895 when she left Sydney with a cargo of wheat for Antwerp. An encounter with ice off Cape Horn was considered the most likely cause of her demise. *Pierre Corneille*, an 1,125-ton full-rigged ship belonging to Rouen owners, was commanded by Captain Leloquet from the time she left the stocks. In 1896, the steel full-rigger had a 50-day run from Australia to the West Coast of America, outpacing 67 other vessels. After leaving San Francisco on 19 February 1898, *Pierre Corneille* disappeared without trace.

In 1901, Chantiers de la Loire launched the 1,728-ton ship *Charlemagne* at Nantes, for Maritime Française of the same city. On the return leg of her maiden voyage, *Charlemagne* left New Caledonia with nickel ore under Captain A Codet on 11 December 1901 and was never seen again.

Other Long Couriers that went missing without trace after leaving New Caledonia in the first decade of the 20th century were the barques *Lamoricière* and *Mistral*. *Lamoricière*, 1,471 tons, was built in 1895 by Laporte of Rouen for Société des Voiliers Nantais. On 3 November 1903, *Lamoricière* left New Caledonia under the command of Captain Christian with a cargo of nickel ore for Glasgow and was never heard of again.

The 2,208-ton four-masted barque *Mistral*, owned by Société Marseillaise de Voiliers, was built by Chantiers de la Loire at Nantes and launched onto the Loire in October 1901. On her fourteenth voyage to New Caledonia, *Mistral* left Tchio for Le Havre with nickel ore under Captain Chevrier on 6 September 1908 and disappeared without trace. Lloyd's posted her missing on 6 February 1909.

A Long Courier lost while on her way to New Caledonia was the 2,254-ton barque *Biessard*. Launched from the Rouen yard of Chantiers de Normandie in 1900, *Biessard* spent thirteen years carrying nickel ore from New Caledonia before she vanished after leaving Le Havre in ballast on 3 February 1914 under Captain Maréchal.

Du Couëdic, a 1,732-ton barque belonging to Société Bretonne de Navigation, Nantes, had a short life. Launched at Nantes on 15 May 1901, *Du Couëdic* was posted missing after failing to arrive in Sydney, having left San Francisco in ballast under Captain Pignorel on 22 December 1902. Wreckage sighted near the

Marshall Islands was presumed to be the remains of *Du Couëdic*.

The 1,740-ton barque *Paris*, belonging to Société des Long-Courriers Français, Le Havre disappeared without trace after three years service. *Paris* left Hamburg with a cargo of cement under Captain Le Guével and 27 crew on 10 May 1903. After calling at Cherbourg, the barque set sail for Honolulu and was last in communication with another vessel at approximately 19°S 37°W in the Atlantic on 26 June. On 4 March 1904 *Paris* was posted missing at Lloyd's.

Lafayette, a 1,766-ton ship built by Dubigeon in 1902 for Société des Armateurs Nantais, was another short-lived vessel. Captain Alexandre Boju commanded her from the beginning. The full-rigger disappeared when on a voyage from New York to Saigon in 1905 with a cargo of case-oil. It is possible that her highly inflammable cargo caught fire and exploded, but there was no evidence to substantiate this.

Yet another short-lived Long Courier was *Saint Donatien*, a 1,259-ton barque launched by Dubigeon for L Bureau & Fils in 1900. *Saint Donatien* developed a reputation as a good passage maker. She was last in communication with another vessel in the Atlantic at 5°N 27°W on 6 July 1905 when on a voyage in ballast from Bordeaux to Adelaide under Captain R Bertrand. *Saint Donatien* was never heard of again, and was posted missing at Lloyds in February 1906. She joined the many sailors and ships of the great sailing ship era that simply disappeared from the high seas without trace.

* * *

European waters, particularly the coastal waters of the North Atlantic Islands of Britain and Ireland, took their toll of Long Couriers.

Maréchal Lannes, a 1,955-ton Nantes barque was launched by Chantiers de la Loire in December 1898 for Guillon & Fleury. A few months later, on 28 March 1899, she left Swansea with a cargo of coal for San Francisco. Soon after she left Swansea dense fog enshrouded the area. On 30 March, three empty boats belonging to *Maréchal Lannes* were washed ashore on the Pembrokeshire coast. Shortly afterwards, her upper masts were seen protruding from the water beside Grassholm reef, part of the hazardous Smalls Rock at the edge of St Georges Channel, about twenty miles off the south-west coast of Wales. Captain C Lepetit and his 24 crew perished in the tragedy.

On 28 December 1900, the eighteen-month-old 1,587-ton Bordes barque *Seine* was nearing the end of the return leg of her maiden voyage, and was 81 days out from Iquique en route to Falmouth with a cargo of nitrate, when she was driven ashore on the north coast of Cornwall during a fierce gale. *Seine* came ashore at Perran Bay, an otherwise picturesque stretch of sand running north from Perranporth. Her crew of 24 were rescued with considerable difficulty.

In 1893, Bordes acquired the 1,112-ton iron ship *Brahmin*, built by Robert Steele in 1876 on the Clyde for J & W Stewart of Greenock. Bordes renamed her *Quillota*. On 12 November 1901, *Quillota* was nearing the end of a relatively short voyage from Nantes to the Tyne in ballast when she was caught in a storm and forced to anchor. Both anchor cables parted and *Quillota* was driven onto the Hendon Rock off Sunderland, and foundered with the loss of nineteen lives.

The 1,447-ton iron ship *Gipsy,* belonging to F Bossière of Nantes, was originally named *Rodney* when she was built for Devitt & Moore by W Pile & Co of Sunderland in 1874. She was acquired by Boissière in 1896 and renamed *Gipsy*. At the beginning of December 1901, *Gipsy* was approaching the English Channel with nitrate from Iquique when she was driven eastwards by a strong south-westerly gale that took her past Falmouth, where Captain Warneck was expecting to pick up orders. Warneck altered course for Plymouth Sound, with the intention of riding out the storm, but the wind backed, and on 7 December *Gipsy* was driven onto the rocks at Downderry on the Cornish coast between Looe and Plymouth, and abandoned without loss of life.

Tragedy struck another Clyde-built Bordes iron ship, the 1,184-ton *Chanaral*. She was launched in 1875 from the J E Scott yard for R W Jamieson of Greenock as *Martin Scott*. On 31 January 1902, *Chanaral's* tow rope parted after a strong easterly gale blew up when she was three days out from the Loire, en route to Port Talbot in ballast. Shortly afterwards, the iron full-rigger capsized and sank about 70 miles north-west of Ushant after her ballast shifted. Captain Loreau and twenty of his crew were lost. The mate, Legrand, managed to survive for twelve hours in extremely cold water before being picked up by the Norwegian steamer *Victoria*.

North Uist in the Outer Hebrides, notorious for its rocky shoreline and treacherous low-lying islands and reefs, in addition to its equally unforgiving offshore shallows known as the Sound of Monach, claimed *Van Stabel* and her crew. *Van Stabel,* a 1,741-ton barque from the Chantiers de la Loire yard at Nantes and belonging to Société des Voiliers Dunkerquois, left Glasgow under the command of Captain Quemper with coal for San Francisco on 17 January 1903. Little progress was made against the strong winter gales that sweep across the Atlantic to the exposed west coast of Scotland. Less than two weeks out, *Van Stabel* lost her main and mizzen masts during a severe storm, and then disabled, was driven north and thrown onto the Durbury Reef off North Uist on 1 February with the loss of Quemper, and the crew of twenty-six.

The 1,731-ton barque *Commandant Marchand*, launched by Chantiers de la Loire on 16 March 1900 for Maritime Française, left Leith under tow by the tug *Oceana* on 25 February 1903 bound for Antwerp. The tow rope parted off the North Yorkshire coast during a storm, and *Oceana* lost sight of her charge. *Commandant Marchand*, with Captain Arnaud and his crew, was not seen again and was subsequently posted as missing.

A similar tragedy struck *Alexandre*, a four-masted 2,419-ton Bordes barque launched by Chantiers de France at Dunkirk on 22 June 1902. The following year, while in the North Sea under tow from Dunkirk to the Tyne, the tow rope parted; *Alexandre* and her crew of 33 disappeared without trace.

At the end of December 1903, *Faulconnier*, a 1,715-ton Nantes barque, approached the Irish coast at the end of a 17-month maiden voyage that had taken her to Philadelphia, Hobart, Hiogo, and San Francisco. On 1 January, a fierce storm blew up and drove *Faulconnier* into Clonakilty Bay where she went aground at Travera, near Seven Heads, and became a total wreck. Captain Hermic and his crew of 25 escaped ashore and were taken to Courtmacsherry.

Cape York was built by Barclay, Curle & Co for Lyle Shipping of Greenock in 1890. Bordes acquired the 2,030-ton four-masted barque and renamed her *Gers* in 1899. In January 1905 *Gers* arrived off the French coast in rough seas and poor visibility with nitrate from Tocopilla under the command of Captain Delépine, and went aground on Ile de Ré. As stormy seas battered the stranded four-master, the crew clung to the rigging throughout the hours of darkness. The following morning they were rescued with considerable difficulty by the French steam trawler *Georgette*. *Georgette's* captain, Fernand Castaing, was afterwards commended for his heroic and skilful action.

Jane Guillon, a 1,717-ton barque, was launched in August 1900 from the yard of Chantiers de la Loire of St Nazaire for N & C Guillon of Nantes. In 1905 most of her crew, including her captain, were afflicted with scurvy when in the South Atlantic, and were obliged to detour to St Helena, where they replenished their Vitamin C reserves with fresh fruit and vegetables. On 25 April 1907, when under the command of Captain Lech'vien, *Jane Guillon* arrived at Queenstown from San Francisco with a cargo of barley, and received orders for Ipswich. Off Beachy Head she found herself unable to maintain progress against strong easterly headwinds, and accepted the services of a tug. Conditions got worse until the early hours of 3 May, when there was an improvement in the weather and Lech'vien found himself beside Gris Nez Lighthouse. For some unexplained reason the tug released the tow and headed off, leaving her charge perilously close to the rocks. The crew immediately started setting sail, but 20 minutes later, before the fully-loaded barque could begin to get under way, she drifted onto the rocks where she was pounded by heavy seas. Shortly afterwards *Jane Guillon* sank. Her rigging stayed above the water, and Lech'vien and his crew were saved by remaining there until they were rescued by the Audresselles lifeboat just after daybreak. The barque became a total loss. At the subsequent inquiry the tug was found to have been at fault for abandoning her tow.

Mal Bay, County Clare, in the West of Ireland, is bounded by a particularly notorious stretch of coast that spelt doom for sailing ships carried north past Loop Head when attempting to enter the River Shannon during an Atlantic storm. The attractive full-rigged ship *Léon XIII*, launched from the Dubigeon yard for Société des Armateurs Nantais in 1902, was thrown onto the Needle Rocks at Quilty in Mal Bay on 2 October 1907 by hurricane force winds sweeping in from the Atlantic. *Léon XIII*, commanded by Captain Emile Lucas, had arrived off the Shannon Estuary with a cargo of wheat from Portland and was driven north into Mal Bay by the storm. An incredible drama unfolded and continued for two days, as local fishermen in their frail canvas currachs (coracles) battled with the raging ocean to come to the aid of *Léon XIII's* crew. The fishermen managed to rescue most of the crew in particularly difficult and dangerous circumstances. By the following morning, when the battle cruiser *HMS Arrogant* under the command of Captain Ralph Huddelston arrived on the scene, the storm had abated. The remaining members of the crew, including the seriously injured captain, were taken off the stranded *Léon XIII* by *Arrogant's* sailors. A couple of months later the strong steel ship, that had withstood the extreme forces of nature as she lay stranded on the jagged rocks off Quilty, broke up under the onslaught of another Atlantic storm.

On 13 November 1908 *Croisset*, a 2,257-ton barque from the Rouen yard of Chantiers de Normandie, was carrying 3,500 tons of nickel ore from New Caledonia to Glasgow when she struck and stranded on South Rock, Cloughey Bay, County Down. *Croisset's* Captain A Kervégan and crew were rescued by the Cloughey lifeboat. But a fine large barque that had given nine years service to the nickel ore trade was lost.

In 1908, Cornwall's Land's End claimed the 1731-ton barque *Alice Marie,* owned by Société des Voiliers Dunkerquois, and built by Chantiers de la Loire in 1901. On 3 October *Alice Marie,* commanded by Captain Cloatre, was rounding Land's End in dense fog, during a voyage from Birkenhead to Antwerp under tow, when she struck the Runnelstone, a treacherous inshore rock, with strong tidal currents in the vicinity. *Alice Marie* was pulled clear by her tug at high water, and towed towards Penzance. But she was badly damaged and sank in Mount's Bay within a couple of miles of the harbor. Her crew was rescued.

On 25 February 1909, the 1,947-ton barque *Surcouf* was sailing north in the Irish Sea in fog, with a cargo of nickel ore from New Caledonia for Glasgow, when she ran aground on the County Down coast at Black Nob. Her 24 crew were saved but she became a total loss. *Surcouf,* built in 1901 by Chantiers Nantes de Constructions Maritimes, belonged to Société des Voiliers Nantais.

Général Mellinet, built for Société des Voiliers Nantais by Laporte of Rouen in 1895, was sold to G C Brövig of Farsund, Norway in 1905. In April 1912, the 1,491-ton barque, then named *Gunvor* and commanded by Captain Salvesen, arrived in the English Channel with a cargo of nitrate from Caleta Buena. On the night of 6 April *Gunvor,* having sailed past Lizard Point on a heading for Falmouth in reduced visibility, ran ashore on the rocks at Beagles Point, Black Head, about five miles north-north-east of Lizard Point. Her crew of 19 escaped by hanging a rope ladder from the bowsprit and climbing down onto dry land. *Gunvor* became a total loss.

A Long Courier that survived being driven aground and abandoned in heavy seas was *Marie,* a 1,958-ton barque belonging to Société Générale d'Armement, launched by Chantiers de la Loire from their St Nazaire yard in 1899. On 19 March 1913, *Marie* was caught in a snowstorm in the North Sea, as she neared the end of a voyage from San Francisco to Hull with a cargo of wheat, and was driven onto Haisborough Sand. *Marie's* crew of 24 were rescued by the Grimsby trawler *Ameer.* Shortly afterwards, the crewless *Marie* freed herself from the sandbank, and was subsequently found by a couple of Dutch trawlers: helped by tugs, they towed her to Cuxhaven. *Marie* was found to have only minor damage and it was not long before she was sailing the high seas again. In December of the same year, *Marie's* crew sighted the abandoned listing hull of the British ship *Dalgonar,* drifting in the Pacific Ocean off Easter Island. On 23 September 1916, *Marie* was in St Georges Channel, about 35 miles south of the Tuskar Rock, as she neared the end of a voyage from Antofagasta to Ellesmere Port, River

Mersey, when she collided with the British steamer *Wheatlands* and sank. Her crew escaped.

After leaving Glasgow on 12 December 1913, the ten-year-old 2,166-ton Nantes barque *Maréchal de Noailles* was headed by gales and forced to take shelter in Lamlash Bay in the Firth of Clyde, and subsequently in Belfast Lough. On 12 January, she left Belfast and was towed to the vicinity of the Tuskar Rock where the tow rope was released. But *Maréchal de Noailles* was unable to work clear of the south-east corner of Ireland, and when another winter storm arrived from the south-west the large barque was swept eastwards by gale-force winds into the Bristol Channel, driven ashore near Minehead in Somerset, and wrecked. Her 24 crew were rescued.

On 21 October 1914 *Guéthary*, a 1,930-ton barque built by Chantiers Nantais de Constructions Maritimes in 1901 for Société Bayonnaise de Navigation, went aground and stranded at Cape Ellen Bay, Isle of Islay, as she neared the end of a voyage from New Caledonia with nickel ore for Glasgow; she became a total loss.

On 5 December 1915, another Chantiers Nantais de Constructions Maritimes barque, the 1,969-ton *Amiral Courbet* commanded by Captain Mazurais, had just left Cork bound for Albany, Western Australia, when she became embayed in Fennels Bay, Myrtleville, to the west of the entrance to Cork Harbor. Shortly afterwards she stranded on Carrig Rocks and subsequently became a total loss. *Amiral Courbet* was owned by Société des Voiliers Nantais.

A tragic loss was the Nantes ship *Hoche*, lost with all hands off the east coast of Scotland in 1915. On 22 October, the 1,941-ton clipper ship, owned by Société Générale d'Armement, left Ipswich in ballast for Leith under tow. As she neared her destination she was engulfed in a storm and her tow rope parted. *Hoche* was last seen off Carnoustie on 28 October. The following day *Hoche's* four boats, with lifebelts and other wreckage, were found on the shore between Arbroath and Carnoustie.

A 1,981-ton barque that started life as the Long Courier *Jean Bart* in 1901, became the Hamburg registered *Heinz* in 1913. In October 1914, *Heinz* was captured as a prize near Port Nolloth, South Africa, by the armed merchant cruiser *Kinfauns Castle*, and subsequently sailed under the Red Ensign as *Tridonia*. Shortly after leaving Belfast for the River Plate under Captain Stewart in early October 1916, *Tridonia* was beset by a storm and took shelter in Cork Harbor. During a lull, Stewart set sail again. But *Tridonia* was barely 100 miles from the Irish coast when the storm gained strength, and the barque received a further battering that swept her eastwards. On this occasion, Stewart sought shelter in the Bristol Channel, anchoring *Tridonia* in Oxwich Bay. Shortly afterwards, on 30 October, *Tridonia's* cables parted and she was swept further eastwards and thrown onto the Mumbles, a couple of rocky outcrops off Mumbles Head in the Gower Peninsula, South Wales. Captain Stewart was drowned; the rest of the crew was saved.

In May 1917 the 1,913-ton *La Pérouse,* another Société Générale d'Armement ship, went ashore on the French coast about 22 miles south of the entrance to the River Gironde, after she arrived there with a load of wheat from Buenos Aires. The crew escaped, but *La Pérouse* became a total loss.

Léon XIII on the rocks at Mal Bay

CHAPTER 13

The *Unterseeboot*

Few boats in recent years have attracted so much attention among naval officers as the *Holland*. If she proves a success she may render the great floating forts of the nations useless, for she has the most powerful of all means of destruction, the torpedo, combined with the most effective of all armors, being invisible under the sea and travelling when in action, beneath the water. She is something in the shape of a cigar.

New York Times, 18 May 1897

The rapid development of the submarine, the *Unterseeboot* (u-Boat), as a weapon of war by the Kaiser's Imperial German Navy signaled the end of the reign of the large sailing merchantmen on the oceans of the world. At the beginning of the

Holland (ILN)

1914–1918 war, France, with over a hundred Long Couriers, operated the only remaining fleet of Cape Horner's. Many of those would be lost to u-boats; German surface raiders accounted for twelve Long Courier losses.

Before the Great War, merchant ships belonging to an enemy could be stopped and taken into the port of the adversary, or the port of a neutral country. It was contrary to International Law to sink an unarmed ship without warning; a merchant ship could be sunk at sea, but only if the crew and passengers had already been safely removed to the attacking ship or another vessel. The accepted conventions of naval warfare required that the crew and passengers of merchant vessels be protected and not abandoned to fate in lifeboats. These conventions changed when the u-Boats were introduced.

Sixty Long Couriers, with a combined registered tonnage of about 115,000 and a capacity to carry over 150,000 tons of cargo, were sunk by German u-Boats during the war. The crews were frequently allowed to get clear before their vessels were sunk. The details of what happened to some Long Couriers and the crews that were lost to enemy submarine action only became available after the war had ended.

One that escaped was *Général de Sonis*. The 1,943-ton Nantes barque had a good turn of speed: on her maiden voyage she logged 6,160 miles in 25 days in the Roaring Forties, an average speed of 10 knots, despite two days of calm. On 8 April 1915 the barque was under tow by the tug *Homer* in the English Channel near St Catherine's Point when she was ordered to stop by *U-32* under the command of Oberleütnant Baron von Spiegel. Captain H Gibson, who was in command of *Homer,* slipped the towline, turned his tug round, and headed straight for the submarine; he was uninjured despite extensive damage to *Homer's* wheelhouse from a hail of bullets. The tug missed *U-32's* stern and escaped. During the confusion Captain Bénard, *Général de Sonis's* commander, set all sail and sped towards Dover. There he picked up another tug and set off on his voyage to Sunderland. *Général de Sonis* continued in service until she was laid up in 1931; she was the last of the Long Couriers to sail under the French tricolor.

But von Spiegel did not remain idle: later that day, *U-32* torpedoed the 2,029-ton ship *Châteaubriand*, commanded by Captain Grondin, about 25 miles south of Beachy Head, as she was setting out on a voyage from London to New York. No casualties were reported. *Châteaubriand* had been launched on 16 January 1901 by Chantiers Maritimes du Sud-Ouest of Bordeaux for Société Générale d'Armement.

Marie Molinos, a 1,715-ton barque launched from the yard of Chantiers de la Loire in 1899, was intercepted by *U-20* and sunk in the North Atlantic on 3 May 1916 at 46°40'N 10°20'W, when on a voyage from Nantes to New York. There was no reported loss of life. *U-20* and her commander Kapitänleutnant Walther Schwieger had gained notoriety a year earlier by torpedoing *RMS Lusitania* on 8 May 1915 off the Irish coast with devastating consequences.

On 10 February 1917, the 2,315-ton Bordes ship *Rancagua*, commanded by Captain Grégoire, was sunk by *U-B-39* in the Bay of Biscay, and lost with all hands.

A Société Générale d'Armement barque last heard of about the same time was the 1,960-ton *Général de Boisdeffre*. On 14 January 1917, *Général de Boisdeffre*, commanded by Captain Pireau, left Mejillones, north of Antofagasta, with a cargo of nitrate for Brest and was never seen again. She was documented as a war loss by the French authorities, although there was no German record to confirm it. It is likely that the barque was sunk by a German submarine that subsequently went missing itself.

Jacqueline, a 2,613-ton Bordes four-masted barque, left Iquique under Captain Y Nicolas on 1 July 1917 with a cargo of nitrate for La Pallice. On 25 September the four-master encountered the British Liner *Victoria*, at 46°25'N 13°10'W, and Nicolas communicated with the captain. Shortly afterwards, as the liner continued on her way, a submarine was sighted nearby just as a bank of fog enveloped the area. After the war it was established that the u-Boat was *U-101*, commanded by Kapitänleutnant Koopman; he lost his target in the fog but found *Jacqueline* the following morning and torpedoed her: she and her crew were lost.

The 1902 Dubigeon-built, 1,389-ton barque, *Saint Rogatein* was under the command of Captain Illiaquer when she was torpedoed by *U-B-40* off Cornwall on 17 November 1916, as she set out for Buenos Aires from Dieppe. *Saint Rogatein* was badly damaged, but Illiaquer, who had been the ship's commander for eleven years, and his loyal boatswain Matelot Huguen, remained on board after he had ordered his crew to abandon ship. Illiaquer and Huguen tried to save *Saint Rogatein* but she sank before they could escape, and they were drowned. The brave captain and boatswain were honored by having two steamers, *Capitaine Illiaquer* and *Matelot Huguen*, named after them in 1921 and 1922.

The large 2,241-ton Chantiers de St Nazaire ship *Bayonne* was lost in the English Channel, in what became a happy hunting ground for u-Boats. In February 1917 *Bayonne* was held up by strong headwinds, following her arrival at the mouth of the English Channel from New York with 3,300 tons of barley and maize for

Ipswich. A few days later, the wind veered to the south-west to become a leading wind that enabled her to make her way up the Channel with ease. On 18 February, *Bayonne* was less than 30 miles east of Start Point when she was captured by *U-84*. *Bayonne's* crew was encouraged to abandon ship before the U-Boat crew sank the fine full-rigger by placing bombs on board. Her crew survived and came ashore near Lyme Regis.

On 1 March 1917, the 1,668-ton Norwegian barque *Hovda*, originally launched from the yard of Chantiers de la Loire as *Jean Baptiste*, was sunk by *U-C-43* off County Cork with no reported loss of life. Nine days later, *U-C-43* was herself lost with all hands off the Shetland Islands, following an encounter with the submarine *HMS G-13*.

When outward bound to New Caledonia with coal from Glasgow, the 2,048-ton Nantes barque *Guerveur*, commanded by Captain Huet, was attacked by *U-48* on 12 March 1917 north-north-west of Tory Island. The barque was armed and fired back, but was hit below the waterline by the third shell from the submarine, and sank. The crew abandoned ship under fire but escaped injury; three days later they landed safely on the coast of Donegal.

Marguerite Elise, a 1,085-ton barque launched by Chantiers de la Loire at Nantes in 1891 for V Vincent, was sold to Seetzen Gebruder of Bremen in July 1903 and renamed *Carl*. In October 1914 she and her cargo of guano were captured by a Royal Navy warship, escorted into Falmouth and impounded. Shortly afterwards she was sold to Norwegian owners, renamed *Lapwing*, and later named *Ivrig*. On 1 May 1917, *Irvig* was attacked and sunk by *U-C-65*, as she was passing through the North Channel between Belfast Lough and the Mull of Galloway when on a voyage from Dublin to Newport News, Virginia, in ballast. There was no reported loss of life.

Mezly, a 1,391-ton Dubigeon barque, was described as an unlucky ship. Captain Dagorne died at sea during her maiden voyage in 1900. In 1902 *Mezly* had a particularly bad passage from Saigon to Dunkirk with rice; it took 255 days: Captain Danval with the mate and the boatswain died at sea, probably from scurvy, an affliction that also incapacitated other members of the crew. *Mezly* was then acquired by Société Générale d'Armement. When laden with coal at Port Talbot in 1907, a firedamp explosion aboard sank her. She was later refloated. In 1910, *Mezly* was partially dismasted when on a voyage from Sunderland to San Francisco, and had to divert to Sydney for repairs that took nearly three months to complete. *Mezly* left Antofagasta at the beginning of 1917 with a cargo of nitrate for Nantes. On 3 May, she was captured and sunk by *U-C-73* about 200 miles south-west of the Fastnet Rock. Captain E Droguet and his crew got away in two boats. Two days later those in the mate's boat were rescued by a steamer. But Droguet and the remainder of the crew endured seven days of considerable hardship before they came ashore in Dingle Bay, County Kerry. There were no deaths or injuries, and Droguet was commended for his actions.

The Long Courier *L'Hermite,* owned by Société des Voiliers Dunkerquois, beat off the advances of a submarine. On 16 May 1917 *L'Hermite* came under attack from *U-C-17* north-west of Ushant. She had been armed a short time previously, and was able to drive off her attacker, before putting into Brest for repairs. In 1923 *L'Hermite* was sold for scrap and broken up.

Jules Verne, a 1,254-ton steel barque, was the first Long Courier to benefit from the enhanced bounty payments when she was launched at Nantes in 1894. On 29 May 1917, the former *Jules Verne,* then sailing under the Danish flag and named *Consul N Nielsen,* was sunk by *U-69* near the Outer Hebrides while on a voyage from Buenos Aires to Copenhagen with a cargo of linseed. There were no reported casualties; *U-69* had sunk *Ernest Reyer* with the loss of all hands a year earlier.

On 31 May 1917, as the unarmed Le Havre barque *Jeanne Cordonnier* under the command of Captain Arnaudtizon, reached the Western Approaches with a load of Chilean nitrate, she was attacked by *U-88.* The u-Boat opened fire while ordering the crew to abandon ship; *Jeanne Cordonnier's* starboard boat was badly damaged, but the crew managed to get away in the port boat, with the exception of one man who drowned. Despite having to cope with very rough seas, the boat-load of survivors reached the Isles of Scilly three days later.

An unidentified sailing vessel sunk in the North Atlantic by *U-30* on 28 July 1917, west of the Fastnet Rock at 51°45'N 14°W, was presumed to be *Atlas,* a four-masted barque that left Glasgow under Captain Le Squeren in ballast for the West Indies on 17 July, and was never heard of again. *Atlas* had been in French ownership for less than tree months when she disappeared. The steel 1,927-ton four-master was launched by Barclay, Curle & Co in 1886 for R Shankland of Greenock with the name *Bannockburn;* her figurehead was a representation of Robert The Bruce. *Bannockburn* was sold to Norwegian owners in 1905, and named *Leif Gundersen.* In March 1917, *Leif Gundersen* was seized by the French Navy and taken into Glasgow on suspicion of being under German control because letters addressed to Germany were found on board. On 10 May, she was declared a war prize, and shortly afterwards was registered in Lorient as *Atlas*.

On 31 July 1917, the 2,264-ton Bordes owned ship *Madeleine*, originally built for Société de Navigation du Sud-Ouest, Bordeaux, was attacked by *U-155* off the coast of North Africa when outward bound to Sydney in ballast. When shelled by the submarine, *Madeleine*'s crew put up a two-hour fight and lost a third of the crew, before Captain Lévèque surrendered. Twenty survivors, including a number of wounded, were rescued by an American steamer. Shortly afterwards, they were transferred to the French trawler *Marakchi*, and taken to Casablanca where they arrived on 7 August. Captain Lévèque and his crew were mentioned in dispatches for their bravery.

In 1908 Bordes acquired the Barclay, Curle & Co's 1892-built *Springburn* and renamed her *Alexandre*. The 2,482-ton four-master survived until 1 August 1917 when she encountered *U-155* about 400 miles north-west of the Canary Islands. She was to become that submarine's second Long Courier victim. *Alexandre* was becalmed and unable to maneuver; in addition her two small guns were no match for the submarine's two five-inch guns. After a short unequal exchange of fire, the crew of 32 abandoned ship. Her guns were transferred to the submarine before she was sunk by gunfire. Captain Lebreton and his crew arrived safely in La Palma.

The Rouen-built four-master *Marthe*, 2,754 tons, had some impressive passages. Her best outward time to the Chilean coast was 70 days. On 6 July 1917, *Marthe* left Le Verdon Roads for Valparaiso in ballast and four weeks later, on 2 August, came under attack from *U-155* at 33°38'N 23°30'W. *Marthe* returned fire, but her guns were no match for the submarine's two five-inch guns, and she was forced to surrender; one crew member was killed and five seriously injured. *Marthe* was sunk by explosives, and her crew set free in the boats. Three days later, they were rescued by a British submarine, and shortly afterwards transferred to a British steamer that landed them in the Azores. Captain Leff and his crew were mentioned in dispatches.

The 2,338-ton *Tarapaca*, built by Thompson on the Clyde in 1886 for Bordes, was one of the first of the large iron four-masted barques to be fitted for water ballast, and her cargo capacity was 4,000 tons. *Tarapaca* was within 50 miles of the mouth of the Gironde on 1 September 1917 with a cargo of nitrate from Iquique for Bordeaux when she was intercepted and sunk by *U-52*. Captain Hunault and his crew made it safely to the French coast the same day.

One of the most determined battles ever fought between a Long Courier and a u-Boat was between the Bordes 2,754-ton four-master *Blanche* and *U-151* on 19 September 1917, north-west of the Bay of Biscay. *Blanche,* commanded by Captain Bailleux, had left La Pallice for Iquique in ballast when she encountered *U-151* at 47°10'N 10°35'W. A two-and-a-half-hour battle ensued in which *Blanche's* crew put up a brave fight against superior firepower, and were only beaten when *Blanche* was torpedoed by the u-Boat. Bailleux and seventeen of his crew were lost. Sixteen survivors, including three wounded men, got away in the boats. Three days later they were rescued by the French naval vessel *Audacieuse,* and taken to Rochefort.

Tijuca, another Bordes four-master, also fought it out with *U-151.* In 1910 Bordes acquired the 2,257-ton Charles Connell built *Marion Joshiah,* and renamed her *Tijuca.* In November 1917, *Tijuca* left La Pallice in ballast for Taltal. Seven days out she came under shell fire from *U-151* about 200 miles west of Cape St Vincent. A short battle ensued; Captain J M Ollivier and his crew were outgunned by the more heavily armed submarine and surrendered. *Tijuca* was torpedoed and sunk.

Babin Chevaye was a 1,930-ton Nantes barque with a history of misadventure. Captain Robert was in command when one man was lost overboard and five were seriously injured off Cape Horn in August 1902, on the return leg of her maiden voyage; in addition, her main topgallant mast came down and she developed a leak, making it necessary to put into Montevideo for repairs. In 1905 *Babin Chevaye's* rudder broke as she doubled the Horn, and Captain Louis Lacroix had to take her into Taltal for repairs. On 23 August 1909, a huge wave swept forward along the full length of her decks as she was running before a fierce storm in the Roaring Forties; two men were lost overboard and the two on the helm were seriously injured. On 14 January 1918, *Babin Chevaye* was attacked and sunk by *U-84* in the Bay of Biscay as she neared her destination, Nantes, with a cargo of nitrate from Chile. Her crew escaped. Twelve days later, *U-84* was rammed and sunk by a British patrol boat in the Irish Sea.

The Nantes barque *Michelet*, 1,965 tons, commanded by Captain M Rose, went missing and was presumed lost to a German submarine during a voyage from South Australia with wheat for Dakar in 1918. She was last seen when in communication with the crew of *HMS Bristol* on 19 April about 220 miles north-north-west of Dakar. She was never seen again. *U-154* was known to have been active in the area and *Michelet* was probably attacked and sunk by *U-154* with the loss of her 28 crew. After the war ended, it became known that *U-154* was torpedoed by *HMS E-35,* and lost with all hands near Cape St Vincent on 11 May 1918 after a two-hour battle.

A minefield laid by U-C-21 claimed the 1,615-ton ship *Coquimbo.* The steel full-rigger, originally named *Burmah,* came from the Russell yard on the Clyde where she was launched in 1890 for Foley & Co of London. In 1907 she was acquired and renamed *Coquimbo* by Bordes. In July 1917, when nearing the end of a voyage from Antofagasta to La Pallice, the wind died and *Coquimbo* was becalmed. On 11 July, having been unable to make way for nearly two days, this fine ship drifted slowly and steadily towards a mine in a minefield about 30 miles west-south-west of Isle de Ré. Captain Le Saux, aware of the imminent danger, ordered the crew to abandon ship. But before the boats could be lowered, *Coquimbo* struck the mine and was destroyed. The clipper sank with Captain Le Saux, the second mate and five sailors still on board. The rest of the crew were rescued by local fishermen and taken to La Rochelle.

No lives were reported lost among the crews of the thirty other Long Couriers sunk by u-Boats during the Great War: *François,* a 1,945-ton barque with the distinction that she had been delayed for 100 days in a persisting Atlantic calm in 1906, was nearing the end of a voyage from Portland with wheat when she was intercepted and sunk by U-35 on 10 August 1915 south-west of the Fastnet Rock; on 22 March 1916 the 1,982-ton barque *Bougainville* was intercepted by U-70 and torpedoed as she approached the Irish coast with wheat from San Francisco; the following month Bordes's 2,258-ton Long Courier and their second to be named *Chanaral* was intercepted and sunk by U-67 about 60 miles from the Isles of Scilly, when nearing the end of a voyage from Chile with nitrate; on 2 May the 2,036-ton barque *Le Pilier* was sunk off Ushant by U-45 when on a voyage to Buenos Aires from London; the 1741-ton barque *Françoise d'Amboise* was sunk by U-22 north-west of the Shetland Islands on 21 June shortly after leaving Leith for Valparaiso; on 10 September the 1,941-ton barque *Maréchal de Villars* was sunk by U-B-18 between Land's End and Ushant as she neared the end of a voyage from Seattle with a cargo of grain; the 1,125-ton Italian-owned barque *Doride,* formerly the Chantiers de la Loire built *Jeanne d'Arc,* was sunk west of the Isles of Scilly by U-35 on 19 September; on 21 October the 1,963-ton barque *Brizeau,* Captain Louis Bourgneuf, loaded with American grain was sunk by U-B-18 near the Casquets; three days later U-B-18 sank the 1,983-ton barque *Cannebière,* Captain Rihouet, about 20 miles south-south-west of the Bishop Rock; on 14 November the 1,954-ton barque *La Rochejaquelein* was sunk off Lizard Point by U-C-17 while en route from San Francisco to Ipswich with wheat; the 1,724-ton barque *Marguerite Dollfus* was sunk by *U-B-37* about 30 miles south of Start Point on 7 December; *Emma Laurans,* a 1,907-ton barque, was captured by *U-52* on 9 December near the Canary Islands and ordered to sail towards the shore, where she was destroyed; on New Year's Day 1917, the Bordes 1,194-ton iron ship *Aconcagua,* Captain Lévèque, was captured and sunk by *U-70* in the Bay of Biscay; the 1,950-ton barque *Brenn,* Captain F Bernot, was sunk by *U-59* on 16 January off the French coast when outward bound to Chile in ballast; the 1,944-ton barque *Duc d'Aumale,* Captain Doublecourt, was inward bound with a cargo of wheat from Bahia Blanca when she was captured and sunk on 22 January by *U-43* in the North Atlantic; the fine 2,234-ton ship *Jules Gommès,* Captain R Nicole, was lost to *U-62* west-south-west of the Bishop Rock on 12 March when on a voyage to Bahia Blanca; the 1,953-ton barque *Eugène Pergeline* was sunk by *U-54* on 15 March about 25 miles south of the Fastnet Rock when inward bound to Glasgow with nickel ore; the 1,419-ton Norwegian owned barque *Sirius,* formerly *Colbert,* was sunk by *U-57* on 22 March off the north of Scotland; also in March the 1,995-ton barque *Sully,* Captain Populaire, was sunk by *U-C-47* near Ushant when inward bound from Bahia Blanca; the Dubigeon built and Norwegian-owned 1,748-ton barque *Sagitta,* formerly *Grande Duchesse Olga,* was sunk by *U-78* south-east of Lerwick in the Shetland Islands on 2 April; on 10 May *Bérangère,* the ship that carried out the brilliant rescue of *Garsdale's* crew off Cape Horn in 1905, was sunk by *U-62* 100 miles south-west of the Fastnet Rock when inward bound with timber to Le Havre; *Marthe Roux,* a 1,726-ton barque, was captured and sunk by *U-34* in the Mediterranean, 25 miles north-north-east of Cape Ivi, on 3 July as she neared the end of a voyage from Black River, Jamaica, with logwood for Port-St-Louis-du-Rhône; on 13 August the 1,698-ton barque *Emilie Galline,* Captain J Frostin, was captured and sunk by *U-C-79* south of the Eddystone Rocks when on a heading for Le Havre with 2,500 tons of Chilian nitrate; in September the 1,266-ton *Bon Premier,* a former German barque and the first French war prize when she was captured on 8 August 1914 when en route from Hamburg to Callao, was sunk by *U-60* west of the Bay of Biscay at 46°06'N 11°25'W, when heading for Bordeaux with rum and logwood; *Edouard Detaille,* a 1,920-ton jubilee-rigged barque, bound for Rochefort with a cargo of Australian wheat, was torpedoed by *U-60* about 150 miles north-west of the Iberian Peninsula on 15 September; *Europe,* a large four-masted barque commanded by Captain Adolphe P Nicolas, was captured and sunk by *U-C-63* in the Atlantic, just west of the Bay of Biscay on 24 September; *U-C-63* struck the Long Courier fleet a second time on 24 September, when she captured and sank the 2,588-ton four-master *Persévérance*, Captain F Béquet, in the Bay of Biscay at 44°22'N 09°10'W; the 1,945-ton barque *Eugènie Fautrel*, loaded with grain from Geelong, was captured and sunk in the Atlantic just west of the Bay of Biscay on 29 September by *U-60*, shortly after the u-Boat sank *Bon Premier* and *Edouard Detaille*; on 30 September the 1,663-ton barque *Amiral Troude*, Captain Forgeard, was torpedoed by *U-B-51* in the North Atlantic at 46°42'N 16°48'W; the 1,126-ton iron barque *Victorine*, Captain A Mathieu, was overcome by superior fire power and sunk by *U-89* on 7 October about 100 miles north-west of the Iberian Peninsula; *La Epoca*, a 2,268-ton Henderson of Glasgow built four-masted barque, was nearing the mouth of the Gironde at the end of a transatlantic voyage from New York on 29 October when she was sunk by *U-93* at 45°10'N, 1°45'W; and the 1,202-ton iron barque *Chili*, Captain J Ollivier, was sunk by *U-B-54* on 14 December at 47°49'N 07°11'W.

* * *

During the Great War armed surface raiders, known as the Kaiser's Pirates and that included one full-rigged ship, roamed the oceans in search of merchant ships belonging to Germany's enemies. On 28 October 1914, during a voyage from South Wales to the River Plate and Valparaiso with coal, the Bordes-owned and Clyde-built 2,023-ton iron four-master *Union* was captured by the armed steamer *Kronprinz Wilhelm* in the South Atlantic at approximately 34°S 52°W, not far from the Plate. *Union's* cargo of coal was a bonus for the German raider. Transferring the coal from the French to the German ship was a difficult and long drawn-out task, and ended on 22 November when *Union* capsized with 800 tons of coal still in her hold. There were no casualties and *Union's* crew was put ashore at Montevideo two days later.

Shortly afterwards, the 1,571-ton barque *Anne de Bretange*, belonging to Société Générale d'Armement and under the command of Captain Picard, was captured by *Kronprinz Wilhelm* at 27°S 33°W. The crew of the captured ship were transferred to the raider. *Kronprinz Wilhelm's* crew spent several days transferring stores from the barque to their ship and then tried to sink *Anne de Bretange* by gunfire and dynamite. They failed, and they also failed to sink the 1,579-ton Dubigeon-built steel barque by ramming her; *Kronprinz Wilhelm's* stem was damaged in the encounter. *Anne de Bretange's* waterlogged hulk was left to sink.

Another surface raider responsible for sinking a number of Long Couriers was *Prinz Eitel Friedrich*. On 10 December 1914, she intercepted the Le Havre barque *Jean* in the Pacific at 44°50'S 81°40'W. *Jean* was carrying a cargo of coal from Port Talbot to Antofagasta. In order to save the coal cargo, a prize crew was put on board and *Prinz Eitel Friedrich,* in company with *Jean,* headed for Easter Island and arrived there on 24 December. *Jean's* topgallants were sawn off to prevent her being seen from a distance, and to make her less top-heavy as her hold was emptied. The slow process of transferring the coal commenced and was completed on 31 December. Then, the 1,994-ton barque was towed offshore, used for target practice, and sunk. *Jean's* crew were marooned on Easter Island until they were rescued by the British steamer *Skerries.* Captain Le Dillinger was not among the rescued: he was enamored with the daughter of a chief on the island and decided to remain rather than return to war-torn Europe.

Shortly afterwards, on 27 January 1915, another Société Générale d'Armement's barque, the 1,926-ton *Pierre Loti,* was captured and sunk by *Prinz Eitel Friedrich* in the South Atlantic at 29°53'S 26°47'W, when on a voyage from San Francisco to Harwich with a cargo of barley.

The following day, *Prinz Eitel Friedrich* captured and sank the 1,950-ton barque *Jacobsen* at 29°44'S 26°57'W. *Jacobsen,* built by Chantiers de la Loire at Nantes, and owned by Société des Voiliers Dunkerquois, was on a voyage to Gloucester on the River Severn with a cargo of barley from San Francisco.

The seventeen-year-old 2,263-ton barque *Nantes* belonging to Société Générale d'Armement left Iquique for London with 3,350 tons of nitrate. On 26 December 1916, *Nantes* was intercepted, captured, and sunk by the surface raider *Moewe* west-south-west of the Cape Verde Islands at 12°37'N 34°W.

A week later, on 2 January 1917, the large 2,715-ton four-masted barque, *Asnières,* built at Le Havre in 1901 and also owned by Société Générale d'Armement, was en route from Bahia Blanca under the command of Captain E Ybert with a cargo of wheat for Bordeaux when she was captured and sunk by *Moewe* at 03°16'N 29°10'W. *Ville du Havre,* also commanded by Captain Ybert and belonging to Société Générale d'Armement, was lost on 7 March 1916 to *U-32* off Ushant. One of *Ville du Havre's* crew lost his life in the encounter.

On 15 December 1917, the Chantiers de la Loire built 1,941-ton barque *Maréchal Davout,* commanded by Captain Bret and belonging to Société Générale d'Armement, was captured and sunk by the raider *Wolf* in the South Atlantic, south-south-east of Bahia Blanca, when on a voyage from Melbourne to Dakar in Senegal with wheat.

One Long Courier was a victim of 'Friendly Fire.' The 2,073-ton barque *Quillota*, the second Bordes vessel to bear that name, was launched from the yard of Chantiers de St Nazaire, Rouen in 1902. On 29 September 1917 she set sail for Fremantle, Western Australia, from St Nazaire Roads in convoy with the four-masted ship *A D Bordes* and the barquentine *Saint Suliac*; the three vessels were escorted by the armed trawler *Chevrette*. The escort returned to St Nazaire the following day. *A D Bordes*, under the command of Captain Joseph Briand, was attacked by a German submarine on 2 October, but beat off the enemy with her guns and escaped.

Four days later a steamer came into view astern of *Quillota* and started firing. *Quillota* was not flying her ensign and Captain A Mal, assuming that his barque was under attack from a German surface raider, returned fire. Forty minutes after the action started, *Quillota*, by then badly damaged, began to sink with the loss of one sailor by drowning. When the crew were taken on board the steamer, Mal and his crew were surprised to find that their attacker was the British armed merchant cruiser *Mantua*, previously a P&O liner. Six of *Mantua's* crew were injured, one seriously, in the exchange of fire. *Mantua's* crew had wrongly identified *Quillota* as the German surface raider *Seeadler*. It was a case of mistaken identity; the loss could have been avoided if *Mantua's* gunnery officer had identified *Quillota* as a classic French barque, and not a three-masted full-rigged ship like *Seeadler*.

A vessel with a relatively long and checkered history was the 1,742-ton ship *Maréchal de Castries*, launched by the Dubigeon yard for Société des Armateurs Nantais on 10 October 1901. On 5 September 1910, *Maréchal de Castries* survived being thrown on her beam ends by a pampero off the River Plate during a voyage from Dublin to Portland, and had to put into the Falklands for repairs. In February 1918 she was attacked by the German surface raider *Norefos* off the African coast, but her crew, using the ship's two guns, managed to keep the armed steamer at bay and escaped. *Maréchal de Castries* was sold to H H Schmidt of Hamburg in 1922, and two years later renamed *Hamburg*. In late 1925 *Hamburg* ended a long voyage at Falmouth with a cargo of Australian wheat for orders. The former Long Courier was directed to Cork but, on the way, encountered a severe storm. *Hamburg* was driven north into the Irish Sea, and on 21 October went aground on the Kish Bank. Her crew was rescued by the local lifeboat. *Hamburg* was refloated, and although she was not badly damaged it was decided to sell her for scrap to a Scottish ship-breaking firm for £2,000, the going rate at the time.

Hamburg's cabin boy was Günther Prien, later known as the fearless 'Bull of Scapa Flow.' He was in command of *U-47* when the u-Boat torpedoed *HMS Royal Oak* on 14 October 1939 with the loss of 810 lives, in an operation planned by Grand Admiral Karl Dönitz, with the intention of striking at the heart of the Royal Navy. Korvettenkapitän Prien and *U-47* were also responsible for sinking the Blue Star Line's *Arandora Star*. She was torpedoed in broad daylight two days out from Liverpool when off Malin Head on 2 June 1940. Eight hundred and five people, mostly German and Italian internees, lost their lives. Prien always wanted to be a sailor and had as his hero Vasca da Gama. He became a casualty of the war on 7 March 1941 when *U-47* and crew were sunk by depth charges dropped by *HMS Wolverine;* the u-Boat was lost with all hands as she was about to attack merchant ships in a westbound Atlantic convoy.

* * *

One sailing ship was commandeered for use as an armed surface raider: the Robert Duncan of Glasgow built ship *Pass of Balmah,* launched onto the Clyde in 1888. In June 1915, when owned by the River Plate Shipping Company of New York and commanded by New Englander Captain Scott, *Pass of Balmah* was conveying a cargo of cotton to Archangel when she was stopped by a British patrol boat and ordered into a Scottish port for examination. She never made it: on the way she was captured and taken to Cuxhaven by *U-36*, under the command of Kapitänleutnant Graefe.

The 1,571-ton steel-hulled full-rigged ship *Pass of Balmah* was renamed *Seeadler,* and fitted out to become the only sailing warship in Kaiser Wilhelm II's Imperial German Navy. Kapitänleutnant Graf Felix von Luckner became her commander. Von Luckner's main qualification for the job was his experience under sail, a career that began when he ran away to sea at the age of thirteen. The young von Luckner served on the Russian full-rigger *Niobe,* the American four-masted schooner *Golden Shore,* the British four-masted barque *Pinmore,* the Canadian schooner *Flying Fish,* and the German *Caesarea;* in addition he crewed on the Krupp yacht *Germania* at Cowes Regatta.

Von Luckner's innocent looking clipper ship was fitted with an auxiliary diesel engine and a powerful radio transmitter. Two 88mm guns were hidden behind false gunwales located immediately behind the forecastle and two other machine guns were mounted out of sight on the poop deck. A large quantity of small arms and ammunition was stowed on board. Space in the hold was arranged so that

von Luckner

armed sailors could hide there when visitors came on board. Unwanted visitors could be captured by lowering the floor of the saloon into the deck at the press of a button. *Seeadler* was disguised as a Norwegian full-rigged ship and crewed by Norwegian-speaking German sailors. Prominently displayed in the saloon were pictures of the King and Queen of Norway, and the late King Edward VII of England.

On 16 December 1916, the full-rigged surface raider set sail on a war mission. *Seeadler* moved fast under canvas; two days out she was charging along before a leading gale when a big sea came aboard and caused damage on deck. This only helped enhance her image as an innocent merchant sailing ship. A week later, von Luckner had an opportunity to test his disguise: *Seeadler* was stopped on Christmas Day by the British armed merchant cruiser *Avenger*, and after a boarding party found nothing untoward von Luckner was allowed to proceed.

Seeadler's true purpose was soon realized with the capture of two British steamers: *Gladys Royle* was taken and sunk on 9 January 1917 when en route to Buenos Aires with coal from Cardiff under Captain Chewn; *Lundy Island*, under the command of Captain George Bannister, suffered a similar fate the following day.

Seeadler's third conquest was the 1,960-ton St Nazaire built barque *Charles Gounod* belonging to Société Générale d'Armement, Nantes. Launched by Chantiers de la Loire, St Nazaire, on 26 January 1900, *Charles Gounod* had a reputation for fast passages; her most notable was a 73-day run from St Nazaire to Newcastle, NSW on her maiden voyage. On 21 January, when in the North Atlantic at about 08°N 26°W, on a heading for Nantes with a cargo of grain from Durban under Captain Rault, *Charles Gounod* was captured and sunk by *Seeadler*. On board, von Luckner found routeing instructions for sailing vessels, information that would enable him to intercept other Long Couriers.

Four sailing vessels fell victim to von Luckner during February 1917. One was the 2,662-ton Dunkirk-built four-masted barque *Antonin,* launched by Chantiers de France for Bordes in 1902. She was on a voyage from Iquique to Brest with nitrate, under the command of Captain F Lecoq, when she was captured and sunk on 3 February in the Atlantic at approximately 07°N 36°W.

The 'Sea Devil', as von Luckner became known, captured the fine British four-masted barque *Pinmore,* commanded by Liverpudlian Captain John Mullen. This was the second time that *Pinmore,* built by Reid of Glasgow in 1882, had become part of von Luckner's life. In 1902 von Luckner had survived a particularly rough passage off Cape Horn as a sailor aboard *Pinmore* during a voyage from San Francisco to Liverpool. After he captured his former ship, von Luckner took her into Buenos Aires for supplies; he avoided signing himself as Captain Mullen, the true captain of *Pinmore,* by having his hand bandaged. *Pinmore* was later sunk by explosive charges. Von Luckner must have had mixed emotions about destroying a sailing ship that had previously served him well. It is reputed that he locked himself in his cabin as the barque with the assumed name he was using in 1902 still there, carved on the stern was sent to her watery grave on his instructions.

Shortly afterwards, on 26 February, *Seeadler* fell in with another British sailer, the full-rigged ship *Yeomen,* whose crew waved enthusiastically to the crowd of captives lining *Seeadler's* decks. To drown out any giveaway information that his captives might try to impart, von Luckner played '*It's a Long Way to Tipperary'* loudly on the phonograph. Then Captain Armstrong was ordered to stop and *Seeadler's* guns were uncovered; *Yeomen* had become another von Luckner casualty.

Early the following day, at about 05°N 31°30'W, *Seeadler* captured another vessel belonging to Société Générale d'Armement, the 1,949-ton barque *La Roche-foucauld,* bound for Rochefort with nitrate under Captain Malbert. Having taken *La Rochefoucauld's* crew captive, von Luckner ordered his gunners to sink the barque by gunfire, to convince his captives that *Seeadler's* guns were real. In 1902, *La Rochefoucauld* had sailed from New York to Europe in a very fast twelve days.

On 5 March, while bound from Tocopilla to Queenstown with nitrate, the 1,935-ton Nantes barque *Dupleix* commanded by Captain Charrier sailed into *Seeadler's* path at 01°30'N 28°W, and was captured and sunk by von Luckner. Back in 1908 *Dupleix's* nitrate cargo had gone on fire and the barque was scuttled, but later she was salvaged and repaired.

Two weeks later, on 21 March, the 1,633-ton Bordes barque *Cambronne,* commanded by Captain Mathieu, encountered *Seeadler* at 20°10'S 28°05'W. But von Luckner did not sink *Cambronne*. He was keen to rid himself of the prisoners he had taken: he had *Cambronne's* topgallants removed, and all her spare sails and spars tipped overboard before loading her with 263 sailors from ships that he had already captured. He put Captain Mullen in charge, with instructions to sail *Cambronne* to Rio de Janeiro. Mullen, much to the chagrin of the ship's French captain, sailed *Cambronne* under the Red Ensign and arrived in Rio de Janeiro on 30 March. After von Luckner's former captives disembarked, Mathieu re-assumed command of his ship. On 14 April *Cambronne* left Rio de Janeiro for Nantes. Less than three months later, she was captured and sunk by *U-C-72* in the North Atlantic at 47°35'N 10°W as she was nearing the French coast. One seriously injured crew member died shortly afterwards.

Seeadler sailed to the Pacific where von Luckner put into Mopelia lagoon in the Tahiti archipelago to rest the crew, and to have weed and barnacles cleaned from the ship's bottom. But *Seeadler* dragged anchor and was wrecked on the reef, bringing to an end von Luckner's career in the Imperial German Navy. He afterwards claimed that *Seeadler* was hit by a tidal wave, although there was no confirmation of an earthquake in the area at that time. Von Luckner eventually arrived back in Germany in 1919 after spending time in New Zealand as a prisoner-of-war.

The flamboyant von Luckner surfaced again during World War II: he found a passport on a bomb site in Berlin and gave it to a Jewish lady, who used it to escape to the United States by way of a neutral country. In April 1945, he negotiated the surrender of the town of Halle with approaching United States forces at the request of the mayor. As a result he was unable to return there until after the occupation because the Nazis had sentenced him to death for his actions.

* * *

The Long Courier *Asie* survived the war. She was a sharp 2,452-ton four-master, built by Laporte of Rouen in 1897 for A d'Orbigny & G Faustin of La Rochelle. In 1908 she passed into Bordes ownership. When in Portland on 31 December 1901 *Asie* fell over on her beam ends after the ballast was removed, despite the log booms that were strapped alongside to prevent this happening. Her spars and rigging were damaged as were the roofs of adjacent warehouses. In December 1919, as *Asie* was nearing the end of a voyage from Iquique to Nantes with nitrate, she veered onto Jardinerts' Rocks at the entrance to St Nazaire Roads when under tow by the tug *Commerce*, and was lost. Her crew escaped.

The English Channel continued to be a collision hazard for sailing ships still in commission in the 1920s. On Christmas night 1926, the 22-year-old 2,039-ton barque *Eugène Schneider* was run down by the British steamer *Burutu* about 30 miles south-west of St Catherine's Point, and sank within three minutes with the loss of Captain Govys and 23 of his crew. The other four crew members were taken aboard the relatively undamaged *Burutu*.

Bossuet, a 1,954-ton Nantes barque, survived the Great War and the breaker's yard when she was laid up in the Canal de la Martinière from 1921 to 1926, only to be lost when what should have been a fairly straightforward maneuver went wrong: on 8 November 1929 *Bossuet*, commanded by Captain Ollivier and owned by M Potet, was outward bound from Dunkirk when she misstayed while sailing close to shore, and went onto the rocks a couple of miles south of Cap Gris Nez. Local fishermen took the crew off, but *Bossuet* was wrecked.

Atlantique, a 2,685-ton four-masted barque built for Bordes by Chantiers de la Loire in 1897, was the last Long Courier to round Cape Horn. Like most other Long Couriers, she had lean times in the early 1920s and was laid up for three years. On 14 April 1925, *Atlantique* left Port Pirrie and rounded Cape Horn for the last time with a cargo of grain for Falmouth. This was the end of the reign of the great French Cape Horners. The following year *Atlantique* went to the breaker's yard.

Maréchal Suchet, a 1,991-ton ship from the yard of Chantiers de la Loire in 1902, survived the Great War and escaped the breaker's yard, only to perish during World War II. In 1924 she was purchased for £3,100 by the Laeisz Flying P Line of Hamburg and renamed *Pellworm*. There was a resurgence in demand for nitrate and *Pellworm* was chartered to collect a cargo later that year but failed to round Cape Horn, and was forced to retreat to Montevideo 119 days out from Nantes. Her difficulties off the Horn were attributed to incorrectly stored ballast and a troublesome crew. On her arrival in Montevideo, *Pellworm* discovered that her nitrate charter had been cancelled, and she was directed to return to Hamburg. It was almost unknown for a Laeisz ship to fail to round the Horn and *Pellworm*, a fine 1,991-ton steel clipper ship with considerable potential, was not given another opportunity by Erich Laeisz. Instead she was used as a hulk.

Pellworm was subsequently fitted out for use as a youth hostel on the Hamburg waterfront and renamed *Hein Godenwind*. On 24 June 1943, an Allied bombing campaign launched against Hamburg developed into a nightly inferno and claimed many lives, including at least one former Laeisz captain. *Hein Godenwind*, one of only a small number of surviving sailing ships with a true clipper hull and rig, was damaged during the raids. Not long afterwards, the once proud clipper ship *Maréchal Suchet* was towed down the Elbe and out into the Baltic Sea to be used as target practice by Luftwaffe pilots, who quickly sent her to the sea floor.

Another notable Cape Horner to end her days as a result of an Allied bombing raid on Hamburg was the 1,615-ton iron four-masted barque and former Long Courier, *Carmen*. Named *County of Inverness* when she was launched by Barclay, Curle & Co in 1877 for R & J Craig, she was later owned by a number of shipping companies in Bordeaux, and operated from there for nine years under the name *Carmen*, before being acquired by Estonian owners and renamed *Nemrac*. In 1940 she was acquired by Emanuele V Parodi of Genoa and given the name *Amicizia*. On the night of 10 April 1945, she was caught in one of the Hamburg bombing raids and sunk. Two years later she was raised, broken up, and sold for scrap.

CHAPTER 14

Sail Training and Museum Ships

Though the ships have gone they still live in the hearts of many of
us who knew their worth and quiet sea beauty, and the worth, too,
of those who sailed them and sailed in them.

Henri Picard, *The Bounty Ships of France*

The days of the great clipper ships have long gone. Of the Yankee clippers that
carried tea from China, adventurers to California, and emigrants and gold to and
from Australia, none remain. The softwood hulls that survived Cape Horn, the
shallows and reefs of the South China Sea, the rigors of the North Atlantic and its
treacherous coastlines, and the other adversities of the oceans were no match for
the march of time. We are fortunate that the finest of these creations were accurately described, beautifully modeled, well sketched, and exquisitely reproduced
on canvas before they foundered or rotted away.

Mud is a great preserver and it has permitted the wooden hulls of sailing
craft from previous ages to survive on the seabed of sheltered waters until their
precise location could be established and their historical worth appreciated. A
small but unique part of the world's maritime heritage has survived by being
embalmed in this way. Two famous ships that have been reclaimed from underwater mud berths are King Henry VIII's *Mary Rose* and Sweden's *Wasa*.

The only original wooden clipper that is known to remain in any way intact is
the 1,066-ton *Egeria*, built at Millidgeville, St John in 1859. In 1898 *Egeria* arrived at
Port Stanley after it was damaged off Cape Horn, and was subsequently used
there as a warehouse. Currently owned by the Falkland Islands Company, the
remains of the sole surviving wooden clipper is incorporated into a wharf at Port
Stanley, with her stern intact and the forward half of her hull cut down.

Ambassador, City of Adelaide, and *Cutty Sark* are the only composite clippers to
have survived, in whole or in part, to the present time. *Cutty Sark* remains in her
permanent dry dock at Greenwich. Willis and Woodget's famous wool clipper

and East London icon was open to the public, fully restored with her teak hull, decks, and rigging intact. It was decided in 2006 that further conservation and maintenance work to her iron frame and parts of her hull was required, and, in order to gain access, her rigging, upper decks, cabins, and other fittings were removed. A fire was discovered on board on 21 May 2007, and she was badly damaged. At the time of writing, *Cutty Sark*, the only original clipper ship that has remained intact, is undergoing a much more extensive reconstruction and refit than was previously planned.

After serving as an isolation hospital in Southampton for ten years, *City of Adelaide* was sold to the Admiralty for £2,500 and renamed *HMS Carrick*. The former clipper was moved to the Firth of Clyde, moored at Irvine, and used by the Royal Navy Volunteer Reserve (RNVR) as a training ship. *HMS Carrick* was subsequently moved to nearby Greenock, and in May 1925 was officially opened as a Royal Naval Drill Ship by the then Marquis of Graham, later the Duke of Montrose. The Duke, commanding officer of the Clyde Division of the RNVR, had sailed before the mast and had served as a junior officer on Devitt & Moore's clipper ship *Hesperus;* he also held a master mariner's certificate and was assistant navigator on Lord Brassey's famous yacht *Sunbeam.*

HMS Carrick was used as an accommodation ship during World War II. Later when she was considered past her usefulness, she was scheduled for the breaker's yard. But through the efforts of the Duke, supported by Admiral Sir Charles Morgan and Vice Admiral Cedric S Holland, *HMS Carrick* was presented to the RNVR Club (Scotland). With subscriptions from a number of the Clydeside ship-builders, she was fitted out as a clubhouse to a high standard at the Harland & Wolff yard at Scotstoun, before being towed to Custom House Quay, Glasgow. Her opening as a floating clubhouse, carried out by Admiral of the Fleet Viscount Cunningham of Hyndhope, is commemorated by a plaque on board. Five years later she was moved to Carlton Place on the opposite side of the river. When *HMS Carrick* was surveyed in 1954, 90 years after she was built, her teak hull and iron frame were found in excellent condition.

In 1990 the former *City of Adelaide* was sold to the Clyde Ship Trust for £1, and two years later was given a Class A heritage listing as part of the National Historic Ships Core. In 1992 her ownership changed, and she became the responsibility of the Scottish Maritime Museum. Since then, it has been difficult to keep her from deteriorating further, and being sent to the breaker's yard. Despite the intervention of the Duke of Edinburgh and Admiral of the Fleet Sir Julian Oswald in 2000, and financial support from businessman Mike Edwards in 2003, there are, as yet, no firm plans to restore the former composite clipper. In 2007 an action group was formed with the aim of saving *City of Adelaide*, and the following year Rear Admiral Kevin Scarce RANR, Governor of South Australia, became patron of the 'Clipper Ship *City of Adelaide* Preservation Trust.'

Ambassador, a composite teak clipper of 692 tons was launched onto the Thames from the yard of William Walker at Rotherhithe in 1869, the same year that *Cutty Sark* was launched onto the Clyde. In 1895, while sailing under the Norwegian flag, *Ambassador* was one of many ships that put back to the Falkland Islands after being damaged off Cape Horn. *Ambassador* never worked under sail again: she was condemned at Port Stanley and subsequently served as a storage hulk in the Straits of Magellan. The remains of the London built clipper now lie on the beach at Punta Arenas beside a sheep ranch; her iron frame is intact, but most of her teak planking is missing.

Three full-rigged three-masted iron ships remain intact and afloat: *Star of India*, the former *Dunboyne* as *af Chapman* in Stockholm, and *Wavertree*. Two other iron sailing vessels have survived; the four-masted barque *Falls of Clyde* and the small barque *Elissa*.

Star of India was launched at Ramsey, Isle of Man in 1863 by Gibson, McDonald & Arnold for Wakefield Nash of Liverpool. This fine clipper of 1,318 tons carried cargo and passengers between Britain and New Zealand for many years. At the beginning of the twentieth century, *Star of India* was acquired by Alaska Packers Association and sailed under the flag of the United States, serving the salmon canning industry of Alaska. *Star of India* is now afloat in San Diego Harbor, where she is maintained by the local Maritime Museum.

The 2,170-ton *Wavertree*, formerly *Southgate* and *Don Ariano N*, was launched from the Southampton yard of Oswald Mordaunt & Co in 1885 to the order of R W Leyland & Co of Liverpool, and was completed for Chadwick & Pritchard, also of Liverpool. The iron clipper ship initially carried jute from the Bay of Bengal. She was dismasted off Cape Horn during a storm in 1901, and forced back to Port Stanley, where she was condemned. From there she was taken to Magellan Strait for use as a storage hulk. In 1948, having been renamed *Don Ariano N*, she was towed to Buenos Aires to become a sand barge. Twenty years later she was acquired by the South Street Museum of New York and taken there. Volunteers carried out restoration work on *Wavertree* over many years, starting in 1970, and she now lies afloat at the museum looking much like she did when she took to the water at Southampton originally.

Falls of Clyde, a 1,809-ton iron four-masted clipper barque, was built in 1878 by Russell & Co of Port Glasgow for the Falls Line of Glasgow. Her maiden voyage was to Karachi, and for the following 21 years she carried general cargo and grain between Britain, India, Australia, New Zealand, and California. In 1899 *Falls of Clyde* was purchased by Captain William Matson of Honolulu and sailed under the flag of Hawaii. When the Republic of Hawaii was annexed by the United States the following year, a special act of Congress was required to enable the Clyde-built ship to sail under the Stars and Stripes. *Falls of Clyde* carried mixed general cargoes between Hawaii and San Francisco until 1907 when she was bought by the Associated Oil Company and became an oil tanker, carrying kerosene from Gaviota, California, to Honolulu, and returning to California with bulk molasses. From 1927 until 1959 the Clyde four-poster was used as a fuel depot in Alaska. She was then towed to Seattle in the hope that she would be acquired by a preservation trust. Insufficient funding was available, and the bank to whom she was mortgaged found a buyer, who had a plan to sink her as part of a breakwater at Vancouver. Karl Kortum, director of the San Francisco Maritime Museum, and Fred Klebingat, who had served on *Falls of Clyde* as first mate in 1915 were determined to save her: they raised funds in Hawaii that became available within days of her scheduled demise.

In October 1964, the skeleton of the old four-master was taken in tow by the Pacific Fleet tug *USS Moctobi,* commanded by Lieutenant Leo Connolly, and towed across the Pacific to Honolulu. During the following decade she was restored; Sir William Lithgow, the grandson and namesake of the original designer, donated masts, yards, and other fittings from his shipyard at Port Glasgow. *Falls of Clyde* now lies afloat in her original splendor at Pier 7, Honolulu Harbor, in the care of the Hawaii Maritime Center,.

The only other recorded remains of an iron clipper is the intact hull of *Falstaff.* Built at Barrow-on-Furness in 1875, and operated by the company of John Beazley of Liverpool, the 1,465-ton *Falstaff* spent her working life on the trade routes of the world before becoming a warehouse in the Magellan Strait. Her iron hull, now owned by the Chilean Navy, is part of a breakwater of ships at Punta Arenas.

Another iron sailing vessel, the flamboyant 400-ton barque *Elissa,* remains afloat, testimony to the shipbuilding skills of the Aberdonians who built her and launched her from the yard of Alexander Hall in 1877. *Elissa* carried cargoes across the oceans of the world for almost 90 years under the flags of Britain, Norway, and Sweden before ending her trading days as a smuggler in the Mediterranean. Later she was rescued from a boatyard at Piraeus, Greece, by the Galveston Historical Society, who was looking for a ship similar to those that sailed along the coast of Texas in earlier days. The dilapidated *Elissa* was restored by volunteers in Galveston, who continue to keep her seaworthy and in beautiful condition. In 1976 she sailed to New York and participated in the Tall Ships sail past the Statue of Liberty. *Elissa*, now the Official Tall Ship of Texas, continues her career, mostly sailing in the Gulf of Mexico.

Brutus, a 1,686-ton full-rigged ship, is probably the oldest surviving steel clipper ship. She was built in 1883 by J Reid & Co of Port Glasgow for Thompson, Anderson & Co of Liverpool and was used as a cargo carrier. Currently owned by British Crown Wrecks, she now lies abandoned, but mostly intact, at Prince Olaf Harbor, South Georgia, Antarctica.

Balclutha, 1,862 tons, is another steel clipper ship that has survived. Built in Glasgow at the Charles Connell & Co yard at Scotstoun in 1886, *Balclutha* set out on her maiden voyage from South Wales with a 2,650-ton cargo of coal for San Francisco, a city with whom she would develop a strong bond in the twentieth century. At San Francisco she loaded a cargo of wheat for the return voyage and delivered it to Fleetwood in Lancashire. *Balclutha* continued in the grain trade, sailing between Britain, California, and Australia. She subsequently served in the nitrate and lumbar trade, rounding Cape Horn thirteen times. From 1902 to 1930 *Balclutha* was based at San Francisco where she was used by Alaska Packers Association, as *Star of Alaska*. She operated as a packet in the salmon trade taking 300 fishermen, cannery workers, sheet tin and other materials to Alaska. At the end of each season, *Star of Alaska* returned with the workforce, and as many as 78,000 cases of tinned salmon. Alaska Packers retained her original full-rigged sail plan, working her as a clipper ship.

After finishing in the Alaska salmon trade, *Star of Alaska* was purchased by Tex Kissinger for $5,000. Kissinger, a carnival promoter, renamed her *Pacific Queen*, painted her in garish colors, hung wax figures purporting to be mutineers from the yardarms, a sideshow that failed to impress local sailors, and opened her to the public. In this way *Pacific Queen* provided her owner with a reasonable income, supplemented by renting her to film companies; she appeared in the movie 'Mutiny on the Bounty' starring Clark Gable and Charles Laughton.

Shortly before Kissinger died, *Pacific Queen* was beached on the Sausalito mud-flats; she was rescued by Karl Kortum, who was determined to have her fully restored for his new maritime museum in San Francisco. Kortum paid Kissinger's widow $25,000 for the wreck, and persuaded the San Francisco business community to contribute $100,000 and the equipment and material needed for her restoration, estimating that *Balclutha* would bring in $100,000 a year. The most significant contribution, however, was made by the fourteen labor unions and their members, who provided 13,000 hours of voluntary work. Harry Lundeberg, then secretary-treasurer of the Sailors' Union of the Pacific and a man who had sailed before the mast, was an outspoken advocate for the restoration project and persuaded the skilled workforce of welders, boilermakers, shipwrights, painters, and their apprentices to offer their time completely free.

In July 1955, the restored *Balclutha* was towed to her berth at the San Francisco Maritime Museum. Shortly afterwards, this imposing Connell of Glasgow steel clipper was opened to the public. In her first ten years, she earned one million dollars, the amount Kortum had predicted. *Balclutha* remains afloat in San Francisco Bay, drawing thousands of visitors every year.

The last survivor of France's bounty ships, the 2,260-ton ship *Suomen Joutsen*, now lies afloat in Finland. She also appears to be the only surviving twentieth century clipper ship. Launched as *Laënnec* in 1902 by Chantiers et Ateliers de St Nazaire for Société des Armateurs at Nantes, she was named after the distinguished physician and inventor of the modern stethoscope, René-Théophile-Hyacynthe Laënnec. *Laënnec* became *Oldenburg* when she was acquired by H H Schmidt of Hamburg for use as a cargo-carrying training ship. In May 1925 *Oldenburg* lost her main topmast and mizzen topgallant mast in a storm off Cape Horn when en route to Callao in ballast, and she had to put back to Montevideo for repairs. *Oldenburg* was acquired by the Finnish Navy in 1930; twin auxiliary engines were added, and for the following 25 years, except during World War II, she provided excellent sail training for naval cadets under her new name *Suomen Joutsen* (Swan of Finland). In 1961 she was moored at Åbo, her accommodation having been modernized, and for a number of years served as a school for the Finnish Merchant Service. Since 1991, *Suomen Joutsen* has been a museum ship in Turku, Finland.

The remains of the 1,087-ton four-masted steel barque *Marjorie Glen* lie high and dry on the seashore at Port Gallegos, Argentina. Built in 1892 at Grangemouth Dockyard on the Firth of Forth just west of Edinburgh, *Marjorie Glen* was beached and abandoned there in 1911 after her cargo caught fire by internal combustion. Her hull remains intact but deformed as a result of the heat generated by the fire.

Six 20th-century four-masted barque-rigged clipper carriers survive intact: the 2,875-ton *Moshulu*, formerly *Kurt*; the 2,346-ton *Pommern*; the 2,760-ton *Viking*; the 3,091-ton *Passat*; the 3,100-ton *Peking*, formerly *Arethusa*; and the 3,545-ton *Kruzenshtern*, formally *Padua*.

Kurt was launched in 1904 from the yard of William Hamilton, Port Glasgow, for G J H Siemers & Co of Hamburg to use as a nitrate clipper. In 1914 *Kurt* was laid up in Astoria following the outbreak of war and impounded by the United States in 1917. Shortly afterwards she was renamed *Moshulu*, and until 1928 traded between the Pacific Northwest, Australia, and South Africa. In 1935 *Moshulu* was acquired by Gustav Erikson for the Australian grain run. Eric Newby joined *Moshulu* as a nineteen-year-old apprentice for her last voyage as an Australian grain carrier in 1939, and afterwards described his experiences in his books: *The Last Grain Race* and *Learning the Ropes: An Apprentice in the Last of the Windjammers*. The following year *Moshulu* was seized by the Germans when she arrived in Norway with a cargo of South American wheat. She never carried another cargo, but served in various capacities until she ended up in Philadelphia as the floating restaurant 'Moshulu', afloat at Penn's Landing. There was a fire on board in 1989. But in 2003 she was back in business as the prestigious new 'Moshulu' restaurant at Penn's Landing.

Pommern, another surviving example of the Clyde's leadership in steel shipbuilding at the turn of the twentieth century, now lies afloat as a museum and tourist attraction at Mariehamn in Finland. Launched in 1903 from the yard of J Reid & Co as *Mneme* for the Hamburg firm of B Wencke Sohne, she spent her final years in service in the Australian grain trade. *Pommern* was subsequently presented to the town of Mariehamn by Edgar Erikson, the eldest son of Gustav Erikson who died in 1947.

Viking was built by Burmeister & Wain of Copenhagen for the Danish Merchant Marine in 1907; her hull and deckhouses were made of steel and the masts of steel and wood. This Danish four-master was employed in the Australian grain trade until 1940. During 1946 and 1947, *Viking* carried timber from the Baltic to South America. She was subsequently purchased by the town of Göteborg for use as a hostel and navigation school, and remains afloat there as a tourist attraction and museum.

Passat and *Arethusa* were launched as sister ships in 1911 from the Hamburg yard of Blohm & Voss for the Flying P Line of Laeisz. The two four-masted barques, constructed of steel throughout, except for the charthouses, were built for the Chilean nitrate trade. *Passat* was sold to Finnish owners in the 1930s and served on the Australian wheat run. In 1949, *Passat* and the 3,020-ton *Pamir* were the last Cape Horners to carry Australian wheat to Europe. The following year they served as floating granaries for the Ministry of Food in Penarth. In 1955, the two four-masted barques were fitted with auxiliary engines and put on the South American run, where they carried grain to Europe in bulk, unlike Australian grain that was loaded in bags. On 21 September 1957, *Pamir* was thrown on her beam ends when her cargo of barley shifted, and she foundered in hurricane force winds, with the loss of 80 lives, during a voyage from Buenos Aires. Two weeks later, *Passat* was also thrown on her beam ends but survived, and made it to port in Spain. The former Flying P Line four-master is now owned by the City of Lübeck where she remains afloat at nearby Travemünde, rigged to royal yards.

The two remaining 20th century four-masted barque-rigged clippers that survive were also Flying P Line ships. *Peking*, launched onto the Elbe as *Arethusa* in 1911, was restored by South Street Seaport Museum, Manhattan, where she is afloat looking as good as new. An even larger clipper barque built for E F Laeisz in 1926, the 3,545-ton four-master *Padua*, was the last true cargo-carrying Cape Horner to be built. At the end of World War II, *Padua* was awarded to Russia, and renamed *Kruzenshtern*. The Russians fitted her with auxiliary engines and converted her into a training ship for the Russian Fishing Fleet. *Kruzenshtern* continues to sail under the Russian flag as a sail-training tall ship.

> They used no resources and consumed nothing she did not carry in her. The use of plain aerofoils called sails set from spars on high masts converted the understood ocean winds into successful long voyages. The ships sailed in peace under God, silently with grace. They destroyed nothing except occasionally themselves, for the price of error was high. They polluted nothing. They made all the great voyages of discovery. They opened up the earth and they shifted peoples.
>
> Alan Villiers, *Last of the Wind Ships*

* * *

During the latter part of the twentieth century, as the great Cape Horners become a distant memory, much smaller sailing craft took to the oceans of the world. Many of their sailors, sometimes single-handed, followed the route of the Australian Clippers, on occasions facing the even greater challenge of sailing in the reverse direction. Only a few have attempted to follow the example of Californian Clippers, and sail the Great Racecourse of the Ocean to San Francisco.

John Kretschmer has a sailing school in Fort Lauderdale, and in 1982 persuaded one of his students, Ty Techera, to consider having a yacht built for the purpose of rounding Cape Horn in the wake of the Californian Clippers. Kretschmer's school had two boats, one of which was a Contessa 32. The Contessa's proven seaworthiness prompted Techera and Kretschmer to have *Gigi* built for the arduous task of sailing from New York to San Francisco. *Gigi* was built at the Lymington boatyard of Jeremy Rogers to Lloyd's 100-A1 specifications. The Contessa 32, a one-design cruiser-racer designed by Rogers and former tank

Kruzenshtern © Colin Sanger

designer David Sadler, made her debut at the 1971 London Boat Show; and the following year, Contessa 32 *Sunmaid IV* won the coveted 'Boat of the Show' award.

Gigi's 15,000-mile voyage was sailed in four legs: Kretschmer was accompanied by Techera on the first and third legs, and Kretschmer's girlfriend, Molly Potter and his friend, Bill Oswald, accompanied him on the second leg; Oswald and Kretschmer sailed the final leg from Valparaiso to San Francisco. GPS was not available then, and Kretschmer had to rely on his celestial navigation skills for the voyage.

Gigi and her crew survived a knockdown off Bermuda and a storm off the coast of Chile but doubled Cape Horn in an excellent 11.5 days. On 27 January 1984, *Gigi* hove-to 30 miles north of Le Maire Strait in gale-force winds, poor visibility, and rain. The barometer plunged from 1005 to 973 millibars in the 12 hours to midnight. But the following morning, though the barometer was at 971 millibars, the expected storm had not arrived, and instead the wind had moderated to a steady 30-knot northeaster. Kretschmer and Techera encountered fickle Cape Horn weather as they approached Le Maire Strait: the wind changed to the south, accompanied by poor visibility. They had experienced Maury's Low Barometer of Cape Horn.

Kretschmer reported how they entered the strait at about 1500 hours when visibility was down to two boat lengths. *Gigi* was forced to retreat after spending a couple of hours doing short tacks into a headwind in short steep seas, resulting from wind over tide that pitched the little Contessa (32-foot) and nearly knocked her over on two occasions. After retreating, *Gigi* sailed north and hove-to in a gale force easterly. Two days later, *Gigi* and her crew of two swept through Le Maire Strait before a north wind, aided by a four knot tidal stream. When the wind died *Gigi's* twelve horsepower Yanmar auxiliary diesel engine was used. Later in the day the wind returned and backed to the east, a favorable wind that enabled *Gigi* to sail west on a course that would take her within three miles due south of Cape Horn, the most written about, feared, and respected seamark in the world. The east wind carried the indomitable yacht and her crew west, until it was time to alter course north for Valparaiso.

Gigi arrived in San Francisco 161 sailing days out from New York, aided only very occasionally by her engine, the first yacht to retrace the entire clipper ship route from New York to San Francisco. The Mayor of San Francisco, Dianne Feinstein, declared 14 May 1984 '*Gigi* arrival day.'

More recently *Gigi*, in near derelict condition, was rescued from a marina in

Gigi finishing under spinnaker

Galveston, Texas, and shipped back to Britain by Jeremy and Fiona Rogers after a friend had spotted her there. *Gigi* was completely refurbished at the Rogers yard, and shortly afterwards was exhibited at the 2007 Earls Court Boat Show in London.

Shortly after *Gigi* set sail on her momentous voyage, Mike Kane left New York in his trimaran *Crusader*, bound for San Francisco in an attempt to break the records set by the clippers. *Crusader* had rounded the Horn and was making excellent time when a backstay shackle parted, bringing down the rig. Kane and his two companions were rescued by the Chilean Coastguard and had to abandon *Crusader*.

In the same year, Chay Blyth's trimaran *Beefeater II* capsized off Cape Horn during an attempt on the clipper records. Blyth and his companion, Eric Blum, were rescued after spending nineteen hours in the water.

The records set by *Flying Cloud* and *Andrew Jackson* were finally broken when, on 11 February 1989, the monohull racing machine Open 60, *Thursday's Child*, swept under the Golden Gate Bridge 80 days 20 hours after leaving New York, beating *Flying Cloud's* two voyages of less than 90 days, her 89 days 8 hours and 89 days 21 hours, and *Andrew Jackson's* record 89 days 4 hours. *Thursday's Child*, skippered by Warren Luhrs and with Lars Bergstrom and Courtney Hazeelton as crew, was forced to put into the Falkland Islands. She spent five days there having repairs carried out, before resuming the race to San Francisco by way of Cape Horn.

Acknowledgements

I am particularly fortunate in having access to a number of great libraries and I am most grateful to the staff of the Bodleian Library, Oxford, the British Library, St Pancras, London, the newspaper section of the British Library at Colindale, the London Library, St James Square, Guildhall Library, London, and the National Maritime Museum's Caird Library at Greenwich.

I very much appreciate the help and expertise of Michael Mitchell and Susan Wightman of Libanus Press who designed the book. My wife, Rosarie, edited and proof read the manuscript and I am most grateful to her.

The following have kindly permitted me to reproduce material: Nancie Villiers, quotations from her late husband's books; Jon Stallworthy, verses from *Rounding the Horn*; John Kretchmer, a quotation and pictures from *Cape Horn to Starboard*; Colin Sanger for the photograph of *Kruzenshtern*; The Society of Authors as the literary representatives of the estate of John Masefield; and Ursula Leslie for the photograph of *Léon XIII* taken by a member of her family, probably Captain Robert Leslie. The photograph of af *Chapman,* credited to Poxnar, is from Wikimedia Commons. The illustration of the clipper ship *City of Adelaide* was supplied by the Antiquarian Print Gallery, Adelaide, South Australia.

Whilst every effort has been made to trace the sources of material reproduced, the publisher will make proper acknowledgement in future editions in the event that any omission has occurred.

Abbreviations and Acronyms

E	East longitude
FRS	Fellow of the Royal Society
GPS	Global positioning system
HIJMS	His Imperial Japanese Majesty's Ship
HMAS	Her/His Majesty's Australian Ship
HMS	Her/His Majesty's Ship
HMSO	Her/His Majesty's Stationary Office
ILN	*Illustrated London News*
MC	Military Cross
N	North latitude
NSW	New South Wales
ODNB	Oxford Dictionary of National Biography
OM	Order of Merit
OUP	Oxford University Press
P&O	Peninsular and Orient Steam Navigation Company
Q-ships	Heavily armed merchant ships used as decoy vessels
RANR	Royal Australian Naval Reserve
RM	Royal Marines
RMS	Royal Mail Steamer
RNVR	Royal Naval Volunteer Reserve
S	South latitude
SS	Steamship
U	U-Boat
U-B	Coastal u-boats small enough to be transported by rail
U-C	Minelaying u-boats that also carried torpedoes
USS	United States Ship
W	West longitude
°	Degrees of angular space
°F	Degrees Fahrenheit
'	Minutes of angular space

Glossary

Aback: When a ship's sails have the wind bearing on their front surfaces; square sails are laid aback to deaden a ship's way, and are taken aback by an unexpected change of wind or inattention of the helmsman.

Abaft: The word generally means behind. Abaft the beam means any direction between an imaginary transverse line amidships and the stern, whether in or out of the ship.

Abeam: At right angles to the fore-and-aft line of a ship.

Aft: An abbreviation of abaft and meaning towards the stern of the vessel.

Aloft: Above; overhead; on high.

Alow: Synonymous with below. Carrying all sail alow and aloft is when the reefs are shaken out and all studding sails set.

Amidships: The middle of the ship, whether in regard to her length or breadth.

Anchorsmith: A forger of anchors.

Awash: The deck of a ship, rock, or reef is said to be awash when it is approximately level with the surface of the sea and waves break over it.

Backs: The wind backs when it changes in an anti-clockwise direction.

Backstays: Long ropes (stays) leading aft from the mastheads to the sides of the ship.

Ballast: A certain amount of stone, gravel, shale, pig-iron, or other such material deposited in an empty ship's hold in order to stabilize the vessel and keep her low in the water.

Bar: An underwater mass of earth, mud, or sand found mostly off the entrance to large rivers. The relative shallowness of the water over the bar, combined with changing tidal streams and strong currents from the outflowing river make it a particularly dangerous place for mariners, which becomes even more hazardous in strong winds when waves break over it.

Barque or bark: A vessel with square sails on her forward masts and fore-and-aft sails on the mizzen mast.

Barquentine: A vessel with three or more masts including a square-rigged foremast.

Beam, On the: Perpendicular to the longitudinal axis of a ship.

Beam ends: A ship is said to be on her beam ends when she has heeled over so much on one side that her beams approach to a vertical position.

Beating: Sailing close to the wind.

Belay, to: To fasten a rope by passing it several times round a cleat.

Belaying pin: Small wooden or iron cylinders, fixed in racks in different parts of the ship for belaying running ropes to.

Bend: To bend a sail is to make it fast to its yard or stay.

Between ('tween) decks: The space between any two whole decks of a ship.

Bight: A loop of rope

Bilge: That part of the floor of the ship nearest to the keel which approaches nearer to a horizontal than to a perpendicular direction, and begins to round upwards.

Billy-boy: A Humber or east-coast boat of river-barge build with a trysail, and usually with the sail tanned; a north-country trader having a vertical or steep broad front; or a large one-masted vessel of burden.

Binnacle: A deck-mounted wooden housing containing the compass, usually mounted in front of the helmsman and with a light to illuminate the compass at night.

Blue-Peter: The signal for sailing, when hoisted at the fore-top-masthead.

Boatswain: The sailor responsible for the sails, rigging, blocks, anchors, cable, and cordage. He gives no orders but reports defects.

Bobstay: A stay of rope or chain extending upwards and forwards from the stem to the bowsprit to hold it in place.

Bolt-rope: A rope sewn into the edge of a sail to prevent the canvas from tearing.

Boom: A spar used to extend the foot of a sail.

Bow: The forward end of a ship.

Bowsprit: The spar running out from the ship's bow and projecting over the stem. The jib-boom extends beyond it, and beyond it in turn the flying-jib boom. To these spars are secured the stays of the foremast, from which the jibs are flown.

Brace about: To turn the yards round for a contrary tack, or because of a change in wind direction.

Braces: Ropes attached to the yards of a ship, two to each yard. The yards are controlled from the deck and swung round to present the optimum sail surface to the wind.

Brigantine: A square-rigged vessel with two masts.

Broach or broach-to: To come up into the wind, often as a result of a ship being driven too hard under too large a press of canvas in strong winds. In extreme cases when the sails were caught flat aback, the masts were in danger of giving way or, even worse, the ship might go down stern first.

Broadside: The side of a ship.

Bulwark: The planking along the side of a ship's upper deck to protect those on deck.

Bunt (of a square sail): The middle part of it formed into a belly so that it can gather more wind; to bunt a sail is to haul up the middle part of it in furling, and secure it by the bunt-gasket.

Buntlines: Ropes on topsails and courses that, when hauled up, spill the wind.

Burgee: A swallow-tailed or broad pennant.

Capstan: A broad cylindrical drum with a vertical axis around which the anchor cable is wound.

Caravel: A lateen-rigged Portuguese boat formerly in use, with square sails only on the foremast.

Carrack: Large, round-built vessels with great depth first built by the Portuguese and Spanish.

Carvel-built: A vessel or boat, the planks of which are all flush and smooth with the edges laid close together and caulked to make them watertight. Clinker-built is where the planks overlap each other.

Chronometer: An accurate time-piece used by navigators.

Clew, originally clue: The two lower corners of a square sail, and the aftermost corner of a fore-and-aft sail. To clew up a sail is to draw the lower end of a sail up to the yard or to the mast ready for furling.

Clew lines: Lines by which the clews of a square-sail are hauled up to the yard when the sail needs to be furled. The sail is then said to be clewed up.

Close-reefed: The last reef of the topsails, or other sails set, being taken in.

Coaming (of the hatches or gratings): Raised woodwork around the hatch openings to prevent water on deck from running down.

Companionway: The steps leading from a ship's deck to the cabin, stateroom, or saloon.

Compass deviation: The influence on a ship's compass card by nearby metal, measured in degrees east or west.

Cotton duck: Heavy plain woven cotton fabric.

Counter (of a ship): Refers to her after-seat on the water.

Courses: The names by which the sails hanging from the lower yards of a ship are usually distinguished: mainsail (main-course), foresail (fore-course), and crossjack (mizzen-course).

Cringle: A short piece of rope worked into the bolt-rope of a sail and containing a metal ring.

Crossjack yard: The lower yard on the mizzen mast.

Cutwater: The foremost part of a vessel's prow; the prow, or bow, refers to the foremost end of a vessel.

Davits: A pair of arms projecting over the ship's side from which a ship's boat is suspended, and from which it is launched or retrieved.

Davy Jones: Sea-devil.

Davy Jones's locker: The ocean to where those who drown or are buried at sea go.

Deadrise, or rise of floor: The angle the ship's sides make with the keel; the base line is a line drawn at right angles to the keel, and the greater the angle between the ship's side and this line the bigger the deadrise.

Doldrums: The parts of the ocean where calms prevail, particularly in the equatorial region between the trade-winds.

Donkey-engine: A small steam engine used for hoisting cargo and for pumping.

Doubling the Horn: Sailing from 50°S in the Atlantic round Cape Horn to 50°S in the Pacific.

Downhaul: A rope led along a stay and attached to the upper corner of a staysail or jib to pull it down when shortening sail.

Downs, The: A sea area adjacent to the Kent coast.

Draft, also **draught:** The depth of water a ship displaces.

Driver: The large square sail flown from the mizzen gaff and often referred to as the spanker.

Earings: Certain small ropes used to fasten the upper corners of a sail to its yard. Below the earings are the reef-earings by which the reef cringles are made fast to the yard when the sail is reefed.

Easting: Distance travelled eastward.

Ebb (tide): The receding or falling of the tide, in contradistinction to the flood.

Embay: A ship is said to be embayed when it is surrounded on most sides by land or an iceberg, with no way of getting out under sail.

Entrance: The shape of the bow under the load waterline.

Fall off: Falling away from the wind.

Fathom: A depth of six feet.

Fid: A square bar of wood or iron, used to support the weight of the topmast when stepped at the head of the lower mast.

Fidded: When a mast has been swayed (hoisted) high enough the fid is then inserted, and the master-rope relieved of its weight.

Flare: Gradually becoming wider.

Flood (tide): The inflowing or rising tide.

Flush deck: A continuous deck laid from stem to stern without a break.

Foot: The lower end of a mast or sail.

Footrope: A rope stretched under the yards and jib-booms on which the sailors stand.

Forecastle: A short deck placed in the forepart of the ship above the upper deck.

Foremast: The forward lower mast on all vessels.

Forepeak: A small part of the vessel's hold, close to the bow.

Foresail: The principal sail set on the foremast, suspended from the foreyard.

Forestays: Long ropes (stays) leading forward from the mastheads to the bow of the ship.

Foreyard: The lowest yard on the foremast.

Frap: To bind tightly together.

Freeboard: The distance from the waterline to the upper deck level, measured at the center of the ship.

Frigate: Originally a light nimble naval ship built to sail swiftly.

Full-rigged: A ship is said to be full-rigged if she carries square sails on three or more masts.

Furl: Roll up and bind a sail neatly to its yard or boom.

Gaff: A spar used in ships to extend the heads of fore-and-aft sails which are not set on stays.

Gasket: A piece of rope, plaited cord, or strip of canvas used to secure a furled sail to its yard.

Great circle sailing: A great circle is the shortest distance on the earth's surface between two points; its plane passes through the earth's center.

Guano: The excrement of sea birds.

Gunwale: The uppermost timber on the sides of a boat or ship.

Guy: A rope extended from the head of shears, and made fast at a distance on each side to steady them; a rope used to steady a weighty body from swinging against a ship's side while it is being hoisted or lowered.

Halyards: Ropes or tackles used to hoist or lower any sail on its respective yard, gaff, or stay.

Hard down: Turn away from the wind

Hard up: Turn towards the wind.

Heave-to: Set the sails to counteract each other, so as to check the ship's way and keep her as still as possible.

Heel: To lie over on one side, usually when canted by the wind. Heel also refers to the after end of a ship's keel and the lower end of a ship's sternpost to which it is connected.

Helm: The tiller, but sometimes used to mean the rudder.

Hold: The interior cavity of the ship, between the floor and the lower deck throughout her length.

Holystone: A piece of sandstone used for scrubbing decks, so called because seamen had to go down on their knees to use it.

Hove-to: The result of heaving-to; the motion of a ship is stopped.

Irons: A ship is said to be in irons if she is permitted to come up into the wind and lose her way, so that without steerage she can neither be brought back to her former tack or fall off on the other without the yards being braced.

376

Jib: A triangular sail set on a forestay. Most clippers could set four jibs: the foremost was the flying jib, followed by the outer jib, the inner jib, and the foretopmast staysail (storm jib). In a vessel with five jibs the foremost was known as the standing jib.

Jib-boom: A spar that continues the bowsprit forward; the flying jib-boom extends beyond the jib-boom.

Jubilee rigged: A full-rigged ship with the royal yards and sails removed.

Junk: The largest boat built by the Chinese. In the past it was bigger than any warship built in Europe. The classic junk has no keel, the hull is divided into watertight compartments, and it is very full at the stern from where a large rudder is suspended. The bow on deck is square and the extreme beam is one-third of the way from the stern. Its huge masts are in one piece and carry heavy lugsails.

Jury rig: A temporary or makeshift rig.

Keel: The lowest and principal timber that supports the frame of the ship and extends its whole length.

Keelson: An internal keel, laid upon the middle of the floor timbers immediately over the keel; it serves to bind them all together by means of long bolts driven from without, and clinched on the upper side of the keelson; in this context 'clinch' is to batter or rivet a bolt's end onto a ring or piece of plate iron.

Knots: Nautical miles per hour.

Lateen sail and yard: A long triangular sail, bent by its foremost leech to a lateen yard which hoists obliquely to the mast.

Latitude: The angular distance of a place north or south of the equator expressed in degrees (°) and minutes (') north (N) or south(S) of the equator. A parallel of latitude is a circle parallel to the equator passing through any place.

Lazarette: A place sectioned off the after part of a ship's hold for stowing provisions and stores.

Leading wind: A good wind abeam or on the quarter.

Lee: The opposite side to that from which the wind is blowing. The side onto which the wind is blowing will be the weather.

Leech: The border of a sail that is either perpendicular or sloping: the vertical borders of a square sail are designated port-leech and starboard-leech; the after edge of a fore-and-aft sail.

Leech lines: Ropes attached to the leeches of the mainsail, foresail, and crossjack that pass through blocks under the tops, and used to truss those sails to the yards.

Lee shore: Shore downwind of the ship.

Leeward: On the lee side. The opposite of lee is weather, and of leeward, windward.

Leeway: The sideways drift of a ship caused by wind, current, tidal stream, or waves.

Lifelines: Lines stretched above the deck in bad weather to prevent the seamen from being washed away.

Lighter: A large open flat-bottomed boat used to carry goods to and from ships.

List: The vessel's angle of tilt to one side caused by a shifted cargo.

Longboat: The largest boat belonging to a sailing ship; carvel-built, and normally furnished with oars, spars, and sails.

Longitude: A meridian of longitude is an imaginary great circle line passing through the poles and cutting the equator and parallels of latitude at right angles. When the sun is on the meridian of any place it is midday there. Meridians of longitude are measured up to 180 degrees (°) east (E) or west (W) of the prime meridian 0 at Greenwich, and represent their angular distance from there.

Loose: Unfurl.

Lorcha: A fast Chinese vessel carrying guns.

Luff: The forward edge of a sail.

Lugger: A small vessel with four-cornered sails set fore-and-aft that may have two or three masts.

Lugsail: A quadrilateral (four-sided) sail bent to a yard that hangs obliquely on the mast.

Lugsails (Chinese): Sails carrying battens that extend the full width of the sail and extend the sail forward of the mast.

Mainyard: The lowermost yard on the mainmast onto which the mainsail, the largest sail carried on the mainmast, is bent.

Marlinspike (also known as a stabber by sail-makers): A conical piece of iron tapering to a point, mostly used to separate strands of a rope when splicing or knotting; when made from a piece of hardwood it is known as a 'fid,' the smaller version of which is used for the bolt-rope of sails.

Maury, Commander Matthew F USN: Oceanographer

Missing stays or **miss-stay**: To fail to go about from one tack to another when, after a ship gets her head to the wind, she fails to go about and begins to fall off on the same tack.

Mizzenmast: The aftermost mast of a ship.

Moonsails: Sails set on yards above the skysails, sometimes called moon-rakers.

Monsoon: Reversal of the trades-winds resulting from heat generated by the sun over large land masses drawing in colder air from over the sea in such places as the China Sea and the Bay of Bengal. When it brings rain it is called the 'wet monsoon.'

Outhaul: A line by which a sail is hauled outboard along a spar: studdingsails and their booms are hauled out along the yard by outhauls.

Pack-ice: A large collection of broken floe huddled together, but constantly changing in position.

Paddle steamer: A steamship propelled through the water by a pair of side paddle-wheels.

Palm: A flat thimble to receive the head of a needle; it is fixed onto a piece of canvas or leather, strapped across the palm of the hand.

Parrals: Those bands of rope, or sometimes iron collars, by which the centers of the yard are fastened at the slings to the masts, so as to slide up and down freely.

Pig iron: Crude iron as first obtained from a smelting furnace.

Pilot: An experienced person with local knowledge, normally a master mariner, charged with a ship's course near coasts, and in harbors, rivers and other confined waters; one who is authorized by the Trinity board to pilot ships of the largest draft.

Pinnace: A small carvel-built boat propelled with oars and sails, of two or even three masts, and forming part of the equipment of a large vessel.

Pin-rail: A horizontal wooden beam with holes to accept belaying pins.

Poop, the: The aftermost and highest part of a ship's hull; also a deck raised over the after-part.

Pooping, or being pooped: The breaking of a heavy sea over the stern or quarter of a ship as she scuds before the wind in a gale or storm. Being pooped is extremely dangerous, particularly if the vessel is heavily laden.

Press of sail: As much sail as the strength of the wind will permit a ship to carry.

Privateers: Men-of-war equipped by private individuals and licensed by a governing authority for cruising against the enemy in time of war or conflict.

Prow: The foremost end of a vessel.

Purchase: Any mechanical power which increases the force applied, such as a pulley, luff-tackle, or capstan.

Quarter: 45° abaft the beam.

Raked masts: Masts set at a sloping angle.

Ratlines: Small lines that traverse the shrouds of a ship horizontally from the deck upwards; they form a series of steps, like the rungs of a ladder.

Reef: Reduce sail in proportion to the increase in strength of the wind. A reef is also the name given to a group or continuous chain of rocks just beneath the surface, or so near the surface that on occasions water may break over them.

Reef-band: A narrow band of canvas sewn onto the reef-line to take some of the strain off the reef-points.

Reef-points: Small lengths of cord attached to a sail, used to secure sail after reefing.

Reef-tackle: Ropes used in reefing.

Rigging: A general name given to all ropes or chains employed to support the masts and arrange the sails according to the direction of the wind; running rigging and standing rigging.

Ringtail: A kind of studding sail hoisted beyond the after edge of the spanker.

Royal yards and sails: Sails set on yards positioned immediately above the topgallant sail.

Rudder: Described by Smyth as an appendage attached by pintles and braces to the sternpost of a vessel that governs a vessel's course through the water; pintles are hooks which enter the braces.

Running rigging: Ropes and chains used to trim the yards, and to control and shorten sail.

Sampan: A Chinese boat with its deck composed mostly of hatches, used for carrying passengers or, with a comfortable cabin, as a houseboat.

Scarph: Joining two pieces of timber by sloping (beveling) the edges to maintain the same thickness throughout the joint's length, is known as scarphing.

Schooner: A vessel rigged with fore-and-aft sails on two or more masts; the mainmast is taller than the foremast in a two-masted schooner.

Scow: A large flat-bottomed boat, used either as a lighter or as a ferry.

Scud: Run before a gale.

Scuppers: Apertures cut through the water-ways and sides of a ship at proper distances, and lined with metal. Their purpose is to carry water off the deck into the sea.

Sextant: A mathematical instrument for measuring the angular distances between the horizon and celestial bodies, and between individual celestial bodies.

Shale: Stratified rock from sedimentary mud or clay.

Sheave: A wheel on which the rope works in a block.

Sheer: Longitudinal curve of a ship's deck or sides.

Sheers: Two or more spars raised at angles, and lashed together near their upper ends, supported by guys, and used for raising or taking in heavy weights.

Sheet: A rope, chain, or wire fastened to one or both lower corners of a sail to tension and retain the clew down to its place.

Shoal: A place where the water is shallow.

Shrouds: Standing rigging which gives the mast its lateral support.

Skylight: A framework in the deck to admit light vertically into the cabin.

Skysails: Small sails set on yards above the royals.

Sling: A rope fitted to encircle any large article such as a yard, and suspend it while hoisting or lowering.

Snatch-block: A single iron-bound block with an opening in one side above the sheave, in which the bight of a rope may be laid.

Spanker: A fore-and-aft sail, with a boom and a gaff, frequently called the driver. It is the aftermost sail of a barque.

Spar: General term used for mast, yard, boom, or gaff.

Spilling lines: Ropes arranged so as to keep the sails from blowing away when they are clewed up.

Splice: Join two ropes together.

Sprit-sail: A sail set on a horizontal yard suspended from the bowsprit, formerly used on a carrack.

Stanchion: Any fixed upright support.

Standing rigging: The ropes that support the masts: backstays, forestays, and shrouds.

Stays: Standing rigging which supports the masts in a fore-and-aft line, forestays support them from forward, and backstays from aft.

Staysail: A triangular sail hoisted on a stay.

Stem: The foremost piece of the ship that unites the bows. Its lower end scarphs into the keel and the bowsprit rests upon its upper end.

Step: An arrangement of timbers on the keelson into which the heel of the mast is fitted.

Step: To step a mast is to erect the mast and fit its heel into the step.

Stern: The after part of a ship.

Sternpost: The post at the center of the stern which is scarphed into the keel and from which the rudder is suspended.

Strake: One breadth of a plank wrought from stem to sternpost.

Strop, or **strap**: A piece of rope, spliced generally into a circular wreath, and used to surround the body of a block, so that the latter may be hung to any particular situation above the masts, yards, or rigging.

Studding sail: Fine weather sails set outside the square sails. They have yards at the head, and are spread at the foot by booms.

Tack: To tack is to go about, to change course from one board to the other by turning the ship's head suddenly into the wind. A ship is said to be sailing on a port tack when the wind is coming over the port side of the vessel, and on a starboard tack when the wind is coming over the starboard side of the vessel.

Taffrail: The curved railing that forms the upper part of a boat's or ship's stern.

Tiller: A straight-grained timber beam, or iron bar, fitted into or round the head of the rudder, by which the latter is moved.

Top: A platform over the head of the lower mast, from which it projects.

Topgallant mast: The third division of a mast above the deck from which topgallant yards, carrying the topgallant sails, are suspended.

Topmast and **topsails:** The second division of a mast above the deck from which topmast yards, carrying the topsails, are suspended.

Topsides: The part of a ship's side above the waterline.

Towson, John T: Inventor and navigation expert

Trades: Abbreviation of trade-winds; currents of air moving from about the 30° of latitude towards the equator.

Trenails: Long cylindrical hardwood, normally oak, pins driven through the planks and timbers to hold them tightly together.

Tumblehome: Inward slope of the upper sides, or swell of the sides, of a ship.

Watch-tackle: A small luff purchase with a short fall, the double block having a tail to it and the single one a hook. It is used for various purposes around the deck.

Water-ways: Deck planks that connect the sides of a ship to her decks, and form a channel to carry off any water by means of scuppers.

Wear ship: To bring a ship round onto the other tack by bringing the wind round the stern, as opposed to tacking when the bow is brought through the wind.

Wheel: The general name for the helm which, by controlling the tiller and rudder, steers the ship.

Winch: A capstan around a drum by which a rope may be employed to increase its power (purchase) when raising a sail or other load.

Windlass: A machine erected on the forepart of a ship which serves to ride by, as well as heave in the cable.

Vang: A rope leading from the end of the gaff to the rails, one on each side, to steady the gaff; when the sail is not set it keeps the gaff amidships.

Veer: The wind veers when it changes in a clockwise direction.

Yard: A long cylindrical pole suspended upon the mast to spread a sail.

Yardarms: The extremities of a yard.

Bibliography

Anderson, Ernest B. *Sailing Ships of Ireland: A Book for Lovers of Sail Being a Record of Irish Sailing Ships in the Nineteenth Century.* Dublin: Morris, 1950.

Anonymous. *The Rime of the Ancyent Marinere, in Seven Parts.* In: Wordsworth, William & Coleridge, Samuel T. *Lyrical Ballads, with a Few Other Poems.* London: J & A Arch, 1798.

Apollonio, Spencer. *The Last of the Cape Horners: Firsthand Accounts of the Last Days of the Commercial Tall Ships.* Washington DC: Brassey's, 2000.

Axelson, Eric. *Congo to Cape: Early Portuguese Explorers.* London: Faber & Faber, 1973.

Baird, Donal. *Women at Sea in the Age of Sail.* Halifax, Nova Scotia: Nimbus, 2001.

Baker, Anne P. *Sir Robert Wigram (1744–1830).* In: Matthew, H C G & Harrison, Brian. Eds. *ODNB.* Oxford: OUP, 2004: 58; 860–861.

Baker, William F. *Running Her Easting Down: A Documentary of the Development and History of the British Tea Clippers Culminating with the Building of the Cutty Sark.* Caldwell, Idaho: Caxton Printers, 1974.

Ballantyne, Tony. Ed. *Science, Empire and the European Exploration of the Pacific.* Aldershot: Ashgate Variorum, 2004

Bascomb, Neal. *Red Mutiny: Mutiny, Revolution and Revenge on the Battleship Potemkin.* London: Weidenfeld & Nicolson, 2007.

Beaufoy, Colonel Mark FRS. *Nautical and Hydraulic Experiments. Vol 1.* London: Henry Beaufoy, 1834.

Belloc, Hilaire. *On Sailing the Sea.* London: Methuin, 1939.

Bigsby, Christopher W E. *Arthur Miller: A Critical Study.* London: Orion, 2008.

Bixel, Patricia Bellis. *Sailing Ship Elissa.* College Station: Texan A&M University Press, 1998.

Blackett, Howard. *The Life of Giuseppe Garibaldi Italian Hero and Patriot.* London: Walter Leigh, 1882.

Blond, Georges. *Admiral Togo.* London: Jarrods, 1961.

Bodley, R V C. *Admiral Togo: The Authorised Life of Admiral of the Fleet, Marquis Heihachiro Togo OM.* London: Jarrolds, 1935.

Bolster, W Jeffrey. *Black Jacks: African American Seamen in the Age of Sail.* Cambridge, Massachusetts & London: Harvard University Press, 1997.

Bonavia, Judy., Hayman, Richard., Bishop, Kevin., Booz, Paddy., Holdsworth, May. *The Yangtze River and the Three Gorges.* Hong Kong: Airphoto International, 2004.

Bourke, Edward J. *Shipwrecks of the Irish Coast. Volume 1, 1105–1993.* Dublin: E J Bourke, 1994.

Bourke, Edward J. *Shipwrecks of the Irish Coast. Volume 2, 932–1997.* Dublin: E J Bourke, 1998.

Brett, Henry. *White Wings: Fifty Years of Sail in the New Zealand Trade, 1850 to 1900.* Auckland: Brett, 1924.

Brinnin, John Malcolm. *The Sway of the Grand Saloon: Social History of the North Atlantic.* London: Macmillan, 1972.

Briot, Claude & Briot, Jacqueline. *Le Clippers Français.* Douarnenez: Chasse-Marée, 2003.

Brouwer, Norman J. *The International Register of Historic Ships.* 3rd edn. New York & London: Sea History Press & Chatham, 1999.

Bruce, Erroll., Steiner, O H M St., Norman, E D. *Cape Horn to Port.* Lymington: Nautical, 1978.

Brunskill, Ian., Liardet, Guy., Tillotson, Michael. Eds. *Great Military Lives: A Century of Obituaries. Togo: Japan's Nelson.* London: Times Books, 2008; 72–77.

Brunskill, Ian., Liardet, Guy., Tillotson, Michael. Eds. *Great Military Lives: A Century of Obituaries. Grand Admiral Karl Dönitz, Architect of German Wartime u-Boat Strategy.* London: Times Books, 2008; 241–246.

Budd, Louis J. *Mark Twain (1835–1910).* In: Garraty, John A & Carnes, Mark C. Eds. *American National Biography.* New York: OUP, 1999: 22; 52–60.

Burnett, Robert. *The Life of Paul Gauguin*. London: Cobden-Sanderson, 1936.

Byron, George G. *The Poetical Works of Lord Byron*. London: Humphrey Milford; OUP, 1921.

Calambokidis, John & Steiger, Gretchen. *Blue Whales*. Grantown-on-Spey, Scotland: Colin Baxter Photography, 1997.

Calderhead, William L. *Donald McKay (1810–1880)*. In: Garraty, John A & Carnes, Mark C. Eds. *American National Biography*. New York: OUP, 1999: 15; 95–96.

Campbell, George F. *China Tea Clippers*. London: Adlard Coles, 1974.

Cartledge, Paul. *Thermopylae: The Battle that Changed the World*. London: Macmillan, 2006.

Chapelle, Howard I. *The Baltimore Clipper: Its Origin and Development*. New York: Dover, 1930.

Chapelle, Howard I. *The History of American Sailing Ships*. New York: Bonanza, 1935.

Chatterton, Edward K. *Sailing Ships: The Story of Their Development from the Earliest Times to the Present Day*. London: Sidgwick & Jackson, 1909.

Chatterton, E Keble. *Old Ship Prints. 2nd edn*. London: Spring Books, 1965.

Christie, W D. Ed. *The Poetical Works of John Dryden*. London: Macmillan, 1870.

Clark, Arthur H. *The Clipper Ship Era*. New York & London: G P Putnam's, 1910.

Clark, Hyla M. *The Tall Ships: A Sailing Celebration*. New York: Tree Communications, 1976.

Clowes, Geoffrey S L. *The Story of Sail*. London: Eyre & Spottiswoode, 1936.

Coles, K Adlard & Bruce, Peter. *Heavy Weather Sailing. 4th edn*. London: Adlard Coles Nautical, 1991.

Compton, Nic. *The Return of a Cape Horn Veteran: Gigi, the Contessa 32 that doubled the Horn, is back, and Renovated by her Builders*. Classic Boat, July 2008; 32–36.

Conrad, Joseph. *Lord Jim*. New York: Doubleday & McClure, 1900.

Conrad, Joseph. *Mirror of the Sea, Memories and Impressions*. London: Methuen, 1906.

Conrad, Joseph. *The Shorter Tales of Joseph Conrad (Youth, The Secret Sharer, The Brutes, Tomorrow, Typhoon, Because of the Dollars)*. New York: Doubleday, Page & Co, 1924.

Conrad, Joseph. *Typhoon and Other Stories*. Leipzig: Bernard Tauchniz, 1928.

Conrad, Joseph. *Heart of Darkness; Nostromo*. Oxford: OUP, 1994.

Cooper, A J. *Sir Alfred Searle Haslam (1844–1927)*. In: Matthew, H C G & Harrison, Brian. Eds. *ODNB*. Oxford: OUP, 2004: 25; 707–708.

Corlett, E. *The Iron Ship: The Story of Brunel's SS Great Britain. 2nd edn*. London: Conway Maritime, 1983.

Course, A G. *Painted Ports: The Story of the Ships of Devitt & Moore*. London: Hollis & Carter, 1961.

Course, A G. *Windjammers of the Horn: The Story of the last British Fleet of Square-Rigged Sailing Vessels*. London: Adlard Coles, 1969.

Crothers, William L. *The American-Built Clipper Ship 1850–1856: Characteristics, Construction, and Details*. Camden, Maine: International Marine, 2000.

Cummins, John G. *Francis Drake: The Lives of a Hero*. London: Weidenfeld & Nicolson, 1995.

Cutler, Carl C. *Greyhounds of the Sea: The Story of the American Clipper Ship*. Annapolis: United States Naval Institute, 1930; Wellingborough, Northants: Patrick Stephens, 1984.

Dana, Richard H. *Two Years Before the Mast*. New York: Harper & Brothers, 1844.

Dana, Richard H. *The Seaman's Manual. 14th edn*. London: Ward, Lock & Co, 1899.

Dear, Ian & Kemp, Peter. Eds. *An A–Z of Sailing Terms*. Oxford: OUP, 1987.

Debenham, Frank. Ed. *Great World Atlas*. London & New York: Reader's Digest.

Delgado, James P & Clifford, J Candace. *Great American Ships*. New York: Preservation Press, 1991.

De Pauw, Linda G. *Seafaring Women*. Boston: Houghton Mifflin, 1982.

Derby, William L A. *The Tall Ships Pass: The Story of the Last Years of Deepwater Square-Rigged Sail, Embodying Herein the History and Detailed Description of the Finnish Four Masted Steel Barque 'Herzogin Cecile.' 2nd. Edn*, London: Jonathon Cape, 1970.

de Tocqueville, Alexis. *Democracy in America. (Translated by Henry Reeve) Vol 2. 2nd edn.* London: Saunders & Otley, 1836.

DeWolfe, Fred. *Impressions of Portland: A Study in Historical Geography.* Portland, Oregon: Multnomah County Library, 1970.

Dicken, Samuel N. *The Making of Oregon.* Portland, Oregon: Oregon Historical Society, 1979.

Dickens, Charles. *American Notes for General Circulation.* Paris: Baudry's European Library, 1842.

Dietrich, William. *Northwest Passage: The Great Columbia River.* New York: Simon & Schuster, 1995.

Domville-Fife, Charles W. *Epics of the Square-rigged Ships: Autobiographies of Sail.* London: Seeley Service, 1958.

Drayton, Michael. *The Poetical Works of Michael Drayton.* Edinburgh: 1793.

Druett, Joan. *Hen Frigates: Wives of Merchant Captains under Sail.* London: Souvenir, 1998.

Dryden, John. *Annus Mirabilis: The Year of Wonders, 1666.* London: Henry Herringman, 1667.

Eaddy, Percy A. *Hull Down.* London: Andrew Melrose, 1933.

Edwards, Bernard. *Dönitz and the Wolf Packs: The u-Boats at War.* London: Cassell, 1999.

Fairbain, William. *Iron Shipbuilding: Its History and Progress.* London: Longman Green, 1865.

Falk, Edwin A. *Togo and the Rise of Japanese Sea Power.* London: Longmans, Green, 1936.

Fernandez-Armesto, Felipe. *Pathfinders: A Global History of Exploration.* Oxford & New York: OUP, 2006.

Fisher, Lawrence M. *Thursday's Child Sails In, Sets Mark.* New York Times: 13 February, 1989.

Galsworthy, John. *Reminiscences of Conrad.* In: *Castles in Spain and Other Screeds.* London: Heinemann, 1928.

Gardiner, Robert J & Greenhill, Basil. *Sail's Last Century: The Merchant Sailing Ship 1830–1930.* London: Conway Maritime, 1993.

Gayford, Martin. *The Yellow House: Van Gough, Gauguin and Nine Turbulent Weeks in Arles.* London: Fig Tree, 2006.

Gervais, David. *John Edward Masefield (1878–1967).* In: Matthew, H C G & Harrison, Brian. Eds. *ODNB.* Oxford: OUP, 2004: 37; 141–144.

Gibbs, Jim. *Pacific Square-Riggers. Pictorial History of the Great Wind Ships of Yesteryear.* Seattle: Superior, 1969.

Giggal, Kenneth. *Great Classic Sailing Ships.* London: Webb & Bower, 1988.

Green, Richard. *Exhibition of Marine Paintings.* London: Richard Green, 1992.

Greenhill, Basil & Hackman, John. *The Herzogin Cecile. The Life and Times of a Four-Masted Barque.* London: Conway Maritime, 1991.

Greenlaw, Joanna. *The Swansea Copper Barques & Cape Horners.* Swansea: Joanna Greenlaw, 1999.

Griffiths, John W. *Treatise on Marine and Naval Architecture, or Theory and Practice Blended in Ship Building. 4th edn.* New York & London: D Appleton, 1854.

Harland, John H. *Seamanship in the Age of Sail: An Account of the Ship Handling of the Sailing Man-of-War 1600–1860 based on Contemporary Sources.* London: Conway Maritime, 1984.

Harland, John H. *Ships and Seamanship: The Maritime Prints of J J Bougean.* London: Chatham, 2000.

Harvey, Geoffrey. *John Galsworthy (1867–1933).* In: Matthew, H C G & Harrison, Brian. Eds. *ODNB.* Oxford: OUP, 2004: 21; 336–338.

Heine, William C. *Historic Ships of the World.* Newton Abbot: David & Charles, 1977.

Hickey, Des & Smith, Gus. *Star of Shame: The Secret Voyage of the Arandora Star.* Dublin: Madison, 1989.

Hocking, Charles. *Dictionary of Disasters at Sea during the Age of Steam. Including Sailing Ships and Ships of War Lost in Action 1824–1942.* London: Lloyds Register of Shipping, 1969.

Hohman, Elmo P. *History of American Merchant Seamen.* Hamden, Connecticut: Shoe String Press, 1956.

Hollenberg, Martin J. *Marco Polo: The Story of the Fastest Clipper.* Halifax, Nova Scotia: Nimbus, 2006.

Hosking, Eric J & Sage, Bryan. *Antarctic Wildlife.* London: Croom Helm, 1982.

Howe, Octavius T & Matthews, Frederick C. *American Clipper Ships 1833–1858, Vols I & II.* Salem, Massachusetts: Marine Research Society, 1926 & 1927.

Hugill, Stan. *Sailortown.* Routledge & Kegan Paul: London, 1967; E P Dutton: New York, 1967.

Hume, Cyril & Armstrong, Malcolm C. *The Cutty Sark and Thermopylae Era of Sail.* Glasgow: Brown, Son & Ferguson, 1987.

Hurst, Alexander A. *Square Riggers: The Final Epoch 1921–1958.* Brighton: Teredo Books, 1972.

Hutton, W M. *Cape Horn Passage.* London: Blackie & Son, 1934.

Irish, Bill. *Shipbuilding in Waterford 1820–1882: A Historical, Technical and Pictorial Study.* Bray, Co Wicklow: Woodwell, 2001.

Jones, William H S. *The Cape Horn Breed: My Experiences as an Apprentice in Sail in the Fully-rigged Ship 'British Isles.'* London: Andrew Melrose, 1956.

Jourdane, John. *Icebergs, Port and Starboard: The Whitebread Round the World Race.* Long Beach, California: Cape Horn Press, 1992.

Joyce, James. *Dubliners.* London: Penguin, 1958.

Kelsey, Harry. *Sir Francis Drake (1540–1596).* In: Matthew, H C G & Harrison, Brian. Eds. *ODNB.* Oxford: OUP, 2004: 16; 858–870.

King, John C & Turner John. *Antarctic Meteorology and Climatology.* Cambridge: Cambridge University Press, 1997.

Knight, Frank. *The Clipper Ship.* London: Collins, 1973.

Knox-Johnson, Robin. *Cape Horn: A Maritime History.* London: Hodder & Stoughton, 1995.

Kretschmer, John. *Cape Horn to Starboard.* Camden, Maine: International Marine, 1986.

Lacroix, Louis. *Les Derniers Grands Voiliers: Histoire des Long-Courriers Nantes 1893 a 1931.* Paris: Amiot Dumont, 1950.

Laing, Alexander. *Clipper Ship Men.* New York: Garden City, 1944.

Lane, Bruce M & Lane, C Gardner. *New Information on Ships Built by Donald McKay.* American Neptune 1982; 42: 118–137.

Learmont, James S. *Master in Sail. 2nd edn.* London: P Marshall, 1954.

Longfellow, Henry Wadsworth. *The Poetical Works of Longfellow.* London: Henry Frowde, 1904.

Longridge, C Nepean. *The 'Cutty Sark': Last of the Famous tea Clippers.* London: Percival Marshall, 1933

Lowe, Keith. *Inferno: The Devastation of Hamburg 1943.* London: Viking, 2007.

Lubbock, Basil. *The China Clippers.* Glasgow: James Brown & Son 1914.

Lubbock, Basil. *The Colonial Clippers.* Glasgow: James Brown & Son, 1921.

Lubbock, Basil. *The Blackwall Frigates.* Glasgow: Brown, Son & Ferguson, 1922.

Lubbock, Basil. *The Western Ocean Packets.* Glasgow: James Brown & Son, 1925.

Lubbock, Basil. *The Last of the Windjammers. Vols I & II.* Brown, Son & Ferguson: Glasgow, 1927 & 1928.

Lubbock, Basil. *The Log of the Cutty Sark.* Glasgow: Brown, Son & Ferguson, 1928.

Lubbock, Basil. *The Opium Clippers.* Glasgow: Brown, Son & Ferguson, 1933.

Lubbock, Basil. *Sail: The Romance of the Clipper Ships. Vol III.* London: Blue Peter, 1936.

Lubbock, Basil. *The Nitrate Clippers.* Glasgow: Brown, Son & Ferguson, 1953.

Lubbock, A Basil. *Round the Horn before the Mast. 3rd edn.* Glasgow: Brown, Son & Ferguson, 1986.

Luckner, Felix Count von. *Out of an Old Sea Chest. (Translated by Edward Fitzgerald)* London: Methuen, 1958.

Lundy, Derek. *The Way of a Ship: A Square-Rigger Voyage in the Last Days of Sail.* London: Jonathan Cape, 2002.

Lyman, William D. *The Columbia River: Its History, its Myths, its Scenery, its Commerce.* New York & London: G P Putnam's Sons, 1909.

Lynn, Madeleine. *Yangtze River: The Wildest, Wickedest River on Earth: An Anthology.* Hong Kong & Oxford: OUP, 1997.

MacColl, E Kilbrook. *Merchants, Money and Power: The Portland Establishment 1843–1913.* Portland, Oregon: Georgian Press, 1988.

MacGregor, David. *The China Bird: The History of Captain Killick and One Hundred Years of Sail & Steam.* London: Chatto & Windus, 1961.

MacGregor, David R. *Fast Sailing Ships: Their Design and Construction, 1775–1875.* Lymington, Hampshire: Nautical, 1973.

MacGregor, David R. *Clipper Ships.* Watford: Argus Books, 1979.

MacGregor, David R. *The Tea Clippers: Their History and Development, 1833–1875.* 2nd edn. London: Conway Maritime, 1983.

MacGregor, David R. *British & American Clippers: A Comparison of their Design, Construction and Performance in the 1850s.* London: Conway Maritime, 1993.

Maginnis, Arthur J. *The Atlantic Ferry: Its Ships, Men, and Working.* 3rd edn. Whittaker: London, 1900.

Major, Richard Henry. *The Discoveries of Prince Henry the Navigator.* London: Sampson, Low, Marston, Searle & Rivington, 1877

Malone, Peter. *Images and Chronicles of the Kerryman Newspaper: A Portrait of Kerry in the 20th Century.* Tralee, Co Kerry: The Kerryman, 2001.

Marr, Ann Whipple. *Mary Ann Brown Patten (1837–1861).* In: Garraty, John A & Carnes, Mark C. Eds. *American National Biography.* New York: OUP, 1999: 17; 128–129.

Masefield, John. *The Collected Poems of John Masefield.* London: William Heinemann, 1938.

Matthews, L Harrison. *Wandering Albatross: Adventures among Albatrosses and Petrels in the Southern Ocean.* London: MacGibbon & Kee; Reinhardt & Evans, 1951.

Maury, Matthew F. *On the Navigation of Cape Horn.* American Journal of Science and Arts 1834: 26; 54–63.

Maury, Matthew F. *The Physical Geography of the Sea.* London: T Nelson, 1855.

Maury, Matthew F. *Explanations and Sailing Directions to Accompany the Wind and Current Charts.* 8th edn. Washington: USN, 1858.

McCutchan, Philip. *Tall Ships: The Golden Age of Sail.* London: Weidenfeld & Nicolson, 1976.

McElliott, M F. *Cape Horn Sunsets.* Dublin & London: Mellifont Press, 1941.

McKay, Richard C. *Some Famous Sailing Ships and Their Builder Donald McKay: A Study of the American Sailing Packet and Clipper Eras, with Biographical Sketches of America's Foremost Designer and Master-Builder of Ships, and a Comprehensive History of His Many Famous Ships. With 10 Color Plates and 48 Other Illustrations.* New York & London: G P Putnam's Sons, 1928.

McKay, Richard C. *South Street: A Maritime History of New York.* New York: G P Putnam's Sons, 1934.

McRae, Bill., Jewell, Judy., Snarski, Jennifer. *Pacific Northwest: Oregon & Washington.* 2nd edn. Hawthorn, Victoria, Australia: Lonely Planet, 1999.

Menzies, Gavin. *1421: The Year China Discovered the World.* London: Bantam Press, 2002.

Menzies, Gavin. *1434: The Year a Magnificent Chinese Fleet Sailed to Italy and Ignited the Renaissance.* London: HarperCollins, 2008.

Miller-Schroeder, Patricia. *Blue Whales.* London: A & C Black, 2000.

Moitessier, Bernard. *Cape Horn: The Logical Route: 14,216 Miles Without Port of Call (Translated by Inge Moor).* London: Grenada, 1977.

Moloney, Senan. *Lusitania: An Irish Tragedy.* Cork: Mercier Press, 2004.

Morrison, Samuel E. *The Maritime History of Massachusetts 1783–1860.* Cambridge, Massachusetts: Riverside Press, 1921.

Murphy, Dallas. *Rounding the Horn: Being the Story of Williwaws and Windjammers, Drake, Darwin, Murdered Missionaries and Naked Natives: A Deck's View of Cape Horn.* London: Weidenfeld & Nicolson, 2004.

Najder, Zdzistaw. *Joseph Conrad: A Life.* Rochester, New York: Camden House, 2007.

Newby, Eric. *The Last Grain Race.* London: Secker & Warburg, 1958.

Newby, Eric. *Learning the Ropes: An Apprentice in the Last of the Windjammers.* London: John Murray, 1999.

Nolan, Daniel J. *Ocean Signposts* (in press)

Nolan, Daniel J. *The Wreck of the Leon* (in press)

Nuttall, Zelia. *New Light on Drake: A Collection of Documents Relating to his Voyage of*

Circumnavigation 1577–1580. London: Hakluyt Society, 1914.

Paine, Ralph D. *The Ships and Sailors of Old Salem, 1871–1925.* London: Heath Cranton, 1924.

Parkin, Stephen. *My Life: Guiseppe Garibaldi.* London: Hesperus Press, 2004

Peaff, Richard W. *Ursula (Mid 5th Century).* In: Matthew, H C G & Harrison, Brian. Eds. *ODNB.* OUP, 2004: 55; 958–959.

Pearsall, Judy. Ed. *The New Oxford Dictionary of English.* Oxford: OUP, 1998.

Preston, Diana. *Wilful Murder: The Sinking of the Lusitania.* London: Doubleday, 2002.

Prien, Günther. *I Sank the Ark Royal* (Translated by Comte de la Vatine). London: Grays Inn Press, 1954.

Raban, Jonathan. *Passage to Juneau: A Sea and its Meanings.* New York: Alfred A Knopf; London: Picador, 1999.

R B. *A Cape Horn Calm and Other Verses.* London: James Nisbet, 1911.

Rees, Colin R. *Our Family of Cape Horners.* Swansea: Colin R Rees, 2000.

Riall, Lucy. *Garibaldi: Invention of a Hero.* Yale University Press: New Haven, Connecticut, 2007.

Riesenberg, Felix. *Cape Horn.* London: Robert Hale, 1941.

Robertson, J Logie. *The Poetical Works of Robert Burns: With Notes, Glossary, Index of the First Lines and Chronological List.* London: Henry Frowde, 1906.

Robinson, Jack. *China Clipper Master: The Story of John Smith of the 'Lahloo.'* Glasgow: Brown, Son & Ferguson, 1995.

Rousmaniere, John. *A Glossary of Modern Sailing Terms.* London: George Allen & Unwin, 1977.

Rydell, Raymond A. *Cape Horn to the Pacific: The Rise and Decline of an Ocean Highway.* Berkeley, California: University of California Press, 1952.

Shaw, David W. *Flying Cloud: The True Story of America's Most Famous Clipper Ship and the Woman Who Guided Her.* New York: Perennial, 2001.

Shultz, Charles R. *Life on Board an American Clipper Ship.* Texas: A&M University, 1983.

Smaridge, Norah. *Master Mariner: The Adventurous Life of Joseph Conrad.* New York: Hawthorn, 1966.

Smith, C Fox. *The Return of the 'Cutty Sark.'* London: Methuin, 1924.

Smyth, William H. *The Sailor's Word-Book: An Alphabetical Digest of Nautical Terms.* London: Blackie & Son, 1867.

Souchez, Ronald A & Lorrain, Reginald D. *Ice Compositions and Glacier Dynamics.* Berlin: Springer-Verlag, 1991.

Stallworthy, Jon. *Rounding the Horn: Collected Poems.* Manchester: Carcanet Press, 1998.

Stein, Douglas L. *Robert Henry Waterman (1808–1884).* In: Garraty, John A & Carnes, Mark C. Eds. *American National Biography.* New York: OUP, 1999: 22; 779–780.

Sunderfeld, Jan & Sehlin, Halvar. *af Chapman: A Full-rigger that Became a Hostel.* Stockholm: Swedish Touring Club, 1988.

Sutton, C W & Baigent, Elizabeth. *John Thomas Towson (1804–1881).* In: Matthew, H C G & Harrison, Brian. Eds. *ODNB.* Oxford: OUP, 2004: 55; 174.

Svensson, Sam & Macfie, Gordon. *Sails through the Centuries.* London & New York: Macmillan, 1965.

Sythes, Desmond G. *Ships of West Cumberland.* Whitehaven, Cumbria: Whitehaven News, 1969; Whitehaven Museum, 1992.

Taylor, John M. *Confederate Raider: Raphael Semmes of the Alabama.* Washington DC: Brassey's, 1994.

Teenstra, Anno. *De Clippers. Ben nieuwe geschiedenis van de snelste Nederlandsche zeilschepen uit de Tweede helft der19E eeuw.* Amsterdam: Holdert , 1946.

Tennyson, Alfred Lord. *The Poetical Works of Alfred Lord Tennyson.* London : Macmillan, 1890.

Thesleff, Holger. *Farewell Windjammer: An Account of the Last Circumnavigation of the Globe and the Last Grain Race from Australia to England.* London & New York: Thames & Hudson, 1951.

Thiesen, William G. *Industrializing American Shipbuilding: The Transformation of Ship Design and Construction, 1820–1920.* Gainsville: University Press of Florida, 2006.

Thomas, David N. *Frozen Oceans: The Floating World of Pack Ice*. London: Natural History Museum, 2004.

Thomas, Phil N. *British Figurehead and Ship Carvers*. Wolverhampton: Waine Research, 1995.

Towson, John T & Atherton John W. *Tables to Facilitate the Practice of Great Circle Sailing*. 6th edn. London: Admiralty Hydrographic Office, 1861.

Twain, Mark. *Life on the Mississippi*. London: Chatto & Windus, 1928.

Underhill, Harold A. *Masting and Rigging the Clipper Ship and Ocean Carrier*. Glasgow: Brown, Son & Ferguson, 1946.

Underhill, Harold A. *Deep Water Sail*. Glasgow: Brown, Son & Ferguson, 1952.

Underhill, Harold A. *Sailing Ship Rigs and Rigging: With Authentic Plans of Famous Vessels of the Nineteenth and Twentieth Centuries and with Illustrations and Plans by the Author*. 2nd edn. Glasgow: Brown, Son & Ferguson, 1955.

Underhill, Harold A. *Sail Training and Cadet Ships*. Glasgow: Brown, Son & Ferguson, 1956.

Villiers, Alan J. *Last of the Wind Ships*. London: George Routledge & Sons, 1934.

Villiers, Alan J. *By Way of Cape Horn*. London: University of London Press, 1952.

Villiers, Alan J. *The Cutty Sark: Last of a Glorious Era*. London: Hodder & Stoughton, 1953.

Villiers, Alan J. *The Way of a Ship: The Story of a Square-Rigged Cape Horner*. London: Hodder & Stoughton, 1954.

Villiers, Alan J. *The War with Cape Horn*. London: Hodder & Stoughton, 1971.

Villiers Alan & Picard Henri. *The Bounty Ships of France: The Story of the French Cape Horn Sailing Ships*. London: Patrick Stevens, 1972.

Villiers Alan. *Voyaging in the Wind: An Introduction to Sailing Large Square-Rigged Ships*. London: HMSO, 1975.

Wallace, Frederick W. *Wooden Ships and Iron Men*. London: Hodder & Stoughton, 1924.

Walter, John. *The Kaiser's Pirates: German Surface Raiders in World War One*. London: Arms & Armour Press, 1994.

Watson, George E. *Birds of the Antarctic and Sub-Antarctic*. Washington: American Geophysical Union, 1971.

Watts Cedric. *Joseph Conrad (1857–1924)*. In: Matthew, H C G & Harrison, Brian. Eds. *ODNB*. Oxford: OUP, 2004: 12; 989–995.

Werner, A. *Autobiography of Giuseppe Garibaldi: Authorised Translation*. London: Walter, Smith & Innes, 1889.

Whipple, Addison B C. *Tall Ships and Great Captains*. London: Victor Gollancz, 1961.

Whipple, Addison B C. *The Clipper Ships*. Amsterdam: Time-Life, 1981.

Wilmore, C Ray. *Square Rigger Round the Horn: The Making of a Sailor*. Camden, Maine: International Marine, 1972.

Winchester, Clarence. Ed. *Shipping Wonders of the World*. 4 Vols. London: Amalgamated Press, 1936.

Winchester, Simon. *River at the Centre of the World: A Journey up the Yangtze, and Back in Chinese Time*. New York: Henry Holt, 1996; London: Viking, 1997.

Woodger, Elin & Toropov, Brandon. *Enclyopedia of the Lewis and Clark Expedition*. New York: Facts on File, 2004.

Woollard, Claude L A. *The Last of the Cape Horners*. Ilfracombe, Devon: Stockwell, 1967.

Lloyds Captains Register 1868–1873.

Lloyds Ships Register 1860.

Ships and Sailors. London: Parker Gallery, 1955.

Boston Daily Atlas, Boston: 31 January, 1854. John Willis Griffith on *Lightening*.

Illustrated London News: The Royal Barge Passing London-Bridge. 3 November 1849.

Illustrated London News: New American-Line Ship 'Cornelius Grinnell.' 31 August 1850.

Illustrated London News: The Ship 'Oriental' of New York. 21 December 1850.

Illustrated London News: The Clipper Ship 'Chrysolite.' 3 January 1852.

Illustrated London News: p336. The American Clipper-Ship 'Witch of the Wave.' 1 May 1852.

Illustrated London News: The Australian Clipper-Ship 'Marco Polo.' 19 February 1853.

Illustrated London News: The Aberdeen Clipper 'Cairngorm". 5 March 1853.

Illustrated London News: The American Clipper-Ship 'Sovereign of the Seas.' 16 July 1853.

Illustrated London News: The New Iron Clipper-Built Ship 'Tayleur', for Australia. 26 November 1853.

Illustrated London News: The New American Clipper 'Great Republic.' 31 March 1855.

Illustrated London News: The New Opium Clipper 'Wild Dayrell.' 10 November 1855.

Illustrated London News: The Royal Mail Clipper 'Schomberg.' 26 April 1856.

Illustrated London News: Chinese Pirate-Boat at Canton – From a Drawing by a Chinese Artist. 31 January 1857.

Illustrated London News: The Black Ball Line Clipper-Ship 'James Baines' with Troops for India. 31 October 1857.

Illustrated London News: The Danish Clipper Ship, the 'Cimber.' 17 April 1858.

Illustrated London News: Striking of the 'Indian Queen' on an Iceberg in the Southern Pacific, on the Morning of April 1. 27 August 1859.

Illustrated London News: The Australian Clipper Ship, 'Royal Family.' 18 October, 1862.

Illustrated London News: The Great Ship-Race from China to London: The Taeping and the Ariel off the Lizard. 22 September, 1866.

Illustrated London News: Steam Yacht Jerome Napoleon, built for Prince Napoleon at Havre. 29 September 1866.

Illustrated London News: Paris International Exhibition: Design for a System of Composite Shipbuilding. 3 August, 1867.

Illustrated London News: The Ariel, Winner of the Ocean Race from China. 5 October 1867.

Illustrated London News: The Tea-Ship Spindrift, Winner of the Ocean Race from China. 12 September 1868.

Illustrated London News: The Sobraon, Australian Packet-Ship. 31 October 1868.

Illustrated London News: The New China Clipper Caliph, Built at Aberdeen. 6 November 1869.

Illustrated London News: The City of Dublin Steam-Packet Company's New Mail Steamer Ireland. 24 October 1885

Illustrated London News: Stern View of Thermopylae from Yacht. 14 March 1891.

Illustrated London News: America's New Armoured Torpedo-Boat, 'Holland.' 7 May 1898.

Illustrated London News: The Largest War-Vessel Afloat: The Japanese Battleship 'Mikasa' Entering Portsmouth Harbour. 11 January 1902.

New York Times: 7 September 1890. *The Days of the Clipper: Fast Ships that Engaged in the California Trade.*

New York Times: 18 May 1897. *Launching of the Holland – A Tiny Torpedo Craft that May Revolutionize Naval Warfare of the World.*

The Times, London: 5 December 1850. Editorial: Oriental's arrival in the West India Docks.

The Times, London: 24, 25, 26 January 1854. Dreadful Shipwreck – 'Tayleur.'

The Times, London: 5 September 1944. Obituary: Alfred Basil Lubbock.

http://chinookindian.com/

http://cityofadelaide.org.au

http://southstreetseaportmuseum.org

http://en.wikipedia.org/wiki/Felix_von_Luckner

http://en.wikipedia.org/wiki/File:Af_Chapman.

http://en.wikipedia.org/wiki/File:Togo_in_ Europe

http://simple.wikipedia.org/wiki/Vasco_da_ Gama

http://www.articlesbase.com/water-sports-articles/star-of-russia-port-vila-967202.html

http://www.bruzelius.info/Nautica/Nautica.html

http://www.eraoftheclipperships.com/

http://www.llgc.org.uk/fga/fga_s01.htm

http://www.uboat.net/men/commanders/ 492.html

http://www.wikipedia.org/

Index

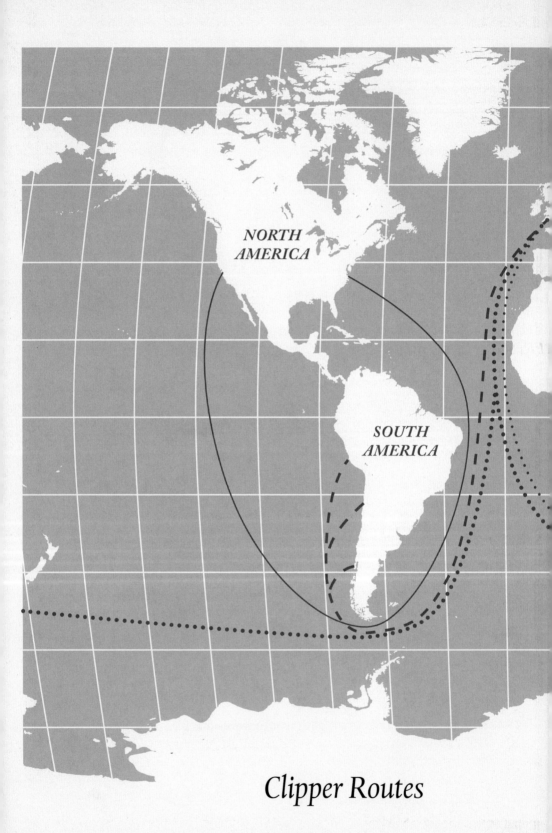

Clipper Routes